THE HACHETTE BOOK OF INDIAN DETECTIVE FICTION

Stories from the subcontinent

Volume 1

Edited by Tarun K. Saint

First published in hardcover in 2024 by Hachette India
(Registered name: Hachette Book Publishing India Pvt. Ltd.)
An Hachette UK company
www.hachetteindia.com

1

This edition published in 2025

Hardback ISBN 978-93-5731-281-3
Paperback ISBN 978-93-5731-760-3

Hachette Book Publishing India Pvt. Ltd
4th/5th Floors, Corporate Centre,
Plot No. 94, Sector 44, Gurugram 122003, India

Typeset in Bembo 11.5/13.5 pt.
by Manipal Technologies Limited, Manipal

Printed and bound in India
by Manipal Technologies Limited

THE HACHETTE BOOK OF INDIAN DETECTIVE FICTION
Volume 1

Tarun K. Saint is an independent scholar and writer born in Kenya, and has been living in India since 1972. His research interests include the literature of the Partition and science fiction. He is the author of *Witnessing Partition: Memory, History, Fiction* (2010), has edited *Bruised Memories: Communal Violence and the Writer* (2002), co-edited *Translating Partition: Stories, Essays, Criticism* (2001) with Ravi Kant and *Looking Back: The 1947 Partition of India, 70 Years On* (2017) in collaboration with Rakhshanda Jalil and Debjani Sengupta. He has also edited *The Gollancz Book of South Asian Science Fiction [Volumes 1 and 2]*.

PRAISE FOR THE BOOK

'Both a voyage of discovery and one of cultural wonder, these volumes unveil unknown territory to even us experts in the history of crime and mystery fiction. Further proof of what we suspected that the genre has roots in all cultures, diversities and thrives through the ages, enlightening and delighting readers, regardless of geography and origins. A major and indispensable contribution to the universality of detective fiction.'

Maxim Jakubowski

'An eclectic collection of some of the best detective stories from the subcontinent, from classic to contemporary, carefully handpicked and beautifully put together in two remarkable volumes that must, must, must adorn the shelves of any mystery fiction enthusiast.'

Bhaskar Chattopadhyay

'*The Hachette Book of Indian Detective Fiction* is a long-needed treasure that delights with its diversity of characters and setting. This anthology shares golden-age and contemporary stories written by bestselling writers and strong stories by emerging authors who are destined to become tomorrow's literary stars. A necessary addition for every mystery lovers' shelf.'

Sujata Massey

'These two volumes offer an introduction to the diversity and skill of writers from the Indian subcontinent. Tarun K. Saint has carefully selected classic and contemporary stories written originally in English, or translated from Bangla and Tamil, from masters like Tagore, Ray and Bandyopadhyay, and placed them alongside the very best contemporary authors like Vikram Chandra, Ambai and Shirshendu Mukhopadhyay. Arranged around five themes – amateur detectives, genre-bending and parody, genre-blurring, police procedurals and historical detective fiction – these stories will delight fans of classic detective fiction everywhere. If you want to learn something about Indian mysteries and the burning issues from colonial times to the present, you need go no further than this outstanding collection.'

Stewart King

'These skilfully edited volumes make an invaluable contribution to the universe of detective stories, presenting a wide range of translated or newly written works from the Indian subcontinent. The history and features of this distinctive but flexible genre are brilliantly introduced in the first volume, in an accessible manner without compromising scholarly rigour. That serves to highlight the nuances with which it has been exploited by Indian authors. Together, the collection registers numerous aspects of the bewildering cultural and linguistic diversity of India – in English. Conventional as well as adventurous takes on the genre's main branches are covered, and in some instances different genres are merged and metanarratives played with. Representative instances from past periods and a tasty range of recent stories are found here. Detectives appear in many guises, ingenious crimes and astute investigations take many pathways. Each story leads the reader into a vividly imagined world, some realistic, some potential, and some patently fictional – none boring.'

Suman Gupta

'From tales of time-travelling murderers to searching for missing diamonds, from amateur sleuths to kidnapped Tamil actresses and much more make up this unique, two-volume compendium of detective fiction stories. From the Bay of Bengal to the backwaters of Kerala, and from the shadows of the Partition to a college campus in Delhi, this collection presents fresh stories of murder, mystery and mayhem.'

Manjula Padmanabhan

'*The Hachette Book of Indian Detective Fiction* is long overdue. Remarkable for its breadth, it brings together classics that defined the genre with new stories that continue to push its boundaries. A vital anthology for afficionados and novice fans alike, the gripping stories make clear that detective fiction has delved deeply into the condition of Indian modernity, navigating critical issues of caste, class, gender, and the nation.'

Laura Rebecca Brueck

'Tarun Saint has embarked on an ambitious and vital project, bringing Indian detective fiction to the fore. From the quintessential sleuth to the deconstructed "whodunnit" to mysteries set in imagined worlds, times and places, these tales draw on the rich history, traditions and culture, brilliantly showcasing an eclectic range of detective fiction both classic and contemporary.'

Ian Mond

'...Saint reminds us of the vastness of crime writing – from its tentative roots to the current day, where it often merges with other genres such as fantasy or historical fiction; from thrill-a-minute mysteries (often condescendingly dismissed as "pulp") to narratives that have deeper sociological underpinnings, or aim for greater realism in their world-building.'

Scroll.in

'The anthology puts a wide variety of language authors at the reader's fingertips through translations... All this makes it a very satisfying read where one tries to guess and outguess the plot.'

Outlook

CONTENTS

INTRODUCTION

Tarun K. Saint

The Hachette Book of Indian Detective Fiction brings together disparate voices in the genre of detective fiction from India and the subcontinent, with selected translations from regional language writing (Bengali in particular, and Tamil). This anthology seeks to fill a long-standing gap in the archive of popular fiction, which may seem somewhat ironic in the context of the popularity of detective fiction, and series and movies (on Netflix, for instance) in contemporary India.[1] Here we showcase some of the best new and original writing in English, while also highlighting the importance of earlier writers who established the standards for the genre in the region.

In a significant recent essay on South Asian crime fiction, Laura Brueck and Francesca Orsini show how the genre unsettles the binaries that often characterize the discourse on World literature (Anglophone/non-Anglophone, domestic/foreign, local/global), as the localization and synthesizing of the form with previous modes of storytelling gave this genre a unique flavour, eventually quite different from either British, European or American precursors.[2] After its arrival on Indian and subcontinental shores in the nineteenth century, this mode rapidly established itself with a niche of dedicated followers. From the late nineteenth century onwards, detective fiction with its characteristic clue–puzzle plot (in which the author sets up a puzzle with clues) found a firm footing, later diversifying into subgenres like historical mystery, police procedural, comic/parodic detective fiction, hinterland noir and feminist detective fiction. Indeed, as the elements of the genre were transformed, the subcontinental detective story at its best became a mode of testimonial literature, bearing witness to the ethical and socio-cultural ramifications of the advent of technological development and modernity in our spaces, especially in the context of the vexed afterlife of traumatic histories, marked by silence, amnesia and erasure, and the denial of justice.

While a comprehensive account of the history of the genre in India and the subcontinent awaits completion by specialists, we can certainly identify some landmarks in the adaptation of the genre across the subcontinent from colonial to postcolonial times. Let us take another look at the origins of the genre. According to several literary historians of Anglophone crime writing, precursors like William Godwin (*Things as They Are; or, The Adventures of Caleb Williams*, 1794, retitled 1831)[3] and Wilkie Collins (*The Moonstone*, 1868)[4] initiated an interest in the subject of crime and detection (also stimulated by the popularity of the Newgate novels detailing true crime stories in often lurid prose). However, modern detective (rather than crime) fiction came to the fore in the nineteenth century with the publication of Edgar Allan Poe's remarkable tales of ratiocination set in Paris such as 'The Murders in the Rue Morgue' (1841) and 'The Purloined Letter' (1844), featuring eccentric amateur sleuth C. Auguste Dupin.[5] The figure of the amateur detective became enshrined in popular culture with the appearance of Sherlock Holmes shortly after (modelled in part on Poe's character Dupin), in Arthur Conan Doyle's novels and short stories (the novel 'A Study in Scarlet' appeared in *Beeton's Christmas Annual* in 1887, while the story 'A Scandal in Bohemia' was published in the *Strand* magazine, in 1891, to immediate popular acclaim).[6]

Between 1911 and 1935, G.K. Chesterton's stories featuring Catholic priest Father Brown posed a challenge to the 'scientific' basis for detection, as spiritual and intuitive methods (at times even entailing a mirroring of the mind of the criminal) proved more efficacious in solving crimes.[7] Agatha Christie's Hercule Poirot was the best known of the detectives of the Golden Age of the genre in the 1920–40s, marked by the clue–puzzle structure and the notion of problem solving as a tacit game with the reader.[8] Indeed, Ronald Knox's Ten Commandments of Detective Fiction (1929) sought to formalize the 'fair play'-based (mock) rules for the genre that were broken famously, earlier by Christie herself in *The Murder of Roger Ackroyd* (1926), in which Dr Sheppard, the Watson-like narrator is eventually disclosed to be the killer.[9]

Children's detective fiction began to appear in the nineteenth century. Indeed, Mark Twain satirized the genre and its readership in *Tom Sawyer, Detective* (1896),[10] emphasizing the 'innocent' perceptions of the child (Huckleberry Finn) at the expense of the craft of the detective (Tom Sawyer).[11] The Golden Age also saw the flourishing of children's detective fiction in the marketplace, as Edward Stratemeyer formed a syndicate with a team of ghost writers, seeking to boost the fortunes of the genre; the first Hardy Boys novel came out in 1927, while Nancy Drew novels were published regularly from 1930 onwards under the Carolyn Keene pseudonym.[12] Christopher Routledge shows how the genre merged with conventions taken from adventure tales and thrillers from the 1940s, exemplified by Enid Blyton's Famous Five from 1942 onwards in England, later succeeded by the Secret Seven, with the ambiguous situation of the child detective vis-à-vis the adult world often decentering assumptions about children's inherent naiveté.[13] Robert Arthur's creation, the Three Investigators, with Alfred Hitchcock as patron, gave an extended lease of life to this subgenre with its greater degree of realism from 1964 to 1987.[14] Children across the Indian subcontinent (as I recall) eagerly devoured these tales, leading to the possibility of constructing counter-narratives and plots of their own as they grew older and became alert to the many stereotypes in such work.

In the hard-boiled detective fiction of Americans, Dashiell Hammett (Sam Spade), Raymond Chandler (Philip Marlowe) and Ross Macdonald (Lew Archer), published initially in magazines like *Black Mask* in the 1920–30s, we can see a greater interest in the subconscious mind and psychopathology, a trend which became more pronounced in the wake of the Great Depression, the two World Wars, and the Cold War.[15] The darker side to the city and human nature became the focus in noir-style narratives that unsettled definitions of good and evil, the law and its supposed antithesis, crime, with emphasis on the visceral rather than the cerebral.

After the second World War, the police procedural or police novel came to the fore with the 87th Precinct series of novels by Ed McBain in particular highlighting the importance of police teamwork, including forensic investigation and the laborious assembling of evidence, while acknowledging institutional imperfections and police corruption.[16] Subsequently, Patricia Cornwell's novels brought in a strong element of forensic science – her character Kay Scarpetta works as a pathologist in the laboratory and morgue, and the novels draw on the author's own experience as a technician in Virginia's Chief Medical Examiner's office.[17] The novels of Kathy Reichs, featuring forensic anthropologist Dr Temperance Brennan (also drawing on the author's professional experience in the field), took forward the emphasis on forensic detail, while Sara Paretsky's series of novels featuring V.I. Warshawski reconstructed the hard-boiled tradition from a feminist standpoint.[18]

Chester Himes (Coffin Ed Johnson and Grave Digger Jones) and Walter Mosley (Easy Rawlins), among others, articulated the Afro-American perspective in their crime and detective novels, underlining the vulnerability of the (often antiheroic) black detective in a racially divided society.[19] Meanwhile, the figure of the antihero in crime and detective fiction has mutated from the gentleman thief Raffles of the nineteenth century and Leslie Charteris's The Saint, through master criminals like Fantômas and Lupin to the more disturbing, even damaged transgressive figures like Patricia Highsmith's Tom Ripley and Jeff Lindsay's serial killer/forensic investigator Dexter Morgan.[20] Indeed, over the years the genre has taken on a plethora of new forms, often resulting in the redoing of genre boundaries, especially in Scandinavia and Latin America.[21]

To invoke a classic reflection from an earlier era, W.H. Auden, in 'The Guilty Vicarage', famously described the genre of detective fiction (the 'whodunit') as an exploration of the dialectic of innocence and guilt. In his account, detective fiction is a mode of escape literature, with magical satisfaction provided by a detective with powers of reasoning akin to a genius, who removes guilt by identifying who is guilty.[22] Yet, Auden conceded that there is a quest for absolution and a return to a lost state of innocence underlying the genre, in effect a pastoralizing impulse unifying aesthetics and ethics. This insight can be further extended and modified in the context of Indian and subcontinental detective fiction, which at its most interesting adapts the clue–puzzle plot to the social and cultural contexts in the region, positing ethnographic puzzles while addressing the problem of violence and the question of justice in local contexts, thus redirecting the quest from the realm of the personal or religious to the socio-political and cultural-collective domains.

The reckoning with criminal activity may be set in colonial times, as in early Bengali detective stories, or may be portrayed in a retrospective way as in postcolonial and historical detective fiction. We can often discern, even in tales with a contemporary setting, a longing for prelapsarian or precolonial innocence, an illustration of a subcontinental variation of the pastoralizing impulse with a different metaphysical and historical basis. In the best work in the genre, the decoding of the ethnographic puzzle involves a sifting of layers of culture and society and a critical questioning of hierarchical structures whether of race, class, caste, or gender. For example, as we will see in Ambai's story 'Sepal' in this volume, detective Sudha Gupta's gaze turns inward to her own personal space, as she unravels with delicacy a mystery pertaining to the situation of those from the LGBTQ community in Mumbai today. Such reinvention of form is often accompanied by a refusal of the closure provided by solving the case as in Golden Age detective fiction. The ambiguities rife in the apparatus of law enforcement inherited from the colonial state come to the fore in the most significant novels and stories, marked by open-endedness and indeterminacy, even an absence of solutions to the mystery at hand.[23]

In the subcontinent, detective fiction came into the regional languages as a result of translations into languages like Bengali, and later Hindi and Urdu, among others. As Shampa Roy shows, the Bengali *bhadralok* were forerunners in adopting the form, with *goyenda* (or detective in Bangla) magazines and novels appearing in the late nineteenth century with the advent of modernity in its colonial avatar (Calcutta was the colonial capital till 1911).[24] Anxieties about colonial law, surveillance and policing as well as racist stereotypes about Bengali 'effeminacy' fed into the construction of at times derivative narratives conjoining (hyper) masculinity and deductive skill, foregrounding the detective's immersion in Bengali culture.[25] Soon after, we also see the emergence on the scene of parodies of the form, as in the case of Rabindranath Tagore's 'Detective' (1898), unsparing of both the formulas of detective fiction as well as of the supposedly pristine cultural context of the genre's origins in colonial Britain.[26]

Francesca Orsini has mapped the coterminous cultural history of borrowing, adaptation and reinvention in Hindi and Urdu (from English and French as well as Bengali), in which the detective is termed *jasus* (or spy).[27] As Brueck and Orsini remind us, the figure of the *ayyar* in the *dastangoi* tradition in Urdu often sent on missions involving investigative work and espionage, resurfaced in the 'introduced genre' of early Hindi and Urdu crime fiction as the *jasus*, albeit with modifications, such as the emphasis on analysing evidence and proof rather than *lakshan* (bodily marks/signs) to attain the truth.[28] Local detective figures did not take long to appear as aspiring authors across the subcontinent sought to emulate western models and templates, also in the wake of the widespread circulation of pulp fiction, for instance at A.H. Wheeler stores at railway stations and the extensive readership that emerged following the publication of the latest story or novel in magazine form or as stand-alone editions. The emergence on the scene of figures like Saradindu Bandyopadhyay's Byomkesh Bakshi,[29] Satyajit Ray's Feluda,[30] and Ibne Safi's (pen name of Asrar Ahmad Narvi) Inspector (later Colonel) Faridi and Sergeant (later Captain) Imraan[31] was a marker of a more complex negotiation with modernity in its colonial, and later, postcolonial guises.[32] The best examples of such writing (Satyajit Ray's work in particular) enabled a critique of both the self and the other, with the genre also becoming a vehicle for social and cultural commentary, especially in Bengali detective fiction. In Ray's 'The Locked Chest', for instance, detective Feluda takes the train from Calcutta via Plassey to village Ghurghutia in the hinterland upon being summoned to help a retired Bengali gentleman, who is an avid reader of works of criminology by Émile Gaboriau, Poe and Conan Doyle. In this short tale, Ray brings in references to the first French detective story, the zamindari system and its style of architecture, as well as English nursery rhymes as Feluda strives to unravel the venal motives underlying the planned theft of a chest's valuable contents, besides deciphering a numerical code involving a parrot.

Brueck and Orsini show how from the 1970s to the 1990s 'hard-boiled' pulp Hindi detective fiction was predominant in North India, also a time of heightened political consciousness leading up to and in the wake of the Emergency (1975–77), with the city becoming identified with violence, both in terms of state-sponsored and communal violence.[33] *Jasoosi kahaniyan* (spy or mystery thrillers) in Urdu and Hindi by writers like Ved

Prakash Sharma, Om Prakash Sharma (both from Meerut), Anil Mohan and Surender Mohan Pathak, outpaced other literary forms in terms of sales.[34] Along the way, ghost writers thrived, especially in the case of the Colonel Ranjit series of stories, actually written by Maqbul Jalandhari, a journalist with the *Milap* daily.[35] Possibly as a result of over-simplistic, often ghost-written plots, as well as on account of the emergence of alternative forms of entertainment with the advent of cable TV and the mobile phone,[36] sales of *lugri sahitya* (Hindi pulp fiction) have gone into a steep decline in the twenty-first century, although the translation into English of bestselling novels by Pathak and others has sought to reverse the trend.[37]

In the wake of economic liberalization from 1991 onwards, we see an increasing sense of self-confidence in writers writing detective fiction in English, not only as imitations of the sleuths in Western precursor narratives, but as an attempt to explore the consequences of the rapid changes overtaking traditional society with the advent of techno-science and modern development, and their often destructive underbelly. A notable trend is the emergence on the scene of a number of women authors and women detectives, absent to a large extent prior to this.[38] Ambai began writing her Sudha Gupta series of detective stories in Tamil after establishing her credentials as a writer of literary short fiction, and has redefined the genre in significant ways in her delicately wrought stories set in Mumbai and its environs.[39]

A host of writers in the English language have published crime and detective fiction in the last two decades. Anuradha Kumar (based in Singapore and the USA, with crime novels set primarily in Orissa), Sujata Massey (based in America, her character Perveen Mistry is a Parsi lawyer in the making turned sleuth in colonial Bombay), Nev March (based in New Jersey, her character Jim Agnihotri, an Anglo-Indian sleuth during the time of the Raj), Swati Kaushal (based in Connecticut, her character Niki Marwah is a police superintendent in Simla), Shweta Taneja (based in the

US now, sleuth Anantya Tantrist), and Kishwar Desai (based in the UK, Simran Singh is a detective in Punjab) belong to the Indian diaspora.[40] Madhulika Liddle (creator of Muzaffar Jang, a maverick amir with deductive skills in Delhi in seventeenth century Mughal India),[41] Kalpana Swaminathan (Inspector Lalli in contemporary Mumbai), Meeti Shroff-Shah (Radhika Zaveri, a detective novelist and amateur sleuth in Mumbai), Anita Nair (Borei Gowda, a detective in Bangalore), Sukanya Datta (Lucky Shome, a detective with scientific training in Bengal), Kiran Manral (Mumbai), Harini Nagendra (colonial Bangalore) and Suchitra Bhattacharya (writing in Bengali, Mitin Mashi in Calcutta), have further consolidated the presence of women in the field, whether in India or abroad, heralding the advent of transnational feminist detective fiction with an Indian anchorage.[42]

Recent times have seen a proliferation of detective fiction in a variegated set of contexts, each with a unique cultural voice and identity. The break out moment for the form in English, albeit as an amalgam of detection and thriller, was the publication of Vikram Chandra's *Sacred Games*, in 2006, and the adaptation of the novel as a Netflix series in Hindi (2018).[43] Besides the authors mentioned above, although British writers H.R.F. Keating (Inspector Ghote) and Tarquin Hall (Vish Puri) chose Indian settings while writing from afar,[44] writers such as Vaseem Khan (based in the UK, his Police Inspector Persis Wadia is a Parsi in post-Independence Bombay, while in another series, detective Ashwin Chopra and Baby Ganesh, his pet elephant, live in contemporary Mumbai), Abir Mukherjee (based in the UK, his detectives Samuel Wyndham and Surendranath Banerjee solve mysteries in colonial Calcutta), A.A. Dhand (based in Scotland, Inspector Harry Virdee investigates crime in the UK and India), Ajay Chowdhury (located in Scotland, detective Kamil Rehman is situated in Kolkata and London), Avtar Singh (now based in Germany, his DCP Sajan Dayal, Kapoor, and Smita Dhingra are Delhi cops), Vish Dhamija (based in the UK, his police detective

Rita Ferreira, from Goa, works on cases in Mumbai), and Sujan DasGupta (based in the US, with stories in Bengali, amateur detective Ekenbabu solves mysteries in the US and occasionally Kolkata) are part of the Indian diaspora in Europe and the US.[45] Arjun Gaind (the Maharaja series during the Raj era), Salil Desai (Inspector Saralkar, in Pune), Ankush Saikia (Arjun Arora, in Delhi and Assam), Bhaskar Chattopadhyay (Janardhan Maity), Jerry Pinto (Inspector Zende and Peter D'Souza), Rajarshi Das Bhowmik (writing in Bengali, Inspector Kanaicharan), Tamilvanan (writing in Tamil, detective Shankarlal) and others in and from India have made effective contributions in this field.[46] We have also seen detective fiction and science fiction meet, with futuristic crimes becoming the subject of investigation (including robot/AI detectives) in times to come as genre hybridization continues to unfold, as the stories in this volume show. Indeed, strong instances of the intersectional potential of the form have begun to appear across the subcontinent, in Sri Lanka, Bangladesh and Pakistan as well, reflected in the selection of stories here by Saad Z. Hossain, Navin Weeraratne and Kehkashan Khalid.

For this anthology authors and translators of detective (rather than crime) fiction from the subcontinent were invited to contribute offbeat short stories in the detective fiction mode (5–7000 words), with emphasis on originality and distinctiveness of treatment of the chosen storyline and setting. While a setting in the subcontinent was not deemed to be crucial, the stories needed to feature a recognizably Indian/subcontinental dimension, whether in terms of character or aspects of the plot. Translations of classic works were welcome. The idea was not to simply tread the beaten path and recapitulate the well-worn clichés of the Golden Age, but to open the genre to experimental treatment, including modes of meta-fiction in Borgesian style,[47] as well as genre mixing. Approaches that encompass both formal innovation and social critique were especially sought. We hoped in the process to set the tone for the further reinvention of the genre of detective fiction in a subcontinental context, with cutting edge work by both upcoming and well-established writers. While not all writers chose to respond, with some expressing their preference for the longer form rather than the short story, many did send stories which extend the scope of the field in distinctive ways. As the luck of the draw (and editorial outreach so far) had it, we were fortunate to get several translations from the strongest regional tradition, Bengali, besides Tamil. We hope to enhance the number of detective stories in other regional languages in future volumes to come.

As we shall see, there is a considerable range in detective fiction emerging from India and the subcontinent in general of which this double volume anthology provides a glimpse. From classic whodunits to police procedurals, from feminist rewriting of the genre to postcolonial reinscriptions of history, as well as genre mixing of science fiction, fantasy and the thriller with detection, the diversity and imaginative versatility coming to the fore in the form is notable. The stories in Volume 1 are subdivided into three sections, classic whodunits with amateur detectives as protagonists, experimental and parodic detective fiction, and hybrid detective or existential or SF or fantasy stories. Volume 2, on the other hand, focuses on police procedurals and historical mysteries.

While early writing in Bengal and elsewhere was inevitably based on European models of detective fiction, the impetus to widen the readership locally has led to a different set of styles and voices emerging, often contesting dominant notions about race, community and class (Vikram Chandra's 'Kama' and Avtar Singh's 'Scandal in Punjab', among others), as well as caste (Shashi Warrier's 'A Murder in the Monsoons') and gender (Giti Chandra's 'A Darkling Plain', among others), even featuring androgynous detective figures (whether amateurs or professionals). The fault lines in our society have come to be interrogated from a distinctive Indian and subcontinental vantage point in the genre. The emergence of an alternative basis for ethics not simply content with the reinforcement of inherited values and codes or judicial precepts can be seen in the most significant detective stories, as modes of fictive testimony.

In the process there is a redefinition of the form, with a redirection of focus from neat solving of puzzles to an exploration of ethnographic complexity and socio-cultural contradictions, particularly in the light of failures to address long standing traumatic memories and silences, as justice continues to go a begging. Indeed, the genre of detective fiction in the region is growing by leaps and bounds, although the critical discourse is perhaps yet to come to terms with this. This double volume should thus be of interest to aficionados, students and general readers who share Auden's sense of being addicted to the form, as well as provide a fillip to new writing to come, as this series unfolds.

---

1. For a listing of popular Bollywood detective films, see Anwesha Tripathy, '15 Bollywood Detective Movies To Keep You On The Edge Of Your Seat!', *ScrollDroll*, 4 October 2021, accessed 3 June 2023. Among the early detective films, CID (dir. Raj Khosla, 1956) is notable, with fine performances by Dev Anand as a CID inspector and Waheeda Rehman as the femme fatale figure who eventually has a change of heart.
2. See Laura Brueck and Francesca Orsini, 'South Asian Crime Fiction', in Jesper Gulddal, Stewart King and Alistair Rolls, eds., *The Cambridge Companion to World Crime Fiction*, Cambridge: CUP, 2022, 141–59, esp. 141.
3. William Godwin, *Things as They Are; or, The Adventures of Caleb Williams,* 1794, retitled 1831, rpt. London: Penguin, 2005.
4. Wilkie Collins, *The Moonstone,* 1868, rpt. London: Penguin, 1994.
5. See John Scaggs's description of the amateur detective as a 'reasoning machine' in *Crime Fiction*, 2005, rpt. New Delhi: Routledge, 2009, esp. 39, also 33–54, Richard Bradford, *Crime Fiction: A Very Short Introduction*, Oxford: OUP, 2015, 1–35, Charles P. Rzpeka and Lee Horsley, eds., *A Companion to Crime Fiction*, Oxford: Blackwell, 2010, esp. 1–42. This British and American centered horizon is broadened in Nels Pearson and Marc Singer, eds., *Detective Fiction in a Postcolonial and Transnational World*, 2009, rpt. Oxon: Routledge, 2016, esp. 31–62, with essays on Vikram Chandra and Amitav Ghosh. An important collection of essays, Janice Allan, Jesper Gulddal, Stuart King and Andrew Pepper, eds. *The Routledge Companion to Crime Fiction*, Oxon: Routledge, 2020 indicates new directions in research, including thinking of crime fiction as a branch of world literature, esp. 1–30. I am indebted to Vaibhav Parel for these references.

6. See https://www.britannica.com/summary/Arthur-Conan-Doyle, accessed 26 April 2023, also Arthur Conan Doyle, 'A Scandal in Bohemia', in *The Adventures of Sherlock Holmes*, https://www.gutenberg.org/files/1661/1661-h/1661-h.htm, accessed 31 March 2023. While the Holmes novels and stories are marred at times by imperial biases and Orientalist stereotypes, for a literary recounting of an episode from Conan Doyle's life in which he confronted institutional racism while attempting to win a pardon for George Edalji, son of a Parsi vicar in Staffordshire, who became victim of a miscarriage of justice after being accused of mutilating animals, see Julian Barnes, *Arthur and George*, London: Vintage, 2005. Also Tim Adams, 'Show me the way to go, Holmes', *The Guardian*, 26 June 2005; Chandrayan Gupta, 'The Most Racist Sherlock Holmes Novel I Have Ever Read', *Medium*, 20 March 2021.
7. See Lee Horsley, 'From Sherlock Holmes to the Present', in Charles P. Rzpeka and Lee Horsley, eds., *A Companion to Crime Fiction*, 28–42, esp. 30.
8. See Scaggs, esp. 46–49. Also see Anthony Howell/Alex Tickell, 'Agatha Christie and the Golden Age of Detective Fiction', file:///C:/Users/Dell/Downloads/agatha_christie_and_the_golden_age_of_detective_fiction_printable.pdf, accessed 20 May 2023.
9. See Susan Rowland, 'The "Classical" Model of the Golden Age' in Charles P. Rzpeka and Lee Horsley, eds., *A Companion to Crime Fiction*, 119. Agatha Christie, *The Murder of* Roger Ackroyd, 1926, https://www.gutenberg.org/ebooks/69087, accessed 18 February 2023.
10. Mark Twain, *Tom Sawyer Abroad & Tom Sawyer, Detective*. 1896, rpt. Ware, Hertsfordshire: Wordsworth, 2009, 125–88.
11. See Christopher Routledge, 'Crime and Detective Fiction for Young Readers' in Charles P. Rzpeka and Lee Horsley, eds., *A Companion to Crime Fiction*, 321–31, esp. 324.
12. Ibid., 325–28.
13. Ibid., 328–31. Recently, among other critics, English Heritage has recognized the 'racism, xenophobia and lack of literary merit' in Enid Blyton's stories for children, citing the figure of Sambo in 'The Little Black Doll' in particular. Alison Flood, 'English Heritage recognises Blyton and Kipling's racism – but blue plaques to stay', *The Guardian*, 17 June 2021.
14. David Barnett, 'On the trail of the Three Investigators', *The Guardian*, 23 September 2010.
15. See Andrew Pepper 'The "Hardboiled" Genre' in Charles P. Rzpeka and Lee Horsley, eds., *A Companion to Crime Fiction*, 140–51. See Dashiell Hammett, *Red Harvest*, 1929, rpt. London: Orion, 2003, Raymond Chandler, *The Big Sleep and other Novels*, including *The Big Sleep* (1939), *Farewell my Lovely* (1940) and *The Long Goodbye* (1953), rpt. as omnibus 1993, London: Penguin Classics, 2000, Ross Macdonald, *The Galton Case*, 1950, London: Penguin Classics, 1950. Also see Fredric Jameson's magisterial account of Chandler's work in historical context, Fredric Jameson, *Raymond Chandler: The Detections of Totality*, 2016, rpt. London: Verso, 2022.
16. See Lee Horsley, 'From Sherlock Holmes to the Present', in Charles P. Rzpeka and Lee Horsley, eds., *A Companion to Crime Fiction*, 28–42, esp. 35, as well as Peter Messent, 'The Police Novel', in Charles P. Rzpeka and Lee Horsley, eds., *A Companion to Crime Fiction*, 175–86.

17. See Sarah Dauncey, 'Crime, Forensics and Modern Science', in Charles P. Rzpeka and Lee Horsley, eds., *A Companion to Crime Fiction*, 164–74, esp. 171–72. Also see Patricia Cornwell, *Predator*, New York: Putnam's, 2005.

18. See Kathy Reichs, *Bones Never Lie*, 2014, rpt. London: Penguin, 2022, Sara Paretsky, *Fire Sale*, New York: Berkley, 2006.

19. See Frankie Bailey, 'Afro-American Detection and Crime Fiction', in Charles P. Rzpeka and Lee Horsley, eds., *A Companion to Crime Fiction*, 270. Also see Chester Himes, *A Rage in Harlem*, 1957, rpt. New York: Vintage, 1991, Walter Mosley, *Rose Gold*, 2014, rpt. New York: Vintage, 2015.

20. Personal communication, Thomas Abraham, also Horsley, 'From Sherlock Holmes to the Present', in Charles P. Rzpeka and Lee Horsley, eds., *A Companion to Crime Fiction*, 28–42, 40–41. Also see Maurice Leblanc, *Arsene Lupin: Gentleman Burglar*, trans. Alexander Texeira de Mattos, rpt. Gurugram: Hachette India, 2021.

21. See Sue Neale, 'Crime Writing in Other Languages' in Charles P. Rzpeka and Lee Horsley, eds., *A Companion to Crime Fiction*, 296–307. Among the most interesting attempts to unpack and reinvent the genre from South America is Gabriel Garcia Marquez's *Chronicle of a Death Foretold*, Trans. Gregory Rabassa, 1982, rpt. New Delhi: Penguin, 1986.

22. W. H. Auden, 'The Guilty Vicarage', 1948, https://harpers.org/archive/1948/05/the-guilty-vicarage/, accessed 6 February 2023.

23. For a brilliant historical analysis of the ambivalences pertaining to colonial law in its encounter with local/subaltern contradictions, with specific reference to gender and caste, in the context of the tragic death of a *bagdi* woman in colonial Bengal named Chandra, see Ranajit Guha, 'Chandra's Death' (1987), in Ranajit Guha, ed., *A Subaltern Studies Reader* (1986–95), Minneapolis: Univ. of Minneapolis, 1997.

24. According to Shampa Roy, this was in the wake of Bangla readers reading English crime/detective fiction or European crime/detective fiction translated into English, including Wilkie Collins, Conan Doyle, Eugene Sue, Gaboriau, as well as Vidocq's *Memoirs*. See Shampa Roy, *Gender and Criminality in Bangla Crime Narratives: Late Nineteenth and Early Twentieth Centuries*, London: Palgrave Macmillan, 2017, Introduction, 6. As Roy says, 'The genre thrived and flourished and detective fictions writers like Sharatchandra Sarkar, Kshetramohan Ghosh, Surendramohan Bhattacharya, Dinendrakumar Ray and Pachkari De became hugely popular and commercially successful.' Roy, Introduction, 37–38.

25. See ibid., also Upamanyu Pablo Mukherjee, 'Introduction', *Crime and Empire: The Colony in Nineteenth Century Fictions of Crime*, Oxford: OUP, 2003, 1–21.

26. Rabindranath Tagore, 'Detective', 1898, trans. Shampa Roy, *Metamorphosis*, Volume 29, Issue 2, Fall/Winter 2021, Ed. Thalia Paniri, 123–31, reprinted in this volume.

27. See Francesca Orsini, 'Detective Novels: A Commercial Genre in Nineteenth Century North India' in Stuart Blackburn and Vasudha Dalmia eds., *India's Literary History: Essays on the Nineteenth Century* (Delhi: Permanent Black, 2004), 436. Also see Francesca Orsini, *Print and Pleasure: Popular Literature and Entertaining Fictions in Colonial North India*. (Delhi: Permanent Black, 2009). Peter Friedlander has a succinct account of the rise and fall of 'Hindi Pulp Detective Fiction' in *Situations* 8.2 (2015):

27–47. For Urdu crime fiction, also see C.M. Naim, *Urdu Crime Fiction: 1890–1950, An Informal History,* New Delhi: Orient Blackswan, 2023.

28. Brueck and Orsini, 'South Asian Crime Fiction', 143–44.

29. Saradindu Bandyopadhyay's stories appeared initially from 1931–36, then again after a break during which he wrote screenplays in Bombay, from 1952–70. Satyajit Ray's adaptation of a story as *Chiriakhana* in 1967 with Uttam Kumar as Byomkesh Bakshi was a major event, followed by the extremely popular Hindi language adaptation of the entire series of 37 stories on Doordashan in 1993 and 1997 by Basu Chatterjee with Rajit Kapur as Byomkesh and K.K. Raina as Ajit, and a Bangla series in 2017 across three seasons with Anirban Bhattacharya as Byomkesh. At least sixteen films have been made as well, including Dibakar Banerjee's Hindi film *Detective Byomkesh Bakshy!* (2015). See Brueck and Orsini, 145–46.

30. Pradosh Chandra Mitter, better known as Feluda, and his assistant Tapesh Ranjan Mitter (nicknamed Topshe, the narrator of the stories) first appeared in a story published in the Bangla magazine *Sandesh* in 1965, and subsequently became immensely popular figures with a pan-Indian fan following. Ibid., 147. Satyajit Ray directed Bengali movies *Sonar Kella* (1974) and *Joi Baba Felunath* (1979), starring Soumitra Chatterjee as Feluda, and many adaptations of Feluda stories for the small screen have since been directed by his son Sandip Ray. For a fine reading of the Ray oeuvre, contrasting his cinematic creations with his SF and crime writing, see Ashis Nandy, 'Satyajit Ray's Secret Guide to Exquisite Murders: Creativity, Social Criticism, and The Partitioning of the Self' in *The Savage Freud and other essays on possible and retrievable selves*, New Delhi: OUP, 1999, 237–66.

31. Inspector Faridi first appeared in 1952 in the monthly *Jasoosi Dunya* (Detective/Spy World) series, shortly before Ibne Safi migrated to Pakistan, with 127 books appearing before the author's death in 1979. These were published simultaneously in Karachi and Allahabad in Urdu and Hindi, with Faridi becoming Vinod and Imran becoming Rajesh in Hindi. See Brueck and Orsini, 147–48. Also see the Faridi novel by Ibne Safi, *The Laughing Corpse*, 1957, trans. Shamsur Rahman Faruqi, Chennai: Blaft, 2011 and the Imran novellas in *The House of Fear*, trans. Bilal Tanveer, Gurugram: Penguin Random House, 2009.

32. See Nishat Zaidi's editorial on Urdu detective fiction 'Detective Fiction in Urdu: Form, Function, Genealogy'. See https://www.thebookreviewindia.org/detective-fiction-in-urdu-form-function-genealogy/, accessed 12 February 2023.

33. Brueck and Orsini, 150–53.

34. Ibid. 151. Also see Sanjay Srivastava's fascinating discussion of 'thrilling affects' and masculinity in Ved Prakash Sharma's work. 'Thrilling Affects: Sexuality, Masculinity, the City and 'Indian Traditions' in the Contemporary Hindi 'Detective' Novel', in *Interventions*, 2013, Vol. 15, No. 4, 567585, http://dx.doi.org/10.1080/136980 1X.2013.849426, accessed 15 February 2023.

35. See 'Pulp Friction', https://economictimes.indiatimes.com/pulp-friction/articleshow/ 1800843.cms?from=mdr, accessed 12 February, 2023. Surender Mohan Pathak's Framed is a crime novel which features his anti-hero Vimal, a master of impersonation and disguise. See S.M. Pathak, *Framed*, translator not mentioned, Noida: HarperCollins, 2017. Also, see Pathak's dismissal of the ghost writers of the 1980s as a short lived phase in an interview, Vijay Chopra, 'Lord of thrillers continues

to pen page turners in digital age', *Times of India*, 12 October 2020, accessed 15 February 2023.

36. See Friedlander, 'Hindi Pulp Detective Fiction', *Situations* 8.2 (2015): 27–47.

37. Brueck and Orsini mention in particular publisher Blaft's attempt to translate Tamil and Urdu fiction in translation as desi kitsch, in their account thus implying irony and nostalgia. Ibid. 157

38. As Brueck and Orsini point out, not many women writing detective fiction can be seen in regional languages. However, Vai. Mu. Kothanayaki Ammal (1901–60), the first female detective novelist in Tamil, began writing in the 1930s. The first English-language detective novel by an Indian woman, *Detective Janaki*, by Kamala Satthianadhan was serialized from 1933 to 1934 in the English-language journal *Indian Ladies' Magazine*. See ibid., 153–55.

39. See the collection by Ambai, *A Meeting on the Andheri Overbridge*, trans. Gita Subramanian, New Delhi: Juggernaut, 2016.

40. See for example Anuradha Kumar (writing as Anu Kumar), *It Takes a Murder*, Gurgaon: Hachette India, 2012, also *The Hottest Summer in Years*, New Delhi: Yoda Press, 2021, Sujata Massey, *A Murder on Malabar Hill: Perveen Mistry Investigates*, New Delhi: Penguin Random House, 2018, Nev March, *Murder in Old Bombay: A Mystery*, 2020, rpt. New Delhi: HarperCollins, 2021, Swati Kaushal, *Drop Dead*, Gurugram: Hachette India, 2012.

41. See Anjana Neira Dev, 'No Cookie-Cutter Criminals Here: In Conversation with Madhulika Liddle', in Shraddha A. Singh, ed., *Speculation and Detection: Explorations in Genre Fiction*, New Delhi: Worldview, 2022, 157–82.

42. For instance, see Madhulika Liddle, *The Eighth Guest and other Muzaffar Jang Mysteries*, 2011, rpt. Gurgaon: Hachette India, 2015, *Crimson City*, Gurgaon: Hachette India, 2015, Meeti Shroff-Shah, *The Death of Kirti Kadakia: A Temple Hill Mystery*, New Delhi: Bloomsbury, 2022, Harini Nagendra, *The Bangalore Detectives Club*, London: Constable, 2022.

43. See Brueck and Orsini, 156. Vikram Chandra, *Sacred Games*, 2006: Gurgaon: Penguin Random House, 2006, and *Sacred Games*, Netflix series based on the novel, dir. Vikramaditya Motane and Anurag Kashyap, starring Saif Ali Khan and Nawazuddin Siddiqui, 2018/2019. For a precursor thriller featuring a nuclear terrorism-based plot, with an IB detective from Bombay investigating the case in Delhi, see Ramesh Menon's *The Hunt for K*, New Delhi: Ravi Dayal, 1992.

44. Between 1964 and 2008, H.R.F. Keating wrote twenty-six Inspector Ghote novels, while Tarquin Hall has published five Vish Puri novels so far. See Brueck and Orsini, 155. The first Inspector Ghote novel, *The Perfect Murder* (1964), was adapted as a film starring Naseeruddin Shah (dir. Zafar Hai, 1988). See https://en.wikipedia.org/wiki/The_Perfect_Murder_(1988_film), accessed 28 May, 2023. Also see for instance Tarquin Hall, *The Case of the Missing Servant*, 2009, rpt. London: Arrow Books, 2010.

45. For example, see Vaseem Khan, *Midnight at Malabar House*, London: Hodder & Stoughton, 2020, Abir Mukherjee, *A Rising Man*, 2016, rpt. London: Vintage, 2017, A.A. Dhand, *The Blood Divide*, London: Transworld, 2021, Ajay Chowdhury, *The Waiter*, London: Harvill Secker, 2021, Avtar Singh, *Necropolis*, Gurugram: Fourth Estate, 2014, Vish Dhamija, *Bhendi Bazaar*, 2014, rpt. Noida: HarperCollins, 2019.

46. See for instance, Arjun Gaind, *A Very Pukka Murder: A Maharajah Mystery*, Noida: HarperCollins, 2016, Salil Desai, *Murder Milestone: An Inspector Saralkar Mystery*, New Delhi: Finger Print, 2020, Ankush Saikia, *Dead Meat*, New Delhi: Penguin Random House, 2015.

47. Borges wrote three remarkable parodies of detective fiction in meta-fictional style. See Jorge Luis Borges, 'The Garden of the Forking Paths' (1941), 'Death and the Compass' (1942), 'Ibn-Hakam al Bokhari, Murdered in his Labyrinth', in *Collected Fictions*, tr. Andrew Hurley, 1998, rpt. Penguin: Harmondsworth, 1999, 119–48, 147–57, 255–62

Volume 1

CLASSIC DETECTIVE FICTION – THE AMATEURS

This section features stories following the whodunit template of Holmes and Christie, with modifications, occasional subversion and cultural re-inflections added.

Satyajit Ray's 'The Locked Chest' (tr. Gopa Majumdar) is a variation on the scenario of a locked chest mystery, with a code carrying – parrot acting as a mnemonic device for local colour.[1] The story narrated by the sidekick Topshe brings in several references to criminology as well as the history of the genre of detective fiction as Feluda (Pradosh C. Mitter), an admirer of Holmes, brings his deductive ability to bear on the problem at hand, conjoining code-breaking and his skill at seeing through disguises and illusions while solving a mystery in the hinterland.

Saradindu Bandyopadhyay's 'The Rhythm of the Riddles' (tr. Arunava Sinha) is a post-Independence tale featuring Calcutta detective Byomkesh Bakshi.[2] The narration by his friend Ajit babu may, to begin with, remind us of Watson's role in the Holmes stories. However, this story, which begins with a lighthearted game of bridge, takes on serious overtones as it summons up memories of Partition-era violence and takes up the problem of retributive justice in an altogether novel, if problematic way.

Ambai is the creator of the Sudha Gupta detective series in Tamil. 'Sepal', translated by Gita Subramanian, is an atypical tale that explicitly recognizes the dreary and wearisome side of amateur detective work in the city of Mumbai. Here we find Sudha's gaze turn inwards, as she deals with a personal situation with respect

---

[1] Satyajit Ray, 'The Locked Chest' in *The Complete Adventures of Feluda*, vol. 1, trans. Gopa Majumdar, 2000, rev. ed. New Delhi: Penguin, 2004, 487-506, reprinted in this volume.

[2] In Saradindu Bandyopadhyay, *The Rhythm of the Riddles: 3 Byomkesh Bakshi Mysteries*, trans. Arunava Sinha, New Delhi: Puffin, 2012, reprinted in this volume.

to the daughter of her helper Chellamal. The ambivalences of gender and the ethical conundrums and questions that may arise in the context of the LGBTQ domain even in a cosmopolitan setting like Mumbai are addressed with finesse.

Meeti Shroff-Shah's recent debut *The Death of Kirti Kadakia* has won critical acclaim. 'Gulmohar House' is a story set in a Mumbai apartment house, with keen psychological insights into the minds of families with the task of looking after someone with a terminal disability. The perspective of a nurse/caretaker allows for the disclosure of the consequences of the advent of empathy fatigue as a death occurs within such a family, not entirely free from doubt.

Ankush Saikia's hinterland noir story 'The River' places amateur detective Arjun Arora in the terrain of the North-East, where Arora's skills help to track down the identity of those involved in a killing embroiled in the politics of dam building in this environmentally sensitive area. High-level corruption and the machinations of corporate interests in collusion with local lobbies contending with anti-dam activists provide a murky contrast to the natural beauty of the location in the North-East (the region where Arjun's mother is from).

Anirudh Kala is a practising psychiatrist, as well as a writer, and his collection of short stories *The Unsafe Asylum* has been noticed by critics and readers alike.[3] In 'No Thermometer for Insanity' we are introduced to a trainee psychiatrist and amateur detective, Dr Baani Sandhu, investigating a suspicious death in a mental asylum. Unravelling the web of deceit underlying the apparent suicide of an inmate requires attention to the politics of land, and the intermeshing of greed, desire and melancholia in provincial Punjab where insanity may be in Mantoesque fashion, set up as a charade to mask dark motivations.

Suchitra Bhattacharya's 'Lethal Air', translated by Radha Chakravarty, brings to the fore the deductive and forensic skills of Mitin Mashi, a woman amateur detective in Kolkata, who

[3] Anirudh Kala, *The Unsafe Asylum: Stories of Partition and Madness*, New Delhi: Speaking Tiger, 2018.

is introduced to what seems to be a straightforward case by a sympathetic police officer. The dilemmas faced by caretakers of someone with a debilitating injury are rendered sensitively with specific reference to the woman's perspective. The story questions the prevalence of masculinist assumptions that wreck the fragile understanding underpinning a marriage in the wake of an accident, also foregrounding Mitin Mashi's intuitive deciphering of psychological motives.

Sujan DasGupta sadly passed away shortly after the completion of the translation of his story 'All that Glitters: An Ekenbabu Story' by Chandana Dutta. DasGupta wrote in Bengali despite being based in the US, and his Ekenbabu series has been popular among expatriates as well as readers of detective fiction in Bengal. Besides the published works, the stories have been adapted as a streaming series and a film.[4] Here we have a story narrated in first person by Bapi, a teacher of Physics at New York University, and a friend and flatmate of Ekenbabu, who helps in the criminology department. The disappearance of diamonds from the shop of a jeweller proves to be a difficult case to crack for the local police, until the amateur skills of Ekenbabu lead to a discovery of the modus operandi in a story that explores the inner workings of the trade in precious stones across international borders.

Tamilvanan's 'Tokyo Rose' (from 1967, trans. Pritham K. Chakravarthy) brings in an element of humour to begin with, as iconic detective Shankarlal tries to find some respite from popular adulation in Japan. The protagonist is nonetheless irresistibly drawn into an ostensible case of kidnapping of a Tamil actress in Tokyo, also solving the mystery of liquids turning blue along the way. This larger-than-life persona of the dashing globetrotting detective owes as much to Ian Fleming and the Bond films as to models in the cinematic traditions of Tamil Nadu in a story that revels in its own kitsch elements and exoticism.

---

[4] Dr Partha Bandopadhyay, 'Creator Sujan Dasgupta leaves "Eken babu" in limbo', *GetBengal*, 18 February 2023.

EXPERIMENTAL/PARODIC DETECTIVE FICTION

In this section we feature experimental, genre bending and parodic treatments of the form, as detective fiction takes a speculative and self-referential turn.

Rabindranath Tagore was a colossus in the field of literature and the arts, renowned as a poet, dramatist, littérateur, and artist, as the Nobel Prize committee recognized in 1913. He did occasionally turn his attention to popular forms such as the ghost story, in 'The Hungry Stones'[5] and detective fiction in his tale 'Detective'. First published in 1898, this story brings in a parodic thrust to the first-person account of the central character, detective Mahimchandra, whose wife is jealous of his devotion to his work. His acute sense of disappointment at the mundane manifestation of criminal tendencies in Bengal in comparison to the sinister criminals of Europe leads our detective to embark on an investigation of a possible criminal mastermind named Manmath, which eventually redounds on himself and his family situation, with comic consequences.

Anil Menon writes speculative fiction, often causing us to reflect on the form he is writing in, as we have seen in his recent collection *The Inconceivable Idea of the Sun*.[6] This meta-fictional tilt can be seen in his story 'A Death Considered', which makes us rethink the structure of the whodunit, positing the notion of a 'whotodoin' as the narrator attempts to redefine the existential detective story with near mathematical precision. The sophisticated and self-reflexive 'writerly' text makes us think afresh about the formulas and plot devices common to the genre, with its wry references and humorous digs at precursors and naïve readers, effectively turning the genre inside out in its refusal to provide closure.

---

[5] Rabindranath Tagore, 'Hungry Stones', trans. of 'Kshudito Pashan' by Ruma Chakravarti, *The Space.ink*, 31 March 2023.

[6] Anil Menon, *The Inconceivable Idea of the Sun*, Gurugram: Hachette India, 2022.

Tanuj Solanki's Mumbai crime novel *Manjhi's Mayhem* has been well received.[7] His story 'The Desire of the Detective' is also set in Mumbai, a self-reflexive tale with a writer of detective fiction as victim and a detective with literary pretensions on the hunt for an elusive killer who may possibly be another writer of detective fiction or even a reader fascinated by the writer's last set of questions about the form. As meta-fiction, this open-ended story makes us think about the nature of construction of meaning and its deconstruction, with the death of the author becoming a telling metaphor, even as the form becomes a pretext for the exploration of desire in such a cosmopolitan context as contemporary Mumbai.

HYBRID SF/FANTASY/EXISTENTIAL DETECTIVE FICTION – MIXED GENRES

The stories here exemplify the porosity and playfulness beginning to manifest itself in popular fiction. The boundaries between the genres are blurred as new hybrid forms take shape, featuring tropes from science fiction, fantasy and the existential thriller.

Saad Z. Hossain from Bangladesh has carved out a niche of his own with his blend of middle Eastern lore, fantasy and science fiction tropes, seasoned with doses of black comedy. In 'The Detective of Black Korail' the Korail slum in Dhaka becomes the locale for a highly unusual murder investigation. In this speculative space, witches, golem and djinns commingle, and advanced nanotechnology is taken for granted. The story achieves an effect of light parody, as elements from various subgenres are blended. Magic and cognition are invoked in the unexpected resolution at the end, with some pointed black humour directed at subcontinental bureaucratic ways, even in an occult setting.

Timeri N. Murari is another established name in Indian

---

[7] Tanuj Solanki, *Manjhi's Mayhem*, New Delhi: Penguin Random House, 2022.

Writing in English.[8] 'She Has My Name' is in the mode of the existential thriller, braiding together elements from detective, crime and spy fiction. The quest is a personal one, as the unnamed operative/protagonist returns to his homeland to reclaim his dead daughter's body, facing sinister antagonists representing the State. This psychological terrain, reminiscent of Graham Greene and Eric Ambler, is ambivalent, marked by shadowy detours and dead ends.

Kehkashan Khalid is a young writer of speculative fiction from Jeddah, Saudi Arabia. 'Andheri Nagri' located in Karachi, is a tale that blends science fiction and detective fiction. We have a time travelling perpetrator/serial killer/vigilante and a detective on her trail, a scenario that leads to several metaphysical and temporal enigmas coming to the fore. The ethical implications of changing timelines through violent action are addressed through the vantage point of the detective traveller through the gateway in the fort, who has considerable personal investment in the quest, as we see.

Navin Weeraratne is a Sri Lankan writer of speculative and science fiction. In the cyberpunk style story 'DeathGPT' he explores the dilemmas of the advent of monetized virtual sexuality in the age of artificial intelligence, with a detective on the trail of the killer of an internet sex symbol. The ethical conundrums inaugurated by ChatGPT style AI with almost limitless possibilities of fakery, simulation and replication online are negotiated with an awareness of the slippery ethical terrain that criminalization of the programmers of such seductive hi-tech machines may open up.

Sumit Bardhan is a bilingual writer from Kolkata who writes in varied genres, including science fiction and steampunk. His story 'Death of an Actress' to begin with unravels the financial maze that underpins the workings of a metropolis like Kolkata, as an investigative journalist seeks to uncover the motivations

---

[8] See for example Timeri N. Murari, *The Taliban Cricket Club*, 2012, rpt. New Delhi: Aleph, 2013.

underlying the death of a Tollywood actress and several other cases of apparent suicide. Pattern recognition plays a crucial role in this story, which is in hybrid SF/detective fiction mode, and has an unexpected twist in conclusion.

Kiran Manral's story 'Witch Hunting' is a blend of science fiction and detective fiction, with an elite squad detective from a future era travelling back to hunt down a time escapee. The story's protagonist is sent back to 1984 Bombay, where she faces an unusual dilemma embodied in the form of the monstrous *chudail* or witch. The story delves into questions of mirroring of identity and the implications on the self of time transfer through portals, as the detective figure deals with the ambiguities that result from (high) technological glitches and split selfhood.

Shweta Taneja writes fantasy and speculative fiction, with several novels featuring Anantya Tantrist, a woman detective with unusual training in the occult arts of Tantrism. Her story 'A Messiah of Tears and Broken Things' is an origin story for Anantya Tantrist, who discovers the extent of her shakti (or power) while tracking a murderer among the aghori Tantriks in the Himalayas.

THE LOCKED CHEST

Satyajit Ray, tr. Gopa Majumdar

Village: Ghurghutia
P.O. Plassey
Dist. Nadia
3 November 1974

To:
Mr Pradosh C. Mitter

Dear Mr Mitter,
I am writing to invite you to my house. I have heard a lot about your work and wish to meet you in person. There is, of course, a special reason for asking you to come at this particular time. You will get to know the details on arrival. If you feel you are able to accept this invitation from a seventy-three-year-old man, please confirm your acceptance in writing immediately. In order to reach Ghurghutia, you need to disembark at Plassey, and travel further south for another five and a half miles. There are several trains from Sealdah, out of which the Up Lalgola Passenger leaves at 1.58 p.m. and reaches Plassey at 6.11 p.m. I will arrange for you to be met at the station and brought here. You can spend the night at my house and catch the same train at 10.30 a.m. the following morning to Calcutta. I look forward to hearing from you.

With good wishes,
Yours sincerely,
Kalikinkar Majumdar

I handed the letter back to Feluda and asked, 'Is it the same Plassey where that famous battle was fought?'

'Yes. There is no other Plassey in Bengal, dear boy. But if you think the place has got any evidence left of that historic battle, you are sadly mistaken. There is absolutely no sign left, not even the palash trees in the woods that stood in Siraj-ud-daula's time. The name "Plassey" came from these trees. Did you know that?'

I nodded. 'Will you go, Feluda?'

Feluda stared at the letter for a few seconds.

'I wonder why an old man wants to see me,' he said thoughtfully. 'It doesn't seem right to refuse. To be honest, I am quite curious. Besides, have you ever been to a village in the winter? Have you seen how the mist gathers in open fields at dawn and dusk? All that remains visible are tree trunks and a little area over one's head. Darkness falls suddenly and it can get really cold... I haven't seen all this for years. Go on, get me a postcard, Topshe.'

Mr Majumdar was told to expect us on 12 November. Feluda chose this date, keeping in mind that a letter from Calcutta would take at least three days to reach him.

We took the 365 Up Lalgola Passenger and reached Plassey at 6.30 p.m. I saw from the train what Feluda had meant by darkness falling quickly. The last lingering rays of the setting sun disappeared from the rice fields almost before I knew it. By the time we left the station after handing over our tickets to the collector at the gate, all lights had been switched on, although the sky still held a faint reddish glow. The car that was parked outside had to be Mr Majumdar's. I had never seen a car like that. Feluda said he might have seen one or two when he was a child. All he knew was that it was an American car. Its colour must have been dark red once, but now the paint had peeled off in many places. The hood, too, bore patches here and there and showed signs of age. In spite of all this, there was something rather impressive about the car. I couldn't help feeling a certain amount of awe.

A car like that ought to have had a chauffeur in uniform. The man who was leaning against it, smoking a cigarette, was dressed in a dhoti and a shirt. He threw away his cigarette when he saw us and straightened himself. 'To see Mr Majumdar?' he asked.

'Yes, to Ghurghutia.'

'Very well, sir. This way, please.'

The driver opened a door for us and we climbed into the forty-year-old car. He then walked over to the front of the car to crank the handle, which made the engine come to life. He got behind the wheel and began driving. We settled ourselves comfortably, but the road being full of potholes and the springs in the seat being old, our comfort did not last for very long. However, once we had passed through the main town of Plassey and were actually out in the country, the scenery became so beautiful that I ceased to feel any discomfort. It wasn't yet totally dark, and I could see tiny villages across large rice fields, surrounded by trees. In their midst, the mist rose from the ground and spread like a smoky blanket a few feet above the ground. 'Pretty as a picture' was the phrase that came to mind.

An old, sprawling mansion in a place like this came as a total surprise. Ten minutes after we started, I realized that we were passing through private land, for the trees were now mango, jamun and jackfruit. The road then turned right. We passed a broken and abandoned temple and suddenly found ourselves facing a huge white, moss-covered gate, on the top of which was a *naubatkhana* (a music room). The driver sounded his horn three times before passing through the gate. The mansion came into view immediately.

The last traces of red had disappeared from the sky, leaving a deep purple hue. The dark house stood against the sky, like a towering cliff. We got out and followed the driver. As we got closer, I realized the whole house could be kept in a museum. Its walls were all damp, plaster had peeled off in several places and small plants had grown out of cracks in the exposed bricks. We stopped before the front door.

'No one in this area has electricity, I take it?' Feluda asked. 'No, sir. For nearly three years, all we've heard are promises. But nothing's happened yet,' the driver replied.

I glanced up. From where I was standing, a lot of windows on the first floor were visible. But each room was in darkness. On our right, through a couple of bushes, a light flickered in a tiny hut. Perhaps that was where a *mali* or *chowkidar* lived. I shivered silently. What sort of a place was this? Perhaps Feluda should have made more enquiries before agreeing to come.

Light from a lantern fell in the doorway. Then an old servant appeared at the door. The driver had gone, possibly to put the car away. The servant glanced at us with a slight frown, then said, 'Please come in.' We stepped in behind him.

There was no doubt that the house sprawled over a large area. But everything inside it seemed surprisingly small. The doors were not high, the windows were half the size of windows in any house in Calcutta and it was almost possible to touch the ceiling if I raised my arm. 'This house clearly belonged to a zamindar.' Feluda remarked. 'All the houses built by zamindars in the villages in Bengal about two hundred years ago were built like this.'

We crossed a long passage, then turned right to go up a flight of stairs. A strange contraption met my eyes as we got to the first floor. 'This is called a "covered door". It's like a trapdoor, really,' Feluda told me. 'These were built to stop burglars and dacoits from getting in. If you shut it, it would cease standing upright. Then it would fold automatically and lie flat, stretching diagonally across, to form a kind of ceiling over our heads. So, anyone trying to climb up would be shut out. See those holes in the door? Spears used to be slipped out of those holes to fight intruders.'

Luckily, the door was now standing wide open. We began crossing another long corridor. An oil lamp burnt in a niche in the wall where it ended. The servant opened a door next to this niche and ushered us in.

The room we stepped into was quite large. It might have seemed even larger had it not been stuffed with so much furniture. Nearly half of it had been taken up by a massive bed. To the left of this bed was a table and a chest. Besides these, there were three chairs, a wardrobe and bookshelves that went right up to the ceiling. Each shelf was crammed with books. An old man was lying on the bed, a blanket drawn upto his chin. In the flickering light of a candle, I saw that through a salt-and-pepper beard and moustache, he was smiling at us.

'Please sit down,' he invited.

'Thank you. This is my cousin, Tapesh. I wrote to you about him,' Feluda said. Mr Majumdar smiled again and nodded. I noticed that he did not fold his hands in reply to my 'namoskar'.

We took the chairs nearest to the bed.

'My letter must have made you curious,' Mr Majumdar observed lightly.

'Yes, it certainly did. Or I'd never have travelled this distance.'

'Good.' Mr Majumdar looked genuinely pleased. 'If you hadn't come, I would have felt very disappointed and thought you to be arrogant; and you would have missed out on something. But perhaps you have read these books already?' Mr Majumdar's eyes turned towards the table. Four bound volumes were arranged in a pile next to a candle. Feluda got up and picked them up. 'Good heavens!' he exclaimed. 'These are all extremely rare and they are all to do with my profession. Did you ever...?'

'No, no,' Mr Majumdar laughed, 'I never tried to become a detective myself. It has always been a hobby. You see, fifty-two years ago, someone in our family was murdered. An English investigator called Malcolm caught the killer. After speaking to Malcolm and learning something about his work, I became interested in criminology. That was when I bought those books. I was also very fond of reading detective novels. Have you heard of Émile Gaboriau?'

'Yes, yes,' Feluda replied with enthusiasm, 'wasn't he a French writer? He wrote the first detective novel, I think.'

'That's right,' Mr Majumdar nodded. 'I've got all his books. And, of course, books by writers like Edgar Allan Poe and Conan Doyle. I bought all these forty years ago. Of late, I believe, there has been a lot of progress and now there are many scientific and technical ways to catch a criminal. But from what little I know of your work, you strike me as one who depends more on old-fashioned methods and uses his brain more than anything else, very successfully. Am I right?'

'I do not know how successful I've been, but you're certainly right about my methods.'

'That is why I asked you to visit me.'

Mr Majumdar paused. Feluda returned to his chair. After a while, Mr Majumdar resumed speaking, staring straight at the flame of the candle. 'I am not only old – I crossed seventy some years ago – but also ailing. God knows what's going to happen to my books when I die. So, I thought if I could give you a few, they'd be appreciated and looked after.'

Feluda looked at the books in the shelves in surprise. 'Are all of those your own?' he asked.

'Yes. I was the only one in my family with an interest in books. Criminology wasn't the only subject that held my interest, as you can see.'

'Yes, of course. I can see books on archaeology, painting, gardening, history, biographies, travelogues... even drama and the theatre! Some of them appear to be new. Do you still buy books?'

'Oh yes. I have a manager called Rajen. He goes to Calcutta two or three times every month. I make him a list of books and he goes and gets them from College Street.'

Feluda looked once more at the books kept on the table. 'I don't know how to thank you.'

'You don't have to. It would have given me a lot of pleasure if I could actually hand them over to you myself, but both my hands are useless.'

Startled, we stared at him. His hands were hidden under the blanket, but I would never have thought that that had a special significance.

'Arthritis,' Mr Majumdar explained, 'has affected all my fingers. My son happens to be visiting me at the moment, so he's looking after me now. Usually, it is my servant, Gokul, who feeds me every day.'

'Did you get your son to write the letter to me?'

'No, Rajen wrote it. He takes care of everything. If I need to see a doctor, he fetches one from Behrampore. Plassey doesn't have good doctors.'

I had noticed Feluda casting frequent glances at the chest kept near the bed while he was talking to Mr Majumdar. 'That chest appears to be different from most,' he said. 'I can't see any provision for a key. Does it have a combination lock?'

'Correct,' Mr Majumdar smiled. 'All it has is a knob, with numbers written around it. The chest opens only if you move the knob to rest against some specific numbers. These areas were once notorious for armed burglars. You knew that, didn't you? In fact, my ancestors became wealthy enough to buy masses of land chiefly by looting others. Years later, we ourselves were attacked by dacoits, more than once. So I thought a chest with a combination lock might be safer than any other.'

Mr Majumdar stopped speaking and frowned for a second. Then he called, 'Gokul!'

The old servant appeared almost instantly. 'Bring that bird over here,' his master commanded. 'I'd like these people to see it.'

Gokul disappeared and came back a minute later with a parrot in a cage. Mr Majumdar turned to it and said softly, 'Go on, sweetie. Say it. Shut the door... say it!'

For a few seconds, nothing happened. Then, suddenly, the parrot spoke in an amazingly clear voice. 'Shut the door!' it said. I gave a start. I had never heard a bird speak so distinctly. But that wasn't all. 'O big fat hen!' the bird added. This time, I saw Feluda turn his head sharply. Before anyone could say anything, the parrot said both things together, very rapidly: 'Shut the door, O big fat hen!'

'What does it mean?' Feluda asked after a moment's pause. Mr Majumdar burst out laughing. 'I am not going to tell you. All I can say is that what you just heard was a code and it has to do with that locked chest over there. You have twelve hours to work it out.'

'I see. May I ask why the bird has been taught to say it?'

'You may indeed and I am going to tell you why. Age does strange things to one's memory. About three years ago, one day, I suddenly discovered that I couldn't remember the combination that would open the chest. Can you believe that? After using the same numbers for years, almost every day, it had simply vanished from my mind, just like that. All day, I tried to remember the numbers. Then, finally, it came back in a flash, in the middle of the night. I could have written it down, but didn't want to, in case it fell into the wrong hands. It was far better to keep it in my head, but now I realized I could no longer depend on my memory. So, the next morning, I made up that code and taught my parrot to say it. Now it says it every now and then, just as other parrots say, *"Radhe Shyam"* or "how are you?"'

Feluda was still staring at the chest. I saw him frown suddenly and get up to peer at it closely. Then he picked up the candle and began examining its lid.

'What is it?' Mr Majumdar asked anxiously. 'What have you found? Do your trained eyes tell you anything?'

'I think, Mr Majumdar, someone tried to force this chest open.'

'Are you sure?' Mr Majumdar had stopped smiling.

Feluda put the candle back on the table. 'There are some marks on it,' he said. 'Ordinary dusting and cleaning couldn't have left marks like those. But is there anyone who'd want to open it?'

Mr Majumdar thought for a moment. Then he said slowly, 'Not many people live here, Mr Mitter. Apart from myself, there's Gokul, Rajen, my driver Monilal, a cook and a *mali*. Vishwanath – that's my son – arrived five days ago. He lives in Calcutta and visits me rarely. He's here now because of my illness. You see, last Monday I had been sitting in the garden. When I tried to get up, everything suddenly went dark and I fell down on the bench. Rajen rang Vishwanath from Plassey and he came the next day with a doctor from Calcutta. It appears to have been a mild stroke. In any case, I know I haven't got long to live. But... don't tell me I have to spend my last few days in doubt and anxiety? Always afraid that a thief might get into my room and force open that chest?'

'No, no. There is no need to jump to conclusions. I may be quite wrong,' Feluda said reassuringly. 'Those marks may have appeared when the chest was first installed in that corner. I can't see very clearly in the light from one candle, so I cannot tell whether those marks are old or new. I'll have another look in the morning. Is your servant trustworthy?'

'Absolutely, he's been with me for thirty years.'

'And Rajen?'

'Rajen has also spent a good many years here. But then, where's the guarantee that someone who has honoured my trust until today won't betray it tomorrow?'

Feluda nodded in agreement. 'No, there's no guarantee at all, unfortunately. Anyway, tell Gokul to keep an eye on things. I don't really think there's any immediate danger.'

'Oh. Good.' Mr Majumdar appeared relieved. We rose.

'Gokul will show you your room,' he said. 'You'll find blankets and quilts and mosquito nets. Vishwanath has gone to Behrampore, he should be getting back soon. You must have your dinner as soon as he returns. Tomorrow morning, if you like, you can go for a ride in my car, though there isn't much to see in this area.'

Feluda picked up the books from the table and thanked him again. Before saying good night, Mr Majumdar reminded him about the code. 'If you can crack it, Mr Mitter, I will give you the whole set by Gaboriau.'

Gokul came back with a lantern and took us to our room. It was smaller than Mr Majumdar's but with less furniture, which made it easier to move about. Two beds had been made with considerable care. A lantern burnt in a corner. Feluda sat down on the spotless sheet that covered his bed and said, 'Can you remember the code?'

'Yes.'

'Very well. Here's my notebook and a pen. Write it down. I would love to get those books by Gaboriau.'

I wrote the words down. None of it made any sense. How on earth was Feluda going to find its meaning?

'I simply cannot see how the numbers for a combination lock can be hidden in this strange message!' I complained. 'I mean, this is pure nonsense, isn't it? How can a hen shut a door?'

'That's where the challenge lies, don't you see? Nobody's actually asking a hen to shut a door. That much is obvious. Each word has a separate meaning. I have to figure it out somehow by tomorrow morning.'

Feluda got up and opened a window. The moon had risen by this time and everything was bathed in moonlight. I went and stood by his side. Our room overlooked the rear portion of the house. 'There's probably a pond over there on the right,' Feluda remarked, pointing. Through a thick growth of plants and shrubs, I could see the shimmering surface of water. The only noise that could be heard was that of jackals calling in the distance and crickets chirping in the bushes. Never before had I visited a place so totally isolated and remote.

Feluda shut the window again to keep out the cold night air. In the same instant, we heard a car arrive. It was obviously a different car, not the American one we had travelled in.

'That's probably Vishwanath Majumdar,' Feluda remarked.

Good, I thought. This might mean we'd soon be called in to dinner. To tell the truth, I was feeling quite hungry. We had left after an early lunch, since our train was at two o'clock. We did get ourselves a cup of tea and some sweets at Ranaghat, but even that was a long time ago. Ordinarily, I would probably not be thinking of food at eight in the evening, but since there was nothing else to do in a place like this, I quite liked the idea of dinner and an early night. Looking around in the room, my eyes suddenly fell upon something I hadn't noticed before. It was the portrait of a man that took up most of the opposite wall. There could be no doubt that he was one of Mr Majumdar's ancestors. He was sitting in a chair, looking rather grim. His torso was bare, which showed to perfection his very broad shoulders. His eyes were large and his moustache thick, its edges turning upwards. His hair rippled down to his shoulders.

'I bet he used to wrestle and use heavy clubs regularly,' Feluda whispered. 'Perhaps he was the first bandit who became a zamindar.'

There were footsteps outside. Both of us looked at the door. Gokul had left a lantern on the veranda. A shadow blocked out its light for a second, then fell on the threshold. It was followed by the figure of a man. Could this be Vishwanath Majumdar? Surely not? This man was wearing a short dhoti and a grey kurta, had a bushy moustache and glasses with thick lenses. He was peering into the room, trying to find us.

'What is it, Rajen babu?' Feluda asked.

Rajen babu finally found what he was looking for. His eyes came to rest upon Feluda.

'Chhoto babu has just returned,' he said in a gruff voice that suggested he might have a cold. 'I have asked Gokul to serve dinner. He'll come and call you in a few minutes.'

He left. 'What is that smell, Feluda?' I asked as soon as he had gone.

'Naphthalene. I think he just took that woollen kurta out of a suitcase and put it on.'

Silence fell once more as the sound of footsteps faded away. Had Feluda not been with me, I could never have spent even five minutes in such an eerie atmosphere. How did Mr Majumdar and the others manage to live here day after day? Suddenly, I remembered someone had been murdered in this house. God knew in which room it had taken place.

Feluda, in the meantime, had dragged the table with the lantern on it closer to his bed and opened his notebook to look at the code. I heard him mutter, 'Shut the door... shut the door...'

a couple of times. Thoroughly bored, I decided to step out of the room and stand on the veranda outside.

Oh god, what was that? My heart nearly jumped into my mouth. Something was moving in the distance, where the faint light from the lantern gave way to complete darkness. I forced myself to stay silent and stared at the moving object. A couple of seconds later, I realized it was only a cat, not black or white, but one with stripes on its body like a tiger. It returned my stare sombrely, then gave a yawn before walking lazily back into the darkness. A few moments later, the parrot gave a raucous cry and then all was silent once more. I wondered where Vishwanath Majumdar's room was. Was it on the ground floor? Where did Rajen babu live? Why had we been given a room from which it was impossible to hear noises in other parts of the house?

I came back to the room. Feluda was sitting crosslegged on the bed, his notebook in his lap. 'Why are they taking so long?' I couldn't help sounding cross. Feluda looked at his watch. 'You're right, Topshe. Rajen babu left at least fifteen minutes ago.' He then went back to staring at his notebook.

I began going through the books Feluda had been given. One was on analysing fingerprints, one was simply called *Criminology* and the third was called *Crime and its Detection*. I picked up the fourth, but could not understand what its name meant. It was full of pictures, chiefly of firearms. Had Feluda brought his revolver?

No, why should he? After all, he hadn't come here to solve a crime. There was no reason for him to have brought his revolver. I put the books in our suitcase and was about to sit down, when the sound of an unfamiliar voice startled me again. Another man was standing at the door. This time, there was no problem in recognizing him. He wasn't Gokul, or Rajen babu, or the driver, Monilal. He had to be Kalikinkar's son, Vishwanath.

'Sorry to have kept you waiting,' he said, folding his hands and looking at Feluda. 'My name is Vishwanath Majumdar.'

Now I could see that he resembled his father to a great degree. He had the same eyes and the same nose. He was probably in his mid-forties. His hair was still black, he was clean-shaven and had very thin lips. I took an instant dislike to him, though I couldn't find a proper reason for it. It was perhaps simply because he had made us wait a long time, and I was tired. Or it could be that – but this could just be my imagination – when he smiled, his eyes remained cold and aloof. He seemed as though he wasn't really pleased to see us. Perhaps it was only our departure that would make him happy.

Feluda and I went with him down to the ground floor to the dining room. I had half expected to be asked to sit down on the floor for a traditional meal, but found to my surprise that there was a dining table. Silver plates and bowls and glasses were placed on it. When we were all seated, Vishwanath Majumdar said, 'I like having a bath twice a day, be it summer or winter. That's what took so long, I'm afraid.'

He was still reeking of perfumed soap and, possibly, an expensive cologne. Clad in grey trousers, a white silk shirt and a dark green sleeveless pullover, he was clearly a man fond of the good things in life.

We began eating. Several little bowls were placed in a semicircle around our plates, each containing a different dish. There were three different vegetables, daal and fish curry.

'Have you spoken to my father?' Vishwanath Majumdar asked.

'Yes. I am rather embarrassed by what he did.'

'You mean the books he gave you?'

'Yes. Even if those books were still available, they would have cost at least a thousand rupees.'

Vishwanath Majumdar laughed. 'When he told me he had asked you to come here, I was at first quite annoyed with him,' he told us. 'I didn't think it was fair to invite people from the city to a place like this.'

'Why not?' Feluda protested. 'Why should you have objected to that? I have lost nothing by coming here. On the contrary, I have gained such a lot!'

Vishwanath Majumdar did not pay much attention to these words. 'Speaking for myself,' he declared, 'I'd be perfectly happy to go back tomorrow. The last four days have been quite enough for me, thank you. I have no idea how my father can live here permanently.'

'Doesn't he go out at all?'

'No. He spends most of his time in that dark room. He used to go out and sit in the garden a couple of times every day. But now the doctor has forbidden all movement.'

'Did you say you were returning tomorrow?'

'Yes. Father is not in any immediate danger. Will you be catching the train at half past ten?'

'Yes.'

'I see. That means I shall leave soon after you get to the station.' Feluda poured daal over his rice. 'Your father is interested in so many different subjects. Are you interested in anything other than your business?'

'No, sir. I simply don't have the time for anything else once my day's work is done. I am entirely happy being a businessman and no more.'

By the time we said good night to Vishwanath Majumdar and returned to our room, it was half past nine. It didn't really matter what time my watch showed, for time seemed to have very little significance here. Seven o'clock had seemed like midnight.

'Do you mind if I keep my pillow on the other side?' I asked Feluda.

'No, but why do you want to do that?'

'I have no wish to see that grim face on the wall the minute I open my eyes in the morning.'

Feluda laughed. 'All right. I think I'll do the same,' he said. 'I must say I don't like the look in his eyes, either.'

Just before going to bed, Feluda picked up the lantern and turned its light down. The room seemed to shrink in size. In just a few minutes, I could feel my eyes growing heavy with sleep. But, just as I was about to drop off, I heard Feluda muttering, which made me open them at once.

'Shut the door... and open the gate... no, that's wrong. Pick up sticks. Yes, that comes first.'

'Feluda!' I cried, slightly alarmed. 'Wake up, Feluda! You are talking in your sleep. What's the matter with you?'

'No, no,' I heard him chuckle in the darkness. 'I am fully awake and no, I haven't gone mad, I assure you. What has just happened, Topshe, is that I think I've won that set by Gaboriau.'

'What! You've cracked the code?'

'Yes, I think so. It was actually ridiculously simple. I should have spotted it at once.'

'It still makes no sense to me.'

'That's only because you aren't thinking. How were you taught to count when you were a child?'

'Very simply. One, two, three, four... that was all.'

'Was it? Think, dear boy, think. Did no one try to make it easier for you? Weren't you taught a rhyme?'

'A rhyme to go with numbers? You mean something that began with one, two... no, I don't think... hey, wait a minute! Feluda, Feluda, I know what you mean! Yes, I've got it.' I sat up in excitement. I could dimly see Feluda turn his head to look at me. He was grinning.

'Very well. Let's have it, then.'

Softly, I began to chant a rhyme I had been taught in nursery school

'One, two
Buckle my shoe.
Three, four
Shut the door.
Five, six
Pick up sticks.
Seven, eight
Open the gate.
Nine, ten

A big fat hen.
Eleven, twelve
Dig and delve...'

'That'll do. Now what do you think the full message means?'

'Shut the door... that would mean three and four. Big fat hen would mean nine and ten. Right?'

'Right. But there's an "O" before "big fat hen". That means the whole number is 340910. Simple, isn't it? Now, go to sleep.'

I lay down again, marvelling at Feluda's cleverness. But just as I began to close my eyes once more, footsteps sounded on the veranda. It was Rajen babu again. What did he want at this time of night?

'Yes, Rajen babu?' Feluda called.

'Chhoto babu told me to find out if you needed anything.'

'No, no. We're fine, thank you.'

Rajen babu disappeared silently. This time, sleep came very quickly. All I was aware of as I closed my eyes was that the moonlight that had seeped through closed shutters had suddenly gone pale. I thought I heard distant thunder and the cat meowed a couple of times. Then I fell asleep.

When I woke in the morning, Feluda was opening the windows. 'It rained last night,' he said. 'Did you hear it?'

I hadn't. But now I could see through the window that the clouds had gone. The sun shone brightly on the leaves I could see from my bed.

Gokul appeared with two cups of tea half an hour later. Looking at him in daylight, I was considerably surprised. Not only did he seem old, but his face held an expression of deep distress.

'Has Kalikinkar babu woken up?' Feluda asked. Perhaps Gokul was hard of hearing. He did not answer Feluda's question at first. All he did was stare at him vacantly. Feluda had to raise his voice and ask again before he nodded and left the room quickly.

We made our way to old Mr Majumdar's room at around seven-thirty and found him exactly as we'd left him the night before. He was still lying in his bed, a blanket covering most of his body including his arms. The window next to his bed was shut, possibly to avoid direct sunlight. The only light that came into the room was through the open door. I noticed a photograph on the wall over his bed. It must have been taken many years ago, for it showed a much younger Kalikinkar Majumdar. His hair and beard were both jet black.

He greeted us with a smile.

'I got Rajen to take out the books by Gaboriau. I knew you could do it,' he said.

'Well, it is for you to decide whether I've got the right number. 340910. Is that it?'

'Well done!' Mr Majumdar's voice held both pleasure and admiration. 'Go on, take those books and put them in your bag. And please take another look at those marks on the chest. I had a look myself. They didn't strike me as anything to worry about.'

'Well then, that settles it. If you're not worried about it, nothing else matters.'

Feluda thanked him once more before collecting the four books written by the first writer of detective fiction.

'Have you had tea?' Mr Majumdar asked.

'Yes, sir.'

'I told the driver to bring the car out. Vishwanath left very early this morning. He said he wanted to reach Calcutta by ten. Rajen has gone to the local market. Gokul will help you with your luggage. Would you like to go for a drive before you catch your train?'

'I was actually thinking of going by an earlier train. We don't really have to wait until ten-thirty. If we left immediately, perhaps we could catch the 372 Down.'

'Very well. I have no wish to keep anyone from the city in this small village any longer than is necessary. But I'm really pleased that you could come. I mean that.'

Soon, we were on our way to the railway station. The road went through rice fields, which glistened in the early morning sun after a rainy night. I was looking at these with admiration, when I heard Feluda ask a question. 'Is there any other way to get to the station?'

'No, sir, this is the only way,' Monilal replied.

Feluda was suddenly looking rather grave. I wanted to ask him if he had noticed anything suspicious, but didn't dare open my mouth. The road being wet and muddy, it took us longer to reach the station. Feluda took the luggage out of the car and thanked the driver, who then drove off. But Feluda made no attempt to go to the ticket counter to buy tickets for our return journey. He found the stationmaster's room instead and left our luggage with him. Then he came out once more and approached one of the cycle-rickshaws that were waiting outside.

'Do you know where the local police station is?'

'Yes, sir.'

'Can you take us there? We're in a hurry.'

We climbed into the rickshaw quickly. The driver began pedalling fast, honking as loudly as he could, weaving his way through the milling crowds, narrowly avoiding collisions more than once. We reached the police station in five minutes. The officer left in charge was Sub-inspector Sarkar. It turned out that he knew Feluda's name. 'We have heard a lot about you, sir,' he said. 'What brings you here?'

'What can you tell me about Kalikinkar Majumdar of Ghurghutia?'

'Kalikinkar Majumdar? As far as I know, he is a perfect gentleman, who keeps himself to himself. Why, I've never heard anything nasty said about him!'

'What about his son, Vishwanath? Does he live here?'

'No. I think he lives in Calcutta. Whatever's the matter, Mr Mitter?'

'Can you take your jeep and come with me? There's something seriously wrong.'

Mr Sarkar did not waste another minute. We began bumping our way back to Ghurghutia in a police jeep, splashing mud everywhere. Feluda's face held a look of suppressed excitement, but he opened his mouth only once. I was the only one who could hear his words.

'Arthritis, those marks on the chest, the late dinner, the hoarseness in Rajen babu's voice, the naphthalene... every little piece has fallen into place, Topshe. I tend to forget sometimes that there are other people just as clever as Felu Mitter.'

The first thing that I noticed with considerable surprise on reaching the old mansion was a black Ambassador standing outside the main gate. It obviously belonged to Vishwanath Majumdar. 'Look at its wheels,' Feluda said as we got out of the jeep. 'There is no trace of mud anywhere. This car has only just come out of a garage.'

A man – possibly its driver, whom I hadn't seen before – was standing near the car. He turned visibly pale and frightened at the sight of our jeep.

'Are you the driver of this car?' Feluda asked him.

'Y-yes, s-sir.'

'Is Vishwanath Majumdar at home?'

The man hesitated. Feluda ignored him and walked straight into the house, followed closely by the inspector, me and a constable.

Together, we ran up the stairs and down the long passage that led to Kalikinkar's room. It was empty. The blanket lay on the bed, all the furniture was in place, but its occupant had vanished.

'Oh no!' Feluda exclaimed. I found him staring at the chest. It was open. Judging by its gaping emptiness, nearly all of its contents had been removed.

Gokul came and stood outside the door. He was trembling violently. There were tears in his eyes. He looked as though he might collapse any minute. Feluda caught him by his shoulders.

'Gokul, where is Vishwanath Majumdar?'

'He... he ran out of the back door!'

'Mr Sarkar!'

The inspector left with the constable without a word.

'Listen,' Feluda shook Gokul gently, 'if you tell me a single lie, you will go to prison. Do you understand? Where is your master?'

Gokul's eyes widened in fear, looking as though they would soon pop out of their sockets.

'He... he has been murdered!' he gasped.

'Who killed him?'

'Chhoto babu.'

'When?'

'The day he arrived, that same night. He had an argument with his father and asked for the numbers to open the chest. The master said, "I am not going to give it to you. Ask my parrot." Then... a while later... Chhoto babu and his driver... they got together...' Gokul choked. He uttered the next few words with great difficulty: 'The two of them dropped the dead body into the lake behind the house. They... they tied a stone round its neck. And Chhoto babu said if I breathed a word to anyone, he'd k-kill me, too!'

'I see,' Feluda helped him sit down. 'Now tell me, am I right in thinking there is no one called Rajen babu at all?'

'Yes, sir. We did once have a manager by that name, but he died two years ago.'

Feluda and I leapt out of the room and began running down the stairs. There was a door to the left where the stairs ended, which led to the rear of the house. We heard Mr Sarkar's voice as we emerged through this door.

'It's no use trying to escape, Mr Majumdar. I have a gun in my hand!' he shouted.

This was followed immediately by a loud splash and the sound of a revolver going off.

We continued running, jumping over small bushes and crashing through thick foliage. Eventually, we found Mr Sarkar standing under a large tamarind tree, with a revolver in his hand. Behind the tree was the lake we had glimpsed last night through our window. Its surface was covered almost totally with weed and algae.

'He jumped before I could fire,' Mr Sarkar said, 'but he cannot swim. Girish, see if you can drag him out.'

Vishwanath Majumdar was fished out in a few minutes by the constable and transferred behind bars, very much like his father's parrot. The money and the jewellery he had stolen from the chest were recovered by the police. It appeared that although he ran a successful business, he used to gamble rather heavily and was up to his neck in debt.

Feluda explained how he had arrived at the truth. 'Rajen babu came to our room twenty minutes after we left Kalikinkar; and we saw Vishwanath Majumdar half an hour after Rajen babu's departure. Then Rajen babu came back briefly after dinner. Not once did we see father and son and their manager together. This made me wonder whether there were indeed three different people, or whether one single person was playing different roles. Then I remembered the books on drama and acting. Perhaps those books belonged to Vishwanath Majumdar? Maybe he was interested in acting and was good at putting on make-up? If so, it wouldn't have been difficult for him to wear a false beard and different wigs and change his voice, to fool a couple of visitors in a dark house. He had to hide his hands, though, for presumably his knowledge of make-up wasn't adequate to turn his own hands into those of a seventy-three-year-old man. But my suspicions were confirmed when I noticed this morning that although he was supposed to have left quite early, there were no tyre marks on the ground.'

'But who had actually written to you, asking you to come here?' I put in.

'Oh, that letter was written by Kalikinkar himself, I am sure. His son knew about it. So, he did nothing to stop our arrival, for he knew he could use me to find out the combination numbers.'

In the end we got so delayed that we couldn't catch a train before half past ten. Before we left, Feluda took out the books he had been given and handed them to me. 'I have no wish to accept gifts from a murderer,' he said. 'Topshe, go and put these back.'

I replaced the books, filling each gap in the shelves and came out quietly. The parrot's cage was still hanging outside in the veranda.

'Shut the door!' it said to me. 'Shut the door... O big fat hen!'

THE RHYTHM OF THE RIDDLES

Saradindu Bandyopadhyay, tr. Arunava Sinha

1.

Byomkesh had been to Cuttack on official work, I had accompanied him too. After a few days, it became evident that the task would not be accomplished quickly, that it would take time to rummage through a mountain of deeds and documents in the government office to unearth the truth. Accordingly, Byomkesh stayed on in Cuttack, while I returned to Calcutta. How could a Bengali household be expected to run without the presence of a man at home?

On my return to Calcutta, however, I had no work. I was feeling a little helpless in Byomkesh's absence. Winter was setting in, the days were getting shorter; and yet the hours refused to pass. Occasionally I would visit the shop, supervise Prabhat, who ran the shop, read new manuscripts if any. But still there was nothing to do for most part of the day.

Then an opportunity to pass the evenings presented itself unexpectedly.

We lived in a three-storeyed building, occupying five rooms on the top floor, while a dozen or so office-goers messed together on the first floor. On the ground floor were the manager's room, the pantry, the kitchen and the dining room, with just one corner room being occupied by a solitary boarder. We were familiar with all of them, but not particularly intimate with any.

That evening, I had just switched on the light after darkness had fallen and opened a magazine, when there was a knock on the door. Opening the door, I discovered a middle-aged gentleman standing outside, smiling deferentially. I had seen him once or twice on the first floor of our building, where he had taken up residence recently. He occupied the best corner room on the floor all by himself. He appeared to be a man of refined tastes, being dressed in a warm Nehru jacket and a silk *churidar*, his hair more black than white. He was well turned out.

Greeting me, he said, 'Excuse me, my name is Bhupesh Chatterjee. I live on the first floor.'

'I've seen you now and then,' I replied, 'though I was not familiar with your name. Do come in.'

I gave him a seat in my room. 'I came to Calcutta a month and a half ago. I work for an insurance company; there's no telling where I'll be next. Tomorrow they might transfer me somewhere else altogether, for all you know.'

'You work for an insurance company,' I said with some unease. 'But I have never taken out a policy, nor am I planning to.'

'That's not what I came for,' he smiled. 'It's true that I work at the insurance office, but I'm not an agent. I came because...' After an awkward pause, he said, 'I'm addicted to bridge. I haven't had a game ever since I came here, I'm dying for one. After much effort I've managed to find two more players. They live in Room No. 3 on the first floor. But we haven't been able to find a fourth. We tried cut-throat bridge for a few days, but that isn't the real thing. I thought I'd find out today whether Ajit babu is interested.'

I was indeed interested in bridge once upon a time. Not merely interested, obsessed. Since I had not played for a long time, the obsession had died. Still, I felt that playing bridge was preferable to passing my companionless evenings reading a dull magazine.

'Very well, very well,' I said. 'I am long out of practice, of course, but still – why not?'

'Then come with me,' said Bhupesh babu, springing to his feet. 'I have made all the arrangements in my room. Why waste time?'

'Please lead the way, I'll follow as soon as I've had my cup of tea,' I said.

'Oh no, you can just as well have your tea in my room. Come along,' he replied.

I was amused by his eagerness. I used to be just as enthusiastic once upon a time; the evenings seemed wasted without a game of bridge.

I got off my chair. Informing Byomkesh's wife Satyabati, I accompanied Bhupesh babu downstairs.

The first room when you went down the stairs to the first floor was Bhupesh babu's. Pausing near his door, he called out loudly, 'Come along, Ram babu, Banamali babu. I've got hold of Ajit babu.'

Two heads popped out of Room No. 3, which was situated halfway down the corridor, then disappeared with the word, 'Coming.' Bhupesh babu took me into his room and switched on the light.

It was a commodious room. There were two barred windows on the wall looking out on the road. On one side of the room was the bed, covered with a bedspread, on the other was a cupboard, on top of which reposed a shining portable stove and everything you needed to make a cup of tea. Four chairs were arranged around a low table in the middle of the room; it was clearly a card table. Besides these, the other small items of furniture, including a dressing table and a chest of drawers, all indicated good taste. Bhupesh babu was slightly Western in his tastes.

Settling me in a chair, he said, 'Let me put the kettle on, the tea will be ready in a few minutes.'

Lighting the stove, he put the kettle on. Meanwhile, Ram babu and Banamali babu had arrived.

Despite our prior acquaintance, Bhupesh babu introduced all of us once more. 'This is Ramchandra Roy and this is Banamali Chanda. They live in the same room and work at the same bank.'

I observed other similarities too; I had not noticed them earlier, possibly because I had not seen them together. Both were aged between forty-five and fifty, both were plump and of medium height, their features cut in the same mould – a thick nose, invisible eyebrows, a square chin. The resemblance was obviously genetic. I was tempted to surprise them. After all, I was a friend of Byomkesh's.

'Are you related?' I asked.

They looked at me in surprise. 'No,' answered Ram babu a little brusquely. 'I'm a Vaidya, Banamali is a Kayastha.'

I was taken aback. Just as I was trying to stammer out an explanation, Bhupesh babu arrived with a plate of snacks to rescue me. Then the tea arrived. Finishing our tea quickly, we got down to the game. The subject of their being cousins was forgotten.

As we played, I discovered I had not forgotten the art of bridge even after all these years; my playing and bidding expertise were both intact. The stakes were low; the most one could win or lose at the end of the rubber was four annas. But playing was no fun without stakes.

Ram babu and I were partners in the first round – or rubber. Ram babu lit a thick cigar, Bhupesh babu and I lit our cigarettes; Banamali babu was content with slices of clove and betelnut.

Then we began to play. After every rubber, the cards were shuffled and the pairs, changed. All three of them were good players; there wasn't much conversation as everyone was immersed in the game. Only the ends of the cigar and the cigarettes glowed constantly. Bhupesh babu rose at one point to open the window and resumed his seat in silence.

When we finished our game, it was past nine; the servant had already reminded everyone twice of dinner. When we totted up, I turned out to have won two annas. Pocketing my winnings, I rose to my feet joyfully. 'We'll play again tomorrow, won't we?' asked Bhupesh babu with a smile.

'We will,' I said.

When I went back upstairs, Satyabati remonstrated with me. Nine-fifteen on a winter night was quite late. But, happy having played bridge after such a long time, I laughed away her scolding.

After this, our games became a daily affair, the session beginning as soon as the evening lamp was lit and continuing until nine at night. After five or six days, I had formed an impression about each of them. Bhupesh babu was kind-hearted, soft-spoken and hospitable, extremely fond of bridge. Ram babu was grave, taciturn, not given to protesting against others' mistakes while playing. Banamali babu held Ram babu in the greatest of regard, trying without success to emulate his gravity. Both were reticent, deeply addicted to bridge. Both had faint Eastern Bengali accents.

We had been happily playing bridge for six days, our sessions on the verge of becoming a permanent institution, when a ghastly incident on the floor below upset our regular gathering. Natabar Nashkar, the only inhabitant of the ground floor, was suddenly murdered. While it is true that we had no direct relationship with him, even when a ship sails along the middle of the river, the waves do reach the banks.

At six-thirty that evening, I was on my way to our evening game, wrapped in a shawl. Because I was a little late, I ran down the stairs, my sandals flapping loudly. Just as I had reached the last step, a bang made me stop in my tracks. I could not identify the source of the sound. It could have been a car backfiring out on the street, but the sound was rather loud. No sound from the street could be as deafening.

After a brief halt I continued on to Bhupesh babu's room. The lights were on. Bhupesh babu was looking out through the window, holding the bars, while behind him Ram babu and Banamali babu were trying to peep through the same window. When I entered, Bhupesh babu was saying excitedly, 'There... there... he ran out of the lane just this minute, did you see him? He had a brown shawl on...'

'What's the matter?' I said from the back.

Everyone turned towards me. 'Did you hear the sound?' asked Bhupesh babu. It came from the lane beneath this window here.

I'd just opened the window when there was a bang down there. I looked out and saw a man running out of the lane.'

Our building was situated on the main road. A narrow, paved blind lane connected the road to our back door; the servants took this route in and out of the house. I felt a misgiving. 'The room beneath this one is occupied. The sound didn't come from that room, did it?'

'No idea,' said Bhupesh babu. 'Someone does live in the room beneath mine, but I don't know his name.'

Ram babu and Banamali babu exchanged glances, after which Ram babu cleared his throat and said, 'The room downstairs is occupied by Natabar Nashkar.'

'Let's go and see,' I said. 'If he's in, he can tell us what the sound was.'

None of the three seemed keen, but I was Byomkesh the truth-seeker's friend. How could I not investigate the source of the sound? 'Let's take a quick look before we start our game,' I said. 'I wouldn't have bothered if it had been an everyday sort of sound, but even if someone came through the lane to throw a cracker into Natabar babu's room, we should find out, shouldn't we?'

They accompanied me reluctantly.

There was a lock on the manager Shibkali babu's door and the door to the pantry was shut too. The dining room was unlocked, for it held nothing but a few low stools. Only the door to Natabar babu's room was closed without being locked. It would not be incorrect to presume that he was in, therefore. 'Natabar babu!' I called out.

There was no reply. When a relatively louder call did not elicit a response either, I pushed on the door gently. The doors parted slightly.

The room was dark, nothing was visible; but there was a faint smell. The smell of gunpowder. We exchanged startled looks.

'There must be a switch by the door,' said Bhupesh babu. 'Wait, let me turn on the light.'

Pushing me aside he peeped into the room, then reached in to grope for the switch. There was a click, and the light came on.

The first thing we saw in the unforgiving overhead light was Natabar babu's corpse. Dressed in a white sweater and a dhoti, he lay on his back in the middle of the room, his limbs splayed out. A thick stream of blood had flowed out of the area near his chest. Natabar Nashkar had not been particularly handsome even when alive; he was of medium build with a protruding stomach, his bloated face deeply pockmarked. But death had made his appearance even more grotesque. I shall not describe that horror. You could tell from his expression how hideous an emotion the fear of death is.

Frozen briefly into a statue by the sight, Ram babu emitted a sound like a hiccup from his throat. He stared at the corpse with unbelieving eyes, as if in a trance. Suddenly sinking his nails into Ram babu's arms, Banamali babu said, 'He's dead, dada!' It wasn't clear to me whether his expression was one of sorrow or wonder or joy.

'There's no doubt he's dead,' Bhupesh babu said, his face pale. 'He died of a gunshot. There. Can you see it on the window sill?'

The window, which had no bars, was open – on its sill lay a pistol. The picture became clear; standing outside the window, the assailant had shot Natabar Nashkar, then left after depositing the pistol on the window sill.

Hearing quick footsteps behind me, I turned. Shibkali Chakraborty, the manager of the boarding house, was approaching. He had an emaciated frame, he walked with undue haste, his eyes were unnecessarily distraught; when he spoke, he wasn't satisfied unless he had repeated himself several times. 'All of you here? Here? What's the matter? What's the matter?' he said when he was near us.

'See for yourself.' We moved away from the door to give him a clear view. Shibkali babu jumped out of his skin when he saw the blood-soaked corpse. 'Oh my god, oh my god! Natabar Nashkar is dead. Blood, blood. How did he die?'

'You can find out for yourself over there,' I said, pointing at the window.

'Oh god, a pistol, a pistol!' Shibkali babu babbled again in terror as soon as he saw the gun. 'Natabar babu has been murdered with a pistol. Who murdered him? When was he murdered?'

'I have no idea who murdered him,' I replied, 'but I do know when he was murdered. About five minutes ago.'

I explained everything to him briefly. He stared at the corpse in distress.

I had not noticed earlier, but suddenly I realized that Shibkali babu was dressed in a brown shawl. My heart leapt into my mouth. Controlling my palpitations, I said, 'Weren't you home? Did you go out?'

'What? Yes, I... was out on work,' he replied in agitation. 'But... but... what is the way out? What is to be done... what is to be done?'

'The first thing to be done is to inform the police,' I said.

'True, true,' responded Shibkali babu. 'That's right, that's right. But I do not have a telephone. You have a telephone, Ajit babu, if you could...'

'I shall telephone the police immediately,' I said. 'But none of you must enter the room; wait here till the police arrive.'

I dashed upstairs. As I was about to enter my room, I saw my own reflection in the mirror. I was dressed in a brown shawl too.

We were acquainted with Pranab Guha, the police-inspector in our locality at that time. A competent, middle-aged man, he was not, however, favourably inclined towards Byomkesh. While he did not express his amiability in any manner of harshness of speech or rudeness, he spoke to Byomkesh with excessive obsequiousness, chuckling softly at the end. Possibly their natures were mutually abhorrent; besides, Pranab babu did not care for the coarse touch of an unofficial hand in official matters.

Having listened to my account on the telephone, he said sarcastically, 'Really! A crime in the detective's den! But when you have Byomkesh babu there, why do you need me? Let him conduct the investigation.'

'Byomkesh is not in Calcutta,' I said testily. 'Had he been here, he would definitely have taken up the case.'

'Oh all right, I'll come round then,' said Inspector Pranab. He put the phone down with a chuckle. I went back downstairs.

Pranab babu arrived with his entourage half an hour later. He chuckled when he caught sight of me, then inspected the corpse gravely. Lifting the pistol gingerly from the window sill, he wrapped it in his handkerchief and put it in his pocket. Eventually, having dispatched the corpse, he occupied the only chair in the room and proceeded to interrogate all the inmates of the house.

I told him whatever I knew. I am summarizing the statements of the others—

Shibkali babu, the manager, was sworn to a vow of celibacy – a bachelor, in other words. He had been running the boarding house for the past twenty-five years; it was his wife, his child, his family... Natabar Nashkar had taken up residence in this ground floor room three years earlier and had occupied it ever since. He was approximately fifty years of age and not given to consorting with the others. Ram babu and Banamali babu used to visit him in his room once in a while. Shibkali babu bore no ill-will towards Natabar Nashkar, for Natabar paid his dues promptly on the first of every month... Shibkali babu had learnt that afternoon of potatoes being sold cheap at a particular warehouse, so he had gone to the godown to purchase potatoes. But the potatoes had been sold out already, so he had returned empty-handed.

Bhupesh babu worked at an insurance office; he had been transferred to Calcutta a month and a half earlier. He was about forty-five, a widower with no children. He had no home to speak of; he had travelled all over the country in course of work. Bhupesh babu gave an accurate account of how he had gathered a group of people to play bridge and of that evening's incidents; he mentioned the man in the brown shawl too. He had not seen the man's face clearly; from the back you cannot see the face of a man who is running away; so he was unlikely to recognize the man were he to see him again.

The statements given by Ramchandra Roy and Banamali Chanda were similar. I observed that although Ram babu remained composed throughout the questioning, Banamali babu appeared somewhat perturbed. Both of them used to live in Dhaka earlier, working in the same British firm. Their wives, children and family had all been killed in the riots at the time of the Partition and they had somehow managed to escape with their lives. Ram babu was forty-eight years old; Banamali babu, forty-five. They had lived in this boarding house after crossing over to Calcutta and worked in a bank. Three years had passed this way.

They were fond of playing bridge, but had not had an opportunity to play since moving to Calcutta. Bhupesh babu had made arrangements for bridge in his room a few days earlier and the evenings had been passing pleasantly since then. Within five minutes of their entering Bhupesh babu's room this evening, there was the sound of an explosion in the lane outside... They had been acquainted with Natabar babu in Dhaka; it had been a slight acquaintance, without any particular closeness. Natabar babu had worked as an agent for various enterprises in Dhaka. By virtue of living in the same boarding house, they used to meet occasionally; Ram babu and Banamali babu would drop in for a chat. They did not know whether Natabar babu had any other friends... They had seen the man in the brown shawl for a split second in the dim light of dusk at the head of the lane; they would not be able to recognize him again.

The remaining inmates were unable to reveal anything. A game of dice had been in progress in a room at the other end of the first floor. Four players and four other spectators had been present there; they had not heard the gunshot. No one else in the boarding house had anything more than a nodding acquaintance with Natabar babu.

Only the servant Haripada said something that could be either irrelevant or significant. At six in the evening, Suren babu from the first floor had sent Haripada to the restaurant on the main road to buy some snacks. On his way back through the back lane, Haripada had heard someone murmuring in Natabar babu's room. He had been unable to see who was inside because the door had been shut; nor had he recognized the voice. Haripada had noticed this specifically because Natabar babu did not usually have many visitors. He could not specify the time, but Suren babu stated clearly that he had asked Haripada to get the snacks at six in the evening.

In other words, Natabar babu had had a visitor in his room half an hour before he died. It wasn't anyone in the boarding house, for no one admitted to visiting him. Therefore it had been an outsider. Perhaps it had been the man in the brown shawl. Or some other person altogether; Haripada's statement proved nothing.

After he had taken everyone's testimony, Inspector Pranab said, 'All of you may leave now, we will search the room. And yes, this is for Ajit babu and Shibkali babu – do not attempt to leave Calcutta without my permission until this murder mystery is solved.'

'What do you mean?' I asked in surprise.

'I mean that both you and Shibkali babu are dressed in brown shawls,' answered Inspector Pranab. 'Heh heh. You may leave now.'

He slammed the door on our faces. We returned to our respective burrows. The game of cards was forgotten.

The following day passed in inactive tedium. The police made no noise. Inspector Pranab had left the previous evening with some documents after searching Natabar babu's room and locking the door. The man was hostile towards us, but he expressed his hostility so courteously that you could say nothing. He knew I had a watertight alibi, but had still used a flimsy pretext to issue instructions forbidding me to leave Calcutta. Since I was a friend of Byomkesh's, harassing me was his only motive.

In the morning, the gentlemen at the boarding house all left for their respective offices. No one seemed the slightest bit perturbed. There was no regret amongst any of them for the death by gunshot of a person named Natabar Nashkar, who had lived in the same boarding house for three years. 'If thou beest born, die thou must' – everyone appeared to harbour a philosophical attitude.

In the evening I went to Bhupesh babu's room. Ram babu and Banamali babu had turned up as well. All of us seemed to be lacking in spirit. No one suggested a rubber. Our session broke up after miserably discussing Natabar Nashkar's death and criticizing the incompetence of the police over a cup of tea.

As I climbed the stairs, a thought occurred to me. No matter how efficient Inspector Pranab was, he would not be able to solve the mystery of Natabar babu's death. Byomkesh wasn't here; the evening sessions were flagging. It would not be a bad idea to write an account of the entire affair instead of sitting by idly. I would have something to do and maybe Byomkesh would be able to get to the bottom of the matter if he could read my account when he returned.

I began writing that very night. Starting at the beginning, I wrote down every last detail from my perspective in a way that would not allow Byomkesh to pick holes in the narrative. I finished writing the next afternoon.

I may have finished writing, but the story was not finished. Who knew when and where the story of Natabar babu's murder would end? Maybe the murderer's identity would never be known. Feeling somewhat dissatisfied, I had barely lit a cigarette when Byomkesh strolled in holding his suitcase.

'Byomkesh! You're back!' I jumped to my feet. 'So your work's done?'

'The work's not even begun,' Byomkesh said. 'Two government departments are at loggerheads with each other. Each wants to be the first to lay down its life for the cause. When I saw all this, I decided to leave. I'll go back when they've finished battling each other.'

Hearing Byomkesh's voice, Satyabati came running, wiping her hand on the end of her sari. They were not newlyweds any more, but even now a joyful light appeared in Satyabati's eyes when Byomkesh appeared unexpectedly.

When the couple's reunion was over, I brought up the subject of Natabar's murder and gave Byomkesh what I had written for him to read. Byomkesh started reading my notes over a cup of tea.

He returned it to me at six in the evening, saying, 'So Inspector Pranab has confined you to the city. What the fellow must think of us! We shall meet him tomorrow. Let us go and meet Bhupesh babu now.'

I realized the case had intrigued Byomkesh. 'By all means,' I said, pleased. 'We may run into Ram babu and Banamali babu too.'

I took Byomkesh to Bhupesh babu's room on the first floor. My assumption had not been incorrect; Ram babu and Banamali babu were indeed there. Byomkesh did not have to be introduced to anyone, for everyone knew who he was. Bhupesh babu welcomed him warmly and put the kettle on for tea. Ram babu's gravity remained intact, but a nervous wariness was occasionally evident in Banamali's eyes.

Taking a seat, Byomkesh said, 'I was once addicted to bridge. Then Ajit taught me chess. But now I no longer enjoy playing.'

Turning to look at him as he was putting the tea leaves into the boiling water in the kettle, Bhupesh babu said, 'Now for only the sport unto death with my life.'

I was startled to hear Bhupesh babu quote Rabindranath Tagore. He not only worked at the insurance office but also read poetry!

'Right you are,' responded Byomkesh quietly. 'Playing against death all my life has ensured that I can no longer train my mind on light-hearted games.'

'It's different for you,' answered Bhupesh babu. 'I deal in death too; what else is insurance but the business of death. But I still enjoy bridge.'

Byomkesh may have been talking to Bhupesh babu, but his eyes kept drifting towards Ram babu and Banamali babu. They sat in silence, unfamiliar with such light but refined conversation.

Bhupesh babu brought the cups of tea and a plate of cream crackers. 'Yours is a different kind of personality too. Bridge is a game for the intelligent; those who are intelligent are naturally attracted to this game. Some people play bridge as a means of respite from the agony of living. Many years ago I knew someone who used to play bridge to forget the agony of his son's death.'

Three pairs of eyes turned mechanically towards Byomkesh. No one spoke, all of them could only stare in surprise. A heavy silence descended on the room.

We finished our cups of tea without a word. Then Byomkesh broke the silence and said matter-of-factly, 'I was in Cuttack, I have only just got back. Ajit informed me of Natabar Nashkar's death as soon as I arrived. I was not acquainted with Natabar babu, but the news of his death made me curious. You do not often have a murder on your own doorstep. So I thought of making your acquaintance.'

'How fortunate then that the murder took place,' said Bhupesh babu, 'or else you'd never have graced my room. But I know nothing about Natabar Nashkar. I had never even set eyes on him when he was alive. Ram babu and Banamali babu knew him a little.'

Byomkesh looked at Ram babu. A shadow of fear seemed to fall over his gravity. He fidgeted, cleared his throat as though about to say something, then shut his mouth. Thereupon Byomkesh turned his glance towards Banamali babu, saying, 'I'm sure you know what kind of a man Natabar babu was.'

Startled, Banamali babu stammered, 'Uh... ar... he wasn't a bad sort... quite a decent sort, in fact... but...'

Ram babu finally regained his power of speech, cutting in on Banamali babu's incomplete sentence. 'Look, we were by no means friends of Natabar babu's. But when we lived in Dhaka, he lived next door to us, so we were acquainted. We know nothing about his character.'

'How long ago did you live in Dhaka?' asked Byomkesh.

'Five or six years ago,' answered Ram babu, gulping. 'Then the Partition riots began and we came away to West Bengal.'

'So you worked in the same firm in Dhaka?' Byomkesh asked Banamali babu.

'Yes we did,' he answered. 'You must have heard of Godfrey-Brown; it's a large British firm. That was where...'

Before he could finish, Ram babu suddenly rose from his chair. 'You haven't forgotten we have to call on Narayan babu at seven, have you, Banamali?... We shall take your leave now.'

Ram babu made a quick exit, with Banamali babu in tow. Byomkesh turned to watch their act of retreat.

Bhupesh babu smiled. 'Your questions sound innocuous, Byomkesh babu,' he said, 'but Ram babu's offended.'

'I cannot understand why,' answered Byomkesh innocently. 'Do you have any idea?'

'I have no idea,' Bhupesh babu shook his head. 'I was in fact in Dhaka during the riots, but I didn't know any of them at the time. I know nothing about their past either.'

'You were in Dhaka too during the riots?'

'Yes, I'd been transferred to Dhaka about a year before the riots. I returned after the Partition.'

Silence reigned for some time. Byomkesh lit a cigarette.

Looking at him for a few minutes, Bhupesh babu asked, 'Is your story about the man who used to play bridge to forget the pain of losing his son true, Byomkesh babu?'

'Yes, it's a true story,' Byomkesh told him. 'It happened a long time ago, when I was in college. Why do you ask?'

Bhupesh babu did not answer. Instead, he rose and fetched a photograph from his drawer, handing it to Byomkesh. It was the photograph of a boy of nine or ten; his face glowing with the brightness of a child. 'My son,' Bhupesh babu mumbled.

'Your son...' Byomkesh said, raising his eyes from the photograph to look at Bhupesh babu in anxiety.

'He's dead,' Bhupesh babu shook his head. 'He had gone to school the day the riots began in Dhaka; he never returned.'

Breaking the unbearable silence, Byomkesh asked half a question. 'Your wife...'

'She's dead too,' answered Bhupesh babu. 'Her heart was weak, she couldn't bear her son's death. I neither died, nor succeeded in forgetting. It's been five or six years, I should have forgotten by now. I go to work, play cards, laugh and joke, but I cannot forget. Is there a medicine to wipe out memories of grief, Byomkesh babu?'

'Eternity is the only medicine,' Byomkesh sighed.

2.

'Let us call on Swami Pranabananda,' said Byomkesh over our morning tea the next day.

I was already under a pall of gloom after hearing of the tragedy of Bhupesh babu's life the previous night; the thought of an encounter with Inspector Pranab depressed me further. 'Is a meeting with Pranabananda absolutely imperative?' I enquired.

'Not if you do not wish to be free of police suspicion,' answered Byomkesh.

'Very well then.'

Taking the stairs to the first floor at nine-thirty, we observed a lock on Bhupesh babu's door. He must have gone to office. Ram babu and Banamali babu were emerging from their room in full finery – they retreated on seeing us. Throwing me a sidelong glance, Byomkesh smiled.

Shibkali babu was going over the account books in his office downstairs. When he saw Byomkesh, he leapt to the door, asking with anguish in his eyes, 'Byomkesh babu! When did you return from Cuttack – what time? Have you heard about Natabar Nashkar! And now look, the police have involved me in the case – they've involved me.'

'Not just you, they have involved Ajit too,' said Byomkesh.

'Yes of course, of course. Brown shawl. Ridiculous... ridiculous. You must save us.'

'I shall try.'

Suddenly stopping on the road, Byomkesh said, 'Come, let us take a look at the lane.'

He was referring to the lane that ran past our home, the one down which the man in the brown shawl had escaped after shooting Natabar babu. It was so narrow that two people couldn't walk abreast in it. We entered the lane in single file. Byomkesh advanced slowly, his eyes fixed on the paved surface. I didn't know what he had in mind, but it was rather far-fetched to expect clues to the murder three days afterwards.

The window to Natabar babu's room was shut. Pausing before it, Byomkesh trained his probing eyes on the paved surface of the lane. The window was at a height of four feet from the ground; it would be easy to fire into the room if the shutters were open.

'What's that stain?'

Following the direction of Byomkesh's finger, I observed a discoloured mark on the ground; star shaped, with a diameter of about three inches. The lane was swept from time to time, but despite the urgency of all the cleaning, the stain had not been obliterated. It appeared to be two or three days old.

'What *is* that stain?' I asked.

Without answering, Byomkesh suddenly lowered himself to the ground like someone doing push-up exercises and planted his nose on the stain. 'What on earth are you doing?' I asked in surprise. 'Why are you rubbing your nose on the ground?'

'I was not rubbing my nose,' said Byomkesh, back on his feet. 'I was sniffing it.'

'Sniffing it! How does it smell?'

'You can sniff if too if you'd like to know.'

'No need.'

'Then let us go to the police station.'

Leaving the lane behind us, we went off towards the police station. I glanced at Byomkesh once or twice out of the corner of my eyes, but it wasn't clear whether he had discovered anything after sniffing the road.

Inspector Pranab was lording it over the police station. He was, on the whole, of pleasing appearance, medium build and not too dark a complexion; the only flaw was that he was barely five feet three inches in height.

At the sight of Byomkesh walking in, his eyes first expressed surprise, followed by feigned humility. 'Byomkesh babu!' he exclaimed. 'How fortunate I am to be in your august company first thing in the morning. Hehe.'

'I am no less fortunate,' countered Byomkesh. 'The scriptures clearly state the outcome of seeing a dwarf in the morning – you are freed from the cycle of rebirth.'

Inspector Pranab was taken aback. Byomkesh had always ignored his jibes, but today he was in a different frame of mind. Unprepared for a riposte, Pranab babu said glumly, 'I admit my appearance does not resemble a lamp post.'

'You have no choice but to admit it,' Byomkesh smiled. 'Lamp posts have lights on their heads; that is where they differ from you.'

Pranab babu's face fell. Forcing out a laugh, he said, 'I can't help it; not everyone is so bright inside their heads, after all. Was there anything you needed?'

'Of course there is,' said Byomkesh. 'First, I have marched Ajit to the police station to prove to you that he is not absconding. You may rest assured that he is under my surveillance; he will not be able to escape under my nose.'

Pranab babu attempted a disarming laugh. 'I do not know what the Commissioner will say if he learns that you have restrained Ajit from leaving the city,' Byomkesh continued without mercy, 'but I would certainly like to know. We have courts of law in this country; even police officers can be punished for unnecessarily interfering with individual freedom. But still, all that can come later. My second question is whether you have been able to gather any information concerning Natabar Nashkar's death.'

Pranab babu debated whether to answer this question rudely. But realizing that it would not be wise to antagonize Byomkesh in his current frame of mind, he answered calmly, 'Do you have any idea of the population of Calcutta, Byomkesh babu?'

'I have never counted,' answered Byomkesh contemptuously. 'Probably five million or so.'

'Let's say it is five million,' said Pranab babu. 'Is it a simple task to apprehend an individual in a brown shawl from these teeming millions? Can you do it?'

'I might be able to if I have all the information.'

'Although it is against our rules to share information with outsiders, I can tell you all I know.'

'Very well, do so. Has Natabar Nashkar's family been located?'

'No. We had advertised in the papers, but no one has come forward.'

'What did the post-mortem reveal?'

'The bullet penetrated the ribs to enter the heart. The bullet was matched with the gun; it was the same pistol.'

'Anything else?'

'He was quite healthy, but on the verge of developing cataract in his eyes.'

'Who's the owner of the pistol?'

'It's an American army pistol, available on the black market. There's no way in which to identify the owner.'

'Did you discover anything significant when you searched the room?'

'All the relevant items are there on that table. A diary, about five rupees in cash, a bank passbook and a true copy of a court judgement. You may take a look if you like.'

There was a table in the corner of the room. Byomkesh went up to it, but I did not. Inspector Pranab was not a decent sort; an unpleasant situation would arise if he objected. From my chair, I saw Byomkesh examine the bank passbook, leaf through the diary and read the court document with the judicial stamp carefully. 'I have seen all I had to,' he said on his return.

By then, the devil in Inspector Pranab had awoken again. Peering at Byomkesh, he said, 'You saw exactly what I did. Have you got to know the name and address of the culprit?'

'Yes, I have,' Byomkesh told him.

'Really!' exclaimed Pranab babu, his eyebrows shooting skywards. 'So soon! You're incredibly clever! Would you be so good as to reveal the culprit's name, so that I may arrest him?'

'I shall not reveal the culprit's name to you, Pranab babu,' Byomkesh said, tightening his jaw. 'That is my own discovery. You are paid a salary for your work; you will have to find out on your own. But I can offer you some help. Search the lane running beside the building.'

'Has the culprit left his footprint in there! Hehe.'

'No, he has left a mark even more incriminating... One more thing. I shall be taking Ajit to Cuttack with me in a few days. Stop him if you dare... Come, Ajit.'

'Have you really identified the culprit?' I asked in excitement when we left the police station.

'I had identified him even before we came to the police station,' Byomkesh nodded, 'but Inspector Pranab is a good-for-nothing. He is not unintelligent, but his intelligence is destructive. He will never be able to get to the bottom of Natabar's murder mystery.'

'Who murdered Natabar Nashkar? Was it someone we know?' I asked.

'I shall tell you later. For now, let me tell you that Natabar Nashkar was a blackmailer by profession. You had better go back home, I am going to the city. Godfrey-Brown has a large office here in Calcutta too. I might get some information there. It may be some time before I am back.' He left with a wave.

I returned home alone. It was 1.30 p.m. by the time Byomkesh came back.

'You have to do something for me,' he said after his bath and lunch. 'You have to invite Ram babu, Banamali babu and Bhupesh babu to tea. We shall gather here in this room this evening?'

'Very well. But what's going on? Why did you go to the Godfrey-Brown office?'

'There was a court judgement among Natabar Nashkar's belongings at the police station. When I read it I discovered that two brothers named Rashbehari Biswas and Banabehari Biswas were the treasurer and assistant-treasurer, respectively, at the Dhaka office of Godfrey-Brown. They were caught embezzling funds seven years ago. They were taken to court. Banabehari was sentenced to two years' imprisonment and Rashbehari, to three. Natabar Nashkar had got hold of this judgement. Then his diary revealed that he used to get eighty rupees every month from Rashbehari and Banabehari Biswas. I went to Godfrey-Brown to verify the misappropriation of funds. It is true. I had no more doubts that Natabar was blackmailing them?

'But... Rashbehari, Banabehari... who are they? Where will you find them?'

'They aren't far away; you only have to go as far as Room No. 3.'

'What! Ram babu and Banamali babu!'

'Yes. You came close to the truth. They are not just related, they are brothers. To honour the idiom, you could say they are not just brothers-in-arms but also thick as thieves.'

'But... but... they could not have murdered Natabar. When Natabar was killed they were...'

'Patience,' said Byomkesh, raising his hand. 'You shall hear the whole story at tea.'

A variety of snacks bought from the Marwari store and tea had been prepared to entertain the guests. Bhupesh babu was the first to arrive. Dressed in a dhoti and kurta, he had a folded grey shawl over his shoulder and an eager smile on his face. 'Have you made arrangements for bridge too?' he asked.

'We can make arrangements if everyone wants to play,' Byomkesh replied.

Ram babu and Banamali babu arrived a little later, their coats buttoned up to their necks, their eyes wary. 'Welcome, welcome,' said Byomkesh.

Byomkesh led a witty conversation over the tea and snacks. I observed after some time that Ram babu and Banamali babu had shed their stiffness. Feeling quite at ease, they were participating in the exchanges.

After twenty minutes or so, when the snacks were exhausted, Ram babu lit a cigar; offering Bhupesh babu a cigarette, Byomkesh then held the tin out to Banamali babu. 'One for you, Banabehari babu?' he said.

'I don't smoke...' said Banamali babu and turned pale. 'Er... my name...'

'The two of you are brothers and I know your real names – Rashbehari and Banabehari Biswas.' Byomkesh sat down in his chair. 'Natabar Nashkar was blackmailing you. You were paying him eighty rupees a month...'

Rashbehari and Banabehari had turned to blocks of wood. Lighting his own cigarette, Byomkesh spoke as he blew the smoke out, 'Natabar Nashkar was a devil. When he was in Dhaka, he was to all appearances an agent, but behind that façade he was a blackmailer whenever he had the opportunity. When the two of you went to jail, he procured a copy of the court judgement, keeping future possibilities in mind. His plan was to wait till you had got jobs again after your release and then start sucking your blood.

'Then the Partition took place. Natabar could no longer continue his business in Dhaka, he escaped to Calcutta. But he did not know too many people here; there was no opportunity to pursue either his legal or his illegal profession as there was no one suitable for blackmailing. His business reached a low ebb. He took a room in this boarding house, surviving on whatever little money he had managed to bring.

'While he was here, he suddenly saw the two of you one day and recognized you. You lived in the same boarding house. On making enquiries, he discovered that you were working at a bank under false identities. Natabar Nashkar found a channel for earning. God seemed to have trussed up the two of you and delivered you to him.

'Pay up, or else I will reveal your real identities to the bank, Natabar told you. Helpless, you began paying him every month. Not a large sum, admittedly, only eighty rupees. But not bad for Natabar – at least it paid for his accommodation and food.

'So it went on. The two of you had no peace, nor could you escape Natabar's clutches. Your only hope lay in his death.'

Byomkesh paused. Breaking the breathless silence, Banabehari burst out, I beg of you Byomkesh babu, we didn't kill Natabar Nashkar. We were in Bhupesh babu's room when he was killed.'

'That is true.' Leaning back in his chair, Byomkesh said carelessly, 'I do not care who killed Natabar. Only the police do. But the two of you work at a bank. If there is ever a discrepancy in the accounts I shall be forced to reveal your true identities.'

'There will be no discrepancy in the bank's accounts,' Ram babu aka Rashbehari babu finally spoke. 'We will not repeat our mistake.'

'Excellent. Ajit and I shall remain silent in that case.' Byomkesh looked at Bhupesh babu. 'What about you?'

A strange smile flitted across Bhupesh babu's face. 'I shall remain silent too,' he said softly. 'Not a word shall escape my lips.'

The room was silent for some time after this. Then Ram babu rose, speaking with his palms joined together, 'We shall never forget your generosity. May we leave now? I am not feeling very well.'

'You may.' Byomkesh saw them to the door, then came back after shutting it.

I saw Bhupesh babu smiling at Byomkesh. Byomkesh returned his smile. 'I did not know there was an illicit connection between Natabar Nashkar and Ram babu and Banamali babu. That is a coincidence. You have probably unravelled everything, have you not?'

'Not everything, but the sum of it,' Byomkesh sighed deeply.

'Why don't you tell the story? If I have anything to add I shall do so afterwards.'

Giving Bhupesh babu a cigarette and lighting one for himself, Byomkesh looked at me and began to speak, slowly. 'You wrote an account of Natabar's death. When I read it, I was struck by a doubt. The sound of a pistol being fired is never so loud. This seemed to be the sound of a shotgun, or a bomb bursting. Yet Natabar had been killed by a pistol shot.

'You had noticed the similarity in appearance between Ram babu and Banamali babu. When I spoke to them, they appeared to be concealing something. Since they used to frequent Natabar's room, I became curious about them.

'But they were in Bhupesh babu's room on the first floor when the gunshot was heard. The atmosphere in Bhupesh babu's room was peaceful, normal. He was in his own room; at 6.25 p.m. Rashbehari and Banabehari came for the game of bridge. But the game could not begin till Ajit had arrived. A couple of minutes later Ajit's sandals were heard flapping on the stairs. Bhupesh babu rose and opened the window looking out on the lane. At once there was an explosion. Rashbehari and Banabehari went up to the window. "There... there... he ran out of the lane just this minute, did you see him? He had a brown shawl on..." Bhupesh babu exclaimed.

'There were several people walking past the lane on the main road. Rashbehari and Banabehari assumed one of them had just run out of the lane. They were left in no doubt that Bhupesh babu was right. It is possible to induce such mistakes if you want to.

'Later the pistol was found on the window sill of Natabar's room. Naturally the question arises, why had the assailant left the pistol behind? There was no justifiable reason. I suspected that there was serious deception at work behind this apparently simple occurrence.

'Haripada, the servant, had heard someone in Natabar's room at six in the evening. What if that person had killed Natabar? And had then pushed back the supposed time of the killing in order to create an alibi for himself? A difference of fifteen minutes in the time of death cannot be detected by a post-mortem.

'I was convinced that the murderer was not an outsider, but someone who lived in the boarding house. But who was it? Was it Shibkali babu? Rashbehari and Banabehari? Or someone else? I did not know who had a motive, but only Shibkali babu had the opportunity. Everyone else had a watertight alibi.

'My mind was fogged; I could not see anything clearly. I had noticed that Natabar babu's room was directly beneath Bhupesh babu's and Natabar babu's window was directly beneath Bhupesh babu's. But the thought of a cracker hadn't even occurred to me then. Yes, a cracker. The kind that explodes when hurled, or when it is dropped from a height on a hard surface.

'I was on my way to the police station this morning in the hope of some fresh information. As I was leaving, I thought of checking for clues in the lane near Natabar's window.

'I did find a clue. The discoloured stain left behind by a cracker which burst on the paved surface of the lane directly beneath Natabar's window. When I sniffed it I discovered a faint tang of gunpowder. All my doubts were now dispelled. An excellent alibi had been created. Who had created the alibi? It could not have been anyone except Bhupesh babu. Because he was the one who had opened the window. Rashbehari and Banabehari had gone up to the window after hearing the bang.

'Bhupesh babu went downstairs quietly at six that evening under cover of darkness. The pistol had already been procured; he entered Natabar's room, introduced himself and shot him. Opening the window looking out on the lane, he placed the pistol on the window sill and returned to his room. Fortunately no one saw him on his journey to and from Natabar's room. But just in case they had, he needed an alibi. Returning to his room, he waited. Rashbehari and Banabehari arrived in ten minutes for their game of bridge. But Ajit had not arrived yet, so the three of them waited for him.

'Then Bhupesh babu heard Ajit's sandals flapping on the staircase. He was prepared, holding a marble-sized cracker in his clenched hand. On the pretext of stuffiness in the room, he opened the window looking out on the lane and dropped the cracker. There was a bang downstairs. Rashbehari and Banabehari rushed to the window; Bhupesh babu showed them the imaginary murderer in the brown shawl.

'Bhupesh babu did not have to do anything more; the corpse was discovered in due course. The police came and took the corpse away. Curtain.'

Byomkesh stopped. Bhupesh babu had been listening without a word, without stirring, he remained the same way. 'Any errors?' Byomkesh asked him, arching his eyebrows.

Bhupesh babu stirred now, shaking his head with a smile. 'None whatsoever. I was the one who made the error. I didn't imagine you'd be back so soon, Byomkesh babu. I had expected Natabar's case to have died down by the time you returned.'

'Two questions remain unanswered,' Byomkesh smiled. 'First, what was your motive? Second, how did you muffle the sound of the pistol being fired? Even if you fire a pistol in a closed room, the sound is likely to be heard outside. Did you take no care to prevent this?'

'I shall answer the second question first.' Removing the shawl folded over his shoulder, he unfolded it and held it out before us with both his hands; we saw a small hole in the new shawl. 'I was dressed in this shawl when I went to Natabar's room, hiding the pistol under it. I shot Natabar without taking the pistol out of my shawl; the sound was muffled by it, no one heard.'

Byomkesh nodded slowly. 'And the answer to my first question?' he said. 'I can guess some of it; you had shown us your son's photograph yesterday. Still, I want to hear it from you.'

A pulse began to beat in Bhupesh babu's forehead, but he spoke calmly. 'I had shown you my son's photograph because I realized you would discover the truth. So I was justifying myself in advance. Natabar tricked my son into accompanying him from school on the day the riots broke out in Dhaka. That evening he came to my house to tell me he would return my son for a ransom of ten thousand rupees. I did not have ten thousand in cash, I gave him whatever I had; my wife took off all her jewellery and handed it to him. Natabar left with all of it, but we did not get our son back. We did not see Natabar either. Several years had passed since then. When I came to Calcutta after losing my wife and son, one day I suddenly spotted Natabar on the road. And then...'

'I see,' said Byomkesh. 'There is no need to say anything more, Bhupesh babu.'

Bhupesh babu remained immobile for a few moments. Then he said, 'What do you wish to do with me?'

Byomkesh looked at the ceiling for a while. Then he said, '"No one hangs for killing a crow," the writer Sarat Chandra Chattopadhyay had said. I believe no one should hang for killing a vulture either. You need not worry.'

SEPAL

Ambai, tr. Gita Subramanian

It was just the kind of morning when it felt that the day had just not dawned properly. There was no breeze to speak of. It was sweltering inside. Even the sea that could be seen at a distance from the window was a dark grey. The bright green leaves of the banyan tree seemed to hurt the eye. Not one bird song could be heard. Sudha Gupta shook her head vigorously; if her mind ran in such contrary directions, how was she to concentrate on her work? It was just her usual routine work: cases of husbands suspecting their wives and wives suspecting their husbands and asking her detective agency to compile a secret dossier on the other. People wanting to form business partnerships asking for secret reports on each other in order to know all there is to know about the other. Lovers spying on each other. Parents arranging a marriage between their offsprings, asking for a report on the prospective groom or bride. And such other similar cases. The usual sort of cases that come to private investigators. The reason why she got so many cases related to relationships could well be because she was the only woman in this line of work. But even though she would tire of it all every now and then, the incentive for her to continue in this line was that the present Assistant Commissioner of Police (ACP), Govind Shelke, regularly involved her in his cases. This was not the norm, yet he would somehow make it possible. He would also make sure that she received the money that was due to her. Though he would make fun of her guru Vidyasagar Rawte's methods and say in jest that he was a veritable Sherlock Holmes, he did have a great deal of respect for him. Anyway, Vidyasagar did not mind it at all. With so many overbridges collapsing in Mumbai these days, Vidyasagar knew the date of construction of every bridge in Mumbai, who built it, when and how they had been rated on inspection. He would say that detective work without conducting research and collecting all the facts available was no detective work at all. Sudha's husband, the scientist Narendra Gupta and her daughter, Aruna, who was studying for her master's degree, appreciated her work. Aruna would sometimes say that her mother's line of work prevented any male student from coming anywhere close to her.

Sudha stepped into the space that she used as her office. At first, she had converted the front portion of one of the flats on the ground floor in her building into an office. The men who lived in the building were dying to find out what sort of an office a woman could have set up in their building. They sent their wives, who like the men were eager to know the details. All of them enquired what they would have to pay to have their own husbands investigated. It seemed like they were indeed men who needed to be investigated. One day, in the morning, Stella had said, 'The uncle who lives in the opposite house thinks he is Salman Khan.' When Sudha had asked her about it, Stella had signalled out the window with her eyes. In the balcony of the first floor opposite their office, wearing striped briefs and nothing on top, staring at their room, was a man with a huge belly, holding a bottle of oil in one hand. 'Now for 15 minutes he will massage his body with oil. A free show for us to watch,' said Stella. To avoid this, Sudha had moved their office to a portion of her own veranda, partitioning it off with a sliding glass door shutter.

To get out of her feeling of mental lethargy, Sudha decided she needed a cup of cinnamon tea. She pressed the button of the electric kettle and grabbed her cup. It was a gift from Aruna and it read: 'Permit me to introduce myself. My name is Hercule Poirot. I am the world's greatest detective.' Sudha put in a tea bag and exactly at that moment, the switch popped up. Listlessly, she poured the water into the cup. The aroma that arose seemed to revive her a little. The file that she needed to check through had been left in readiness by Stella. This was a slightly different kind of job. A rich industrialist's daughter, who was her father's partner, wanted someone to keep an eye on the activities going on around him. It was one of those cases which involved property matters of wealthy families. The father was in the ICU and the mother herself was a doctor. At first, they could not quite make out what was at stake and how to go about it. The nurse who had been looking after him happened to be a classmate of Stella. It was through her that they could gather some details. On the previous evening, she had sent them a shocking three-minute video. The industrialist's doctor-wife and another man had taken his thumb impression on a document. After wiping his thumb clean, they had closed the tube that was connected to his vein, through which essential drugs were being given. The nurse stood outside the room and was able to film what was going on inside. She had managed to get the flow of the fluid started again and then immediately called in the doctors. Without telling them the details of what had just happened, she had asked them to examine him. As the patient's wife was a doctor, the nurse must have been confused as to what would be the correct course of action. The video had been sent to the daughter as soon as it had arrived. Now they had to send her the full report.

As she sipped her tea and opened the file, she realized that Chellammal had not yet come in. Normally, she would have dropped in by that time and come to her with a cup of tea and sat by her side, chatting for a little while before going in. Till some time ago, Stella would also have come in by this time, but she had started coming in a little late these days as she had to feed her baby, little Anandi. Besides, today she had to take Anandi in for some inoculations, so she was sure to be late. But still, Chellammal should have arrived by now. Just as Sudha was thinking this, the door opened and Chellammal entered, muttering something under her breath. As she moved towards the kitchen, Sudha called out, 'What, Chellamma? Are you ill? I was just thinking that you had not come in today.'

'What can go wrong with my body? After all, if I walk, it comes with me,' Chellammal answered in a frustrated tone.

'What happened, Chellamma? Come here, let us have some tea.'

'I'll go and make some for myself. Your cinnamon tea will not suit me.'

She soon came out with a cup of tea and sat on the little *rattan* stool by Sudha's side. Her face looked drawn.

'What is the matter, Chellamma?'

'What can I say? This ass Mallika is giving me a lot of trouble.'

Chellammal, who always referred to her daughter as gold, pet, darling, sugarcane, pearl, princess and so on, calling Mallika an ass today surprised Sudha. Mallika was a schoolteacher. Chellammal had worked very hard after her husband's death to raise her with great care and affection.

'What is this, Chellamma? Calling Mallika an ass and all that...'

'Then what should I call her? She keeps on rejecting all of the men I choose for her on some ground or the other. I let it go thinking we can wait. But now she is crying and saying she does not want to get married at all. I asked her, "Are you in love with somebody? Just tell me and be done with it. I will marry you off to whoever that is," I told her. She has refused to say anything and is just crying. Isn't she getting old? Stella is married to Singaravelu, whom I had rejected for Mallika and she is now even the mother of a little baby. And Mallika is losing weight day by day. Her face looks like someone who has lost everything in a card game. I don't understand anything.'

'Shall I speak to her?'

'You can try talking to her if you like. She is not in town today. She left this morning for Mahabaleshwar. Holi festival holidays are approaching, aren't they? She has taken two additional days off and gone.'

'Alone?'

'No, with some teacher from her school...'

'Which teacher? Just one teacher or two or three?'

'I don't know. You are always telling me: "Don't ask a girl who is old enough to go to work, nagging questions." That is why I didn't ask.'

'Well, all I said was don't keep poking your nose into what she is doing all the time. Let her live as she wishes to. But if she is going out of town, don't you have to find out how and why. If something happens, don't we have to know the details?'

'Yes, yes, you will speak for both sides,' Chellammal muttered in anger.

'What time did she leave in the morning?'

'Around six o'clock.'

'She would have reached by now. I will call her. I'll have my phone on speaker. Wait.'

She called Mallika's number.

'Hello, Sudhamma. Is anything the matter?'

'Is Mahabaleshwar nice? I just called, no special reason.'

'Has my mother come there? It is very nice here, Sudhamma.'

'Where are you staying? In a hotel?'

There was silence for a while and then she said in a low voice, 'Yes.'

'There are many good hotels there. One can rest comfortably and look at the hills around. Which hotel are you staying in?'

At once Mallika asked, 'Did Amma ask you to ask me?'

Chellammal wagged her index finger, mouthing the words, 'Didn't I tell you so?'

'Che, Che! We are planning to go. That is why I asked you. Just to get an idea.'

'J.P. Farm House. It is like a real farm. Very nice.'

'Okay. Enjoy yourself with the other teachers. After all, teachers need a break too, right?'

'Thank you, Sudhamma,' said Mallika and ended the conversation.

'I think that two or three of them have gone there together, Chellamma.'

'What kind of detective work do you do, Sudhamma? Didn't you notice how she cut you off as soon as you mentioned other teachers? You didn't get that?'

'Let it go. This is a question of her privacy. Don't worry about it.'

'No, Sudhamma. You don't understand. That girl is hiding something. Make some enquiries.'

'Right, we'll do that. But don't fret yourself over this for no reason.'

Chellammal picked up Sudha's empty cup as well as hers and went back in.

She called out from the kitchen after some time. 'There are leftovers from the *kozhambu*, fried vegetables and *koottu* made two or three days ago. Shall I add some fresh rice and dhal and mix them all up together, add some tamarind juice and make it into a mixed rice dish?'

'Do that, Chellamma. You can powder some *bisi bele bath* spices and add that. It will have a good aroma then.'

'That is what I was planning to do. "Gadbad" rice,' she said and laughed. 'Gadbad' means something that is not in proper order, a hotch potch of many things. Aruna had given this name to a dish made with all sorts of leftovers mixed into rice.

Exactly as if she were told to come at that moment, Stella walked in.

'Aunty, you are making gadbad rice, do make some extra. I love it,' she said as she walked in. She had brought little Anandi with her. Anandi leapt towards Chellammal. Chellammal gathered her in her arms and said, 'Baby Anandi and Chellamma Paatti are going to cook,' in baby talk. Then she asked Stella, 'Have you brought her formula milk, or should I make some porridge for her?'

'Aunty, I just had no time in the morning. Could you make her some porridge, please?'

'I will. But how come you had no time? What great feats are you accomplishing with your big detective work? You can't even find out why a girl has changed to the extent of saying she does not want to marry at all,' muttered Chellammal angrily.

Stella looked at Sudha quizzically. Sudha gestured to her to say that she would tell her later. Stella came in and after checking whether the electric kettle had water in it, switched it on, put a tea bag of the tulsi tea that she liked into a cup. She closed the sliding glass door, poured boiling water into the cup, dipped the teabag, pressed it, then removed it, before coming to sit with the tea in front of Sudha.

Sudha started telling her about Mallika.

The case of the industrialist had become quite a sensational one, and besides that they also had many other cases to work on; with all that, they did not take Chellammal's worry about Mallika very seriously. Chellammal was a very emotional person. And if there was anything related to Mallika, her worry would be unimaginable. She would worry about things with no reason at all. Thinking that this worry was just the same as all those others, Stella and Sudha had done nothing about it. Then one day in the evening there was a call from Govind Shelke.

'Didi, how are you? Has Chellamma Mausi left?'

'She has left, why?'

'Didi, could you come over to our place?'

'Why, what has happened? Is Meena...?'

'No, no. You just come.'

Stella had left. There was time before Naren and Aruna would come home. Anyway, they both had their own keys. She messaged both of them to say that she was going to Govind's house.

She locked up and went down and took her car. His house was in the police quarters in D.N. Nagar. It took her hardly ten minutes to get there. Govind himself opened the door when she rang the bell. When she saw Mallika in front of her sitting in the living room, Sudha got the shock of her life. Mallika's hair was all messed up; her face was totally pale and drawn. She sat staring at the floor. Very gently, Meenabai was trying to persuade her to drink the tea that she had placed on a stool in front of her.

Sudha walked in very slowly and came and sat on the sofa. When she placed her hand on Mallika's shoulder, the tears began to roll down Mallika's eyes. Sudha took a tissue from the box on the table and gave it her saying, 'Drink your tea first,' and picked up the teacup. Mallika wiped her eyes and then began to sip the tea very slowly.

Govind began to speak in a very soft voice. 'Meena and I were on our way to visit relatives in Worli and were driving along the Sea Link. Mallika was standing there. She had tried to jump and commit suicide. Some people had seen her and stopped her. The police too had arrived on the scene. I knew she was Chellamma Mausi's daughter. I spoke to them and brought her home. She refuses to say anything. That is why I called you.'

'What happened, Mallika? What is the matter? Tell me. It doesn't matter what it is. Tell me without fear,' Sudha said.

Mallika maintained her silence and drank her tea.

'Did Amma say something to you?'

Mallika shook her head to say no.

'Did somebody else say something to you?'

Again, she shook her head to say no.

'Any problem in school?'

'No,' she said in a whisper.

'There must be a reason for you to want to commit suicide. Are you in love with someone?'

She gave no reply to that question.

It did not look as if she would say anything more after that. Sudha got up.

'Thanks, Govind. I will take her home,' she said.

Mallika got up and said, 'Thank you, *Bhai Saheb*, thank you, *Bhabhi ji*.' Her words were slurred and indistinct, as the attempt to commit suicide, the fact that many people had come to save her, coming to Govind's house, everything had affected her. She had been badly shaken up. Govind patted her on the back. Meena embraced her.

'Whatever the problem is, don't worry about it, Mallika. Aren't we all there for you?' said Govind as he saw her off.

Once they sat in the car, instead of taking her home, Sudha took her to the Versova beach. Sudha bought two packets of *Chana Jor Garam,* made of cooked chickpeas slightly mashed and fried with spices and as soon as they were seated in a secluded area, gave one to Mallika. Mallika began to eat it very slowly. Sudha hugged her with an arm around her shoulder and said, 'Mallika, don't say anything now. Too many things have happened in the space of one evening. Just calm yourself now. But whatever your problem may be, open your heart and tell me all about it when you feel up to it. But you have to make one promise to me; don't ever even think of committing suicide again. Your mother will be totally heartbroken. Who else does she have besides you? Tell me.' As soon as she said this, Mallika put the packet down and started crying with long sobs. Sudha patted her back all the while.

'Tell me if there is something that is bothering you or frightening you. I know a very good psychiatrist, I will take you to her,' she said in a consoling tone.

Mallika did not say anything. Then, 'Let us go home, Sudhamma,' she said.

Sudha got up and bought a bottle of water and asked Sudha to wash her face. Once she did that and also drank some water, her face seemed much clearer. Getting back into the car, Mallika said, 'Sudhamma, don't tell Amma.'

'No, I won't tell her. I won't even come to the house. Just tell her that you had work and got late.' As soon as she said that, Mallika's phone rang. It was Chellammal.

'I am on my way home, Amma. I got late today,' Mallika said.

Sudha dropped her at a short distance from her home.

'Thank you, Sudhamma,' Mallika said.

'Silly girl! Why do you need to thank me? Go home carefully,' Sudha said.

When she reached home, Naren was sitting in the living room drinking a cup of tea and watching TV. Aruna was in her room working on her computer. She waved her hand from there.

'Work?' asked Naren.

Saying yes, she went in to have a wash. She came back and sat beside Naren. Aruna also came and sat by her side. News of the industrialist continued on the TV. They started discussing that case and then the conversation ran into many different areas. Naren switched off the TV. Then Aruna said, 'Amma, I saw Mallika didi two days ago.'

'Where?'

'You know Aman, the son of Mehmood Kaka who runs a bakery and a vegetable shop? I saw her with him.'

'She must have come to buy bread or something like that.'

'No, ma, you know, that small lane by the side of the bakery, I happened to go that way. I saw the two of them together ahead of me, holding hands as they walked.'

'They went to school together, didn't they? They must have been discussing something.' She quickly redirected the conversation.

Everybody who lived around there was very fond of Mehmood Kaka. He ran the bakery and the vegetable shop. In the bakery, you could get some tea as well. Delicious masala tea. Once you bought vegetables, he would give you quite a bit of green coriander, green chillies, curry leaves and ginger gratis. Not just that, tea and some khari biscuits as well. Sudha would tease him by saying, 'Kaka ji, you'll start making a loss in your business if you give so many freebies,' in answer to which he would say, 'Allah will provide, Sudha madam.' He was a great admirer of the saint-poet Kabir. He would never let a conversation go without a Kabir *doha*. Aman was his son.

The next day, Sudha left to go to the bakery to buy bread before Chellammal arrived. Aman welcomed her with a smiling face.

She bought some wheat bread and then asked, in Hindi, 'Aman, I hope you won't be angry if I ask you something?' They were in a corner of the shop. The shop assistant was serving the other customers.

'What is this, aunty? Will I ever get angry with you? You are like my ammi to me.'

She lowered her voice further and asked, 'Is there anything going on between you and Mallika?'

He looked shocked. Then he said softly, 'Yes, aunty.'

'Did you go to Mahabaleshwar with her?'

That question really shook him up.

'Never ever, aunty. I am not one who does such secretive things. What is there to be secretive about going on a picnic? Last month some of us went on a picnic to Karjat. Her mother knew all about it.'

'Did you have a fight recently?' she asked.

He hesitated a bit.

'After knowing each other for such a long time, when I ask her to marry me, she refuses. She won't tell me the reason. When I asked her about it, she got angry.'

'Did you ask her to convert to your religion? By you, I mean your family.'

'Not at all, aunty. My ammi and baba don't like all that.'

'Perhaps she is worried about what some others may say or do.'

'Aunty, I have many Hindu friends. None of them has any objection to such things.'

'No, maybe somebody spoke of love jihad or something like that...'

'Aunty, there are people who cheat girls and take them away. But I don't want to change her in any way. Last year at my sister's *nikah* ceremony, my ammi bought Mallika a new dress. Chellamma Aunty had also come to the wedding. You too were there, aunty. Ammi had bought a new dress for Aruna as well, don't you remember?'

'Then why this fight?'

'She kept saying, "Not now, not now" and I got angry and said "Okay then; if not now let us say never and leave it",' he said, hesitantly.

When she told him about how that probably resulted in the suicide attempt and told him about all that had happened the day before, he was in real agony.

She comforted him and told him to wait patiently till they could find out what was in her mind. Something was definitely tormenting her. Till they could find out what that is, she told him not to say anything to her about marriage.

'Sorry, aunty, sorry, aunty,' he repeated many times. Then he asked her not to say anything to his baba.

She walked home in a very confused state.

Chellammal had not come in yet. She felt like talking to Govind. She called him and told him about Aman. 'There is some tangle somewhere in this, Govind. I am not that sure that Aman told me everything. There is some serious worry that has led her to this extreme step of a suicide attempt.' She continued in this vein.

'Didi, don't panic like this. We will see.'

'No, Govind. Her suicide attempt has given me a big shock. Poor Chellamma! If she finds out, she may not survive the shock.'

'True.'

'Shall we do something? Shall we find out who went with her to Mahabaleshwar? The hotel she went to is called J.P. Farm House. She went two days before Holi and stayed for about three days. I suspect she went with Aman...'

'What is this, Didi? When two people love each other what is wrong with their going away together for two days? What do you suspect in this? Mallika may have kept it secret because Chellamma Mausi will not understand all that.'

'What is this, Govind? Did I say that it was wrong for her to go? Perhaps they had a very big fight there. I suspect that perhaps it was because of that that this suicide attempt happened.'

'Well, all right. I will make enquiries.'

'Thanks, Govind.'

'There is nothing for you to get so alarmed about, didi. She is a young girl. Some sort of mental confusion. We'll wait and see.'

Even after speaking to Govind, things did not clear in her mind. Suicide was a dreadful act. What could push a girl like Mallika towards this extreme step?

Chellammal arrived. Seeing the unopened packet with a loaf of bread, she said, 'The bread packet seems unopened. Did Aruna and Naren babu go away without eating anything?'

'Remember, there were some *pav* buns? They ate eggs and *pav* buns. I went and got this now for myself. You know I don't like pav buns.'

'What, you still haven't had your breakfast? Shall I toast the bread?' Chellammal asked.

'Okay.'

'I'll toast the bread and make some ginger tea. Have your cinnamon tea later. Have you had your bath? Don't you have any work to do? Your face is so drawn. And, there at home, Mallika came late yesterday and today she is sleeping in, totally exhausted.'

That was a shock.

'Has she not woken up at all?'

'She woke up but went back to sleep. She has a lot of notebooks to correct.'

While she was talking, Chellammal toasted the bread, buttered it and put it on the dining table with the ginger tea. Then she came and sat at the table with her own cup.

When they were discussing the menu for the day, Stella entered.

'Hey, is there no tea for me?' she asked.

'There is some in the kettle. Take it,' said Chellammal.

When Stella came and joined them, Chellammal went in saying, 'I better go and see to my work.' Malu came and started her work.

Stella and Sudha went to their office space. Sudha shut the sliding glass door and told Stella about what had happened with Mallika the evening before and about speaking to Aman that morning. The suicide attempt shook Stella up as well.

'This has become a much bigger thing than we imagined, Sudhamma!'

'There is something here, Stella, that we just haven't understood.'

Sudha's mobile phone rang. The screen said 'Govind'.

'*Bola*, Govind,' she said.

'Didi, according to the hotel records, it was Mallika and Nirmala Chitre who were in that hotel on those dates.'

'Who is that?'

'I have checked. She is the headmistress of her school. A woman with an excellent reputation. She won the Teacher's Award last year.'

'Okay.'

As usual, a dead end.

Even as her mind was preoccupied with thoughts of Mallika, Sudha was trying to do her other jobs when a call from Vidyasagar Rawte came through. He asked her about the industrialist's case. He knew some juicy titbits about the man, the sort of things that don't get reported in the daily papers. As usual, he told her those stories and made her laugh. As they were talking, she asked him if he happened to know Nirmala Chitre who won the Teacher's

Award last year. He said he knew her well. She was a brilliant teacher, one who was always willing to help others. Sudha knew that such unstinted praise would always be followed by a 'but', so she prompted him with a 'but...'

'About 15–20 years ago a very unfortunate incident happened.'

'What was it?'

'Not many in those days understood such things. That untoward incident happened because of that.'

'What kind of thing?'

'Nirmala has no interest in men...'

'Oh!'

'There is nothing wrong with that. Nirmala and her closest friend were living together without saying anything to anybody. But the members of both the friend's family and Nirmala's family began to suggest suitable bridegrooms who were engineers or IAS officers and pressuring them to get married. They planned to commit suicide. They actually made the attempt. But Nirmala was saved. That girl died. Somehow, they managed to get any news related to it suppressed before it got blown into a very big issue.'

'How did they manage that?'

'Just take it that I helped them.'

'Okay.'

'Why are you asking so much about Nirmala now?'

When she told him about Mallika, he said, 'There is something not quite right in this. Sudha, please go and see Nirmala. She is a wonderful lady. Very well-read.'

'Will she agree to meet me?'

'She definitely will. She has a very good heart. Don't tell her what you want to meet her for and just ask her if you can meet her. There is some complication in this.'

'Okay, Guruji.'

After a little while, he sent her Nirmala's number.

With some hesitation she pressed the numbers on the phone keyboard. At once a gentle voice said, 'Hello, *mi* Nirmala *boltei*.'

When she introduced herself as a journalist, Nirmala gave her an appointment to meet straightaway. Before meeting her, she decided that she would collect as much information as she could get about her and got on to the net. She found many articles on her on winning the Teacher's Award. In the corner of one newspaper, her name appeared among the names of participants in a rally of mainly transsexuals, homosexuals, lesbians and bisexuals, opposing Article 377. When she went deeper into her research, she found a short article in Marathi written by her. A short note very movingly written:

Sunanda,

I don't know. What should I write about you? Today is the same day. The day we had decided to die together. The name Sunanda has many interpretations right from Matsya Purana to Mahabharata. There are many Sunandas in the ancient Puranas. Both as human beings and as goddesses. For me, you were someone who always delighted the heart, someone brimming over with joy. From the day you turned around with your twinkling eyes and smiled at me in college for the first time till the day you turned towards me and smiled just before you were about to swallow a whole lot of sleeping pills that you held in your palm, you remained joyful. How was that possible for you?

I am not in the same house where we lived together from 1996 to 1999. That is not because I could see you in every corner of that house. But it is because that is where you went away from me. Embracing, we lay in each other's arms after we consumed the tablets. You told me that death would be like flying. I said it was like falling headlong off a fast-moving swing. You laughed. You kissed me. How did I live, how did you die, Sunanda, my love!

Who will understand this love? Its tenderness; its poignancy, its touch; its compassion; its fulfilment – what words can possibly suffice to describe all this? We had kept it a secret. It was something that belonged to us alone.

Among married couples if one dies and the other survives, we say the survivor is widowed. We call her a widow and him a widower. But in our kind of relationship, if one dies what is the other? I have found a suitable word for that. That word is Sunanda. A word that contains all the happiness and sorrows of the world. After you, I have become a Sunanda. Did we not have our fights? We certainly did. Anger, jealousy, sulking, fury, indifference; all these were there between us. But again and again, it was just the two of us for the two of us. We fought. We made peace. After getting angry we spoke sweetly to each other. I got a job. You did not get a proper one. You only wanted to be a freelancer. You were interested in alternative methods of teaching. We had problems with money. 'Why don't you take up a job? Do I have to be the only one to slog?' I shouted one day. As soon as I shouted, I apologized. You went out. When you came back, you placed some hundred-rupee notes in my hand. You had sold your bangles. I cried. You comforted me saying, 'When I get a job that I like, we can buy them back.' In an earthen pot covered with plastic, you had bought rasmalai from a Bengali sweet shop. That was our pact, wasn't it? Soon after a fight we would have to eat something sweet.

Our parents could not understand. Every day we got calls recommending some prospective groom. Your parents found one particularly good match. 'If you refuse this too, I will consume poison,' your Aai said. That is when we took the decision.

When everything was over, I don't know why, your parents gave me a bit of your ashes in a small earthen jar. I kept it for a very long time. Then one year, on this day, in the evening, I immersed your ashes in the sea. That is the time of the day you liked the most. You would say that it is the time everything melts and streaks down in red in the sky.

Now I am still here. I, a Sunanda.

Sudha rang the bell and waited. The woman who opened the door was around forty to forty-five years old. A calm smiling face. She was wearing a red kameez with yellow flowers embroidered on one side and a yellow salwar. She asked Sudha to sit down and said, 'Why don't we have some tea,' and went in to prepare the tea. A room that was decorated in an uncluttered manner. Maybe she was interested in minimalism, thought Sudha. On a low table there was a photograph of a young woman. It could be Sunanda.

She came out with a tray with two cups of tea, some pieces of mawa cake and some Shrewsbury biscuits. They were the specialities of Kayani Bakery in Pune. As if she had read Sudha's mind, Nirmala said, in English, 'They had closed Kayani Bakery for a while, hadn't they? They have reopened it now in the same place. My brother had gone to Pune. He brought these.'

The mawa cake melted in the mouth.

'You said you wanted to talk to me about something?' she continued in English.

'Yes, I wanted to talk to you about your award.'

'Is it for some magazine?'

'Yes, I freelance sometimes and write some pieces.'

'How do you know of me?'

'Vidyasagar Rawte told me. Besides, I know Mallika, who is a teacher in your school, very well,' Sudha said in Marathi.

Her face that had bloomed when she heard the name of Vidyasagar Rawte, became expressionless when Mallika's name was mentioned.

After a short silence, Nirmala said, in Marathi, 'I don't think you are a journalist.'

After a slight pause, Sudha said, 'No, I am not a journalist. I am a close friend of Mallika's family.'

A trace of anger swept over her face. But she steadied herself and said, 'You could have told me that openly.'

'This is a rather complicated situation,' said Sudha and told her about Mallika's suicide attempt.

Nirmala Chitre was profoundly shocked by this.

'Do you have any idea why this happened, Nirmala ji?'

'How can I know anything about this?'

After a few moments of silence, Sudha asked, 'Mallika and you had gone to Mahabaleshwar, right?'

'You have found out everything before coming here.'

'No, Nirmala ji. Vidyasagar ji spoke about you in such glowing terms that I have the greatest respect for you. I really don't know all the facts of the case. Please don't take me amiss.'

'Did Mallika say anything?'

Sudha did not say anything about the article she had read or about meeting Mallika before coming to meet her.

Before speaking to Nirmala about anything, Sudha had thought it was necessary to talk to Mallika. She had asked her to come to Cafe Moshe's in Bandra. It was a place where one could talk in peace. Mallika seemed listless when she arrived. Sudha ordered snacks and hot milk chocolate and stayed silent for a while. Then she told Mallika about speaking to Aman and about what she knew about Nirmala Chitre and about her being a much-respected person. After that she asked Mallika how she had gone to Mahabaleshwar with her.

Mallika did not reply at once. When Sudha told her that if she did not speak at once, things could go terribly awry, Mallika said, 'She is someone who has helped me a lot. She encouraged me a lot. She is our headmistress as well. I thought I might lose my job. So I agreed when she asked me. I didn't want it. But I did it for her. For the sake of her good heart. She calls me Sunanda...' Her voice quivered as she spoke.

'Couldn't you have said that you were not interested?'

'I didn't know how I should say that. I kept postponing it, thinking I will tell her later. Amma began to look for a groom for me. How could I tell Nirmala ji that? In Mahabaleshwar, she put a ring on my finger...'

She took it out of her bag and showed it. It was a ring with many pearls set on it. It was her mother's ring, Nirmala had told her.

'I just didn't know how to refuse. She lavishes so much affection on me. In Mahabaleshwar she asked me, 'Shall we live together? Move in with me to my place.'

'Don't you think you need to tell someone who loves you so much that you were not interested?'

Mallika remained quiet.

'If that is what you want, tell me, Mallika. There is nothing wrong with it. I will explain it to Chellammal. What is on your mind? Tell me. Do you feel you want Aman and you also want Nirmala?'

She shook her head to say no.

'There are people who feel that way. Look here; tell me what exactly is confusing you.'

'I only agreed because I found it impossible to say no. I did not want her feelings to be hurt. But I don't want it now. But I couldn't say it. When she put the ring on my finger, she cried. And the other day Aman shouted and said he did not want me at all. That is why that day...' Her eyes were brimming over.

'Okay, let us see if we can do this without hurting anybody,' she said and tried to cheer her up.

Now Sudha was in front of Nirmala.

'Did Mallika say anything?' Nirmala asked again.

In order to ascertain what was on Nirmala's mind, Sudha said, 'No. She did not say anything. I have come to you because I wanted to find out what is bothering her so much.'

She was quiet for a while. Then slowly she said, 'She is a very innocent girl. A little bud. I guarded her to make sure nobody should hurt her. Since she was the only Madarasi teacher in the school, I vigilantly made sure that nobody, even in jest, would tease her or treat her without respect. After many years, I had found someone who was calm, patient, always with a smiling face...'

Sudha looked at the photograph on the table and said, 'Like Sunanda?'

Nirmala was taken aback.

She said in a soft voice, 'Yes, I saw my Sunanda in Mallika. She is my treasure. A big treasure. What worry did she have in her mind that made her try to commit suicide like that? I looked after her like she was a flower that was about to bloom...' Her voice broke and perhaps because she felt ashamed of breaking down in front of a stranger, she bent her head down.

She continued speaking with her head down.

'Sudha ji, do you think this kind of relationship is bad?'

'No, not at all. I never thought like that. If you won't misunderstand me, may I say something?'

'Go ahead.'

Sudha moved forward a little and held Nirmala's hands in hers.

'Mallika is a very young girl. She is timid by nature. She could not refuse someone who showed her so much love. She loves a boy who studied with her. She just doesn't know how to get out of this relationship without hurting you...'

'She doesn't like this relationship?' Nirmala seemed jolted by this. 'She could have told me she did not like it, couldn't she?'

'Some kind of fear. Confusion. She was worried that the way things were in the school may change. You should forgive her, Nirmala ji.'

Nirmala freed her hands.

'I feel badly humiliated, Sudha ji,' she said in a muttering tone.

'Please, don't think like that. None of this was planned.'

Sudha took out the ring that was now in her handbag and placed it in front of Sunanda's photograph.

Nirmala was sitting with her head bent down.

Sudha got up slowly and went out and shut the door from outside.

Seen from above, the sea appeared like a black mat flung out. She had parked her car in a corner and walked up to the sea. When she peered into the sea, Sunanda leapt up with a wave and laughed. She waved her hand and beckoned to her. 'Just coming,' said Nirmala. When Sunanda rose from the waves and spread her arms wide she leapt across and ensconced herself in them.

Sudha woke up with a start. It was two o'clock at night. Black waves were still arising in her mind. She turned around. Naren was fast sleep. She got up without making a sound and slowly went into the living room. She opened the window. A breeze blew on to her face. She saw the sea at a distance.

She sat on the sofa for a little while. Then she called Nirmala's number. It was a while before it was answered. Then in a voice not yet completely out of sleep, Nirmala asked in a slightly panicked tone, 'Hello, Sudha ji. Why at this time? I hope there is no problem...'

Sudha apologized and then narrated her dream. 'I got scared, Nirmala ji,' she said.

She could hear Nirmala laugh softly.

'Sudha ji, when Sunanda and I decided to commit suicide, we were both quite young. Of course, what you told me about Mallika was a major shock. I shrank in shame when you told me that she had been in this relationship with me unwillingly. But not for a moment did I contemplate dying. Suicide does not solve anything. I am sad. But I am not angry. Congratulate Mallika on my behalf. Tell her that she can come to school without any worries. When she gets married to Aman, I will surely come. I will give her a wedding gift as well. The same pearl ring that you left here. I cannot change my love, can I?'

'Thank you so much, Nirmala ji,' Sudha's voice stumbled over the words.

'It is two-thirty. Life goes on regardless. *Aata jaa ani zopa shant. Kalaji karu naka.*' (Go now and sleep peacefully. Don't worry.) Nirmala ended the conversation.

Outside the window, the twinkling lights of the fishing vessels on the sea were glowing. Little dots of light scattered here and there on the dark sea.

THE RIVER

Ankush Saikia

The hanging bridge above the river was shrouded in the early-morning mist. Then it swayed and a figure appeared out of the whiteness, hands holding onto the cane rings. It was a slim tribal girl in jeans and a windcheater. Without glancing down at the roaring waters, she crossed the bridge which had been made by people from her village during the winter. It was a 30-minute walk to her village, but today she was headed in the opposite direction.

She climbed up a steep path while holding on to creepers and shrubs, till she came to the road that went towards the town. There was a shed with motorcycles belonging to people from her village: there was no road to the village. She took out her phone, saw it had caught the network and made a call. Then she waited. She kept looking back at the hanging bridge and the mist obscuring the wet forested hillsides.

She felt sad that she was leaving the village and her parents behind, but she was young and also wanted to get back to her life in the town. She had heard talk about a dam being constructed on the river and wondered how it would change things if it was built. Maybe there would finally be a road to their village.

About 20 minutes later, a Sumo taxi playing loud Hindi pop came to a halt in front of the shed. The girl, Oyin, got down from the motorcycle she had been sitting on. Picking up her backpack, she smiled at the handsome young driver and got in with the other passengers.

The body was found early in the morning lying at a bend on the highway. The man who spotted the body later told his friends that he had seen it only because he had slowed down his motorcycle at the turn. He had touched the brakes, looking at the roaring waters of the river down below, then looked to his left and saw the body lying at the roadside. It was a smooth road, save for the occasional landslide and had been upgraded recently by the Centre to make it easier for army trucks to go up near the border with China. He hit the brakes and then got down to take a few photos of the corpse. The body was of an outsider, about 50 to 60 years old, short and dark complexioned with greying hair, maybe a contractor or an army supplier – that was what the man told the officer-in-charge when he reached the police station in town, only about 10 km from there.

Arjun Arora was steadily working his way through a bottle of Blenders Pride when the call came. The person on the other end, Dinesh Sethi, wanted to meet straight away. His old army training and his regular drinking habit, had allowed Arora to sober up quickly. An expensive sedan was sent to pick him up from C.R. Park and bring him to a luxury hotel in central Delhi. Arora had told Sethi that he didn't want to be stopped and given a breath-analyser test.

Sethi was a big man running to fat and his eyes were red as though he'd been drinking too. He was eating a large pastry when Arora arrived at the nearly empty coffee shop. Sethi asked for two black coffees and then told Arora that his business associate,

Pawan Gupta, had turned up dead that morning on a roadside in Arunachal Pradesh.

Sethi was the promoter of Himalaya Power, which had built hydropower projects on rivers in Himachal Pradesh, Sikkim and Bhutan. He owned other companies too: transport, real estate and packaging. Arora had heard of him, had read about HP or Himalaya Power in the business pages. Gupta had been the director of HP.

In Arunachal, Sethi told him, they were planning an 800 MW project. Sethi and Gupta had met the chief minister (CM) and the state power minister in Delhi two years ago, and, as was the practice, a memorandum of understanding or MoU had been quietly prepared between HP and the power minister (representing the state government) upon payment by HP of 10 crore: 25 per cent of 40 crore, which was the total amount at the going under-the-table rate of 5 lakh per MW. The project itself would cost a few hundred crores, and was based on a design of an energy PSU which had since dropped the idea (and from whose offices Sethi had smuggled out the plans).

The balance 30 crore was to be paid to the power minister once work started. However, the project never took off due to public opposition and the denial of environmental clearances. Sethi decided to get back the 10 crore HP had paid. It helped that he had contacts in the army, which had influence in the state.

Sethi said to Arora, about the power minister, '*Thik hai*, you might have spent some money on *chai pani*, but at least half of the amount return to us, *hai na*? Nothing that duffer could do in two years! All our equipment and trucks are gathering rust in the work camp.'

After some persuasion from HP's security chief, Dabholkar, an ex-army colonel, the power minister agreed to return half of the advance. Gupta had then gone to Arunachal, collected the money from the minister and was returning to Assam (from where he would fly to Delhi) when the incident happened. Above the same river where the project had been planned.

'He would have carried 5 crores with him on the plane?' Arora asked.

Sethi cleared his throat noisily. 'HP has a private jet. Anyway, he would have deposited the money in Tinsukia. Hawala type. You'll know where Tinsukia is, you served that side.'

Arora's assignment, explained Sethi, was to recover a file Gupta had with him, to recover the money and to find out who had killed the HP director – in that order of importance. The file had the original copy of the MoU and the original plans of the energy PSU.

'Anyone you suspect?' Arora asked.

'Gupta's taxi and the driver are missing,' Sethi said. 'But a driver won't take such risks. The power minister must be behind this. He has his money back with him now. They can do anything for money, these people.'

So can you, Arora said, to himself. He had his doubts – too many angles, too many players in the shadows – but Sethi was paying well, half upfront, so the next morning he called Sethi and said yes.

They had booked him on a mid-day flight to Dibrugarh. One of Sethi's men met him in the airport parking and handed over an HP identity card, identifying Arora as a 'Consultant', an Inner Line Permit for Arunachal for 7 days, besides some money in an envelope.

He slept soon after they were in the air and woke up while they were above north Bengal, by his own calculation. He had a window seat, but on the right, so he couldn't see the Himalayas. In any case, there was heavy cloud cover, especially over Assam. There was plenty of turbulence too as they came in to land. From the airport, he took a taxi to cross over to the neighbouring state.

They drove over the Brahmaputra on a very long, recently built bridge to get to the north bank. The river was grey like the colour of the vast sky above and swollen by the rains. It was like a basin here at the upper end of the valley, the rivers from the surrounding mountains running down to create the vast floodplains of the Brahmaputra.

Everything was green – paddy fields and tea gardens – but the humidity was high. They left the bridge behind and turned onto the highway that ran across the length of the north bank; the evening sky had cleared up. Beyond the paddy fields rose up the hills of Arunachal.

After they drove past the last railway station and the market town, they reached the border-crossing: no one at the police post bothered to check the taxi. The town at the foothills was some 30 km away, through a stretch of forest and then paddy fields with scattered longhouses. It was as he remembered it, a spread-out and sleepy place similar to other foothill towns in eastern Arunachal. Only now on the outskirts there were the usual workshops, rubbish dumps, wine shops and Sumo taxi counters.

The bridge was as he remembered too, spanning the wide river – which HP wanted to dam – flowing down to the plains, the high mountains standing guard on the other side in the fading light. He asked the taxi driver to stop, got down, and lit a cigarette, cupping the flame from the lighter in his hands because of the strong wind off the river. A hundred years ago, the British had gone up into these hills to subdue the natives, accompanied by Nepali troops and Naga porters. As Arora got back into the taxi, two motorcycles tore past, none of the four youngsters on them wearing helmets.

The HP work camp was a few kilometres ahead in a clearing beside the road, which continued up to the China border, an almost two-day journey. By the headlights Arora saw rusty tin sheets screening off the perimeter of the camp; they had been fixed to the gate too. The taxi driver honked several times before a *chowkidar* came to open the gate. There was the bright glare of a light coming from behind him. Arora paid the driver, took his backpack and got down. Another person appeared: a sparely built man with a receding hairline, the HP 'liaison officer', Tsering. He took Arora to a prefabricated block within the compound after making sure the *chowkidar* had locked the gate.

'They tried to burn down the camp,' he told Arora. 'Just two of us here, we have to be careful.'

'Who tried to burn it down?'

'Local public. Led by one student leader.'

Two floodlights pointed ahead and behind the prefabricated unit, Arora had to squint his eyes as they approached. The unit had an office and three smaller rooms. Tsering opened one for Arora: it was a narrow space with a bed and a plastic table and a tube light. At the end of the unit was a tiny bathroom where Arora freshened up. Towards the rear of the compound, he saw the half-lit shapes of JCBs and dump trucks and large cement mixers. He returned to his room and stretched out on the bed.

Tsering knocked half-an-hour later – Arora had almost fallen asleep – and led him to the *chowkidar*'s hut at the end of the compound. The grass was squelchy underfoot and Arora could now see that some of the trucks had been damaged in the fire. The hut, with split-bamboo walls and a tin roof, was dimly lit with a bed on one side and a fireplace on the other, where the *chowkidar* had something on the fire. He was a lean, muscled man in an old olive-coloured sweater and had close-cropped hair. Tsering spoke in Nepali to the *chowkidar* and he rose from the fireplace to get a bottle of rum from under his bed.

'From the army canteen,' Tsering said.

Arora accepted a large peg in a stainless-steel glass. They sat on wooden stools near the fireplace, the *chowkidar* and Tsering talking about visiting the office of the SP, or superintendent of police. Tsering noticed him following their conversation.

'You understand Nepali?' he asked.

Arora nodded, not caring to elaborate.

'Chettri here was in the army,' Tsering told him and added, 'my father is Nepali, mother Arunachali. They live in Lakhimpur now.'

Arora drank the strong rum and stared into the smoking fire. He felt comfortable here, in this forgotten place with these forgotten men. It reminded him of his past in the army and the construction camps his father would stay in.

'Was Gupta staying here?' he asked.

'Yes, he stayed one night. In your room.'

'Where was he coming from that early in the morning?'

'Hornbill Resort. About 10 km from here. Belongs to the power minister's brother. Gupta stayed there the second night.'

'Are there hornbills here?'

'The brother's wife is from Nagaland,' Tsering said by way of explanation.

'Sethi told me they haven't found the taxi and the driver?'

Tsering shook his head. 'No. Arunachal-registered Sumo. New driver from Assam. The regular driver was sick, so he called another driver.'

'Who do you think is behind it?' Arora asked.

Tsering shrugged. 'Can't say. Where there's money involved... but you should talk to Dabholkar. He knows all the details.'

Arora wondered if Tsering was hinting at something. 'All right. You're going to the SP's office tomorrow?'

Tsering sipped his rum and nodded.

'I'll come along,' said Arora.

Chettri lifted the lid off the *degchi* on the fire, stirred and ladled out steaming khichdi on a plate which he handed to Arora, along with a spoon and some mango pickle. Arora finished his rum and dug in.

The SP's office in town looked newly constructed, with orange painted walls and cheap aluminium door and window frames. There were piles of sand, stones and bricks in the wet forecourt area (it had rained at night). They had got there in a battered old

HP pick-up truck driven by Tsering. Arora followed him down echoing corridors, their shoes leaving muddy imprints on the concrete floor.

The SP was a tall, young south Indian by the single name of Vijay and Tsering had told Arora that he was one of CM's men. When they entered the room there was an elderly Arunachali inspector present.

'All formalities complete, Tsering,' the SP said from behind his desk. 'Mr Gupta's family are collecting the body today.'

'They are here?' Tsering asked.

'Yes, reached yesterday. Staying in circuit house. I met them,' said the SP, studying Arora.

'We were hoping to look at the body,' Arora said mildly.

'And you are?' the SP queried.

'HP consultant, he's come from Delhi,' said Tsering quickly.

'I have to write a report for the head office,' Arora said.

'Hmm. You can go and see,' said the SP. 'Inspector Lego will go with you.'

Arora noticed a look pass between the SP and the inspector.

'Any news about Gupta's taxi and the driver?' he asked the SP.

'We are looking. We have asked our counterparts in Assam for help too.'

'The overall status of the investigation?' Arora asked, looking at the inspector and the SP. 'You've filed an FIR?'

'Tsering filed the FIR,' said the SP.

'Have you interviewed anyone?' Arora asked.

The SP smirked. 'You go see the body and write your report. You can also go to the incident site with Tsering. Leave the investigation to us. Okay?'

Arora forced himself to smile politely. He looked at Tsering and both men stood up.

'Okay, sir, we will take your leave,' said Tsering.

The SP raised a hand magnanimously and indicated that the inspector should accompany them.

Once they were outside, Tsering looked back to see where the inspector was, then hissed, 'Be careful! I told you he's the CM's man.'

'Yes, I remember! Do you think he's questioned the power minister?'

'He's the CM's man too,' Tsering said.

Arora remembered the answer to his query about hornbills. As they waited for the inspector to join them, a shiny black Scorpio entered the parking area and two tribal youths got down. Both were well-built, dressed in semi-formals, and sported expensive sunglasses. One had short hair parted to the side, while the driver had longer hair which was dyed blonde. They got down from the SUV and approached the pick-up truck.

'Tsering ji, any news?' the short-haired one asked, in Hindi.

Arora was introduced by Tsering: the blonde-haired one was David, a local student leader, and the other was a local journalist, Prem.

David studied Arora, nodding his head. Arora wondered why he looked familiar, then remembered: he had been one of the boys on the two bikes the previous evening.

'Very sad, what happened to Gupta ji,' David said, in Hindi. They spoke Hindi fluently, which they were taught in school. 'But if you come to tribal areas and try to forcefully implement projects, this is what will happen.'

'End up murdered?' Arora asked in English. 'Who do you think killed him?'

David glared at Arora; he obviously wasn't used to being challenged. Inspector Lego joined them. Outdoors, Arora saw that above his lined, weathered face he had a full head of thick, naturally black hair. Something in the genes, or in the water; one hardly saw men here with grey hair, or even bald men. The three of them got into the pick-up truck, Arora in the back. As Tsering drove out of the office compound, the inspector rolled down his window and lit a cigarette. Arora looked back and saw the journalist and the student leader entering the office building.

'Useless people,' the inspector said to Tsering, in Hindi. 'Just seeing them spoils my day.'

'Any NGO people here?' Arora asked the inspector. 'Anti-dam activists?'

Tsering answered, glancing at the inspector, 'There's one girl, Priya Pandey. From Future India. She's been meeting all the anti-dam people.'

The inspector spat out of the open window. 'She's another useless person.'

'She left for Delhi the day the body was found,' Tsering said.

It was a short drive to the civil hospital through the older parts of the town. They passed government quarters with faded tin roofs and overgrown gardens. Outside the gate of one quarter stood a man in a vest with a child slung on his back in a shawl.

The civil hospital, a one-storey construction with several wings, was built on top of a low hill, with the green-clad mountains visible nearby. As Arora got down, he noticed, among the other vehicles, an Innova taxi and an ambulance. Standing beside the vehicles were a knot of outsiders, Delhiites by the look of them.

With the inspector and Tsering handling things, Arora was able to go with them straight to the run-down morgue room, which had a row of four freezers against one wall. Only one was occupied, by the late Mr Gupta. That tray had been pulled out and around it were two hospital attendants and a few more people from the parking-lot group, including a middle-aged woman with a thick jacket over her salwar kameez. Her eyes were swollen from crying. A young female doctor was helping one of the men fill up a form.

The inspector spoke to the attendants and indicated that Arora could come take a look. Gupta, whom he had never met while alive, looked unassuming in death. He lay there under a dark-blue sheet as though sedated and awaiting surgery. Only a slight depression at the top of his head hinted at the nature of his death: Sethi had said that Gupta had been struck several times on the back of the head. Tsering got the autopsy report from the doctor, which he handed to Arora.

Arora stepped outside and lit a cigarette to get the acrid odour of formaldehyde out of his nostrils. He went through the report, which said that death had occurred due to severe blunt force trauma to the back of the skull. The middle-aged woman now stepped out of the morgue room.

'You've come from Delhi?' she asked, in Hindi, adding, 'I'm Mrs Gupta.'

Arora threw away his cigarette. 'Yes. The company sent me to have a look.'

'What is there to look at,' she said sadly. 'I don't know why they had to send him to this place instead of someone else, someone younger.'

'Did he tell you anything? On the phone?'

'He just said he wanted to get home soon. He was worried about the money.'

'Any reason?'

'It was a lot of money. And this place…' she said, looking around with distaste.

The doctor came out, followed by Tsering and told Mrs Gupta that they could take the body. Arora handed her the report and she took it and quickly walked off, as if glad to leave the whole business behind her. Mrs Gupta went back inside the morgue room.

'The body will go by air ambulance to Delhi,' Tsering said. 'HP is arranging it.'

Arora nodded. The inspector joined them.

'Are you done?' he asked Arora and to Tsering, 'Come on, let's go.'

They dropped Inspector Lego at the SP's office before crossing the bridge over the river and driving out of town. The clouds had come down from the nearby mountains. Tsering was silent on the way, but Arora didn't mind; he was turning the pieces of the puzzle around in his head.

They passed the HP work camp, a few houses and the occasional shop and then the river was down below them to the left while the mountains rose up on the right. The greyish waters flowed between the rocky banks with a muted roar, while on the far side was a narrower road passing below lower hills. Tsering drove fast on the empty highway, slowing down at places with small landslips and rocks which had come down from the friable mountainsides and soon they were at the 'incident site'.

He parked on the right margin of the road some distance before a sharp turn to the right and they got down and walked ahead. There was a fine drizzle on the wind, and Arora breathed in the cold damp air. Tsering stopped at the turning.

'His body was found here that morning. No sign of the Sumo taxi.'

The road, the cemented drain beside it, the bare earth of the mountainside – Arora felt the hopelessness of his task. Across the surging river was a patch of terraced rice cultivation with a tiny hut in the middle. It was a place still wild and free: people like Gupta and Sethi wouldn't have understood that.

They went back and got into the pick-up truck. A Sumo taxi full of passengers came speeding round the bend honking wildly. As they set off, Arora noticed a thin plume of smoke rising up from the lonely hut across the river.

A little way ahead the road turned away from the river and Tsering turned left onto a gravelled track that went up and then down a hill with scattered trees, including fruit trees – papaya and orange. The track ran diagonally down the hillside to a grassy clearing where to one side was a row of connected wooden cabins and on the other a glass-fronted wooden structure with a covered deck out front. A few SUVs were parked at the end of the clearing. As Tsering drew up alongside them, Arora noticed a downward path, past a couple of tall old trees, leading to a sandy beach by the river. This was the Hornbill Resort.

Tsering got down, frowning at a dusty Scorpio with an Assam registration number parked beside three Arunachal-registered Toyota Fortuner SUVs. Arora asked him what the matter was.

'Dabholkar is here. I thought he was in Tinsukia.'

He took out his phone to make a call, while walking towards the covered deck. Arora followed him. There seemed to have been a party the previous night: empty Japanese single malt and Australian wine bottles on the floor and soiled plates on the tables along with the remnants of a garishly decorated cake. A log was still smoking on an ash-piled tin tray. Arora lit a cigarette and took a seat at a clean corner table. The drizzle had stopped and a little sunlight filtered through the clouds and the treetops rustled in the wind.

Tsering opened a tinted-glass door and went in. He returned with a sleepy worker who started cleaning the mess half-heartedly. Meanwhile, a tall man in a purple fleece jacket came swaggering along from one of the cabins.

'Tsering, didn't come for the party yesterday?' he asked, stomping up to the deck. 'It was *bhabhi ji's* birthday. Still having a hangover, *yaar*,' he chuckled.

'I wasn't invited,' Tsering said testily.

The tall man appeared not to hear. Though balding, his hair was trimmed in a crew cut.

'You're the guy who's come from Delhi?' he asked Arora.

'Yes. I have to write a report for Sethi.'

The tall man sat down at an adjoining table and introduced himself as Dabholkar.

'Police in upper Assam are looking for the taxi driver,' he said.

'Have they traced his number?'

'Switched off since that morning. He must have got rid of it.'

'Last seen?'

Dabholkar shrugged. 'Here. When he left that morning with Gupta.'

Arora was reminded of an incident from Nagaland, back when he had been in the army. A family was selling a large plot of land. A customer appeared, someone with ties to one of the groups, but that wasn't such a big deal in Nagaland. On the day of the sale, the person made an excuse about not being able to present a cheque and said he would pay in cash; then there was an excuse about the cash too, some problem in collecting it. The payment was finally made in the evening, by which time the banks were closed (for the family to deposit the money). That night a couple of armed masked men turned up, searched the house and left with the money. The customer of course later swore he had nothing to do with it.

By then a couple of youths who looked like local toughs had tumbled out of the restaurant, where it seemed they had spent the night; they stood outside smoking and laughing, making light of their hangovers. Arora and the two HP men were joined on the deck by the power minister, a stout man with short hair wearing an expensive down jacket, his face puffy from the night's enjoyment. His brother and the brother's wife, came along. They were equally stout and bleary-eyed.

Tea and coffee were brought to the tables by a worker while the revellers attempted to make sense of the previous night, about the guests who had left at night and early in the morning. Arora noticed a young girl come out briefly from Dabholkar's cabin, then go in again. He was introduced to the minister by Tsering, under Dabholkar's watchful eye.

Arora could have asked the minister why they had been celebrating when a death had just occurred. Instead, he asked why the payment hadn't been done online, or in Delhi or even in town and why Gupta himself had to come and not an employee of HP (even Tsering or Dabholkar for that matter)?

The power minister sighed and leaned forward on the table.

'You're asking the right questions,' he said, in chaste Hindi. He was smooth, a diplomat. 'Online, or in Delhi; yes, if it was four or five years ago. With this new government, it's not possible. The CBI would be on my trail straightaway. In the town? Too dangerous, my enemies, also the anti-dam activists. The cash itself I had to arrange from the state capital. It came here directly. And as far as Gupta is concerned, Sethi was the one who sent him.' He sat back in his chair with a faint smile.

'Why no security for him?' Arora asked Dabholkar. 'Till he got to Tinsukia.'

'He himself didn't want it,' Dabholkar said. 'Didn't trust anyone. See what happened.'

'The regular driver, was he really sick?' Arora asked.

Dabholkar nodded. 'I checked. He was bedridden. He sent this other driver, said he thought he was an honest boy. But who knows...'

With the tea and coffee finished, the minister and his brother were getting restless. The brother's wife returned to their cabin to get ready to leave, giving them a chance to take out another bottle of scotch.

'Let's fix this hangover,' the minister said, after one of the youths had brought him the bottle. 'Arora ji, please join us.'

But Arora stood up and looked at Tsering.

'Thank you, but we have some work.'

On the way back from the resort, he asked Tsering what might have happened.

'Those people have played some game,' Tsering replied, his eyes fixed on the road.

He slowed down as he took the turn where the body had been found and Arora noticed a small lone figure in the rice fields across the wide river.

'So, what work now?' Tsering asked.

'Nothing. Let's have lunch,' said Arora.

They went to a 'nice hotel' in town, where they had a few cans of beer followed by a simple but filling lunch of rice, dal, boiled vegetables and fried *mithun* meat. When they came out, Arora stopped to light a cigarette and noticed the Sumo taxi that had passed them earlier in the day, now parked near a rubbish dump. He turned to Tsering.

'Do you know where the regular taxi driver stays?'

Tsering led Arora to a nearby commercial building. They went through a corridor on the ground floor past several shops and came out to a rundown old house. Loud Hindi pop music was playing inside; on the veranda a few young men were lounging, drinking beer from cans. A couple of kids were playing Ludo and there was a pretty, young girl beside one of the youths. Tsering beckoned, and he got up and sauntered over. He was lean, brown-complexioned and nonchalant, wearing tight jeans and an open shirt. His name was Krishna; Arora felt he was of mixed parentage, maybe a child from one of the road-crews up in the mountains.

Tsering asked if there was any news of Gopal, the other driver.

There was none, said Krishna, he had disappeared.

'You were sick?' Arora asked. 'What happened to you?'

'Are you a doctor?' Krishna shot back. 'I wasn't well, it happens sometimes.'

The other youths were looking their way. Arora noticed that the girl whom Krishna had been sitting with looked worried. She wore black trousers and a red-and-black shirt, possibly some sort of uniform.

'I was in bed for almost three days,' Krishna said. 'You can check with the pharmacy doctor.'

'You stay here? Who are the other people?' Arora asked.

'Yes, I stay here with some friends.'

'How come you're not driving today?' Tsering asked.

Krishna shrugged. 'Haven't got a trip.'

With that he walked back to his friends. He said something and they laughed. All except for the girl.

Tsering and Arora drove back to the work camp and later Arora lay on the small bed catching up on news from the outside world through his phone (his mobile data connection worked – Tsering said it worked till about 3/4th of the way to the border).

He looked up Priya Pandey, the anti-dam activist. She was of a recognizable type, from a privileged background with links to the West (Future India was foreign-funded), burning to remove inequalities (but it wouldn't be at the expense of her privileges) and a great critic – especially in foreign media – of the present government. She had criticized the HP group, in connection with the planned dam in Arunachal and had harsh words for both Sethi and Gupta. To Arora, the HP group was essentially a product of a corrupt Delhi, built on easy loans; it had simply found ways to take advantage of the current dispensation. Still, Pandey's criticism of Gupta and her sudden disappearance were interesting. Arora called the HP staffer who had met him at the airport and asked him to look her up.

Late in the afternoon, Arora took a long walk to the banks of the river. Tsering was watching a Hindi movie on the desktop television in his room. Arora walked along the almost deserted highway, through fields and past vegetable patches and old houses with woven bamboo walls and palm-leaf roofs, outside which families were relaxing at the end of the day. It was cloudy and windy. On a sandy patch by the wide river, already at the plains here, a couple of children were playing football. Arora had all but given up on the case.

It was dark by the time he got back to the camp. Tsering was going out in the pick-up; Arora noticed he had shaved and changed his clothes. Later, while he was drinking rum with Chettri by the fire, the *chowkidar* said with a leering smile that Tsering had gone to meet a woman. Arora asked him who she was, but Chettri would only say that she was a widow who worked in a government office.

Tsering got back in the early hours of the morning. Arora was woken by the growl of the pick-up entering the camp. His mouth was parched from the strong rum and cigarettes and he got up to drink some water. Afterwards, as he lay on the bed in the dark, unable to sleep, he suddenly knew what he would do in the morning.

At 8 a.m., after two cups of Chettri's black tea, he asked the *chowkidar* to get the keys to the pick-up from Tsering. He drove out of the camp and crossed the bridge into the town, where he went past the SP's office and the civil hospital to take the road that ran along the far bank of the river. It was a narrow road that wound through a scruffy residential area and then climbed up to the hillsides above the river. After almost half an hour on the potholed road, he saw the terraced rice field and the hut below him and, across the river, the sharp turn on the highway where Tsering had stopped the previous day.

There was an old Hero Honda motorcycle parked against the hillside; Arora parked behind it and got down. A wiry middle-aged man in a faded blue shirt and trackpants was bent over in one of the narrow terraces. He straightened himself to look at Arora standing by the roadside, then returned to his task. Arora lit a cigarette and waited.

About 10 minutes later, the man stepped out of the terrace, flung a handful of weeds down the hillside and went into the small hut, from which he then came out puffing on a pipe and approached Arora. A local dog that had been waiting outside the hut followed him and growled at Arora. The man sharply told it to be quiet. Arora saw that he was elderly, with a lined and creased face, but still in good shape, the contours of his muscled body noticeable under his old clothes. He studied Arora with alert, mischievous-looking eyes and asked him in Hindi who he was.

'I'm with HP. Got here from Delhi two days ago on some work,' Arora said.

'You want to buy my land? For your project? I'll be getting compensation if you people build the dam anyway,' the man said, his eyes twinkling. 'But my wife has a nice big plot if you're interested. On the highway near the town. It would be a good location for a hotel. We don't have any five-star hotels here.'

Arora smiled. He was starting to like this elderly rogue.

'I'm not here to buy anything. I came to find out something. Is this your *kheti*?'

'Yes, it is. And I still work it myself. My sons are useless, no help from them.'

'You come here every day?'

'Yes. Early in the morning, then I leave by 9 or 10 a.m. Why? Has HP run out of rice? But there's only Tsering and that Nepali *chowkidar* in the camp now.'

'Someone from HP was killed. A company director who had come from Delhi.' Arora pointed across the river. 'At that turning in the road. Early in the morning, three days ago.'

A sly grin spread across the man's face.

'You've been here two days and you came to ask me about it?' he said. 'Even the police here haven't come.' He looked at the pick-up truck. 'That must belong to HP?'

Arjun understood. He nodded. 'Let me know what happened, and there'll be a reward from the company for you.'

The man sucked on his pipe and grinned, showing even white teeth. He then told Arora what had happened that day.

He had got there early as usual and worked for a while in his field before taking a break to make a cup of black tea in his hut, which he had outside with a few biscuits. It was a cloudy morning and then he saw, across the river, one Sumo taxi rashly overtake another at the turning.

'I thought the fellow was drunk. He stopped in the middle of the road, blocking the other Sumo. The driver got down and another person got down – could have been a girl, looked skinny. Two people also got down from the other Sumo. It looked like they were arguing, then they started pushing and shoving. I couldn't see properly after that because they went to the other side of the two vehicles.

'Then the driver of the first Sumo came running around and got in and drove off. The driver of the other Sumo was walking this way and that, like he didn't know what to do. Now I thought he was drunk. Then he got into the Sumo and drove off very fast. Very strange! But then I forgot about it. Later that day I hear that a dead body had been found at the turning.'

'Someone going past on a motorcycle found the body,' Arora said. 'Did you see?'

'I wouldn't have noticed a motorcycle stopping. Anyway, I left early that day.'

'Could you see the body from here?' Arora asked.

The man grinned again. 'Do you think you could have made out?'

Arora strained his eyes across the river and had to admit that it would be hard. He shook his head.

'You're a smart fellow,' the man said. 'You might be from Delhi, too, but I don't think you'll end up dead like him.'

'Good,' said Arora and took a couple of notes from his wallet and handed them to him. 'Thank you.'

The man counted the money, then said, 'HP is a big company.'

Suddenly Arora had had enough, of the grasping elderly man, of the rainy skies.

'The dam is never going to be built, do you understand?' he snapped.

'I knew that from the beginning,' the man snapped back.

He turned and went back to the hut followed by the dog. Arora got into the pick-up, reversed it roughly and headed back towards town. As he drove, he calmed down.

Just before he reached the outskirts of the town, there was a call from the HP staffer. Priya Pandey was in Delhi, staying with her parents in Vasant Vihar instead of her rented flat in GK-1 Enclave, keeping a low profile. When she was in town, the staffer said, she always stayed at Hotel Mirbuk. She was friendly with the politician who owned the hotel, an old rival of the present power minister.

'Should we talk to this girl?' the staffer asked. 'Do you want me to tell Sethi?'

'Wait till I get back,' Arora said. 'I need to check a few things.'

He remembered he had seen the hotel in town and on his way back, he took the side street leading to it and parked outside. Hotel Mirbuk was a glitzy four-storey building with a parking lot beside it, where there were the usual mud-splattered SUVs. Arora walked up the front steps and into the lobby. Almost instantly something jumped out at him: the girl at the reception wore a uniform he had seen before, black trousers with a red-and-black shirt.

He went up to her and asked about Priya Pandey, saying she was a friend. No, they didn't know when ma'am would be back. Yes, she always stayed here, in Room 103 on the first floor.

A girl in the same uniform was coming down the wide steps beside the reception and faltered when she saw Arora. She was the one he had seen with the driver Krishna. The receptionist smiled at her.

'Oyin, this is Priya ma'am's friend,' she said. 'Have you spoken to her? When is she coming back?'

Oyin shook her head and muttered something, then hurried off down the corridor. The receptionist stared after her, puzzled.

'What's happened to her?' she said and turned back to Arora. 'Priya ma'am was very friendly with Oyin. She had even gone to her village to do research on the HP dam.'

'*Achchha*. Where is her village?'

'You have to walk from the highway, about half an hour. From here, about 25 kilometres to the spot. There's a waiting shed there.'

Arora thanked her and left the hotel. Part of him had wanted to go after Oyin and question her, but experience told him it was better he waited. Just ahead of where he had parked was a grocery store and a tea shop; he sat at a table from where he could see the hotel and asked the Bihari owner for tea.

Several cigarettes and glasses of tea later, he saw Oyin come out of the hotel. She looked around, before starting to walk quickly toward the main road. Arora got up and paid. He followed her. He had a hunch about where she was headed. About 10 minutes later she came to the same commercial building beside the road and after a quick glance back (Arora ducked behind a car parked beside the footpath), went inside.

Arora hurried through the corridor that ran along the length of the ground floor. A female voice shouted from a shop selling jackets and sneakers: 'There he is!' Inside were Oyin and Krishna and two more boys from the house.

'Take the bastard behind!' Krishna told them and, grabbing Oyin's hand, pulled her out of the shop.

The other two youths came forward punching and kicking; taken by surprise, Arora stumbled and fell on the cemented floor. Then he got back the advantage: two well-aimed kicks and the two of them were down on the floor. Arora got up and hurried out of the building past the shopkeepers who had come out on hearing the commotion.

As he stepped out to the road, a Sumo taxi sped past him: it was empty except for Krishna and Oyin. Arora ran back towards the hotel. It took him around five minutes to get there and he was breathing so hard he had to wait a few a moments before getting into the truck.

The Sumo had headed in the direction of the bridge and Arora followed. The two youths were standing outside the building and scowled when they saw him, but Arora didn't have time for them now. He drove out of town and as he approached the bridge, called Tsering and told him to wait outside the camp with his licensed pistol.

He picked up Tsering and carried on, heading in the direction of the Hornbill Resort. As he drove, Arora briefly told him about the developments of the morning.

'How do you know they're going this side?' Tsering asked.

'Because the girl's village is this side. I think they're headed there.'

'And the other Sumo and driver?'

'He must be hiding somewhere, maybe in Assam. He'll be scared.'

'The bastard,' swore Tsering. 'I had got him work with HP. But how did he know?'

'Through the girl. She might have heard it from Priya Pandey, who might have been told by the politician who owns the hotel – he could have found out about it.'

They sped on: with every kilometre Arjun grew more worried. Had he miscalculated? Tsering, alarmed at the way Arora was driving, kept quiet and held on to the dashboard. The road climbed up at one point past a cleft in the hillside and then there was the waiting shed – with the Sumo taxi parked near it.

Soon Arora was hurrying along the swaying hanging bridge over the river followed by Tsering. The pistol was jammed into the back of Arora's jeans.

'Why has he come here?' Tsering shouted above the roar of the river.

'They might have hidden the money here,' Arora replied.

It was a tough trek on a stony path along the river and then up a steep forested hillside on a muddy track. As they came down the track, Arora could see, beyond terraced rice-fields that gently sloped up above the river, the thatch-and-palm-roofed longhouses of the village.

The village dogs started barking as they approached and snotty-nosed children came out to look at them. Tsering knew the people – it was one of the villages that would be submerged if the dam was built – and asked where Oyin's house was.

As they made their way towards the rear of the village, Arora noticed a commotion outside one of the longhouses. The driver Krishna, with two black duffel bags slung on his shoulders, was brandishing a double-barrelled shotgun, while the girl Oyin was kneeling beside an elderly man bleeding from the nose: he looked like her father. An elderly woman was shouting and the villagers were coming out.

When he saw the two of them, Krishna raised the shotgun. Before Arora could react, he fired. Tsering let out a cry and fell, clutching his stomach. The driver shifted the shotgun towards Arora, but he had already drawn the pistol and fired first. The bullet hit Krishna on the chest, spinning him around and the shotgun went off in the air, while the girl screamed. Arora dropped to his knees beside Tsering.

'Are you okay?'

There was blood seeping through his fingers, but Tsering nodded. 'Get him.'

Krishna had tossed the now-empty shotgun away and was hurrying through the village. Arora got up to follow him, but by now men with shotguns and old rifles had appeared and blocked his way. Tsering with much effort yelled at them to let him go – the actual culprit was getting away.

Arora ran forward and when he reached the green rice fields, he saw that Krishna had already disappeared into the track through the forest. Cursing, he gave chase. There was no sign of the driver along the way and Arora grudgingly admired his toughness.

He ran, tripping and falling on the stony path above the river. Krishna was almost at the hanging bridge. But when Arora reached the bridge, it was tilted dangerously to one side: the youth had collapsed onto the cane rings wound around the bridge.

Arora advanced along the bridge slowly, then stopped. it was swaying dangerously and had turned halfway in the middle. Then he saw Krishna unzipping one of the bags.

'What are you doing?' Arora yelled. 'Have you gone mad?'

It seemed he had, for he grinned at Arora, blood spewing out of his mouth – a lung was likely to have been hit, it was amazing he had made it so far. Krishna then tugged at the bag and the 500-rupee notes floated like snow into the foaming waters below. Arora watched, horrified. Krishna repeated the procedure with the second bag. The waters below the hanging bridge turned white with the 500-rupee notes. Then he pulled at the cane rings. Arora shouted again, but the driver just laughed at him and toppled into the water below. He disappeared instantly under the notes floating on the water.

It turned out as Arora had suspected: Priya Pandey had been told about the deal by the hotel owner and rival of the power minister and Oyin, who had gotten friendly with the NGO activist, had heard her mention it on the phone. Oyin had told her boyfriend Krishna and he had hatched the plan. The two of them had waited near the turning that morning and Krishna had followed and overtaken the other Sumo. A blood-stained wrench with which he had battered Gupta was found in the back of his Sumo.

No charges were brought against Oyin, but she lost her job at the hotel. Gossip in the village made her leave for the state capital after a few weeks, where she found work in another hotel. Her boyfriend Krishna's bloated body had been fished out of the Brahmaputra in Assam after some fishermen spotted it. As for the money, there was a rush among people downstream for several days to try and recover the notes. Some people became very rich – and later lost the money too when the police came to recover it. The happiest were children who managed to pick up a note or two from the river's edge.

The other driver and the Sumo taxi were found in a village near Lakhimpur in Assam, where he had been hiding at a friend's place. He was let off by the police and Sethi managed to obtain the file which was recovered from the vehicle. Sethi got back about 1.5 crore from the police in both states (they kept some of the recovered money too). Tsering was taken to the hospital, but survived.

A couple of months later, Arora called up the liaison officer one night. Tsering said he had recovered, quit his job with HP, married the widow he had been seeing and started his own business: a transport service with two Sumo taxis, one of which was driven by the driver who had been with Gupta that morning.

GULMOHAR HOUSE

Meeti Shroff-Shah

'*PERFIDIOUS*? How do you even think of these words?' BG frowned as he studied the Scrabble board between us.

'Oh, they just come to me,' I said airily and stuck my hand back into the red bag of letters to draw more tiles.

I'd meant it as a joke and yet, in this instance, it was true – the word had just floated into my head, as if like me, my subconscious was also trying to warn BG of the danger he was in. From my spot across the table, I considered his shrivelled legs and downturned mouth and reminded myself that holding back was really the right thing to do. He'd been so downcast ever since his physiotherapist told him that he'd probably never walk again that I worried about how he'd react to what I'd discovered.

'*PELICAN*,' BG arranged his tiles below my 'P' to spell out his word on the board.

'Every time, huh?' I shook my head wonderingly and earned a slight glimmer of a smile. When we first started playing, I'd been amazed at the regularity with which BG found finches and falcons amongst his Scrabble tiles. But since then, I'd learnt that he'd been a most avid birder before his accident.

Now, he shifted uncomfortably in his wheelchair and I knew from experience that he was beginning to tire.

'Should we resume in the afternoon?' I suggested.

He nodded, letting the tiles in his hands drop back into the bag, and I wheeled him out of the balcony and back into his room.

'How about some *khajoor* milk, sir?' I asked once I had helped him climb into the bed and propped pillows behind his back.

But before he could answer, there was a soft knock at the door and his wife, Rashi Ganatra, poked her head into the room with a hesitant smile.

'Just wanted to see how you were doing,' she opened the door wider and walked into the room. 'Morning, Mary.' She said glancing in my direction before turning her attention back to her husband.

A small and fit woman of slender built, she was about a decade younger than BG, but looked half his age.

BG shrugged, as if how he was doing was hardly worth getting into and gave her formal clothes a once-over.

'I'm off to meet Nisha and Parul from the Rotaract for that breast cancer awareness fundraiser we are organizing.' She said following his gaze. 'And then I plan to stop by the club for a workout and a massage. And I'll pick up some groceries for the dinner as well. I'll be home in time for lunch.'

'That's fine, you don't have to give me a whole report.' BG picked up his phone and began to scroll through it.

Rashi flinched and her eyes lost their warmth, 'I wasn't giving you a report. Just telling you what my day looked like.' She turned and headed to the door, where she stopped once more, 'You seem to have lost your civility along with your legs.' She stepped out of the room, shutting the door softly behind her. A calm gesture despite the heated exchange, it reminded me again of how measured she could be.

'Sorry you had to see that,' BG threw his phone aside the minute she'd gone and ran a frustrated hand through his hair.

'Don't be, sir. I understand… when everyone else is moving ahead with their life, it's natural to feel a little left behind.'

BG didn't answer.

'Would you like some *khajoor* milk, sir?' I tried again.

'No, no, nothing,' he murmured, his attention already on the photo album lying open beside him. I glanced at the picture that had caught his eye and immediately felt sorry for him. It was from one of his cycling trips and he was holding a Tibetan prayer flag against a stunning mountainous landscape. His cheeks were red with exertion and his whole body radiated good health.

'Thank you, Mary, that'll be all.' BG had caught the pity on my face and his voice was stiff with displeasure.

I left the room with an apologetic smile and immediately bumped into BG's brother, Saket Ganatra. He brushed past me without so much as a glance or a word of apology, confident as usual that anyone he could afford to employ was below his notice. Saket was also BG's business partner, but in my view, partner was just a polite way to describe the minor 20 per cent stake he held in their sporting goods company.

In any case, I was relieved he was here, because he'd involve BG in some work-related paperwork and BG, who'd been in an awful sort of funk lately, could really do with the diversion. Besides, with BG busy, I would get some spare time to plan.

19.12.21

Diary entry – 1

I, Mary D'Souza, am writing this down so that there is a record of what has happened and what may still transpire at 14/B Gulmohar House, Worli. I've been employed here as a full-time nurse to sixty-nine-year-old Brijesh Ganatra (BG) – father of two. About two years ago, BG was in a near-fatal biking accident that left him paralysed from the waist below and confined to a wheelchair with a urostomy pouch attached to a catheter to collect his urine. At first his family tried to care for him, but a crippled old man can be a difficult patient and soon it became clear to them that they needed professional help. This is when I came into the picture. I've been given the room adjoining BG's so that I can go to him as soon as he rings the bell. Now, I'm a rather sprightly fifty-year-old, but I admit I'm glad of this proximity, because for some time now, I've suspected that someone is trying to murder BG. I have no proof of this – just two unrelated incidents coupled with a terrible feeling in the pit of my stomach that he is in danger.

The first was an Amazon gift hamper that came for BG a few weeks ago, on Diwali. The servants gave it to me, along with the other Diwali gifts he had received and I took it to his room, where we opened it during our daily game of Scrabble. It contained the usual assorted pouches of almonds and cashews as well as a large box of vegan cookies. BG has a sweet tooth and he'd have gone right for the cookies had I not picked up the box at that very moment to read the ingredients at the back and in effect, saved his life. For the cookies were made of cocoa and peanut butter and BG is fatally allergic to peanuts. I admonished him to be more careful then and he ignored me in that absent way of his and I'd have forgotten all about it, had I not reached out for the gift card and found that it didn't say who had sent the hamper. There were just general Diwali and New Year wishes on a standard Amazon card, addressed to Brijesh Ganatra along with a picture of a traditional diya. When I asked BG who the gift could be from, he had scanned the gift card, shrugged disinterestedly and handed it back, before playing 'HAWK' *on the Scrabble board in front of us. I'd slipped the gift card into the pocket of my nurse's uniform to mull over it later, but I probably wouldn't have made much of it, had it not been for what happened a week later.*

'May I come in?' I knocked harder on BG's door. Nobody had responded to the first two gentler knocks, but I could hear raised voices inside.

'Sir?' I called out louder still.

The voices fell quiet. A few seconds later the door flew open and Saket strode out of the room, his face like thunder.

BG was pale, as if after two years on a wheelchair even the figurative act of standing up to his brother had tired him out.

'Thinks he knows what's best for the business now.' BG jerked his head towards the door his brother had just stomped out of. 'Had to explain to him that my legs may not work, but my head still does!'

I smiled sympathetically and handed him a glass of water along with the first of the three tablets he was meant to take every morning. Ever since the two incidents, I'd become suspicious of everyone in BG's family. While anyone in the world could've sent BG that hamper, it seemed to me that his family had the most to gain from his death. Not to mention, they had every opportunity. I did not like Saket Ganatra. He resented taking instructions from BG – that much anyone could see. He was also ambitious. Which, coupled with his impatience, was a dangerous combination. But somehow, I didn't think it was him. He was loud and abrasive, while the two attempts on BG's life had been subtle. Not really his style I thought… unless… unless…

'Mary?' BG was holding out the empty glass of water towards me, looking at me with concern, 'Are you okay?'

My hands and face had grown all cold as I considered the possibility that Saket could've been working with someone else. I forced myself to smile. 'Sorry, just a little lost. Were you saying something?'

'Can you please check if Prateek is up?' he asked, glancing up at the clock on the wall.

It was 10 a.m., and I knew his son would most likely still be in bed, but I went down to the floor he occupied with his family. Finding the door to his room shut, I wandered towards the main living area in the hope of bumping into his wife, but found his son, instead.

'Hi Krish, is your dad awake?' I asked the quiet, thirteen-year-old child, who was sitting at the dining table with his sketchbook, wondering if the strange boy would answer this time.

He looked up, stared at me for a full minute before resuming his sketch of the Nataraja statue on the TV mantle in front of him. Not entirely surprised, I turned to make my way out of the room. At the door, however, I felt the hair on my arms stand up and I glanced behind to find him staring at me again. When I first came to live here, the servants had insinuated that he wasn't completely right in the head; however, no one else, including BG, ever spoke about him, so I was never sure of what was wrong.

Gulmohar House was a two-storeyed bungalow built in colonial style, with the living room, kitchen and three bedrooms on the ground floor and an almost equal number of rooms on the second, connected to each other by a staircase on one end and a more recently installed elevator on the other. Prateek and his family shared the lower floor with Saket and his wife, Sumitra, whose only son was studying at a university in America.

On the second floor, BG, his wife and I, had three rooms, while the other two had been given to Riddhi, BG's daughter, who, in an unconventional arrangement, lived in her father's house with her husband and children, instead of with her in-laws. She taught in the same school that her twins studied at and left the house with them each morning. The house was quiet and restful at this time of the day and I decided to make my way towards the kitchen to cut some papaya for BG. I hadn't checked if he wanted any, but with him I had realized that sometimes it was best to just leave the food within arm's reach and more often than not, the bowls and plates would come back empty.

In the kitchen, the cook Mohanlal was watching a YouTube video. From the alacrity with which he shut it, I presumed it wasn't a *Satyanarayan Katha*.

'All set for the dinner tonight?' I asked as I examined the papaya in the fruit basket for ripeness. It was BG's birthday the next day and the family had planned to bring it in together that evening, over a nice dinner.

'They're still arguing over the menu.' He shrugged and busied himself cleaning coriander.

I knew who he meant when he said 'they' and I nodded, not surprised. It was a joy to watch Sumitra and Poonam, Prateek's wife in the same room. Poonam was simpering sweet while Sumitra had the disposition of a bitter gourd and both were stubborn as hell.

I diced the papaya into neat cubes and transferred the fruit into a bowl.

'Is that for papa ji?' Poonam enquired, from the door of the kitchen, just as I had placed the bowl onto a tray.

I nodded, 'He didn't want any milk today, so I thought I'd try some fruit.'

'Thank you, Mary, you are a treasure.' Poonam made to take the tray from me with a bright, fake smile. 'I can take that to him,' I relinquished my hold on the tray reluctantly. Ever since the two incidents, I had become more vigilant about who served BG his food and who he was alone in the room with. 'By the way, ma'am, Brijesh sir was asking for Prateek sir.'

Poonam's expression soured at the sound of her husband's name, 'I'll let him know.'

As Mohanlal and I watched Poonam's receding back, the cook smirked, 'That husband of hers is her biggest mistake. Otherwise, she's as sharp as a razor. Knows exactly how to get what she wants from her father-in-law.'

I rolled my eyes but held my tongue. I had plenty to say on the subject but not to Mohanlal. He'd been with the Ganatras much longer than I had but didn't have a discrete bone in his body. What the cook probably didn't realize was that Poonam got her way with BG, only because her father-in-law was always anxious to get rid of her. I proceeded to boil some water to make tea for myself.

'Is that for Brijesh bhai?' this time an older voice enquired from behind me.

I turned around to see Sumitra at the door. Tall, with a straight back, she had thick wiry hair and lips that were always pursed as if she was permanently sulking with the world.

'It's for me,' I turned back to the stove, irritated.

She knew perfectly well that BG had neither tea nor coffee, this was just her way of letting me know that she'd noticed that I had made myself an extra cup. She liked to keep a close eye on us, the staff and all the goings-on in the kitchen. I liked to think that I was in a more elevated position than the servants, what with my convent-school English and nursing diploma, but I knew it bothered her that BG had instructed that I eat with the family at the main dining table.

'Why haven't you started on the *gajar ka halwa* for the dinner, yet?' she turned to ask Mohanlal.

'Poonam *bhabhi* said to wait, she's checking with Brijesh *bhai* to see what he prefers.'

Sumitra's nose flared, 'And where is she now?'

'She just went up to Brijesh sir's room with some fruit,' I stirred my tea and lowered the flame.

Without a word Sumitra turned on her heels and stomped off in the direction of BG's room.

Despite her unpleasantness, I felt sorry for Sumitra. As the wife of the younger, less successful brother, she'd always played second fiddle at Gulmohar House. Rashi had always had more clout over the staff and kitchen and now it seemed, with Rashi increasingly busy in her fundraising work, Poonam was taking over. For someone with Sumitra's temperament, I imagined it would be hard to ignore the slights she probably faced when the servants did Poonam's bidding before her own.

With Poonam and Sumitra both in BG's room, I was certainly not needed there. I thought for a moment, that he would appreciate being rescued, but there was a more real danger I hoped to save him from. I decided to take my cup of tea up to my room and resumed writing in my diary.

19.12.21

Diary entry – 2

The second attempt on BG's life took place last Friday. While BG and I were on our daily evening walk, the brakes of his wheelchair failed. Our usual route involves walking down the steep slope at the end of our lane and then crossing a busy, traffic-ridden road to reach the sea facing promenade where we like to walk. BG, who is always desperate to salvage any remnants of his dignity, usually insists on manoeuvring the wheelchair himself. Which is why I was walking beside him when it happened and not behind with my hands on the push handles of the wheelchair – like I would've liked. We were fine till the end of our lane, but the minute we turned into the slope, BG's wheelchair went hurtling down like some hellish, cartoon film and he would've crashed right into the oncoming rush hour traffic on the main road below, had it not been for the fast-thinking banana-seller who pushed his cart full of bananas right into the path of the wheelchair and stopped its terrifying plunge. If BG had any sensation in his legs, he'd have been hurt from the impact with the banana cart, but as things were, he was only terribly shaken. We both were. Once I'd ascertained that BG was all right and thanked the banana seller a million times, we made our way back home where Sumitra and Poonam listened gravely to our story and then promptly began to bicker on the best way to care for him. His sister-in-law wanted him to have a glass of warm turmeric milk while Poonam wanted to call his doctor and have him do a full once-over. I left an increasingly irritated BG to their ministrations and went to examine the wheelchair and what I discovered, chilled my blood. There was a neat cut in the brake line because of which the brake fluid seemed to have leaked out. My first thought was to alert the family, but my very next instinct was to not say anything. I took the wheelchair to the local garage where the mechanic who took a look at it, seemed grim. He could not be a hundred per cent certain, but even to him the cut seemed deliberate.

I spent the next two nights in agony wondering who to confide in and then decided that there was no one in his family I actually trusted. I'd just have to keep a closer eye on him and as soon as I could I'd have to put my plan into action. Luckily, the opportunity presented itself earlier than I had expected when the family planned BG's birthday dinner. I could lay my little trap then.

'Why aren't you in school?' BG asked his grandson as he squeezed some lemon juice over his yellow dal, before mixing it with his rice.

Krish looked up from the comic he was reading and stared mutely at his grandfather.

'Oh, the poor boy had a terrible tummy ache in the morning,' Poonam chimed in.

'It's amazing how his stomach's always better by lunchtime.' Sumitra bit into a cucumber, ignoring the look of pure hatred that Poonam shot her.

'Sorry, I'm late,' Prateek murmured as he pulled a chair to his father's right.

In his late thirties, he had his mother's slender built, and fortunately for him, his father's above average height. Poonam had once told me that his guitar and boy-band looks were what had first attracted her to Prateek in college. Now, however, I knew, they were the bane of her existence.

'Why aren't you in school?' he asked his son, just as his father had done before him.

'You'd know if you'd been awake in the morning.' BG said sharply.

A muscle in Prateek's jaw tightened, but he said lightly, 'Come on papa, not that again. You know I work at night.'

'Beating on a few drums in the garage is not considered work.'

Prateek, who'd been about to take a bite of his salad, lowered his spoon and fixed his father with a cold look. 'Do we really have to do this every single day?'

'Come now, Brijesh, he's been getting regular work with his radio jingles now, you know that.' Rashi protested from the seat next to mine.

BG ignored her, continuing to glare at his son, 'I hope you remember our deal. You have until tonight to let me know what you decide.'

Prateek stopped eating, Krish lifted his head up from his comic book to stare at his grandfather and Poonam turned pale. Only Sumitra continued to eat, her face a carefully constructed mask of disinterest, apparent only to someone whose judgement wasn't clouded by high emotion – like me.

'Why do you always have to be so harsh with him?' Rashi flung the door of the room open and began without preamble.

I had just wheeled BG into his room after the disastrous lunch and was now emptying his urostomy pouch in the bathroom. The door was slightly ajar and I could see Rashi standing with her hands on her hips.

'And what deal were you talking about? Surely, not that ridiculous proposition from last year?'

'He agreed to it,' BG said quietly.

'Brijesh, you can't be serious!'

'Saket wants a higher stake in the company – says he has taken on a larger share of the responsibility and wants to be compensated for that.'

'It's true, no? He *is* doing more…' Rashi sat down on the edge of the bed.

'He wouldn't have to if Prateek had stepped up!' BG hit the handle of his wheelchair with a fist. 'I didn't build this company to just give it away, Rashi.' He added softly. 'I really thought he'd settle down by now.'

The two of them fell silent and I took the opportunity to step out of the bathroom. If they realized that I'd overheard their conversation, they didn't seem to mind. I busied myself with attaching a fresh pouch to BG's catheter.

'Would you like to sit in the balcony?' I asked when I was done.

We usually played a game of Scrabble at this time, but I knew he wasn't going to be in the mood for it today.

'I'll just take my nap now.' He suddenly looked very tired and every bit his age.

Rashi and I helped him climb into bed, after which, we both stepped out of the room.

'Never thought I'd have to choose between my husband and son.' She sighed.

I wasn't sure what their 'deal' was, but I felt sorry for Rashi. 'Every family is complicated in its own way.'

She smiled at me. 'A famous Russian author said something very similar.'

Patting my arm, she left to go to her room while I made my way to the kitchen, in the hope of fixing myself another cup of tea.

'Add some cashews to the paneer gravy to make it thicker,' Sumitra's voice floated out into the corridor outside the kitchen, making me do an about turn.

I wanted the tea but not enough to make it under Sumitra's hawkish gaze.

'But Poonam *bhabhi* said the *malai* will make it thicker,' I heard Mohanlal protest.

'And since when is Poonam *bhabhi* the expert? Hmm? If you know what's good for you, you'll do what I say.'

I couldn't hear what Mohanlal said because by then I had made my way to the other side of the floor and was listening to a different set of voices.

'Where will we go, but?' Poonam sounded almost hysterical.

'Nowhere. We aren't going anywhere! I've told you a dozen times, I'll figure something.' Prateek replied.

'You know what your father said. If you can't make enough money to support us, you can either join his company or…'

'Leave this house,' Prateek interrupted, 'I know what he said, I was there!'

'Good, so what's…'

The doorbell rang then and I quickly began to walk away from their room. It would be embarrassing to be caught eavesdropping. But just as I was about to round the corner, the hair on my arms rose again and I turned to see Krish staring at me from the living room. He'd not only heard his parents fight but he'd seen me loiter around to listen to it. Cheeks burning, I walked briskly to the elevator, only to bump into Riddhi and her twins who'd just come home from school. Short, with golden highlights in her hair and plump, dimpled cheeks, Riddhi had the cheerful disposition of someone who didn't think about things too deeply. Harmless enough, I'd always thought, except for the man she had married.

'How is his mood?' Riddhi asked me when we had reached our floor and the kids had run ahead towards their room.

I knew she meant BG. I screwed up my face and shook my head.

'Why? What happened?'

Very briefly, I told her about the argument at lunch, leaving out the bits I'd overheard in BG's room.

Her face fell. 'Oh, that's a pity, Girish wanted to talk to him about something important.' She said referring to her husband.

She walked ahead to her room while I stopped outside my own.

19.12.21

Diary entry – 3

I know exactly what Girish wants to talk to BG about. He has a business proposition and he'd like BG to invest money in it. I've heard him expound upon his idea in great detail, because I was in the room, changing the sheets and pillowcases on the bed, when he made his pitch to BG. This is why, I also know what BG thinks of the idea – he used a word I prefer not to repeat. But luckily, he said it after Girish had left the room – to him, BG only promised to 'think about it'.

It seems to me that everyone wants something from BG. Prateek and Poonam, Saket and Sumitra, and Riddhi and Girish – all need BG to relent. But who would benefit most from his death? And would one of them actually kill for what they want? I suppose, I'll find out soon enough.

BG was in a dark mood when I wheeled him down for dinner that evening. The whole family was already seated around the table, but nobody seemed to be talking much. The food had been laid out in ornate dinnerware made of real silver. It seemed Sumitra had won the menu argument against Poonam – it was a traditional Gujarati meal with the winter special *undhiyu*, made of eight or nine winter vegetables and served with pearl millet rotis, a tart yogurt-based *kadhi* and crispy, rice flour *khichiya*s.

'Happy birthday, nana!' Riddhi's twins broke the uncomfortable silence as they scrambled out of their chairs and rushed to their grandfather with birthday cards in their hands.

BG's face lit up as he opened one card and then the other, pausing to give each rainbow and heart the appropriate amount of attention.

'Here,' he said, handing me his phone before lifting the five-year-olds to his lap, 'Take a photo of me with these monkeys.'

'Krish, go join your grandfather and your cousins,' Poonam urged her son to be a part of the picture.

But Krish shook his head wordlessly.

For a moment I thought that Poonam would yell at him, but she let it pass and the rest of the dinner went off surprisingly smoothly. Sumitra and Poonam were civil to each other. Rashi was sitting between BG and Prateek, which ensured BG's interaction with his son was limited. And Saket told everyone an absurd story about a client who'd bought himself a peacock for his fiftieth birthday. The food was delicious, but I was too nervous about the evening ahead to eat properly. I was wondering how to set my plan in motion, when Poonam literally dropped the opportunity into my lap.

'Mary, I must compliment you on your flower arrangement, today. It's exquisite.' She smiled at me from across the table.

'Thank you,' I smiled back.

Over the last two years, I'd gotten into a weekly habit of picking up flowers from our local florist while BG and I were on our evening walk.

'I really love the colours!' Poonam declared, 'Are those Asiatic lilies?'

'Lilies, yes. But they're Oriental lilies, also called tree lilies because of their height.' I sipped on a spoonful of the *kadhi* before adding, 'And those in the middle are of course, white roses, but the most interesting ones are these oleanders.' I pointed to the seven delicate yellow stalks I had scattered throughout the bouquet.

'Why interesting?' Poonam inquired in between bites of her *gajar ka halwa*.

'Because of their poison,' I murmured, purposely soft, so that she'd have to ask me to repeat.

'What's that?'

'Because they're poisonous,' I said again, loudly this time, so everyone heard.

It was not my imagination that the table suddenly seemed to grow ever so slightly quieter. As if everyone's brains, even those engaged in conversations with others, had registered the word.

'Poisonous to touch?' Sumitra, who was closest to the flower arrangement, leaned back in alarm.

'No, no…' I reassured her, 'Only if it is ingested. But yes, flower, stem, leaf – the entire flower is extremely toxic.'

'It's true,' Girish boomed from the other end of the table, 'Do you know that the Oleander is the official flower of Hiroshima? It was the first flower to bloom after the city was devastated by the atom bombs.'

'Isn't your papa very clever?' Riddhi beamed at her children who ignored her. But Girish smiled broadly and glanced at BG to see if he'd noticed. I leaned back into my chair relaxed for the moment now that my plan was underway.

It was when dinner was cleared and BG's cake was cut that things started to go horribly wrong. One of Riddhi's twins dropped cake on his brother's pants, who in turn retaliated by smashing cake on his brother's face. And before the adults could even register what had happened, both children were covered in chocolate and pulling each other's hair.

'Oh, Mary could you possibly take the kids to their room and help them clean up?' Rashi requested, 'That way, Riddhi can stay with us for a bit. I'll send Mohanlal upstairs, with your cake.'

'And please don't bring them down again,' Girish added, 'They're just sleepy now and won't let us talk in peace.'

'Uh… I… yes, sure,' I glanced in BG's direction, wondering desperately how to get out of going with the twins.

'We can take papa to his room, Mary,' Poonam offered, 'You're sweet to always be worrying about him.'

I forced myself to smile as I ushered the children out of the room, but my mind was in a panic. I had told the family about the oleanders only to see if any one of them tried to sneak one. I'd counted the number of oleander stalks before adding them to the arrangement. There were seven. The plan had been to keep the flowers in sight all evening. Not for a moment had I imagined I'd get stuck in the kids' room. My mind worked furiously as I tuned out the twins' bickering and helped them get out of their soiled clothes. In any case I reasoned, I hadn't really expected someone to steal the oleander while we were all still in the room. I imagined that whoever it was, would come back once the lights were out and everyone had retired for the night. I'd planned to camp in the dining room for the night and catch them then. But what if I was wrong? What if someone did manage to get to the oleander while I was here? While the kids brushed their teeth and put on their pyjamas, I spent a tortured half an hour kissing the cross I wore on my gold chain and getting increasingly desperate, until finally, Jesus put me out of my misery.

'I want my mummy,' one of the boy's lips quivered and his eyes turned watery.

Seeing his brother tearing up was all the other child needed to have his own meltdown. And in a matter of seconds, I had two children howling to the high heavens for their mother. Promising them that I'd bring her to them, I rushed downstairs, taking the stairs two at a time.

'Riddhi… sorry but the kids want you,' I entered the dining room to find Girish flipping through a magazine, Saket on his phone and Riddhi and Sumitra chatting quietly on the sofa. Everything seemed to be in order.

'Oh well, it was good while it lasted.' Riddhi got up with a smile and left the room.

'Rashi and Prateek just took Brijesh up to the room,' Sumitra volunteered before I asked.

I nodded absently and turned towards the dining table, my eyes already scanning the flower arrangement. But even as I approached it, I could tell, there were fewer oleanders than I had put in there. I dug my nails into my palms to control my reaction, one flower had been stolen.

The only person to notice how upset I was, was Krish. His eyes met mine for a moment before he looked down. My eyes travelled to the sketch he was working on – it was a birthday card with a flower vase full of white roses and yellow oleanders and his grandfather's face in the background.

Heart beating wildly, I rode the elevator up to BG's room. There was no thought in my mind, just blind panic. I could hear raised voices inside, but I knocked and entered the room without waiting for a response.

'Oh, I can come back later,' I pretended to be apologetic as I scanned BG's face.

He seemed furious but otherwise in perfect health.

'Yes, pl…' Rashi started to say but BG interrupted her, 'No, Prateek was just about to leave.'

His son glared at him angrily, before stomping off and banging the door hard behind him.

'Mary, Poonam was making some *khajoor* milk for Brijesh, could you please see if its ready?' Rashi asked.

'Yes, ma'am,' I left the room with one final appraisal of BG.

Back on the first floor, I willed myself to calm down. No harm had come to BG yet, but I had to keep my wits about to consider my next steps. In the kitchen, I found Poonam stirring the milk on the stove.

'Oh, Mary, it's you,' Poonam started when I walked up behind her.

'Sorry, didn't mean to startle you,' I smiled, 'Just wanted that milk for sir.'

'I still need to blend the dates in,' Poonam said, 'Why don't I bring it up, when its ready?'

I had no intention of letting BG drink this milk, but I couldn't think of an excuse and once again I was saved by a child in need of his mother. This time Krish came to the kitchen, insisting that his mother come and see his birthday card.

'Sorry, Mary. Will you?' Poonam handed me the blender.

I sighed in relief and waited until she had left. Then I checked the kitchen counters as well as the dustbin – there were no traces of flowers or leaves anywhere – not that I was about to take a chance. I chucked the milk down the drain. If Sumitra had come at that moment to see who was making what in the kitchen, I would've had a hard time explaining what I was doing. But luckily, I was left alone for the ten minutes it took me to make the milk again.

It was in the elevator, while I was taking BG's milk to him that my luck seemed to run out. There was a power cut and the whole house was suddenly plunged into darkness. I gasped as the elevator came to a halt with a lurch. If someone in this house, indeed wished BG harm, this would be the perfect time to do something. The thought that I had put those oleanders there and made it even simpler for them, made my chest hurt and I found it difficult to breathe. I opened the top button of my nurse's uniform and began to recite the Lord's prayer.

Ten more minutes passed before the power finally came back on. But it had felt like some sort of hellish eternity. I made my way shakily down the corridor, blinded by the sudden glare of the bright lights and almost bumped into Sumitra and Saket. Their heads were bent deep in conversation and for once I didn't try to eavesdrop. I hurried past them and entered BG's room without even a perfunctory knock.

He glanced at the milk and me without comment and continued to remain preoccupied as I helped him change and get into bed. The multiple conversations he'd had with his family, seemed to have completely drained him. But other than that, he appeared unharmed and at that moment, that was all that mattered to me.

'Happy birthday, sir,' I said to him when I had dimmed the lights and drawn the curtains.

'Thank you, Mary.' He smiled then as if snapping out of a reverie.

I went back to my room knowing fully well that my respite from danger was temporary. Whoever had stolen the oleander would try to use it tomorrow or in the coming days. My only hope now of catching them was to take someone into confidence. I could tell Mohanlal. He had a loose tongue, but he'd been with the family for many years now. Surely, he felt some loyalty towards BG. And there was always Rashi. Despite their recent arguments, I'd seen enough pictures of BG and her on cycling and birding trips to know that there'd once been a real love there. Could I trust her, I wondered, as I fell into a fitful sleep.

When I woke up an hour later, my back was drenched with sweat despite the cool December breeze blowing in from the window. Somewhere between sleep and wakefulness, my subconscious mind had seen what I'd been blind to. I knew now who had sent BG the hamper, who had taken the oleander and who had the most to gain from his death. Stumbling in the dark,

I patted the uniform I'd discarded the night before and found what I was looking for in my pocket. In a few seconds, I had the proof I'd needed all along. Silently, I hurried to BG's room and let myself in. Just as I had feared, he had been poisoned. He was lying on the floor in a pool of his own vomit. But I put a finger below his nose to check – again, just as I'd hoped, he was still breathing.

21.12.21

Diary entry – 4

From the beginning, I had wondered about who had the most to gain from BG's death, when all along the answer had been staring at me right in the face. Who else but the cripple who'd once climbed mountains, chased birds across continents and cycled his way through deserts and forests and who was now confined in utter misery to a chair akin to a cage? I had seen how wretched BG had been, especially once his physiotherapist told him that he wouldn't walk again. I had observed him bristle at my pity and envy his own wife for leading the life that they should've been living together. But in my fervour to protect him from his family, I'd failed to see the threat he had posed to himself. I still wouldn't have thought of him, had I not seen Krish's sketch and realized that the boy had drawn what he'd actually seen. At some point during the evening, his grandfather had approached the flowers and Krish had captured that moment on his card.

Once I had digested this truth about BG, finding proof was easy. In the pocket of my nurse's uniform, I'd found BG's phone with which I had clicked his pictures with the twins. A quick search of his Amazon account had revealed that he had indeed sent the Diwali gift hamper to himself. And when I had foiled that plan, he'd grown more desperate and tampered with his wheelchair brakes. And then, of course, I had handed him an opportunity on a golden platter. He'd swiped the oleander right after dinner and waited until he was alone at night to eat its leaves. The doctors said it was lucky I found him when I did, any later and it would've been much too late. But

I wonder if it isn't too late already. Once a man has decided that he doesn't want to live, are a few failed attempts enough to deter him? To me, BG doesn't seem the kind to give up easily.

LETHAL AIR

Suchitra Bhattacharya, tr. Radha Chakravarty

Of late, Mitin had been popping into Lalbazar whenever she visited the office area for work. She'd spend some time chatting over a cup of tea in Deputy Commissioner, Detective Department Anishchay Majumdar's room. In the course of their professional interaction, her relations with Anishchay had grown much more cordial. If not too busy, Anishchay too was very happy to see her and engaged her in informal chat with great gusto. Mitin rather enjoyed these sessions. She also learned a lot from them. After all, listening to Anishchay's stories about his long experience in the police force was also a kind of education.

That evening, the moment she stepped into his chamber, the DC cried, '*Arrey*, madam, come in, come in. You have chosen a good day to come by. Today, we've captured an extraordinary bird in our cage.'

'A bird?' Mitin frowned.

'Yes. A bird. You could even call it a bulbul.'

'What's this case about? Tell me about it,' Mitin said, taking a chair and adjusting the dupatta around her shoulders.

'Did you read the newspapers last Wednesday? About the mysterious death of a disabled young man in the multi-storeyed building, Akashleena, in Alipur?'

'Soumyarup Chaudhuri? Thirty-three years old, found dead in his room, no marks of violence on his body, apparently died of a heart attack, but the doctors suspect foul play…'

'Baah, baah! You have read the details very minutely, I must say!' Anishchay twirled the paperweight on his table. 'We had sent the body for post-mortem. It's a case of planned homicide.'

'Is that so?'

'Hmm, yes. Our Kolkata Police force has a bad reputation. They say we're so slow that our year has 18 months, not 12. Yet the murderer in this case has already been caught, this very day. Within 96 hours.'

'*Achchha*? Really? So, you and your team have indeed woken up now!' Mitin couldn't resist a bit of sarcasm. 'Who is that evil creature by the way?' she asked, still smiling.

'You earn so much money from this detective agency you have started – can't you guess who the killer is?'

'How can I tell? What do I know about the case, after all?' Mitin's hair rippled as she shook her head. 'Must be some sort of enemy.'

'Enemy indeed. Born enemy, as they say.' Anishchay grinned, baring his teeth. 'Haha, you didn't get it, did you? A married man has only one born enemy. His wife.'

'The wife is the murderer?' Mitin became instantly alert.

'Yes indeed. All of you make such a fuss about bride killings. At the drop of a hat, you register a case against the husband under Section 498A of IPC. But the very mention of a case of husband being killed by his wife sounds jarring to the ear, right?'

'That's not it. But still, I read in the papers… the man was crippled…'

'Madam, you women are capable of everything. There is no word for kindness and compassion in the female dictionary.' Anishchay rearranged himself on his chair. 'You can't imagine how she murdered him. Absolute cold-blooded murder.' He added in English: 'In the most savage manner.'

'How?'

'Air embolism. Pushing air from an empty syringe into the victim's body… leading to instant cardiac arrest. He's dead.'

'Oh no! But it's hard to detect this mode of killing.'

'That's why she took the chance. But how could she evade the eyes of a seasoned doctor! Several drops of blood had been sucked into the syringe. The moment he spotted it, the doctor declared: "This is not how a normal injection is administered."'

'This sounds awfully interesting!'

'Interesting indeed, but simple. The facts add up neatly.'

'How? How is that so?'

'Aroused your curiosity, didn't it? Hahaha, curiosity, thy name is woman.'

'Aha, you may as well tell me.'

'I will, I will. I went personally to conduct the investigation. Let me share the full details. See if you can find any gaps. But before that, tell me whether you'll have tea or coffee.'

'Let's go with coffee.'

Anishchay rang a bell and ordered coffee and biscuits. He then launched forth on the saga of Soumyarup. His narrative style was quite dramatic. With embellishments and exaggerations, he would recount part of the story, then pause suddenly, to take note of the listener's reactions. From time to time, he would also add small personal comments of his own. Officers would come in with files from time to time and depart after taking his noting or signature. Every now and then, the telephone would ring.

The story, in a broad outline, was the following:

Soumyarup Chaudhury and Chitralekha had married about four years ago. Not a love marriage, but an arranged one. Chitralekha's father was a railway officer, her mother a schoolteacher. Chitralekha was their only child. Her family was quite well off – they owned a double-storeyed house in Behala. Soumyarup also came from an affluent family. His father was a doctor, a neurologist, with a considerable income. The mother also well-qualified, with an MA degree, but a housewife. Soumyarup also had a brother, Abhirup. In Anishchay's view, he was good for nothing. Twenty-six or twenty-seven years old, he had made no attempt to find a job, thriving on the inheritance he received from his father. Eating, drinking, making merry. Going about town with some band – pop music or rap – jangling his guitar. Education limited to his undergraduate degree, which he barely managed to obtain.

Soumyarup had been a brilliant student. Ranked among the first hundred in the higher secondary examination. He wasn't doing badly in his profession either. Just twenty-nine and he was already the deputy marketing manager for Peterson India. Chitralekha was also highly qualified, with an MSc degree in Physiology. In other words, Soumyarup and Chitralekha were a perfectly well-matched couple.

As a married couple, they got along fine at first. The problems began about six months after their marriage. They had gone to Darjeeling and Gangtok on holiday. There, Soumyarup had apparently suffered a fall on a stony path. That was the beginning of his ailment. Sacroiliitis at first. Unbearable pain in the lower back. Unable to stand upright, unable to walk… He consulted a doctor in Gangtok and after his return to Kolkata, his father took over his treatment. At this juncture, Chitralekha got a job in a college. The father-in-law and mother-in-law were not really in favour of her taking it up. Soumyarup was dead against it. But ignoring everyone's objections, the girl accepted the job. That was probably when things began to turn sour in their marriage.

For his wife to get a good job offer just when he was on the brink of losing his own job – how many husbands can accept such a situation with pleasure!

Meanwhile, Soumyarup's condition was deteriorating. His father continued to treat him of course, simultaneously consulting a number of specialists. Nothing worked, though. In about a half year, Soumyarup became bedridden. Spine completely stiff – what they call bamboo spine. Constant tingling in the limbs, pain in the neck and lower back… ankylosing spondylitis turned the poor man into a complete invalid.

When things had come to such a pass, Soumyarup's father died. It was very sudden. A cerebral attack. He used to remain terribly anxious for his son – perhaps that was the cause. Within a year of the gentleman's death, Chitralekha left her marital home and went off to her parents' house. After that she completely stopped visiting Soumyarup.

Then suddenly, on the previous Monday, Chitralekha had turned up at Soumyarup's house in the evening to get his signature on the divorce papers. She was there for a half hour, or an hour, maybe. Immediately after her departure, the young man was found dead. Thinking that he had suffered a heart attack, Soumyarup's mother had immediately called the doctor. But the doctor, upon arrival, had given the matter a murky twist. For about two years, a scalp vein set had been inserted in Soumyarup's arm. After repeated injections, it had become difficult to find the veins in his arm, hence the scalp vein set was used to administer injections to the patient. Anyone in the house could give the injection. Injections for sleep, injections for pain. On that day, a 50cc syringe was found fixed to the scalp vein set. It had a drop of blood in it. Chitralekha's fingerprints had also been found on that syringe. After laying their hands on such a clinching piece of evidence, the police had wasted no time arresting the woman.

Mitin heard the entire story in almost complete silence. Coffee had arrived. She was sipping it, lost in thought.

'So?' Anishchay Majumdar cocked an eyebrow. 'Did you find any holes in the story? Anything in the girl's favour?'

'Holes? I can see some yawning gaps. What time did the woman arrive, what time did she leave, when was the dead body discovered – you say nothing about these things.'

'Those details are foolproof. We have sounded them out. She came between a quarter past eight and eight thirty and left exactly at nine. The guard at the apartment block is a witness to her arrival and departure. The dead body was discovered at around ten thirty.'

'Who discovered it?'

'Soumyarup's mother.'

'Why an hour and a half after his death?'

'As soon as she saw Chitralekha, Soumyarup's mother had gone to the adjacent flat. You can quite understand – the daughter-in-law wanting to divorce her son when he is in such a condition. Which mother-in-law would want to see the face of such a daughter-in-law? She did return to the flat though, at around nine thirty. She even parted the curtains to take a peek at her son. She thought that he was asleep, so she didn't speak to him. Soumyarup used to have dinner at around ten thirty. But when she found him unresponsive even at that hour, she panicked and called for the doctor. He arrived at around eleven. Rigor mortis had just set in. It was the doctor who certified Soumyarup's time of death – 9 p.m.'

Anishchay drained his coffee and placed the cup and saucer on the table. He withdrew a cigarette pouch from the drawer. Crushing the tobacco between his palms, he said: 'Having inserted the injection, that wily woman fled the scene. She didn't have the sense, at that moment, to realize that the syringe needed to be removed. As you know very well, a murderer always makes some mistake or the other.'

'But still…'

'But what?'

'What was the motive for the murder? Why needlessly murder someone when a separation is already on the cards?'

'That is the stunt. That's why I called her a special kind of bird.' Placing the rolled cigarette between his lips, Anishchay flicked the lighter on. He winked. 'The divorce papers were a camouflage. A pretext to gain entry into that flat. She knew she was bound to find her husband alone. She had no need for divorce or anything of that sort. If her husband died, every bit of his share of the property would come into her hands, as natural inheritance from her spouse. And with that, she would dance her way to her new marital home. What a flawless plan!'

'Was Chitralekha going to marry again?'

'What else am I trying to say? That talented young woman was embroiled in an affair indeed. Poor Soumyarup had become a dog in the manger. She hatched such an elaborate plan: the dog would be bumped off, the spoils would fall into her hands and people wouldn't be able to blame her either. Everyone would say, aha, the poor woman, if a young widow begins her life anew, what's wrong with that… Everything was in order, she had even taken the jewellery out of the almirah, but if only she had just removed that syringe and taken it away with her…'

'Wait a second. Was that 50cc syringe used to administer all injections, including Soumyarup's painkillers, sedatives, everything? They are small doses after all. A 5cc syringe should have sufficed.'

'That giant syringe was kept for other purposes. Whenever Soumyarup's condition became acute, he would be fed through a nasal tube.'

'A Ryle's tube?'

'Yes, yes. Soup and other such stuff would be filled in the 50cc syringe and fed to the patient via a Ryle's tube. Imagine how cunning the woman was. She knew an air embolism could not be managed without a big syringe… She was a physiology student, after all…'

'Hmm.' After a short silence, Mitin asked, 'One question. How long had it been since she left Soumyarup?'

'Just before the last Pujo… say eight or nine months ago.'

'Why did she leave him?'

'She found a lover, that's why. It had become difficult, managing a love affair while staying in her marital home. Though her own parents tell a different story. They claim that Soumyarup had become impossibly bad tempered, that he would abuse his wife in abominable language, say uncouth things… that he would shout so much, even the nurses wouldn't stay on.' Anishchay took two puffs of his cigarette, then extinguished it in the ashtray. 'But the parents would of course say these things to prove their daughter innocent.'

'But what they say may not be untrue, after all.'

'It doesn't matter. That Chitralekha was having an affair of late is something even her parents couldn't deny. For us, that is enough.'

'Mmm... And where was this brother of Soumyarup's, that day? In the evening?'

'As I told you: he was into pop music, part of a band. On that day, Babu was performing with his troupe at the Jadavpur University annual function. I have cross-checked. The lad was indeed present there at that time.'

'When did he return?'

'After midnight. Our team from Alipur *thana* had reached the crime scene by that time. The young man trembled violently at the sight of the police, I'm told. He had received a severe shock, in other words. Whatever you might say, it was his dada's death, after all...'

'What is the condition of Soumyarup's mother, now?'

'A stone. She's frozen, as if turned to stone. Two huge blows, within the space of just two years. Having first lost her husband and then her son...' A shadow crossed Anishchay's face. 'I feel bad thinking about Chitralekha's parents, too. I believe they have been making frantic visits to the court, but still, she didn't get bail. Now, she's in police custody for seven days... What misfortune. Because of that wicked daughter, the parents' reputation is turned to dust.'

'Has the woman given a statement yet? Has she confessed to everything?'

'Uff, what a brazen woman! She has completely sealed her mouth. Just repeats the same thing, like a parrot: "I didn't kill Soumya. As I left, he was writhing in pain. So, I measured out and administered an injection of 2cc of Calmpose, upon Soumya's own request. I don't know anything more."'

Mitin seemed lost in thought for a while. She checked the time on her watch. Her husband Partho would be home early today. They were to visit Didi's house with their son Bumbum in the evening. But she didn't feel like leaving. The case seemed to draw her like a magnet. Ultimately, Mitin couldn't stop herself from asking, 'Police custody means Chitralekha is here right now, isn't she? Right here, in Lalbazar itself?'

Anishchay spread his hands. 'Where else could she go? She is now gracing the lock-up with the radiance of her being.'

'Can we get her here for a bit?'

'Why?'

'I would like to check her out. Talk to her for a while.'

'So, you want to discover something new with your third eye, is that it?' Anishchay guffawed. '*Arrey*, madam, no matter how much praise is heaped upon people like you – professional detectives, I mean – it's we who do the real work. We recognize criminals, as a jeweller recognizes gems. We don't easily make mistakes. You can't save her, even if you try a hundred ways.'

'Who says I want to save her? I just want to test the waters. My sixth sense tells me there is a gap somewhere. The motive doesn't emerge with perfect clarity.'

'Okay, sure. Try to check things out. If coal can turn to diamonds…'

Summoning an officer, Anishchay gave him orders in a low voice. Within fifteen minutes, the female prisoner appeared before them, escorted by two female guards in uniform.

For a few minutes, Mitin gazed intently at Chitralekha. Age, twenty-seven or twenty-eight at most. A little taller than average Bengali women, well-built, complexion quite fair, appearance very charming, full of grace. But her face was now as dark with gloom as the cloudy sky outside. Chitralekha's hair was dishevelled. Dark smudges under her misty eyes. Just a few hours had done this to her. Whitish streaks down both cheeks. Had she been weeping?

'Do you understand why you have been summoned here?' Anishchay asked in a booming voice.

Chitralekha did not answer. She had turned away her face.

'This lady wishes to speak to you. Whatever she asks, please give proper answers.'

Chitralekha's expression remained blank.

'I'm told you teach in a college,' Mitin said gently. 'Which college?'

Chitralekha didn't even turn her head. She continued staring at the wall.

'What's this? Let's have your answer!' roared Anishchay.

The onslaught seemed to send a shiver down Chitralekha's spine. She turned her head once. Her jaw was clenched tight, but a pulse throbbed in her throat. Then she quickly turned her face away again.

Mitin rose to her feet, looking embarrassed. Going up to Chitralekha, she placed a light hand on her back and drew her to the chair beside her own.

'Why are you getting so nervous?' she asked gently. 'I am your well-wisher.'

The words did not seem to even enter Chitralekha's ears. She sat there like a wooden doll.

'Won't you speak?' Mitin adopted an even softer tone.

Chitralekha's lips moved. 'I have nothing to say. I've already been identified as the culprit, after all.'

'Not at all. Until the judge pronounces a verdict, you are not guilty. Will you answer my question? How had Soumyarup reacted when he saw you that day?'

'What use is it telling you anything? Who will believe me?' Chitralekha sniffed. 'Soumya was extraordinarily calm that day. He had signed the papers immediately, upon my first request. It was he who asked me to take away the jewellery box.'

'Very well. Now tell me, why did you use such a huge syringe to administer the injection?'

Chitralekha frowned. 'Because I couldn't find a smaller syringe. That one was readily available, near at hand... It was Soumya who said...'

'Are you aware that, if the syringe has bubbles in it, a person can die?'

'I know. But I didn't kill Soumya.'

'The same old story!' Anishchay thundered, his voice reverberating across the room. 'If you didn't kill him, then who did? A ghost?'

Chitralekha darted a piercing glance at Anishchay. Then she continued sitting, with her head hanging.

'Did your husband know that you were coming with divorce papers?' Mitin asked, after a pause.

Chitralekha remained silent.

'Had your mother-in-law returned by the time you left the flat?'

No answer.

'What were your relations like, with your mother-in-law and brother-in-law?'

Again, no answer, as though Chitralekha had turned into a granite wall. Every question ricocheted back to Mitin, like an echo. After a few more queries, Mitin gave up. She leaned back in her chair.

At a signal from Anishchay, the female guards led Chitralekha away. As soon as they had left the room, Anishchay spluttered, 'Do you see now, how cussed she is? Husband dead, you'd expect some tears, some penitence, but no… I'll have her hanged, just you watch.'

Mitin lapsed into a gloomy silence. Then suddenly, she asked, 'May I make a request, Mr Majumdar?'

'Fire away.'

'May I meet some members of her household? Unofficially, I mean.'

'Do you still have any doubts?'

'Mm-hm… No. Just curiosity. Please, I want to study this case a for a bit,' wheedled Mitin. 'It may prove useful for me at some later time.'

'Okay. You may go ahead, as long as you don't disturb our investigation.'

Mitin didn't waste any time. After a few more pleasantries, she rose to her feet. Her face had a worried expression. Stepping out on to the street, she took the slip of paper from her pocket and glanced at it. An Alipur Avenue address. Quite a posh area. Should she drop by there that very day?

No, let it be. Partho would get worried. Tomorrow would be better.

The Akashleena building was gigantic. Eight floors high. Six flats on every floor. A pair of lifts, one on either side, in continuous motion, going up and down. Hawk-eyed security guards at the gate. They were the watchmen for the apartment block. Strangers entering the gate had to first enter their name in the register along with their destination. That was the rule.

Mitin didn't take the lift, though. She took the stairs to the fourth floor. Every floor had a long, vast corridor. Mitin observed this as she climbed. What a beautiful, sparkling building. Not a speck of dust to be seen. Ah, when would Mitin and her family possess a home of their own!

A young man answered the doorbell of the designated apartment. Glowing fair complexion, dressed in panjabi-pyjama, face carefully clean shaven. Head full of puffed-up hair. The eyes were puffy too, as if he had just awakened from slumber.

'Yes?' enquired the young man, with great style.

'You must be Abhirup Chaudhuri?' Mitin asked him, brightly.

The young man's eyes narrowed. 'And you…?'

'My name is Pragyaparamita Mukhopadhyay. I have come from Lalbazar. I have a few questions about the death of your dada, Soumyarup Chaudhuri.'

Abhirup's expression underwent an instant transformation. His face grew pale.

'What is there to ask?' he demanded. 'The murderer has already been arrested, after all.'

'Yes, indeed she has. But to prepare a case, one needs some more information, after all. I hope you all will cooperate.'

'Oh, sure.' Abhirup moved away from the doorway. 'Come in.'

As she entered the flat, Mitin was wonderstruck. Enormous drawing-room, marble floor, king-size furniture and an aquarium in the corner, covering the entire height of the wall. The whole place seemed to exude an aura of opulence. It was entirely possible that the temptation to gain this property might instigate a murder or two.

Mitin seated herself on the long, plush sofa. Abhirup went inside and re-emerged with a middle-aged lady. She was not particularly beautiful, rather unattractive in fact. But her complexion was startlingly fair. Her expression was lifeless, her gaze vacant. Clearly, she had not yet recovered her composure after the bereavement.

Mitin rose to her feet.

'I know I am intruding,' she said. 'But without asking a few questions...'

'No, please go ahead,' said the lady as she sat down on the sofa on the opposite side. 'I'm okay.'

'I'd like to ask each of you some questions, but separately.' Mitin glanced quickly at Abhirup. 'If you don't mind...'

'No problem. I'll go inside.' Abhirup paused, as he was about to leave. 'Shall I send you some tea, or some juice?'

'No thanks. You could give me some water. Cold water, please.'

As soon as Abhirup vanished from the scene, Mitin began, 'Look, Mrs Chaudhuri, you must have heard that your daughter-in-law was arrested yesterday, in the morning?'

'I know. There was a call from Lalbazar.'

'Could you have imagined that your daughter-in-law was capable of such an act?'

'No.' The lady's voice wavered. 'I can't think straight about anything.'

'What was your relationship with her like?'

'Not very good, I'd say. Someone who has caused such suffering to my son – how can I...?'

'Has she tormented your son right from the beginning of their marriage?'

'No, why would she do that! They were quite involved with each other. I too had cherished and pampered Lekha at the time.

But ever since my son developed health problems, Lekha has neglected him terribly.'

'You didn't like the fact that Chitralekha had a job either, did you?'

'My husband didn't like it either.'

'That is to be expected. There is no particular financial need in your family, after all.'

'Tell me. You tell me!' The lady wiped her eyes with the corner of her sari. 'Somu was desperately hungry for love. He wanted his wife's company. Wanted his wife to be near him, all the time. But see how cruelly the girl abandoned him and went away.'

The attendant had brought some water on a tray. A dark-skinned woman, about thirty-five years old. She waited until Mitin had drained her glass, then took the tray away, glancing over her shoulder as she departed.

'Is she your full-time help?' Mitin asked casually.

'No. She comes in the morning, leaves in the evening.'

'Does she handle all the housework alone?'

'There's one more. He comes from somewhere near Gopalnagar. Does the laundry, does some cleaning… It's Subala who handles all the cooking.'

'Yes. As I was saying,' Mitin resumed, 'Exactly when did your relationship with your daughter-in-law change? From the very beginning of his illness?'

'You could say so.'

'So, how long would that be?'

'Say, about three and a half years.'

'But Chitralekha left this home only eight or nine months ago. So why did she languish here for all that time?'

'My husband had a strong personality. She defied him and went out to work, indeed, but didn't have the guts to leave this home. And in her general conduct, Lekha was much more civilized then. After my husband's demise, Lekha began to behave like an unbridled horse. Didn't want to go into Somu's room even for a couple of minutes. Slept separately, amused herself according to her own whims and fancies. That my son was choking to death, all alone, all by himself…'

'Didn't you try to persuade your daughter-in-law?'

'Look, once a woman's mind turns wayward, she enters a different realm. Why would she care about her mother-in-law any more?'

'In other words, you had spoken your mind?'

'Yes. As much as one could say, without losing one's self-respect.'

'*Achchha*, you knew Chitralekha would be coming to this flat that day, right?'

'She had called up Abhi to inform him. My younger son, that is…'

'Did you know why she was coming?'

'I had heard, from Abhi.'

'Did Chitralekha stay in touch on the phone, or otherwise, after she left this place?'

'It was Somu who stayed in touch. I would call her on the phone and give the handset to Somu.'

Mitin was observing the lady. Now her eyes showed no hint of tears. Her voice also sounded much firmer.

'Did you speak to Chitralekha on that day, after she arrived?'

'No. I had told myself all day that I would keep myself under control, but the moment I saw her, I felt a surge of anger in my head.'

'So, you went out.'

'Yes. I went to the adjacent flat.'

'What time would that be?'

'I didn't look at the clock. But it would be eight twenty, or twenty-five.'

'Your son died at 9 p.m., right?'

'So Dr Panja says.'

'You were in the adjacent flat at that time?'

'Yes. I was talking to Rani di. Her clock struck nine while we were speaking, I remember.'

'At what time did you return from there?'

'Almost nine thirty. Lekha had left by then.'

'And then you went to your son?'

'Somu loved Lekha immensely. He suffered a lot in her absence. And that same Lekha comes to get the divorce papers signed. Getting married again too, I hear…' The lady's voice suddenly wavered. 'I couldn't bring myself to set foot in that room. But still, a mother's heart… I came to the door once and stood there. Somu was asleep, I saw…'

'Did you know Chitralekha was planning to marry again?'

'That girl had no shame or decency. She herself told Somu on the phone, once.'

'Oh, *achchha*.' Mitin casually glanced around the room. Above the handsome wooden showcase hung a young man's smiling photograph, with a garland around it.

Gazing at the photograph, Mitin asked, 'What was your son's reaction upon hearing that Chitralekha wanted to remarry?'

'Please don't ask me that question. It breaks my heart.'

'Sorry.' Mitin felt faintly embarrassed. 'So, after peeping into your son's room, where did you go?' she asked, after pausing to reflect for a while.

'To my own room. I switched off the light and went to bed.'

'Didn't you notice, from the door, that the syringe was fixed to the scalp vein set?'

'I should have noticed. I didn't pay heed. And what if I had? Somu was no more, by then, after all.'

'Afterwards, when you went to feed your son, you found…'

The lady nodded, with what sounded like a long sigh.

'What food had been prepared for your son that night?'

'Chicken… no, no, vegetable stew. And toast. Somu could no longer digest spicy food.'

'One last question. Since your son was bedridden, why didn't you employ a nurse?'

'A nurse would be engaged, from time to time. On occasions when Somu's condition took a turn for the worse… Somu didn't like to be cared for by a nurse.'

'Who took care of all these duties at normal times?'

'I did.'

'You?'

'Who else? Who else was there for Somu?'

'Oh yes, another question. Did your husband leave a will?'

'He didn't get time to make a will, did he? But this flat, the car, everything is in my name. There's also a plot of land in my name, at Salt Lake. The bank account was jointly in our names. Now I handle it myself.'

'One more question. The last one. Did your son have a life insurance policy in his name?'

'Yes, he did. Of about two lakh rupees.'

'Your daughter-in-law must be the nominee?'

'No. He had got the policy immediately after getting a job. Before marriage. My younger son is the nominee. Perhaps Somu would have transferred it to his wife's name, but he didn't get the opportunity, did he?'

Mitin closed her eyes for a couple of seconds, then said, 'You may go now. Kindly send your younger son to me.'

The lady rose to her feet and walked away unhurriedly. Her room was probably the one at the far corner, beyond the drawing room. She parted the curtains and went inside. From the same room, Abhirup emerged, almost immediately.

Leaning back, he spread his arms across the back of the sofa.

'You're a private detective, right?'

Mitin was quite taken aback. 'How did you know?'

'I just called up Lalbazar…'

'Oh. To confirm if my identity is genuine?'

'That is necessary, after all. The press is proving such a nuisance.' Abhirup pulled a face. 'Tell me, what do you want to know?'

Well, he was rather smart, wasn't he? Mitin wanted to test him a bit. She frowned.

'You had a programme at Jadavpur University on the day of the incident, right?'

'The police have already verified that.'

'At what time was the programme held?'

'Around nine or thereabouts. I didn't look at my watch before going on stage.'

'Your pop concerts and the like are generally held rather late in the night, aren't they? They generally don't start before ten or eleven. Am I right?'

'On that evening, it began earlier.'

'The police haven't confirmed that, though.'

'What do you mean? What are you implying?'

'I know that your event started at ten thirty.' Mitin took a shot in the dark. 'Between nine and ten thirty, where were you?'

Abhirup's face turned ashen. He began to stutter. 'Wh-who told you?'

The wild shot had hit the mark. Mitin smiled inwardly. 'There is no need for you to know that,' she declared sternly. 'Please answer my question.'

'I... I was with a friend.'

'Friend?'

'No, I mean... a girlfriend.'

'What's her name?'

'Pallavi. Pallavi Sen. Believe me, I was with her until nine thirty. Then I went and joined the group. I'll give you her name and phone number, you can check it out. We were together, at the Golpark corner...'

'Your girlfriend's testimony will not be tenable. She will be counted an interested party.'

'Why are you trying to frighten me?' Abhirup's tone had changed to one of pleading. 'Am I capable of murdering Dada?'

'Why not? Fratricide is very common, in this world.'

'But why would I kill him? Given the physical state he was in and his mental condition, Dada could have died of heart failure any day.'

'And if your Dada died, you too would inherit his LIC policy. Moreover, there wouldn't be any other heir left to claim a share of the paternal property.'

'What are you talking about? Not even in my dreams have I ever thought of such things.'

'That might be true. But there's sufficient reason to suspect you, isn't there?'

'Believe me, I'm not the culprit. I don't get involved with anyone's affairs. When I think of Dada, I want to weep.'

'And when you think of your Boudi, your sister-in-law?' Mitin's voice was icy. 'You must be pleased with her arrest?'

'Why? Why would I be pleased?'

'Firstly, it saves you from harassment. From the clutches of the police and their strongarm tactics, I mean. Secondly, one more possible claimant to the money gets removed from the reckoning. Thirdly, she has caused your Dada a lot of suffering. You can naturally be expected to rejoice at her being caught in a difficult predicament.'

Abhirup remained tight-lipped for a while. He glanced up once at the revolving ceiling fan overhead. Then, lowering his gaze, he said in a low voice, 'Can I say something frankly? I can't quite believe, even now, that Boudi has murdered Dada.'

'Why? She was a very cruel woman, wasn't she? To abandon your Dada when he was in that condition?'

'This is not the time to say such things, but still, I'll tell you. It's not as if my Dada didn't inflict mental torture on Boudi, either. Always irritable, temperamental, given to unmentionable abuses... Why would a dignified woman like Boudi tolerate that? For how long could she tolerate it? Just because they had lived together for a mere six months, why would she have to handle an invalid for the rest of her life? And have to live with a short-tempered, disabled husband? Though from his own point of view, Dada was also right. After all, if a full-blooded young man suddenly becomes permanently disabled, it is hardly surprising that he should develop some psychological problems. In similar circumstances, the same thing may have happened to me as well.'

This young man did not seem as much of a wastrel as Anishchay Majumdar had made him out to be. Indeed, the lad was quite rational and intelligent.

Mitin cast him a sidelong glance. 'Does that mean you want to say your Boudi is not the murderer?'

'I didn't say that, after all. Maybe Boudi was the one who… What happened on that day, at that moment, how can I say? Maybe Dada had done something so provoking, that Boudi, in the heat of the moment…' Abhirup swallowed. 'I was trying to say, I don't like thinking of Boudi as the culprit.'

'You seem to have quite a weakness for Boudi, it appears?'

'No. I'm neutral. I'm telling you what I have observed and understood.'

'Are you aware that your Boudi was contemplating a second marriage?'

'I know everything. I see nothing wrong in it either. After all, she also has a life. Why must she languish in hell for a man who has become an invalid? Everyone has the right to live on their own terms. When Boudi called up the other day to speak of divorce, I had said to her: "You should have taken this decision even earlier."'

No, it must be said the young man compelled one to respect him.

'What was your mother's relationship with your Boudi?' she asked, narrowing her eyes.

'Ma is by nature rather reserved. But she'd give her life for Dada. If Dada suffers… Though Ma never openly said anything to Boudi. At least, not as far as I know.'

'Hmm, the entire episode is very sad.' Mitin rose to her feet. '*Achchha*, your mother said she was in Rani di's flat at the time of Dada's death. Which one is Rani di's flat?'

'The door just opposite our own… Will you be going there now?'

'Just for a few minutes. A few things I need to discuss, that's all.'

'But with whom will you discuss anything there? She is a doddering old woman, after all. I wonder how Ma communicates with her. Can't see a thing, keeps muttering to herself endlessly…'

Mitin stopped in her tracks for a few seconds. 'Who else lives in that flat?'

'A half-deaf maidservant, the old woman's companion. Annada Masi.' Abhirup accompanied her to the door. 'The old woman was the bride of a very eminent family. The wife to the only son of the zamindar of Singhagarh. This whole compound of ours was part of their land, once. The old woman's sons are also well-to-do. One in the States, one in Canada… she has grown-up grandchildren.'

Mitin listened without comment. When they reached the door, she said, 'Say goodbye to your mother on my behalf. I'll take my leave. But, if need be, I will come and torment you again.'

Abhirup nodded. He smiled but did not say anything in response.

Entering Rani di's flat, Mitin almost fainted in shock. A miniature palace, indeed! Gigantic oil paintings on the walls, along with bull's heads, tiger-skins and a grand chandelier hanging from the ceiling. A massive brass replica of a tiger. But covering everything was a heavy layer of dust.

Annada led Mitin to Rani Lahiri's room. On an enormous ebony bed reclined the aged Rani. Wrinkled skin, hair like ropes of flax, a once-glowing complexion, now faded and sallow. The pupils of her eyes were green, like opaque marbles.

'Ma, someone from the police is here,' Annada shouted at the top of her voice.

'Tell me, *bachha*, what's the fuss all about?' Rani bristled. 'Asked so many questions the other day and now you're back again?'

'No interrogation today,' Mitin assured her. 'Today I've come to chat with you.'

'O ma! A woman police officer! So much has changed over time. Pigs can fly! Even a woman becomes a cop! So, tell me, *bachha*, why are you all coming to me again and again because Somu has died?'

'Well, Somu's mother is your friend, after all, isn't she?'

'Are you speaking of Aparna? Ah, poor woman, so unhappy. What a crisis she endured for all those years, because of her son.'

'So, she'd often come and cry on your shoulder, wouldn't she?'

'A woman must unburden herself somewhere. My sons are absent even in their presence and Aparna's son was dead even when he was alive. The two of us used to salve our sorrowing hearts by telling each other our innermost thoughts. What a cruel blow of fate. Even a son in that condition gets murdered by his wife. That damned woman! Serves her right, to get caught. There is a god above our heads, after all…' Rani was rushing through her narrative like a mail train.

Suddenly, the wall clock began to chime. A strange, foreign tune. As soon as the music stopped, the clock struck twelve. Ding, dong, ding, dong. Mitin glanced at her own wristwatch to check the time.

'I must say your clock has quite a loud chime,' she observed, to interrupt the old woman's prattle.

'My younger son sent it to me. From Canada. The sound is too loud. Makes one's heart tremble.' Rani grinned, exposing her gums. 'But there's a trick to deal with that. If you darken the room, the clock won't strike.'

Mitin glanced at the clock inquisitively. It had two black buttons: one above, one below. Could they be photocells? These days, of course, such clocks were a dime a dozen, even in Kolkata. As the clock chimes, just switch off the light and the sound stops at once.

The old woman continued muttering to herself. 'I don't even turn on the light, for fear of these clock chimes. During the day, I manage somehow, blocking my ears. But as soon as it's evening, I can relax. After all, even if the lights are off, what difference does it make to me? What's day or night to a blind woman?'

'True, indeed.' Mitin was about to nod in assent, then paused abruptly. 'Why, but Aparna Devi told me that your clock had struck nine that evening?'

'It did, of course. Aparna said, it's nine o'clock, now let me slowly head back to my flat… Maybe our *bahu*, my daughter-in-law, has left by now…'

'Did Aparna leave as soon as the clock had struck?'

'No, she was here for a while longer.'

'Had she come just before the clock struck?'

'Wait, let me think.' The old woman frowned in an effort to remember. Then she beamed. 'I remember now. She had come long before the clock chimed. She wept profusely. I kept stroking her head… After she had recovered somewhat, she calmed down and sent Annada to buy some *paan*. She left for her own apartment right after the *paan* arrived.'

'Oh! *achchha*, Mashima, during her visits, did Aparna Devi criticize her *bahu* a lot?'

'She never criticized anyone, *bachha*. She used to curse her own fate.'

'Were you acquainted with her *bahu*?'

'Yes, slightly. Very conceited about her education, that wretched woman. Spoke to me so arrogantly. Go, woman! Now go get a taste of gruel in jail!'

At that moment, Annada walked in with a cup of tea. Mitin took a sip, then rose to her feet. She left the room, chatting with Annada. This time, on her way down, she took the lift, not the stairs. Lost in her own thoughts, she didn't even notice when she had walked out of the gate. She was walking on the broad pavement. Dark monsoon sky above and a gloomy day below. The darkness of this cloudy month of Shravan seemed to penetrate deep into Mitin's very heart. In her mind's eye, a picture began to dimly take shape, then vanished again.

Suddenly, she felt a flash of lightning in her brain. Mitin stopped in her tracks. For a second, she paused for thought, blinking. The next moment, she turned around and rushed off in the opposite direction. Straight to Akashleena. Panting, she charged into the security guard's cell.

Ten minutes later, Mitin emerged from the security room. Her face was as thunderous as the monsoon sky.

Abhirup opened the door.

'You, again?' He looked startled.

'I told you I might come again, if necessary,' Mitin replied, in a heavy voice.

'What is it? Tell me, what brings you here?'

'Ask your mother to join us. I will speak to both of you together.'

Aparna had emerged from her room, probably upon hearing voices. She gazed at Mitin in surprise.

Ignoring the two of them, Mitin went straight to the sofa and took a seat.

'If Chitralekha hangs at the gallows, will it please you, Aparna Devi?' she asked, in a sharp, staccato tone.

Aparna returned her gaze with indifference. 'She has to suffer for all her sins, of course.'

'But you have committed an even greater sin. It is you who killed Soumyarup.'

'What madness is this!' Abhirup shouted. 'Do you know what you are saying?'

'I am speaking the truth. Aparna Devi has, in full possession of her faculties, in a pre-meditated manner, in cold blood, murdered your Dada.' Mitin gazed straight into Aparna's eyes. 'You had made your calculations very well, but couldn't see it through to the end.'

Aparna stood there, hanging her head. Abhirup stared wide-eyed at his mother, then at Mitin.

'But I don't understand anything of all this.'

'You will understand. Let me explain. I will lay out the scenes, in proper sequence. If I make a mistake, Aparna Devi will correct me. That evening, as soon as Chitralekha entered the flat, Aparna Devi had walked out. But not for long. She came back. Listened silently from behind the curtain as husband and wife exchanged words. Her heart was bursting with tears, but also with rage. Aparna Devi saw Chitralekha inject the sedative. Unable to find the smaller syringe, Chitralekha had indeed used the 50cc syringe meant for the Ryle's tube, to put Soumyarup to sleep. He was writhing in pain. Not just in physical pain, but also in mental agony. Aparna Devi couldn't bear the sight. She moved away to her own room, just before Chitralekha emerged. Her room is in the far corner, barely visible to anyone coming out of Soumyarup's room. As soon as Chitralekha had left, Aparna came to her son's room, this time with gloved hands. Or maybe carrying a handkerchief. The sight of her daughter-in-law sedating her husband out of pity had set Aparna Devi's mind aflame. Having been a doctor's wife, she knew how to cause air embolism. Hardening herself, Aparna Devi injected air into the arm of her own sleeping son. Her brain is also razor-sharp. After waiting for ten to fifteen minutes, she raced to the opposite flat. Rani Lahiri was lying in her darkened room. Aparna Devi switched on the light and began speaking to her. Her heart was in turmoil at the time. She couldn't speak properly. Only tears kept welling up from within... But even as she wept, she had not forgotten her calculations. Just a few minutes before ten, she sent Annada off to fetch *paan*. At exactly 10 p.m., the clock began to chime. One, two, three, four... As she was speaking, Aparna Devi started stealing towards the switchboard. At the ninth stroke of the clock, she switched off the light. The tenth stroke was silenced. The blind Rani Lahiri didn't sense any of this, but Aparna Devi made sure to mention that the clock had struck nine. And she returned to her own flat after Annada came back. By then it was almost ten-thirty. She immediately called the doctor, then the police... Everything followed in sequence, exactly as Aparna had wanted. For one thing, she was the mother. And then there was the alibi she had created, fixing 9 p.m. as the time. So, from beginning to end, she remained totally above suspicion. But one point had not occurred to her. She had indeed, by a ruse, removed Annada from the scene, but the fact that Annada had left the apartment block almost an hour after Chitralekha's departure can be easily ascertained from the security guard. Hence, it would be impossible to establish that Chitralekha and Annada, both left the building exactly at nine. Besides, the woman who was so concerned for her son, couldn't quite recall whether she fed him vegetable stew or chicken stew. Because, she had not fed him at all that evening! By then, he was…'

Mitin paused briefly, to catch her breath. Then she resumed, 'Why such bitterness against Chitralekha, Aparna Devi? Why did you want to trap the harmless young woman in such a way?'

Suddenly, a change came over Aparna's face and expression.

'Whatever I've done, I'm glad I did it!' she screamed, her voice distorted. 'I did it for my son's own good. I liberated him from a slow and painful death. And why would I spare the one who has caused him so much suffering?'

Her screaming had slowly turned into a wail. Aparna was heaving with heart-rending sobs. The entire flat was echoing with her anguished cries.

Mitin's heart was also twisting in pain. Aha, how much torment the mother must have suffered, to be able to do such violence to her own son! How powerful a mother's love could be!

What would Mitin do now? Leave the scene quietly, without a sound?

No, that was not possible. She had to rescue Chitralekha too.

With trembling footsteps, Mitin walked towards the telephone.

A DIAMOND IS FOREVER

Sujan DasGupta, tr. Chandana Dutta

Promotho and Francesca seem to be serious this time around. They've been dating for a while now, although Promotho doesn't usually talk about it. This morning however, at breakfast, he suddenly brings up the matter of an engagement ring, I'm not sure why.

Those of you who have not read an Ekenbabu story so far, won't be familiar with us. So let me give you a quick introduction. I'm Bapi and I teach Physics at New York University. Promotho, my childhood friend, is a post-doc scholar in the Chemistry department at the same university. We stay in a rented apartment near the university. Our third resident is Ekenbabu. The guy's a detective and does some utterly ridiculous work with the criminology department, something like deciphering horse's eggs perhaps. Without doubt, he's a peculiar character.

'Engagement ring!' Ekenbabu pipes up instantly. 'A diamond is forever, sir. You must give madam a diamond ring.'

'You think you can get away with that suggestion, do you, Moshai?[1] Do you have any idea how much a good diamond ring costs?' Typical Promotho reaction. Measured responses are not part of his DNA.

'No, sir, but I'm sure you'll get a good bargain from Mr Chugani.'

---

[1] Moshai, a Bangla honorific, meaning Mister; later Ekenbabu's wife is referred to as Boudi, sister-in-law.

We know Hemant Chugani as Raju's husband. And Raju works in our main library. Perhaps the last name is Chughani with an 'h', but at work, Chugani it is. Hemant has a huge jewellery store in New York. Ekenbabu believes Raju's reference will certainly fetch a discount. But the problem is that Promotho is not telling us clearly what he wants. The guy's not usually sentimental about his heritage, but now we can see that he wants to gift Francesca something that is somewhat Indian. Not bought from Zales or Tiffany or Helzberg.

Having deduced this, Ekenbabu ventures, 'Mr Hemant is after all from our country, he will certainly be able to manage genuine stuff from home. And if Bapi babu too buys a ring for Bev madam, then perhaps you'll get a good discount.'

Ekenbabu's absurd concern with our marriages is becoming quite exasperating. But I don't need to interject. Promotho scolds him, 'Please keep to your thefts and murders, don't concern yourself with our marriages.'

'Oh, sir, how can you say that! Marriages are such interesting cases, no – two hearts warmly meeting…'

'Nonsense!'

Having brought up the matter of the engagement ring once, Promotho now zips up. But does that stop Ekenbabu? Every day at the dining table, he presents news of some or the other jewellery store – God knows where he gets his information.

One day, Ekenbabu brings home some catalogues as well. Promotho sits sulking, he doesn't even look. Then he challenges Ekenbabu, 'Don't you have a case to focus on?'

Tch, tch, is this any way to talk? This Promotho is becoming cruder by the day. I feel terrible though I don't need to. I begin leafing through the catalogues and remark to Ekenbabu, 'Really, I had no clue there were so many jewellery shops in this tri-state of ours. Who in New York, New Jersey and Connecticut owns these shops?'

'Most are Sindhis and Gujaratis and only one Bengali shop, Montu Ghosh's in White Plains.'

This last bit I know, from one of Ekenbabu's previous cases. Promotho, irritated, stomps off to his room to get ready for work. I continue to look through the catalogues.

Ekenbabu whispers, 'Promotho babu didn't even look at these.'

I respond, 'Now, here, Ekenbabu, Promotho is hardly the type to rush into things, he's not into "have feet, will travel" kind of stuff. He thinks through everything carefully by himself. It'll be better if we select some and then talk to him. He'll decide where he wants to go.'

Ekenbabu seems mollified by my suggestion, 'Fine, sir, if you say so.'

We proceed without telling Promotho and take Bev, our department secretary, along. She'd know better the likes and dislikes of a woman. I don't know what mantra Ekenbabu has chanted, but Bev seems super enthusiastic. Perhaps more because it's all such a secret from Promotho and Francesca. Bev gives us ideas about the prices of engagement rings in this country. 'You'll get a reasonably good ring for about five-thousand dollars,' she preps us.

Ekenbabu seems ready to have a heart attack when he hears the number.

'Fffi…iivvv…eee… thousand, madam!'

I tell Bev as much, 'Five thousand is too much, can't we find something cheaper?'

'You won't find anything cheaper than that at Tiffany's.'

'Arrey, we won't go to Tiffany, madam, Promotho babu is looking for something Indian.'

'Then maybe, yes. Tiffany marks up by two to three hundred per cent.'

'Why then do people go there?' I query.

'Oh, they have excellent quality and cut grade.'

I understand little of what Bev's saying. I believe that India has excellent diamonds and Surat is now known for its cuts. How's it even possible not to find a good diamond in an Indian shop? But I don't need to say anything because Bev suggests, 'Then why don't we go to Hemant's shop?'

Hemant's shop, H.C. Jewelers, is on the twentieth floor of a large building on 44th Street. Bev's already told Raju about our visit that evening, but she didn't mention the reason. Raju has instantly assumed that we're going to get Bev an engagement ring. We've just reached when Hemant hurtles towards us with a loud and hearty welcome. We've been to Hemant's shop before, to get Ekenbabu a sapphire. The shop has grown enormously since. Its display has changed completely. Or am I getting it wrong, is this a different shop? My puzzled expression doesn't escape Hemant. 'The shop's changed a lot,' he promptly explains. 'A year back there were four shops on this floor. I took over the space next door, only half of it, when it shut down. The other half I subleased, thanks to a deal with the owner.'

Almost immediately Hemant excuses himself to attend to a call. We busy ourselves with a quick look at the shop next-door from the outside. A small shop, Indian jewellery. Owned by a friend of Hemant's. True, I think as I peep in through the glass. Sindhis, Gujaratis, Marwaris do help each other grow successful in business. It couldn't have been simple to find such a space in this part of Manhattan. It's his because he's Hemant's friend. Not like the Bengalis, with their crab mentality – if I don't have it, neither will you. Of course, Promotho completely dismisses this theory. Whenever they discuss it, he retorts, 'Do you know what your biggest problem is? You are a Vibhishan,[2] the enemy within! A Bengali yourself, you go about abusing the stock you come from. Remember, whatever these folks do, they do it for selfish reasons. Everything is give-and-take. I give you now, you give back later, that's the unwritten rule.'

I respond, 'Maybe, but Bengalis don't even do that.'

We go on arguing. Promotho, the universal cribber, looks for faults in everyone. But a single negative comment about Bengalis and he takes on a peculiar position. He transforms into a chest-all-out-Bengali. When the quarrel is at its peak, Ekenbabu comes to the rescue. He says, 'Aha! Let it be, na, you aren't getting into business, are you? You are seekers of knowledge.'

But Promotho is not one to melt at these honeyed words. 'Fine one to say, Moshai, while happily running that detective agency business of yours!'

'Oh, sir, what are you saying, how can you even call it a business!'

I jump to Ekenbabu's defence, 'It's called a professional service.'

'My foot! Don't you need references when you go scouting for clients? Don't the Bengalis give you that? And in return, Ekenbabu gives a discount to those who bring their cases to him. Isn't that give-and-take!'

I retort, 'There you go again, bunkum!'

Is Ekenbabu omniscient! As I wonder, he whispers, '*Achchha*, sir, you just called Promotho babu a nonsense-spewing universal cribber. Why then did you drive us all so far?'

'As atonement for a childhood buddy.'

---

[2] Vibhishan, the younger brother of Ravan, defected from his brother's side to support King Ram and thus gave birth to the saying that even our closest family can bring us to ruin.

'No, sir, this too is because of Promotho babu's give-and-take theory. As you look for a ring for Bev madam, you are really asking for Promotho babu to help.'

'One day I'm going to slaughter you. And you'll fail to unmask the murderer. Tell me why?'

'Hmm... why!'

'Because you'll already be dead!'

Mercifully, Bev is standing some distance away. She hasn't heard a word.

'What are you talking about,' she asks, curious.

'Nothing at all.'

Hemant is now free.

'Sorry, I kept you waiting. It was an urgent call.' He ushers us very warmly into his office.

We fill in Hemant about the kind of ring we're looking for. It must carry its Indianness openly, not something off the shelf from Zales or Tiffany or Helzberg. And priced only at around two and a half thousand.

Hemant shows us some rings, but I can't spot anything 'Indian' in them. He's a shrewd businessman though – takes one look at me and senses my reservations. 'These are not Indian enough, right? 'Cause these diamonds are not from our country, but from Botswana, Russia, South Africa, Tanzania, Australia, Canada; though they've all been cut in Surat. I could bring you a stone from Golconda, but it'll cost you more.'

'No, no, it's not about the diamond, it's the style. Doesn't seem too Indian. What do you say, Bev?'

I don't think Bev is taken in by any of the rings.

'And you, Ekenbabu?'

'What do I know, sir, Bev madam's say is what matters.'

'Should I suggest something,' Hemant shoots off and brings back two silver-gold bangles, encrusted with tiny diamonds. 'Made by artisans from back home, a beautiful blend of the traditional and contemporary.' He turns to Bev, 'Try it, it'll look good on you.'

As she tries on one, Bev quips to Hemant, 'This is not for me though.' She twirls it around her wrist. 'This is neat, an engagement bangle, quite a modern idea.'

'Price?' I ask.

'These aren't expensive diamonds, around two thousand dollars or so.'

'And what if they were quality diamonds, sir?' Ekenbabu prompts.

'At least four thousand, if Type 2.'

I've heard something about Type 2 diamonds but can't recall where. So, I pose another question, 'Does it mean sending the bangles back to India?'

'Nope, we just need to get the diamonds. The setting can be done right here. I have all the equipment in place.'

Meanwhile, Ekenbabu is poking around. Hemant grins, 'Not here, not in the showroom or office. There's a separate room next door for repair and setting.'

The office wall is all glass. The repair room can be seen through the chinks in the vertical blinds; I hadn't noticed it until now. A work bench with a lit-up magnifying glass clamped to it, two jeweller's loops, pliers, cutter, a jeweller's saw, a brazing torch spread on it. I don't even recognize all the instruments. Ekenbabu is more excited than I am. He shoots up, looks around hawk-eyed. Bev's perhaps delighted with the bangle, she's still twirling it around her wrist. Meanwhile, Hemant has brought out a couple more from the showcase for her. But, without a doubt, the first one is tops. I take a pic of Bev's bangle-adorned arm. I'll show it to Promotho later.

Bev jokes with Hemant, 'You'll have to pay me modelling fee, after all, Bapi just took a picture.'

'Of course, the very day I receive good news.'

Hemant still doesn't believe Bev. He thinks this is for her. It's obvious from his next question, 'What's the budget?'

I scratch my head as Bev answers. 'Three, maybe four thousand!'

'Then there's no problem, I have spare diamonds in stock.'

As we take our leave, Ekenbabu suddenly asks, 'How is your father-in-law doing?'

I'm taken aback at this question.

Hemant responds, 'Oh, good! Thanks to your contact, he's found a decent concentrator in Pune. I'm really grateful to you both.'

The mystery clears up on our way home. While visiting his daughter four months back, Raju's father had suffered breathing difficulties. A chronic obstructive pulmonary disease (COPD) patient, New York's pollen allergen had been a deadly combination for him. A portable oxygen cylinder came to his rescue. But it needed frequent recharging – a terrible nuisance. An oxygen concentrator was found at Bev's, one her father had used when alive. She passed it on to Raju.

'What exactly is it?' I ask Bev.

'Special medical equipment to provide oxygen support. Sucks in fresh air and filters out nitrogen to supply pure oxygen. Works like an oxygen cylinder but on electricity.'

'How does it filter nitrogen?'

'With a zeolite.'

Zeolite! That's a first for me. I'm impressed with Bev's scientific knowledge, but a diffident me can't praise her. And if I try, she'll shoot me down, 'You think I'm a dumb blonde?'

'Interesting! But why buy it in Pune again? Couldn't yours be taken there?'

'I'd asked Raju to take it, but Hemant said it wouldn't work there. The voltages are different. We were discussing all this when our dear detective came visiting the library. He mentioned a Pune connection who could help.'

I can't hold back. 'That wouldn't have been necessary, a step-down transformer would've done the job.'

'Sir, how could we know this when you weren't with Bev madam. Anyway, no harm in having more. There's one here and another there. When he visits, he can use the one here.'

'Exactly, I've asked Raju to keep it,' adds Bev.

'She has, madam, I saw it in the repair shop.'

These days, many girls in America get their ears pierced. I don't remember where I read about it, but the figure is about eighty per cent, that is eight out of ten. So far, I hadn't paid any attention to this information but now I do. It's true, I see many women with piercings, particularly, in this area of New York where we live. Even Bev wears earrings. But, of course, hers are usually tiny – a pearl drop, or ruby set in silver or platinum. Today, I notice, she's wearing a filigreed gold basket earring. It looks great on her.

I say, 'I've never seen you wear this earring before.'

'Do you even notice what I wear?'

'Of course, why wouldn't I?'

She seems happy with my answer. 'I'd gone to Hemant's shop yesterday with Raju. He's the one who suggested this. I picked up quite a few.'

'It seems Hemant has landed a keen customer.'

'His products are excellent and much cheaper than Tiffany's.' Then she chuckles, 'You should buy a few too, you'll look good wearing them. Of course, you'll have to get your ears pierced first.'

'No, thanks! But really, what news of Raju, how's she doing?'

'She's fine, just worried about her dad.'

'But why?'

'The oxygen machine in India doesn't work too well, so they need portable cylinders. They're thinking of importing one from here.' And then she dives headlong into a completely different matter, 'Hey, tell me, should I wear a bangle from now on?'

'Why not, it looked good on you.'

'Raju wears it all the time.' She trots off to attend to a call and returns soon. 'Wanted to let you know that I checked out several American jewellery sites on the net. They're selling diamond bangles for about ten to fifteen thousand dollars, while the ones Hemant promised were only three to four.'

'That must be because of differences in quality.'

'Perhaps, but I think it's better to go for India-made gold-plated Minakari, the enameled bangles. Guess how much they cost?'

'Two hundred?' I suggest tentatively.

'Under twenty-five dollars,' Bev counters, a triumphant smile lighting her up.

'My kind of price. But ten or fifteen thousand dollars is hardly a problem for you.'

I hadn't intended to make a dig at her. Among my acquaintances, undeniably, she is the richest: an heir having finally agreed to accept her mother's share of her grandfather's estate. An inheritance worth not just a couple of millions, but multi-million dollars. But Bev's face has clouded over. It's a sensitive point for her. For years she'd avoided accepting her share, but finally… under her uncle's pressures… forget it, that's an old story.

Words can't be taken back, but the hurt can be minimized. I quickly interject, 'Tiffany's, Blue Nile, or even Hemant's, for that matter, I won't be able to gift you these. But, yes, I can get you Amazon gold-plated enameled bangles. Would you accept it?'

Her eyes brighten, 'Of course! Gift it and I'll wear it.'

At dinner that night, Promotho asks, '*Arrey*, what glories of Ekenbabu are you writing of now?'

These days Promotho is keen to know about my writing. He makes me read out whatever I write. I think he wants to know if there's anything damaging about him in it.

'*Arrey na*, not Ekenbabu, I'm writing about you.'

'Meaning? Listen, nothing about me can leave this house without my permission. Show it to me first.'

As soon as I slide the laptop towards him, the file of stories opens, his brows crinkle and after a quick glance he says, 'What rubbish is this! Who told you I'm scouting for an engagement ring for Francesca? One small question and you start writing a Mahabharat here?'

'You aren't scouting?'

'Even if I am, what's there to write about? Don't you have other topics to write about? And why's there so much of Bev in this story, *hyan*[3]? Seems you should be the one to buy an engagement ring, or a bangle!'

'Maybe I have written a tad much,' I agree.

'A tad much? Now listen, just give up writing these Ekenbabu mysteries. Is this even a story? From what I read, there is neither suspense nor romance.'

'Oh ho! This is just the beginning.'

'The morning shows the day. You'll not be able to climb out of the pit you've fallen into.'

You may ask why I ignore such a deadly prophecy and continue with the story. It'll become clear from what follows. We've become involved in the investigation of a theft, one that involves Hemant too.

Let me elaborate. That morning as I sit in my office, Bev rushes in with an extremely agitated Raju.

'What's the matter?'

'Raju's diamond ring's gone missing. She's trying to get hold of Ekenbabu but can't find him.'

---

[3] The slightly nasal hyan is the Bangla word for yes. It has been retained here to maintain cultural specificity.

I know why. Ekenbabu has an all-day meeting at Captain Stewart's office today. His phone will be switched off, he said.

'You can't contact him before this evening, but you could tell me what's happened.'

I understand a little of what Raju narrates, not everything. There may be a slip or two in what I'm writing now. In fact, Promotho enters the room while Raju's explaining things. He's always eager to show off his knowledge about everything. No doubt he knows a lot, but he lies too. But let me first put down what Raju says – her ring is a gift from Hemant's mother, that's her mother-in-law, who in-turn has received it from her mother-in-law. The diamond is not an ordinary one, it's a Golconda. God knows how that makes it extra special. I, of course, think the value of the ring perhaps lies elsewhere. A family heirloom carries with it a lot of emotions and sentiments, which can't be calculated in terms of money. But since Raju has mentioned Golconda a couple of times, the next question slips out, 'This must be priceless because it's your mother-in-law's mother-in-law's, right? Not because it's a Golconda, or Kimberley, isn't it?'

No sooner do the words leave my mouth than Promotho interrupts, 'Don't speak like an idiot! A Golconda diamond is a super special Type 2a stone. Only one per cent of diamonds in the world are Type 2a.' He goes on to unload a ton of wisdom on me. 'The Kohinoor, the Hope, they are all the same lineage. It seems there is hardly any or no nitrogen impurities in their crystal lattices. Hence, they don't easily absorb short wave ultraviolet light wavelengths.'

'What's the meaning of this gibberish, this *agrom-bagrom?*'

'It means when light strikes it, it radiates out without interruption. Understand?' After doling out such remarkable blather, Promotho turns to Raju, 'I have a question. If this is a Golconda, it must be very old, at least three to four hundred years. How did it come into your family?'

Poor Raju! She looks mortified, 'I've heard it's a Golconda. I can't be hundred per cent sure, perhaps I'm mistaken.'

At last, it enters Promotho's thick skull that not only has he deviated from the main issue but he's also dragging Raju's family honour through the mud. He now tries to set things right, '*Aarey na!* You aren't wrong. Several Type 2a diamonds were found in Golconda many hundred years ago. So, other types of 2as are also labelled Golconda. Such stones are also found in other different places. In fact, smaller ones are created artificially. But forget all that. How did you lose the ring?'

Raju meanders through her answer. I'll share with you what I salvaged from it. A well-heeled client of Hemant's was enquiring about a Golconda diamond. Hemant didn't have one the size his client wanted. Asking him to come back later, Hemant requested Raju for her ring as a sample. If it suited his customer's requirement, Hemant would get a matching one of the same quality from Surat. Upon this, Raju handed over her ring to Hemant.

The client is thrilled to see Raju's diamond ring. He wants it for himself. The man is obstinate; Hemant's insistence that it's only a sample is of no use. 'Give this one to me and I'll pay twenty thousand dollars for it.'

'Twenty thousand dollars?' I almost fall off my chair. 'I've seen you wear the ring, it wasn't too large, was it?'

On cue, Promotho interjects, 'A diamond is priced for its carat, colour, clarity and cut. But it's also all about fancy pricing – not just size.'

I've heard something to this effect but have forgotten it now. Anyhow, Hemant discusses the problem with Raju and she feels that if the man is willing to pay this exorbitant amount, Hemant should just sell the diamond off. Even an artificial diamond could be set in the band later, at less than half the price.

Hemant objects, becoming furious in fact. His mother has lovingly gifted her own ring to the daughter-in-law, and now the son is going to sell it!

The long and short of it is that Hemant finally convinces his client for a twenty-day respite to get him a diamond almost like this one.

'But why almost like this one? Why not an exact substitute?' I query. 'The two diamond earrings you're wearing, they look exactly the same.'

'These aren't diamonds, they're cubic zirconia. Only a hundred, or hundred and fifty dollars. If diamonds, they'd have cost almost twenty thousand.'

'Oh gosh! They look just like diamonds.'

'Thank you but these aren't copies. You'll notice their variations only under a microscope. Hemant was certain that this man would bring another jeweller with him to verify the quality before paying. The GIA Certificate wouldn't be enough. So, he hadn't even tried to cheat him. But the man said something to Hemant that floored him completely. If Hemant could get him a dozen of the same stones, he'd pay the same rate for all of them. He wished to impress a Hollywood celebrity who was to be married soon. He would like Hemant to design a necklace or a bracelet or something with those diamonds.'

But I can't understand a thing about what exactly happened even after this long-winded explanation. A couple more questions, but only my IQ goes up slightly – a GIA Certificate is awarded by the Gemology Institute of America and that my knowledge of diamonds-shaimonds is not even a fourth of Raju's.

'When did the robbery take place?'

'We came to know of it last night. My ring had been lying in Hemant's shop for almost a month now. A few days earlier we'd received twelve diamonds from Surat. And last night, we discovered that my ring and all the diamonds were missing.'

'But how only last night?'

'Our showroom was closed in the morning. Hemant had gone to set up a place he has rented in the diamond district. Customers prefer to visit there. In this country, if you wish to be a noted diamond merchant, that's the place to be.'

I've visited Manhattan's diamond district a few times – row after row of shops in a wide area between the Fifth Avenue and the Avenue of the Americas. Diamonds and diamond jewellery glittering along the street, abuzz with retail and wholesale buyers and sellers.

'I understand, but wasn't there any security at the main shop?'

'There was, the usual. Two guards and two employees, doing repair work and setting.'

'Trustworthy?'

'Totally. Men from Hemant's village, working as part-timers for several years now. Even the guards are from a bonded security agency – responsible 24/7.'

I don't understand the details completely. From what I know when something is stolen from a shop, compensation is the responsibility of the security agency. But are they still responsible when there are others present at the time of the theft? Another question that bothers me: was each diamond separately insured?

Raju isn't sure. But I am, as much as I can be, that in such cases, matters of compensation are never uncomplicated. Someone once had his expensive video camera, laptop and other things stolen and the poor guy felt barely alive by the time he'd recovered his compensation. And then, he never received his replacement cost. After much calculation and computation, he was handed over a small amount. And all this for a camera, laptop and so on, at most worth thousand, maybe five hundred dollars more. And what about this case? If each of the twelve tiny diamonds cost twenty thousand dollars, it'll be an astounding 2.4 million. No matter who's stolen them, it's certainly a neat figure! Even if I teach for twenty years, I won't make such an amount.

The minute I mention this to Promotho, he responds, 'You could, if you married Bev.'

Bev's standing right in front. Thankfully, she doesn't understand Bangla, nor does Raju – but I wish Promotho used some common sense!

'Has Hemant informed the police?' I ask.

'Yes,' Raju replies.

I finally send Raju off with a promise to tell Ekenbabu everything that evening. Bev's filling in for someone, so she's left as well. Promotho leaves too. He'd peeped into my office on his way somewhere. I now sit down with my thoughts: how could the diamonds disappear? I can't think of reasonable possibilities. But I do recall that Ekenbabu had spoken of a similar case earlier where the night guard fed his pet dog a diamond coated in peanut butter. When the guard was searched, nothing was found on him. He'd planned to give the dog laxatives and recover the diamond. But Ekenbabu foiled the plan. But there's no dog here, that much is obvious. And it is daylight robbery with two workers present on spot. Would the guard be able to swallow so many diamonds without the workers noticing? Maybe one, or two, but so many together? A dozen! Unless... unless... they're all in it together!

In the evening when I tell Ekenbabu about Raju's stolen diamond the poor man's face falls, 'Oho, such a beautiful diamond.'

Promotho is making coffee, 'You've seen it?'

'Why wouldn't I, sir? A pale pink diamond, quite a bit like the famous Graff Pink.'

'Now what on earth is that?' I am perplexed.

'That's the name of a famous diamond, na? I don't know, sir, maybe I've got the name wrong.'

'No, you're not wrong,' interjects Promotho, 'but I didn't know that you're such a keen observer of beautiful women's fingers.'

'Oh, sir, what are you saying! They are all like my sisters.'

'You can tell your family that!'

Family meant Ekenboudi, his wife, we all know that now.

'Aah! Now let it be,' I chide Promotho and turn to Ekenbabu, 'You must find those diamonds. Even if not all, at least Raju's.'

God knows what is going through Promotho's mind, but he suddenly declares, 'I understand it's about Raju's ring and a matter of sentiment, but I find this obsession with diamonds intolerable.'

'Why, eh? Because you'll lose money on an engagement ring?'

'Don't be stupid! It's meaningless to spend lakhs of rupees over a tiny piece of carbon. Just think, if pencil lead cost you ten lakhs, would you buy it? It's graphite, that's carbon. Same, same.'

'No sir, there's a difference. Just think, there are so many madams in the world, but these two – Francesca madam and Bev madam – they're different.'

'What nonsense is this! Anyway, no point in this conversation anymore. Now please look for Raju madam's ring.'

Ekenbabu, flustered, begins to scratch his head. 'Actually, sir, Captain Stewart has given me some very urgent work. I won't be able to take up anything else before that's done.'

Almost on cue, Bev calls on Ekenbabu's mobile.

'Yes, madam… Bapi babu was just telling me about it. Actually, I'm tied up in a big thing… no, no, madam, why are you saying this. I will try. As much as I can. Hyan, hyan, I'll talk tomorrow itself… yes, in the morning.'

It isn't difficult to figure out what Bev's saying. Promotho charges, 'Hello, mister, Bapi requests you and it's a no and when Bev says, it's an immediate yes.'

'Please sir, madam doesn't understand no.'

'Enough of your frivolous excuses. In truth, you melt as soon as you see a beautiful woman.'

'Bapi babu, look how Promotho babu is speaking.' Ekenbabu looks at me, puppy faced.

The next day I find Bev is on leave, that is, she's not available at work. She hardly ever takes a day off. She likes coming to the office. Strange! I'm forced to come because I need to feed myself. I love the teaching part, yes, but checking exam papers, grading them, attending boring departmental meetings – I just hate all that. But, Bev! Sometimes she comes in to work even when on leave. She wanders in and out of rooms to gossip, visits the library, chit-chats in the cafeteria. She pitches in for other secretaries too. Difficult to figure out if she's on leave, or at work. Occasionally, even when she's informed me, I've taken a memo to her simply because I've spotted her at her desk. My English is sometimes awkward. Bev doesn't mind correcting it, she in fact emails my memos too. Now, she looks at it and says, 'I can't do this, I'm on leave.'

I'm embarrassed of course, 'So sorry,' and try to take the memo back.

She stops me, smiles, 'I'll do it.'

'No, no, you're on leave.'

'Just sitting around. Let me.'

Today she walks in as soon as I enter my office. 'You don't have class this morning, no meetings either.'

'Correct.'

'The Detective's coming. He will go with us to Hemant's store. Poor Raju can't join us today, too many on leave in her department.'

'In search of Raju's stolen ring?' I ask although I know the answer.

'Yes.'

'Does Hemant know we're going?'

'Yes, Raju called him. His shop opens at 10 a.m., but he'll be there earlier. I've also spoken to him. He'll be waiting.'

Promotho calls just then. 'Listen, call me as soon as you return from Hemant's shop.'

'How do you know I'm going there?'

'I spoke to the commander-in-chief this morning.'

Promotho has started calling Bev commander-in-chief since last night. Apparently, she has an immense capacity to keep everyone in line by ordering them about, pretending to be angry, or even by playing vain.

'How'd you get out of it?' I ask him in Bangla.

'I've work in the lab. Our C-in-C is extremely considerate. I was immediately excused. But I'm with you in this mission.'

'Mission my foot!'

Ekenbabu appears a few minutes later.

'So sorry for the delay, madam.'

'Not at all. Bapi is coming too.'

'Bah, wonderful. I was just about to ask you that. How can we proceed without Bapi babu?' Humility personified, this Ekenbabu!

'We'll go in my new car today. You haven't even seen it.' This last line is directed at me.

Oh, I'd forgotten to mention it, Bev's uncle gifted her a Tesla. It's not exactly a cheap car. I'm not surprised. When an heiress refuses her inheritance worth millions simply out of pride, this is a way to win her over. Bev is the beloved niece of her only uncle. Her tycoon grandfather passed away some time ago and, finally, Bev's agreed to accept her inheritance. I don't drive to work, I walk. Bev too doesn't normally drive. She's tried to show me the car a couple of times, it just hasn't worked out.

Ekenbabu answers excitedly, 'Of course, madam. It's a Tesla after all!'

These days one can see many Tesla cars on the road. At one time people were doubtful about the future of these cars. They didn't run on gas or petrol and had to be taken to charging stations when their batteries ran out. There were very few charging points unlike the countless gas stations. Who knew what one would have to do if the battery ran out in the middle of nowhere.

As soon as he gets into the car, Ekenbabu says, 'Madam, but for you I would never in my life be sitting in an electric Tesla. It's very expensive, no?'

Bev is visibly embarrassed. 'Not really, Detective, this is a model 3, not too pricey, around 50,000.'

'Is that cheap, madam? I've heard this is self-driving, all you need to do is to tell it your destination.'

Bev giggles at this, 'There's a software package, FSD, but that works on highways, not so well inside the city yet.'

I've heard of this, so I ask, 'Is that the full self-driving package?'

'Yup. It changes lanes on its own, brakes if it senses something too close, even parks on the side. It's a very obedient car.'

'Is that so, madam?'

'Want to see?' says Bev and then orders, 'Lock the door.'

The doors lock instantly.

'Open boot.' And the boot opens.

'Fold mirrors.' Promptly the rear-view mirrors fold up.

'Great, really great,' Ekenbabu nods. '*Achchha*, madam, can you say, "Catch the diamond thief?"'

Bev guffaws, 'It can't do everything, Detective, that's why we need you.'

'Absolutely correct, Bev,' I say, 'and I too would like you to drive, I don't at all trust a self-driving car.'

'You trust me?' Bev twinkles.

I'd never expected such a question. I grin like an idiot. Thank god Promotho isn't present or else I wouldn't hear the last of it.

Bev smiles again, 'Don't worry, I'm driving.'

Hemant is waiting for us at the entrance to his shop. It's obvious he's broken. As it is he's shouldering the problems of a new shop and now so many diamonds have been stolen. He's not just worried, he's devastated.

'I can't figure anything out, Ekenbabu. Nothing of this sort has happened in the last fifteen years since I started my business. I pay massive amounts for security and still...'

'What does the police say, sir?' Ekenbabu asks as he enters the shop.

'Nothing reassuring. Nothing suspicious on the security cameras. The shop was locked from the inside. Two of the men were setting stones, two guards were stationed outside. The workers hadn't even stepped out. No one had come in either...'

'Where were the diamonds and Raju madam's ring, sir?'

'In a jewellery box in the repair shop. A few urgent settings were pending. I had instructed the workmen to complete those and then clean Raju's ring and the diamonds. The client was to visit the next day – I wanted everything ready in advance.'

'Does cleaning mean polishing, sir?'

'No. When we touch the stones with our hands, they become dirty, oily, their brightness diminishes. I wanted the diamonds in picture-perfect condition.'

'That means the ring and diamonds were available to the workmen.'

'Yes, true, but the men are very trustworthy. When I came to the shop and discovered the diamonds were missing, they were as shaken as I was. They swore to god that they had no clue about how the diamonds had vanished. The police have already interrogated them. They're ready to take a lie detector test. And really, I'm wondering too, if they had stolen the diamonds where could they have hidden them? We turned the shop upside down. We found Raju's ring, of course, but the diamonds are still missing. We've not told Raju yet.'

'Where did you find it, sir?'

'In my office, in the desk drawer. It was the first to be cleaned and kept there. When I was desperately rummaging around looking for the diamonds, the workmen got scared and forgot to mention it to me.'

'And where was the jewellery box, sir?'

'In the repair shop vault. We have two vaults. The large one is kept in the office and the small, in the repair shop. If work is not complete, the workmen keep the jewels back in the vault before locking up. Nothing is left outside. The jewellery box was in the vault, but empty.'

'Does the vault stay open, sir?'

'In the morning yes, but it's locked when we leave at night.'

I blurt, 'People can swallow diamonds. Ekenbabu solved such a case some years back.'

'The police did a quick scan last night with a portable instrument. Had they found something suspicious, they would have done a full body scan, maybe an ultrasound or X-Ray, god knows what. Basically, found nothing.'

Ekenbabu responds, 'Understood, sir. Now let's take a good look around the repair shop.'

On our previous visit, I'd seen the shop through the office window. The instruments here were very like watch-repair instruments. I've seen such delicate instruments in a Kolkata watch-repair shop once. But there's equipment here for welding, braising and soldering too. I spot two broken gold chains on the table. These tools will be required to fix the chains, I suppose.

I notice Ekenbabu staring meditatively at the corner of a wall.

'What are you looking at so carefully, there's nothing there.'

'Yes, sir, there's nothing here.'

'Then?'

Ekenbabu doesn't respond but looks around a little and then says to Hemant, 'Could you show me the jewellery box, sir, the one that had the diamonds?'

'Of course, it's now in my office.'

Hemant takes us there and hands over an empty box lined with soft velvet. Ekenbabu studies it for a while, turning it this way and that. Something's going on in his mind, it's obvious.

'*Achchha*, sir, has the police examined the air vents in the shop, the underside of the table, the wall plugs?'

'Yes, they spent a lot of time on those. When they were kneeling under the table, I asked and they said that thieves tape tiny objects or stick them with chewing gum at the base.'

'But clearly they didn't find anything?'

'I knew they wouldn't because before calling them I'd brushed the entire room, just in case. I would have spotted it.'

'Didn't the police use something like a diamond detector?' I question.

'There's no instrument like that,' replies Hemant. 'A detector can be used to find a ring or even earrings because there's metal in them. But loose diamonds, no.'

I hadn't known this. I see Ekenbabu is silent. But suddenly he says, '*Achchha*, sir, don't you use a vacuum cleaner for the floors?'

'Of course, we do.'

'Where is it?'

'The police have taken it away to check its hose, dust bag, other parts.'

'I'm assuming, sir, that nothing has been found there too.'

'Why assume, it's certain, or else I would've heard something.'

'What are you thinking of, Detective?' Bev probes.

'About Promotho babu.'

'Suddenly, now?'

'Nothing, madam, come, let's leave now.'

Hemant prods, 'Do you sense something, Ekenbabu?'

'Not yet, sir. Let's talk about something else. How's your father-in-law now?'

'Oh good! It was your person who fixed the machine, had to change the filter from what I understood.'

'What a relief! May I ask you a financial question, sir?'

'Financial? Sure.'

'Is there an insurance on the diamonds?'

'Yes. Larceny, mysterious disappearance, accidental loss, theft: everything's covered. But all these only apply to what I've spent on the diamonds. I can't recover any profits from sales now.'

'Where is the problem then, sir, you can get some new diamonds again.'

'I'll have lost my client if I wait to recover the insurance money before I buy the diamonds again. I found out that he's already paid an advance to someone else now that he knows I'm not delivering on time. Time is a huge factor in this case.'

'Very interesting, sir,' Ekenbabu replies scratching his head.

I can't figure out what's so interesting in this. But from his manner I can see that there's nothing more for him here.

As we leave, Bev asks Hemant, 'I have a pendant that's come loose from my necklace. Surely your people will be able to fix it.'

'Even I can do that. Bring it over or send it through Raju.'

'So sweet of you, thank you.'

I understand that Hemant takes care of such repairs himself, rather than depending entirely on his workmen.

Hemant comes to see us off. At the exit, Ekenbabu thinks of something again, '*Achchha*, from whom is your client buying the diamonds now?'

Hemant mentions a familiar name. They have a huge shop in Jackson Heights. I see their commercials in the local Queens paper. After a pause, Hemant says again, 'Back home, they live in the town next to ours. That's how I found out. We have several common clients.'

On our way back, Ekenbabu suddenly mumbles 'I have work' and disappears. Only Bev and I are in the car now. Bev asks me, 'What do you think, are the Jackson Heights folk involved in this theft?'

'I won't be surprised, but how did they manage it?'

My day is full of worries about the diamonds, but not one idea proves fruitful. Meanwhile, Bev has spoken with Ekenbabu. I believe the police are proceeding with their own theories.

They suspect the workmen strongly. They somehow must have smuggled the diamonds out of the shop. Interesting info, the two workmen are freelancers. They're attached to several shops. Apparently, they're considered super artisans and no shop has the means to hire them exclusively. They're called for special assignments only. They've been working for years in this New York–New Jersey region. They're both educated, in fact, one of them studied Promotho's subject. But Chemistry graduates from our country don't easily find well-paid jobs here. The other, although educated, had chosen to work in his father's jewellery shop in Gujarat. He's the master artisan, while the other learnt on the job. No one has any complaints against either. Hemant doesn't even suspect them. In this profession, it will be impossible to find work if one were to lose one's reputation. And diamond theft! No way they can live through that. Of course, there's a risk of getting caught, but no shop owner in this country will buy or sell diamonds without authentic papers either. That's why even the police are unable to get to the bottom of the problem. About this last bit, I've a niggling doubt.

So, as soon as Ekenbabu returns home that evening, I question him, 'I believe you told Bev that no one in this country will buy without authentic papers?'

'Yes, sir.'

'But how's one to know that the papers are for these specific diamonds?'

'Why not, by checking the numbers, sir.'

'Numbers?'

'The ID number mentioned in the GIA Certificate is embossed with laser on the side of the diamond in tiny lettering.'

'Side?'

'Let me explain, sir. The diamond top is the crown, the base, a pavilion. The middle part around the stone is the *gher*, or girdle. That's where the number is, microscopic.'

'*Baba re!* I had no idea. I'm super impressed with your knowledge.'

'I didn't know too, sir. An expert explained it to me at Captain Stewart's office today. It's after all a matter of millions and millions of dollars.'

'But wait! What if the numbers are erased exactly as they're embossed?'

'Of course, possible, but there's a problem.'

But before he can proceed, his mobile phone rings. 'Oh, is that so, sir? Yes, that's what I was thinking too. Did you count? All twelve? *Aarey*, no, no, sir, the debt should be to Promotho babu… Hyan, yes, I'm just coming.'

'Where are you off to?'

'Just coming, sir.'

Promotho is in the kitchen. As soon as Ekenbabu leaves, I go in and question him, 'What is it that you said to Ekenbabu? He was all praises for you.'

'What… nothing!'

'Day by day, Ekenbabu is becoming more secretive. Seems there's a positive development with your information.'

'Information? To that chatterbox?'

'We'll know only when he returns.'

Ekenbabu returns in a couple of hours. Not alone, but with Bev. I'm surprised. 'You?'

It's Ekenbabu who answers, 'It's Bev madam's case, sir, how would I solve it without her.'

Bev smiles slyly. And then she clears up the mystery. It seems when she got to Hemant's shop to drop Raju off, she saw Ekenbabu arrive with Captain Stewart to arrest the two workmen. The case of the vanished diamonds had evidently been solved, but the knotted matter of how the money moved had yet to be untangled. Turning to Promotho, Bev continues. 'And thanks to you, the case has been solved.'

'So said Bapi, but I can't figure out how. Now stop behaving like a Mouni Baba, Ekenbabu. Unmute yourself and enlighten us!'

'What are you saying, sir, you who know everything.'

'Know what?'

'Only this, sir, that no matter how overpriced, a diamond is after all pure carbon. And if it can be set on fire, it'll dissolve into the atmosphere as carbon dioxide, leaving no trace behind.'

'I've never told you all this. It's hardly a joke to set a diamond on fire.'

'Absolutely right, but that knowledge came from my own college pass course Chemistry class.'

'Aah! Then say what you really want to say.'

'In a minute, sir. I was doing a little research. I saw that setting a diamond on fire is not at all easy, it would need a huge amount of oxygen. And just then, the worry that was foremost on my mind, vanished. I don't know if you remember, sir, but on that first day, in a corner of the shop, stood the oxygen concentrator that Bev madam had given away. On the second day, it wasn't there. I was slightly surprised. Bapi babu, maybe you don't remember but you questioned me about what I was looking at when there was nothing in front. And I had answered, yes, nothing.'

'I definitely remember that unfocussed look of yours.'

'Yes, sir, I was a little confused. I was trying to figure out why it had been moved from that corner. Then as soon as I saw it in front of the braising table, it clicked. Normally, one can't set diamonds on fire, but if you start a concentrator on full strength and oxygen flows over the diamonds while a braising torch ignites them, then they will burn. Possibly in about four to five hours the diamonds will evaporate into thin air as carbon dioxide.'

'How would it even profit anyone to destroy that many costly diamonds?'

'That's such a fitting observation, sir! This is exactly where the dollar angle comes in. And they must've made a neat profit because of this. Either in this country or back home. But who is paying them? Surely the same businessman who now has this order worth two and a half million dollars. To get that order, he wouldn't mind spending ten or twenty thousand dollars. Now I'm very poor at mathematics, sir, so how much is twenty-five per cent of two and a half million dollars?'

'Five hundred thousand.'

'And there certainly is a profit of twenty to twenty-five per cent in this business, right? With a tiny portion of this amount, he managed to get these workmen on his side. Also, the businessman doesn't have to worry about stolen goods. He is following the law and selling his goods legally. As for the workmen, what is the chance of getting caught with stolen goods? In this case the stones have vanished into the atmosphere, beyond being caught!'

'Even if we accept it right now, how can you be so sure that this is what really happened?'

'Plain good luck, sir. They showed inexperience in burning the diamonds.'

'Correct,' agrees Promotho, 'absolute amateurs. If only they had put liquid oxygen in a quartz beaker and dropped the burning hot diamonds after a braising torch treatment, the stones would have evaporated as carbon dioxide in no time.'

'But there's a problem with that, sir. It would have been difficult to evade the guard while bringing in a liquid oxygen cylinder and the CCTV would have caught it too. But they were sure about the oxygen angle and they were aware that an oxygen concentrator could work. Only time was an issue. Just a few more hours and the diamonds would indeed have evaporated. Tiny bits were left over just because they didn't have enough time. Now, you wouldn't know them as diamond bits. The plan was to vacuum these up and throw them away later. But as soon as the diamond particles showed up in the dustbag, the problem was solved.'

As we speak, Captain Stewart calls Ekenbabu – both workmen have confessed. The Jackson Heights shop owner has been arrested. Captain Stewart hadn't dreamt of the case being solved so swiftly.

Promotho speaks as soon as Ekenbabu hangs up. 'All this is fine, but isn't Stewart sir giving you some medal-shedal?'

'What can I say, sir!'

'Only that which should be said. Please stop all this free service to the cops, will you! And listen, this proves another thing.'

'What, sir?'

'Do you agree now that all your whining the other day about "A diamond is forever" is bogus?'

'I agree, sir, but true love isn't!'

'Really? Do you really believe that true love is forever?'

'Yes, sir, yes, there is no doubt.'

'Now, Bev, you must arrange for your dear detective to be packed off home. Can you see how much he is missing boudi?'

'How cute,' twinkles Bev, and hugs Ekenbabu.

NO THERMOMETER FOR INSANITY

Anirudh Kala

It was a clear winter night and the glow from the signage on top of a shopping mall a short distance away filled the doctors' duty room. Dr Baani Sandhu was on night duty at the sprawling state mental hospital with 257 patients admitted in several wards on the campus. All the patients were asleep after their night medication, as she had been informed on the intercom by the ward nurses.

There were no blinds on the window and when someone had mentioned it to the medical superintendent at the staff meeting, he had snapped, 'Curtains in a mental hospital are a suicide risk and blinds are costly. This is a state hospital in Punjab and not the Mayo Clinic in Minnesota,' reminding all of them that he had spent a month there as an intern twenty years back. 'That is the duty doctor's room,' he had gone on, 'duty doctors do not sleep. And it is not the ground floor, nobody can peep in.'

It had been a hectic day for Baani. She had followed on her scooter, through dusty roads, a wayward husband to a town twenty kilometers away and managed to take pictures of him going into a seedy hotel with a garishly dressed young woman. The money Baani got paid was not much, but the work was exciting. There was a time when this was what she had wanted to become, a detective, preferably a police detective. 'How mundane,' the boyfriend, also a trainee psychiatrist had said, 'identifying with the father.'

It was, however, a bitter father who wanted her to become anything but a police detective. The result, she thought ironically, was the mishmash that she was, a half-hearted trainee psychiatrist and a part-time rookie detective who, courtesy of divorce lawyers, got a trickle of cases.

She cursed the light from the brightly lit signage of the Diamond Mall and wondered almost aloud, 'Who builds a mental hospital next to a shopping mall?' The medical superintendent would have told her it was the other way around. Many years back, the hospital had several old buildings scattered over a vast expanse of land and no money. Land sharks bought most of the land from the government and parcelled it out as a mall, a multiplex and a hotel. The government had made a new building for the hospital and kept the rest of the money. The mental hospital and the glitzy sprawl stood cheek by jowl since then in an uncomfortable juxtaposition. The watchmen at the mall swore that on some nights, in the dark corridor behind the Van Heusen showroom, they heard shrieks of mental patients from earlier times.

She had been away for four days to look after her father who was recovering from a stroke, and there was a lot to catch up on. Nobody expected the night doctor to take rounds of all the patients every night, but she decided to go and see at least the new admissions. That is how she spent the next hour, going from ward to ward, on the women's side first and then the men's side. Male admissions outnumbered females – three to one – and that had always been so. Probably because women were less disruptive when mentally ill and could be managed at home, or, as Baani thought, nobody bothered about women anyway.

The light in the ward had been dimmed. All the patients were deep asleep. Approaching the last bed, her feet stopped abruptly and the nurse carrying the treatment charts stumbled into her. Her surprise was caused by there being a new patient in the bed next to the ward door where Kartar Singh should have been. He was to be discharged the next morning. In fact, she had planned her leave so that she could talk to Kartar Singh before his discharge. A taciturn man, she was the only doctor he talked to.

For all others, when addressed during ward rounds, his response was a stoic silence and a bow with folded hands as if to make up for the rudeness of his silence. The discharge date was sometimes postponed if a patient deteriorated unexpectedly but here it was the opposite. The patient had been discharged early.

'Kartar Singh committed suicide,' the nurse blurted out, 'by jumping down the stairwell. Police came, there was an internal enquiry too. You were on leave.'

Baani went down to the record room and pulled out Kartar Singh's file. She knew everything that was in there because she was the one who had written it, except for the outpatient department (OPD) notes just before admission and the long notations of the previous night written by her substitute right after the 'incident'. Another patient who had woken up at three to go to bathroom had raised the alarm because Kartar Singh was neither in the bathroom nor in his bed. The ward nurse who had gone to another ward to borrow an injection had come running back. On hearing the commotion, the security guard who was manning the exit of the inpatient block had rushed in, only to discover Kartar Singh's frail body lying at the bottom of the stairwell on the basement floor. Since his bed was next to the door, it was just a few steps from his bed to the railing.

After reading the note several times, Baani came up to the duty room and dozed off on the couch, tired as she was from driving around the countryside. When she got up, it was six.

In her three years in Psychiatry, she had not seen any patient less likely to kill himself and she decided to meet the medical superintendent when he came for work at eight.

The medical superintendent was wearing a tie, colour synced with his turban. 'It is his birthday', the clerk had said. And Kartar Singh already seemed far from his mind.

'Oh him, right. What a pity! He would have been discharged today. His wife came yesterday and she was so distraught. She was looking forward to him coming home recovered, after all that unpleasantness.'

'But why would he do that?' she wanted to know.

The medical superintendent was in a teaching mood, 'Psychiatric patients commit suicide far more often than normal people, you know that. And he had a history. There was a serious attempt long before he was married. He did not know how to swim and had jumped into a canal at midnight. An auto driver returning home rescued him. He was admitted for a month under a psychiatrist and recovered, but only after being given electro-convulsive therapy. Come on, you are the one who told us all of this at the case conference!'

'But he was fine till three days before,' Baani tried to interject.

'A previous suicide attempt is a risk factor for a future suicide. You should read about it. It is a common question in an MD examination. And recovering patients are paradoxically more prone to suicide. Probably with treatment, executive functions of the brain recover early on, and while the patient is still in a dark place, he can think better of a plan.

'He was not a recovering patient,' she insisted, 'he was a recovered patient. I had been talking to him every day.' She was already regretting having been away for the last few days.

The MS did not seem to hear her, 'Maybe with recovery, the guilt over having suspected his wife of a non-existent affair had dawned on him. And for having beaten her black and blue for months for that. The last time was bad, the gash on her arm needed to be stitched. He was a sensitive, introspective man. Such people are guilt prone.'

'He was not unduly guilty when I last talked to him. Of course, he said she had suffered a lot, but he rightly blamed his illness and said he was sure his wife understood.'

'I can understand you being upset because he was your favourite patient. All of us have a favourite patient occasionally,' he added not very honestly. He had never had a favourite patient.

Just then his phone rang. It seemed to be his wife, confirming restaurant bookings for the evening.

While he was still on the phone, Baani wished him a happy birthday, came out and drove home. She slept like a log despite the bustling traffic in the lane outside the window of her room. The house was in the maze of lanes around the Golden Temple. When her mother woke her up to eat, it was four. She peeped into her father's room; he was deep asleep with his face to the wall. After his stroke, he had been sleeping during the day. At night he talked to an empty room about fingerprints, suspects, clues and arrests.

She left for the police station early in the morning to avoid traffic. Besides, Inspector Balraj Grewal (Grewal Uncle, as she called him) might go home if there was no active case going on. Balraj Grewal was her father's friend, and he had known Baani since she was a toddler. He was also her father's replacement in the department and was about to retire.

She parked her scooter outside the dhaba next to the police station, waving to the owner and pointing to her scooter. She had been doing this for years. Inside the police station, the yard was filled with cars, jeeps and motorbikes impounded over the years and left to rot in the open. Balraj had worked under Baani's father for years and was a frequent visitor to their house. They discussed work over drinks and even as a schoolgirl, Baani found reasons to hover around him. Balraj always thought she would be a police officer one day. But when she got ninety-three per cent in her school examinations, her father said she would be wasted in the police department. Over the years, he had grown bitter about political meddling in police work. He had let go more suspects than he had arrested.

Balraj had not seen her for months; she had been at work the few times he had gone to meet her father. He did not know about the case, suicides in the mentally ill were below his pay grade. He went out to another room and came back with a slim file. The autopsy report had just come in, the cause of death was blunt injury to the back of the head, probably sustained as the result of impact with the railing during the fall. The contents of the viscera had been sent to the laboratory to rule out poisoning, but that report would take some days. And that was that.

'Seems to be routine.'

'He was my patient,' she said simply.

'And?'

'And I do not think he committed suicide.'

'He had a known history of mental illness and was so disturbed, he needed to be admitted to a mental hospital. So why not? Sometimes things are simple. You are letting your hobby cloud your professional judgment. Trust your boss and let it be.'

Back on night duty, she went down to the record room and pulled out Kartar Singh's file. The outpatient notes, written three months back on the day he was brought in by neighbours, described him as 'dishevelled, frail man of medium height with long hair and beard left open'. The men accompanying him explained that his turban had come off because they had to bring him forcibly as he had refused to board the tractor trolley. The wife was not there with them because another neighbour had taken her to a doctor to get her arm wound stitched. The injury was the result of Kartar Singh having been violent.

The 'current illness' had started four months prior, 'when the patient started accusing his wife of having an affair with an unknown man, whom he had never seen'. He would point to some stains on the bedsheet which he said were semen stains and a proof that a man had been with her. The 'stains' were just patterns in the fabric of the bedsheet. He was also convinced that at night she went to the backyard to signal 'him' in.

When the wife came to the OPD after getting her arm stitched, she said the two times he saw her coming back, she had gone to the toilet in the backyard. The OPD resident had told Baani later that the tall and slim Sarabjeet said candidly that her husband had a low sex drive and it was she who had to initiate the 'playfulness' which she had stopped some months back. Never a talkative man, he had become even more withdrawn and had once said that she must be having sex elsewhere, since 'she could not live without it'. She told him it was because she had a bad back. There were frequent arguments, quarrels and beatings. The outpatient psychiatrist had made a note of bruises of various hues on her legs, arms and back. He had even drawn a diagram.

Kartar Singh went through her phone to check for calls and messages, but he never found anything. He then started staying awake at night to keep a close watch on her. On the previous night, he shook her awake at three in the morning. There was mud on his trousers, his eyes were red and he was breathless. He had kept saying that he had seen some movement in the fields which, according to him, meant a man was lurking there. On seeing Kartar Singh instead of her, the man had run away. He said he had chased after him, but he got away. That is when he slapped her and pushed her against the wall shouting, 'I was right all this time.' A nail in the wall had cut into her arm.

She said his suspiciousness was the result of his own impotence. She showed the doctor a strip of some tablets which he had been taking without any effect. It was a local brand of Viagra.

The OPD psychiatrist had advised admission 'in view of his having been violent and the wife fearing further violence'. Medication was started in the ward, but all it did was keep him groggy. Whenever he was alert, he would be steadfast in his belief that his wife was having a torrid affair. Sarabjeet came to the hospital once a week to see him, but went back after talking to the doctors who advised her against meeting him, as it would upset him further. After the third week, she had stopped coming. Two months had passed with no change in his condition.

However, in the beginning of the third month, it was explained to him that a new medicine for his condition had been formulated the previous year and had now become available in India. When he agreed, the medication was started. The very next day, he showed dramatic improvement. He accepted the possibility that he could have been wrong all along. On the second day, he regretted having suspected his wife over 'absolutely nothing'. It was indeed a mental illness, he said, probably a relapse of the same which had made him jump into a canal many years back, long before he was married.

He still talked remarkably little with nurses or with other patients. But that was his original temperament, his 'pre-morbid personality', the seniors said. After Kartar Singh had been stable for more than two weeks, his wife was called in so she could meet him. She too found him recovered and completely rid of his suspicions. He apologized for having treated her badly because of his illness and promised to take the medication for as long as the doctors advised him to. That was when his discharge was planned and Sarabjeet was told he would be sent home the following week.

Baani read the two short notes written by her on two consecutive days about his dramatic improvement several times. There was something amiss there.

It was already 2 a.m. She went back to the duty room, made coffee, and stood near the window, looking through the fog at the blood red Levi's sign on top of the mall. It was going to be another cold day, the forecast had said. Cold and grey.

And then the obvious explanation struck her – Kartar Singh had faked his recovery. To get out of the hospital. In his mind, he was not ill, never was. And if he kept telling the truth, his truth, he would never be discharged. So why not speak the truth the doctors were so keen to hear after the new drug was started. And they – Baani included – were so excited with the result, they forgot that no anti-psychotic drug made delusions vanish in one day. Drugs produced changes in the brain chemicals and that took a few days at least.

So far so good; but why would he kill himself? The thing furthest from the mind of a person, who has successfully cheated highly qualified doctors in order to go home, would be to kill himself two days before his discharge.

Guilt, the MS had said. Guilt over having blamed his wife of an abominable deed she had never committed. But why would there be any guilt if he still believed his wife did have an affair behind his back?

Jumping from a height of thirty feet to the basement floor was neither a neat nor a sure way of dying, she thought. The back of his head had hit the railing as he was falling, but suppose it had not. He could have ended up with a fractured spine, paralysed for life. Maybe that was the reason why no patient had tried it before, although two had killed themselves over the last ten years by hanging themselves with their turbans from the shower in the bathroom. And a man who jumps on his own, aims for the floor, is less likely to hit a railing on the way down, than a struggling man who is hefted and thrown down.

Baani knew what she was going to do. She also knew it could come to nothing. There was a week left of her night duty, and after that she would be working morning till evening and there would be no daytime left, as Grewal Uncle put it, to 'pursue her hobby'. Kartar Singh's admission form had been signed by one Surinder Singh since his wife was still getting her arm stitched when the formalities were being gone through. The 'relationship to patient' was filled in as 'neighbour', who had even provided his phone number.

Baani went home and waited for the fog to clear. It would be worse in the countryside because of moisture in the fields. By the time she reached the village, it was ten. She had been told by Surinder Singh on phone that their bunch of houses was not in the village proper but spread out in the middle of the field half a kilometre away. The path to Surinder Singh's house was all slush from the rain a few days back. He turned out to be a sprightly man of seventy-five who lived there with his wife. A son and daughter lived in Canada and the old couple were waiting for their immigration papers to come through so they could join them. He offered her tea and was apologetic for the access to the house being difficult. The farmers who lived in the fields were not keen to invest money on laying down proper roads to their house because all of them were going to sell their lands sooner or later, she was told. It seemed the land prices had sky-rocketed after a four-lane highway had come up not far from their fields.

She managed to steer the conversation to Kartar Singh.

'Yes, what a tragedy. His wife is devastated, and they have an eight-year-old child! Even on the parents' side, she only has an aged father living in U.P.'

'We at the hospital are a bit curious about Kartar Singh's suicide and wondered if you could help us with some information. We could not find any reason at our end.' This was rather stretching it since nobody at the hospital was curious except her. In fact, doctors were not supposed to visit homes or neighbourhoods of patients, dead or alive.

Pulling his chair closer to Baani's, Surinder Singh asked his wife for more tea.

'We are old people and we keep to ourselves. It was different when Bahadur Singh, Kartar's father, was alive. He came over every other evening and we would have a drink. He, unlike his son, liked to meet people. He was a panchayat member and very helpful even towards strangers. When his wife died, Kartar was just fifteen. The next crisis in that house was seven years later when Kartar jumped into a canal and was rescued by a passer-by. He got electric treatments and recovered. Bahadur Singh was a wise and far-sighted man. He had been told by the doctors that future relapses were highly likely. With that in mind, Bahadur Singh wrote a will that after his death all his land should be transferred not just to his son Kartar as the sole heir but jointly to him and Sarabjeet, since he considered her wise and prudent.

'I wondered if you could tell me something about Kartar's suspicions against his wife and the fights the two had.'

'Well, like I said, we are an old couple and keep to ourselves. Kartar Singh hardly ever came to meet us. Sarabjeet did. She would often pass through here on her scooter as she dropped off her son at the bus stop and she would often drop by on her way back. She is friendly and peppy, the exact opposite of what her husband was. Right now, she is crestfallen and my wife says she has not eaten for three days.'

'The women in the village like her. She used to go to all the family functions and celebrations in the village. Both husband and wife were invited, of course, but most of the times, she would turn up alone. She was the one who went to school for parent teacher meetings, for shopping. Also, Kartar, unlike his father, was a teetotaller and that, you know, in these parts, can reduce the number of men you fraternize with by a lot.'

Baani was getting impatient. The fog had disappeared, there would be traffic on the way back and she needed to sleep before her night duty, 'Did she say anything about…'

'Beeba ji,' Surinder's tone had become patronizing now, 'the misunderstanding between husband and wife that you mention, we know very little about. Most people admired Sarabjeet for living all these years with a man as difficult as him. I do not want to speak ill of the dead, especially so soon, but that was the opinion of most people in the village, even the women. Particularly the women. The whole village turned up for the cremation, more for her than for him, to be frank.'

'We are not even the nearest neighbours. Succha and his family are, and his son Davinder goes to that house a lot, I have heard. He would know.' Baani thought there was an amused twinkle in his eyes just for a fleeting moment when he said that.

'He works in the city as a tourist guide, probably part time, since I see him loitering around here most of the time. I can give you his number, but do not tell him you got it from me.' Baani was not sure if he was pointing her towards something or just trying to get rid of her. 'Those villagers', her father had once said, 'hide more and tell less.'

Balraj told her, when she called him, she was wasting her time and he was worried for her. 'Your MD examination is in one year. Your father, when he recovers, is going to be angry with me for not having stopped you from wasting your time. He is going to ask, "I was not well, but what had happened to you?"'

He was right, Baani thought. She studied after night rounds and managed to cover a lot of ground. When the night duty finished, she had two days all to herself. While scrolling through her phone, she came upon the name Davinder and promised herself, she will wait for two rings and no more. The phone was picked up right away.

Baani introduced herself. 'I am from the mental hospital, following up on the tragic suicide of Kartar Singh, we call it psychological autopsy. This understanding helps us to prevent future suicides.'

She was getting better at that at least, she thought.

They met at a cafe inside the Diamond Mall. Davinder was a tall and good-looking man, clean-shaven with a crew cut and not the turbaned farmer with a beard that she had expected. As it turned out, he had never been a farmer. It was his father who looked after all the farmwork. Davinder had been in the army and now worked as a tour guide at the city heritage walk. He said they were the same age and went to the same school. 'He was very good at studies and everybody thought he would go to college.' There was this thing again about Kartar Singh being a highly introverted man who hardly ever started a conversation. 'But he was quite playful with his son.' Davinder had seen him teaching his son badminton in the backyard where he had set up a proper net.

'I rather liked him; he could be aloof but also intimate. We talked across the vegetable patch regularly, and sometimes I would go over to join them for badminton.'

'No, I did not see anyone come to meet her. Very few people come that way because the path peters out. It is the last house and any stranger would have been noticed.'

'And at night? In the backyard through the fields?'

'There is no light in the fields and half the time, the crops are tall enough to hide a person if he does not want to be seen. In the winters, it is impossible because of the fog.'

'How often did you see Sarabjeet?' It seemed abrupt and out of context, but she thought she had to ask.

Just then his phone, which was lying on table, rang. Davinder excused himself and walked several feet away to take the call. When he came back, he looked distracted and told her, 'That is pretty much all I know. I have been called back to work. There is a group of tourists ready and waiting for me.' That was a lie because Baani had seen the name Sarabjeet flash on the screen before he had hurriedly picked up the phone.

Her first thought was, of course, nobody saw a man going to Kartar Singh's house at night, because the man was from right next door. When she called Balraj he was dismissive, 'Just because the neighbour is good looking does not mean Sarabjeet is having an affair with him. And it is understandable for neighbours to call each other.'

'But why hide it?'

'My guess is you scared him with your awkward questioning. You are not trained; this is not your job anyway.' That made her feel low for the rest of the day and she was surprised when in the evening, she received a call from Davinder's phone, but it was his wife wanting to meet her. They met the next morning in the hospital cafeteria.

'My husband has a feeling you suspect him of having an affair with Sarabjeet. This is not true. I can assure you. When he was talking to you, she called him just to remind him about some arrangements at the gurudwara about Kartar's memorial service.'

There was a pause, while she kept stirring sugar in her tea. 'However, Sarabjeet does have an affair. And I do not blame her. What does one do if one's husband not only has a sexual problem but also does not talk for days and the only time he opens his mouth is to suspect her of meeting someone at night? His suspicions and the fights had started long before she met this man.'

The affair, she said, was a reaction to and not the cause of his morbid suspicions. 'Like he is going to keep suspecting and beating me anyway for having sex with someone, so why not! It was also her way of getting back at Kartar.'

'He, his name is Jinda, never came to meet her in the middle of the night, that part was Kartar's madness. He did not have to, they met outside. Almost every day at his friend's apartment when her son was in school. I did not tell my husband because he liked Kartar Singh and would have told him. Also, because Sarabjeet talked to me woman to woman, even if she did not tell me all the details. She did show me his picture on her phone. He is good looking and quite well built, like a gym instructor. I know that he is not from our village. I do not know his full name or what he does for a living, but I know that he is planning to migrate to Canada where his uncle owns a petrol pump. It is a fling since both know he is going away soon.'

After her OPD, Baani stopped by at Balraj's office. 'I told you something was amiss. You should take some action. At least call in Sarabjeet for questioning.'

'For what? Since when is an extra-marital affair a crime?' Baani was unhappy because Balraj was not even acknowledging that her instinct had been at least partially right.

'But she railroaded her husband to a forced admission in a mental hospital based on him having a delusion of infidelity which she knew to be factual not delusional.'

'An act in which psychiatrists of the mental hospital including you collaborated, not knowingly of course.'

She was now defensive on behalf of her whole discipline. 'It is far more complex than that. His delusion started long before the affair which was a reaction of a wife trapped in an abusive marriage. What made us believe that it was a delusion from day one was the bizarreness of his ideas, his insistence that a man came to their home at the dead of night to meet her knowing he would be home. A man nobody saw and the dogs did not bark at. The delusion of infidelity predated the actual infidelity by a year and then both got intertwined. In the end, there was no way to know how much was real and how much imagined. Unfortunately, there is no test for mental illness and no thermometer for insanity.'

Balraj was not impressed, 'I get it. But it is your mess and I hope you all learn from it. Where is the crime though? The man is dead. He killed himself. The viscera report has come in, he was not poisoned. The main door of the inpatient block remains locked from the inside till six in the morning. From ten at night to six in the morning, that whole block is like one locked room. As far as I am concerned, the case is closed. There never was one. Unless you are suggesting the preposterous possibility that another patient or a well-built staffer picked him up and threw him down the stairwell just for the heck of it, since there could not have been any motive.'

What stayed with her were words, 'locked room', 'motive' and 'well built'. Well built, like a gym instructor. With a motive. She called up her colleague who was going to be on duty that night and offered to do it for him, since she had to sit up at night and study and there was a noisy '*jagrata*' next to her house. Exchanging night duties was a common practice.

It was 1.30 a.m. by the time she finished her rounds. The tubelight in the record room was flickering and she had to use the torch on her phone. According to Davinder's wife, the man's name was Jinda which is often a nickname in Punjab for men whose names end with 'jinder' such as Rajinder, Harjinder, Gurjinder and so on. Baani knew it was not easy for a person pretending to be mentally ill to be admitted to the hospital. But it had been done before when the hospital was in the old building and patients were kept in poor conditions. A journalist, posing as a patient of schizophrenia, wanted to write about the human rights violations of the mentally ill and had gotten himself admitted to the hospital. He had managed to stay for a whole month and his article about bad food, corruption and the beating up of patients had created a furore.

In Kartar Singh's file, she looked for the date on which his discharge from the hospital had been finalized and communicated to his wife. Next, she looked for male patients admitted between that date and the day of Kartar Singh's death. With the records computerized two years back, it took her two minutes to find what she was looking for. There were nineteen male patients admitted in those six days and the names of three of them ended with 'jinder'. And one of those three was a 'voluntary' patient and had come to the hospital alone! Complaints? Intense sadness, unable to sleep and suicidal thoughts There were many patients who came to the OPD alone for consultations, but when it came to the ones needing admission, they were always accompanied by someone, and involuntary admission was the rule, voluntary, exception. But here he was, Japinder Singh, 35 years, male, physical education teacher by occupation, purportedly suicidal, had come alone and was admitted as a voluntary patient.

He was admitted two days after Kartar Singh's discharge was finalized and he had been sent to the ward just across the landing from his ward! Baani tried to look for the date of discharge and a shudder went down her body. The column was blank, which meant that he was still there!

Baani came out of the record room praying the lights would not go off and walked quickly past the spot where Kartar Singh's body had been found on the basement floor. She sprinted up the stairs and had a strong urge to peep into the ward where Japinder would be. From there to Kartar's bed in the ward across the landing would have been a twenty-second walk.

It was 2.30 a.m. She grabbed her phone and called Balraj. Balraj was alert in an instant and listened intently for what must have been two or three minutes and then told her to stay put in the duty room. 'Do not come out. You have done your job.'

Japinder Singh was taken into custody half an hour later, on the suspicion of having murdered Kartar Singh. Next day, Sarabjeet, when called to the police station, confessed to having an affair with Japinder for more than six months. She said she had been accused of and beaten up for being unfaithful for a whole year before she had even met Japinder at her son's school where he was a physical training instructor. He had bought her a phone which Kartar Singh was not aware of and they talked and messaged several times a day.

After Kartar's admission to the hospital, she was told by Japinder and many other friends too that such an illness was untreatable. At that point, the two started talking about her getting a divorce from Kartar Singh on the grounds of his insanity, getting married and immigrating to Canada along with her son. Preliminary enquiries with immigration agents had already been made, she said, which the police later confirmed. However, when she met Kartar Singh in the hospital after his unexpected recovery, she had second thoughts. She just wanted a normal family life and she had her eight-year-old son to think about. She had told Japinder about her hospital visit and Kartar's recovery. According to her, Japinder looked crestfallen after he heard this. However, she had no inkling about his intentions or that he had gotten himself admitted to the hospital. He had told her he was going to meet a cousin in a remote village in the hills of Garhwal where the phone signal was poor. The phone records proved they had not been in touch after that day.

Japinder, according to her, was counting on Kartar Singh being in the hospital for a long time, probably permanently, as he could not have foreseen him saying he was wrong about the affair since he was not.

According to the police, when he heard about Kartar Singh having recovered unexpectedly, Japinder's whole plan came unstuck. The untreatable mental illness as grounds for a divorce had disappeared overnight as had the property, half of which would have come to Sarabjeet after the divorce, since she was the joint owner. Balraj's opinion during a meeting with his superior was that Sarabjeet may not have been a co-conspirator in the plan, but she suspected what Japinder was going to do and could have stopped him if she wanted to.

'*Suspected* is just a state of mind,' his superior had said, 'it needs proof and there is none. Let us not be overambitious.'

According to the prosecution, as the government lawyer explained in court, the real motive of the murder was the forty acres of land that Kartar and Sarabjeet jointly owned, price of which had skyrocketed after a highway had come up nearby. And the money invested in Canada would have helped not just in getting fast track immigration visas for all three of them but also a snug future.

During the trial, the defence argued that Japinder's mental illness was real and him being in the hospital at the same time as the unfortunate incident of another patient's suicide, happened to be a coincidence. The psychiatrist who had admitted him testified that Japinder was indeed depressed and suicidal at the time of admission. No laboratory investigation was done to confirm it since none was available. The prosecutor argued that the psychiatrist could not have said anything else in the court, without proving his incompetence and possible debarment by the medical council.

Japinder was convicted of murder by the sessions court and sentenced to life imprisonment. However, the High Court upturned the conviction saying, in the absence of any actual evidence or witness, mere presence of the accused in the same building did not connect him to the actual murder beyond reasonable doubt. The judges also expressed doubt about how the accused could have forcibly carried the victim away from his bed without waking up other patients, even if the nurse had gone to another ward to borrow an injection. About his pretending to be mentally ill and getting himself admitted to the hospital at the opportune time, the court said there was nothing on record to say that the mental illness was feigned. He was examined by a duly qualified government psychiatrist and then admitted to the mental hospital. The medical board which had examined Japinder six months after his arrest had been equivocal in its findings saying: although he did not have any mental illness at the time of examination, a mental illness in the recent past could neither be confirmed nor ruled out.

Baani's father has long recovered and when told by Balraj about the case which his daughter helped crack even if conviction was later set aside, said while sipping his whiskey, 'It seems to be an easy case. Whenever lucre, woman and land appear together, a murder must be around the corner.' The words he used were Punjabi words '*zar, joru* and *zameen*'.

Japinder and Sarabjeet are married and live in Calgary, Canada along with her teenage son and their three-year-old daughter. They own four petrol pumps and are planning to buy another one.

Dr Baani Sandhu is a forensic psychiatrist and works at the police training institute.

TOKYO ROSE

Tamilvanan, tr. Pritham K. Chakravarthy

Tokyo, capital of Japan! The cars seemed to outnumber the people. A few pedestrians, having parked their cars on the side of the road, went about their shopping like pretty butterflies. The roads were jammed full of automobiles of many different makes and models.

One of them was driven by Shankarlal, king of detectives, with his beautiful wife, Indra, seated beside him. Indra was eyeing the shop windows as the car crept slowly forward. Shankarlal, irritated, loosened his tie. The traffic jam was so bad it had taken over half an hour to move just a furlong. The car in front of him stopped completely and he cut the engine.

The shop owners were just beginning to open their shops, displaying their wares lined up in the windows.

'Indra,' said Shankarlal. She turned towards him, smiling. 'Looks like we might be spending the whole day here! It seems that every fourth person in Japan owns a car now,' he continued.

'What's this road called?' Indra asked.

'The names of these Japanese streets are very difficult to remember – let alone the names of Japanese people! But at the last crossing we passed a signboard that said Mitsubishi Avenue. Didn't you see it?'

'I did see it, but I forgot it already,' replied Indra.

The car ahead of them moved an inch. Shankarlal followed it.

'It's nine o'clock, people are in a hurry to get to work. The traffic will be backed up for another couple of hours,' said Shankarlal.

'So let them be in a hurry. Why do we have to join the battle?' asked Indra. 'We came here for a holiday.'

Shankarlal had a good idea of what was coming next. He asked her anyway. 'What do you want to do, Indra?'

'Let's just park the car here and go into one of these shops and browse around for a while. The traffic will ease up by that time,' said Indra.

Shankarlal laughed. 'I've heard that there's nothing you can't find here on Mitsubishi Avenue. It's hard to resist. You're right, it'll be better than sitting stuck in this traffic.'

He parked along the white line and they got out. The car had been their first purchase upon arriving in Tokyo. Indra looked at it with pride. '*Athaan*, we must take this car back to India with us when we return,' she said.

'I'm going to need to hire a separate cargo ship to take back all your purchases,' he teased. He locked the car and they headed toward the shops.

The stores were stocked with everything from the latest car models to the newest games and catered to tourists from all over the world. The salespersons were Japanese, well trained in Western etiquette.

Indra entered a toy shop. There were four beautiful saleswomen. One of them walked up to them and gave a silent gesture of welcome. Shankarlal and Indra walked through the aisles eyeing the toys.

Another saleswoman was wiping away some invisible dust from a countertop with a wet rag. Suddenly, the rag turned blue! The woman's clothes turned blue too. Yelling, she rushed to a sink at the back of the store to wash. Blue water gushed from the tap.

Pandemonium broke out. Indra looked around fearfully, but Shankarlal remained calm. Another saleswoman had touched the countertop and found her hands turning blue as well.

'What's going on? Why is everything turning blue?' wondered Indra.

'Be patient. Take care not to touch anything, or lean on the shelves,' replied Shankarlal and went to take a closer look.

Just then, loud screams were heard from the road outside. He rushed out. At the hotel next door, there was a crowd of Japanese talking excitedly amongst themselves. Shankarlal went up to them. He could not understand exactly what was being said, but their panic was obvious. He peered into the hotel. On the tables were teacups with blue tea in them.

'What happened?' he asked.

'I don't know!' the agitated manager replied. 'The tables have all been suddenly stained blue. The tea's turned blue too. The customers think I'm trying to poison them.'

Shankarlal came back out and joined Indra.

'I'm scared to even stand here,' said Indra. 'The saleswomen have fled the shop! One girl was saying that this is all because of the nuclear experiments that America and Russia are carrying out; she said invisible particles of the atom bomb are floating in the air and turning everything blue. Could it be true?' she asked.

Shankarlal looked back at the road. A thick crowd had gathered. Terrified that another nuclear holocaust had hit, the people ran around in circles, gripped by abject fear. A man came rushing out of a barbershop, his face covered with foam. 'The soap in the salon has turned blue!' he shouted. 'It must be the atom bomb! No one who's touched the blue stuff will survive!' He took to his heels, not even pausing to wipe the foam off his face.

In the following few minutes, the cars lining the road disappeared. A police squad arrived and began making inquiries in the shops. Not knowing how to respond to the widespread terror, the police called on the fire squad for help. Fire trucks drew up, clanging their bells, but when they began to hose down the shops, the water that gushed out from the tanks was blue. The policemen and firemen stood with their mouths hanging open, scared to move.

'*Athaan*, please! Let's get away from here! I'm frightened,' said Indra.

Silent and determined, Shankarlal walked back to the car. The police commissioner had arrived; they ducked quickly into his vehicle to avoid being spotted.

Shankarlal sped away from the scene, never taking his eyes off the road.

'It's bizarre. Why did everything turn blue? Do you think it really could have been caused by an atom bomb?' asked Indra.

Shankarlal did not reply; he just concentrated on his driving. He turned the car down a side street.

'Where are you going? This isn't the way to our house,' said Indra. The car turned again, down a narrow lane and came to halt in front of an apartment building.

Shankarlal got out and Indra followed. 'Who are we visiting?'

'Just follow me. I'll explain later.'

They climbed the steps. Shankarlal's leather-soled shoes made no noise. They walked up to the fourth floor, where he began checking the nameplates on each door. He stopped at a door which had a bicycle propped against the wall next to it. The nameplate read HIROSHI WAKIYAMA.

Shankarlal knocked. A thick Japanese voice replied from within and the door opened. A man looked out at them curiously. Shankarlal shoved his way past him into the room. He seemed to be searching for something.

'What do you want? What are you looking for?' asked Wakiyama, in English.

Shankarlal did not reply; he walked straight into an adjoining room. On the floor was a blue sack, open at the mouth. Dark blue powder had spilled from the sack onto the floor.

Smiling, Shankarlal turned back to Wakiyama. 'Did you come home just now, with this sack on the back of your cycle?'

'Yes,' replied Wakiyama. 'Why do you ask?'

'Because you have sent the entire city of Tokyo into a panic!'

'What kind of powder is that?' asked Indra.

'Indra, be patient. Mr Wakiyama, am I correct in surmising that while you were riding down Mitsubishi Avenue, this sack fell off your cycle?' asked Shankarlal.

'Yes,' replied Wakiyama, still not understanding what this was all about.

'And there was a heavy gust of breeze?' asked Shankarlal.

'Yes, you're right. The sack broke open and a lot of the powder spilled out. So what?'

'You should go have a look down Mitsubishi Avenue. You've nearly caused a riot. Everything there has turned blue! The fire squad has started washing the avenue down. The people are scared that it's nuclear fallout. When the powder fell on the road, it wasn't visible to the naked eye. But if even a tiny amount comes in contact with water, it turns the water blue.'

Wakiyama laughed out loud. Indra still looked worried and confused.

Only Shankarlal stayed calm. 'See? My hand has turned blue now, because of the sweat.'

Wakiyama said with a smile, 'You still don't get what it is?'

'Yes, I think I know.'

'Tell me, then.'

'Ink powder, correct?'

'Absolutely! I invented this stuff. The ink is bright and clear when mixed with water; the letters glow and can even be read in the dark. I had taken it over to a pen company, to try to sell it to them. But they rejected my invention. I was on my way back, disappointed, when it all happened as you said.'

'I followed your cycle tracks. That was how I found you. Please contact the police immediately and tell them what happened. They might never guess this.'

'I will, at once. Please tell me who you are. You both look very familiar, but I don't seem to recall your names. Do you visit Tokyo frequently?' asked Wakiyama.

Shankarlal replied with a smile, 'I've been here a few times, but I don't think I've had the pleasure of meeting you before. I am Shankarlal and this is my wife, Indra.'

Wakiyama was taken aback. 'Shankarlal? Really? The famous detective? Yes, I've often seen your photos in the newspaper! Now that I think of it, I did read that you were visiting Tokyo. Please, have a seat! I've heard you're fond of tea. We Japanese make the best tea in the world.'

Excitedly, he rushed to kitchen to make tea. He lit the stove and then came back to make a telephone call. He spoke to the police commissioner for over five minutes, explaining what had happened.

He returned with three cups of hot tea. But just as Shankarlal was going to take a sip, the tea turned blue. He set his cup aside with a laugh.

'What's wrong?' asked Wakiyama anxiously.

'It's okay, Wakiyama. Just the effects of your new invention. I suppose this will last for a few more days – but not to worry. We should be going.'

Shankarlal and Indra had rented a bungalow in the quiet suburbs of Tokyo. That evening, the police commissioner dropped by to thank Shankarlal for his help in solving that morning's mystery. Madhu, Shankarlal's elderly butler, served them tea. On seeing him, the commissioner asked, 'So, you've brought Madhu along too. How about Kathrikai and Manickam,[4] what have you done with them?'

'If we had brought them, we would have had to bring their wives along as well. Then we would never have been able to get any rest,' said Indra.

After the commissioner had left, the telephone rang. Madhu answered the phone, but quickly put the receiver down and walked back to Shankarlal. 'I don't think I'm of any use to you here in Japan. I can't understand a word of what the person at the other end of the line is saying! It's a woman's voice, but I don't know what she wants.'

---

[4] Kathrikai and Manickam are Shankarlal's driver and gardener, respectively, back home in Chennai. The nickname Kathrikai, which means 'eggplant', derives from the fact that he is rather portly and has a tuft of hair which sticks up from his head.

Indra took the call instead. The woman spoke rapidly in Japanese.

'What do you want? Please speak in English. Do you know English?'

'I do, I do. I'm sorry; I didn't even realize I was speaking in Japanese. Is this Indra? Shankarlal's wife?' the woman said in English.

'Yes, this is she. What do you want?'

'I need your help. You are the only ones who can help me now. I'm in great danger. Please save me!'

'How did you get this number?'

'I'll explain that later. Please, promise that you will help me! I need to give you some important information.'

'What kind of danger are you in?'

'There's no time to give you details. Please, will you please come to my house immediately?'

'Right now?'

'Yes, now! This very moment! You can save a woman's life. Please bring Shankarlal along.'

'Why don't you go to the police?'

'That wouldn't be of any use. Besides, I can't go to them…'

Even as the woman was speaking, there was the loud *rat-a-tat-a-tatn* of a machine gun, the sound of shattering glass and then a dull thud.

'Hello? Hello?' called Indra. But there was no reply, only the sound of a car speeding away.

'*Athaan*!' she shouted.

Shankarlal was by her side at once.

'Indra, what happened?'

'There was a woman at the other end who said she was in danger and wanted to see us at once. Then I heard gunfire. Now the line is silent,' she replied fearfully.

'Don't disconnect the call. I will try to find out where the call was made from using the other telephone in the bedroom.'

Within a few moments, he learned from the telephone operator that the call was made from a public booth, at an intersection a mile away from their bungalow.

They ran out to the car. He tried asking Indra to stay behind, but to no avail. 'I have to know who this woman is and if she is safe. I'll drive, you tell me the way,' she insisted.

Indra drove and she drove fast. The bright streetlamps bathed the city in light.

There was a crowd gathered at the shattered phone booth. Police vans were already at the scene.

'Is she dead?' Indra gasped.

'You stay in the car. I'll go and find out,' Shankarlal told her and hurried to the scene.

The police investigator recognized him. 'Welcome, Mr Shankarlal. I'm glad you're here in Tokyo, to help us with this murder case.'

He looked inside the booth. A Japanese woman lay dead on the ground. Her back and the walls of the phone booth were riddled with bullet holes.

'Who is this woman?' he asked the policeman.

'We don't know that yet.'

'Who are you waiting for?'

'For the commissioner. We've been told not to remove the body until he can inspect the scene of the crime. He should be here soon.'

'Will you let me know as soon as you get some details about this woman? I am very interested in this case.'

He rushed back to the car. The crowd had recognized him by now and ran forward to shake his hand and get his autograph. He jumped into the passenger seat and told Indra to drive away fast.

'Why don't we wait for the commissioner?' asked Indra.

'We're just here as visitors in Tokyo. I don't want to step on any toes.'

'How did the murder happen?'

'That's not difficult to guess. She was shot while she was speaking to you on the phone.'

When they returned to their bungalow, Madhu asked, '*Thambi*, this is such a beautiful city, with such lovely people. How could such a horrible crime happen here?'

Shankarlal replied with a wry smile, 'Madhu, you have not yet understood Tokyo. We must accept the fact that there are as many evil people here as there are good ones.'

At that moment, the telephone rang. Madhu answered it apprehensively. He heard a male voice, speaking in Tamil, say he was coming to meet Shankarlal at once.

'Did he give his name?' asked Shankarlal.

'No, he didn't. But he sounded frightened,' replied Madhu.

It was already ten, well past Indra's bedtime. Shankarlal often went to bed much later, staying up with a book. But tonight, he was not interested in reading and Indra was too rattled to sleep.

'I thought we came to Tokyo to rest and have a holiday,' grumbled Indra, disgustedly.

Madhu intervened with a laugh. 'I used to have the same complaint before *thambi* got married. Now it's your turn. I seriously think that to get any real rest and relaxation, the two of you will need to travel to a deserted island somewhere. Even then the police may track you down for help.'

'Madhu, people look to us when they are in danger. It is our duty to help them. People come running to me when they know I am the only one who can save them. But look what happened to this poor woman, this evening! She died before I could even find out her name. How can I rest until I find the killer?' asked Shankarlal.

'That woman is dead. She cannot be brought back to life. I have no doubt you will find the murderer. But I can't understand who this Tamil man could be, demanding to see you at this late hour,' said Indra.

'Be patient,' advised Shankarlal. 'We'll find out soon enough.' He was now expecting two visitors: the police commissioner and the stranger.

He stayed silent throughout his dinner. Shankarlal was used to crime scene investigations and dead bodies. He could drive the most horrible scenes out of his mind and casually sit down for a meal. But Indra was not so indifferent; had she laid eyes on the murdered woman, she would not have been able to eat.

Just as they finished their dinner, the doorbell rang. Madhu opened the door to reveal a man of about thirty – tall, with strong features, dressed in expensive clothes and shoes.

'I have come to meet Shankarlal. I called earlier.'

Madhu let him in. When the stranger saw Shankarlal, he looked apologetic. 'I am sorry to disturb you at this hour,' he said.

Shankarlal could tell the man was greatly disturbed; he was sweating profusely.

'Can I get you some water?'

The man nodded. Madhu brought a glass of water, which the man drank in one gulp.

'You look as if you've had a good scare.'

'It's true.'

'What's your name?' asked Shankarlal.

'My name is Mudikondan. You've probably never heard of me in Tamil Nadu. But you would have heard of my wife. We came to Tokyo very recently,' said the man.

'Who is your wife?'

He took a moment before responding. 'Neelavalli, the film actress.'

Indra sat up in surprise. 'Neelavalli? I haven't missed a single one of her films! But when did she get married? I never read anything about that!' she exclaimed.

Mudikondan replied with a smile, 'We got married three months back. But we kept it under wraps. We had planned to make an announcement after we returned from our honeymoon.'

'But why would you keep your marriage a secret?' asked Shankarlal.

'Because that was what Neelavalli wanted to do.'

'But why?'

'She was a little superstitious about it. She had an idea that her popularity would wane if the marriage was publicized. There are four of her films to be released over the next three months. She wanted the marriage to remain a secret until then,' said Mudikondan.

'How funny! I thought secret relationships like that only happened in Hollywood. To think that our film stars are the same!' said Indra.

'But I can't keep it a secret any longer. I have come to beg for Shankarlal's help. I believe that my wife is in great danger.'

'What's the trouble?' asked Shankarlal calmly.

'This morning we went shopping on Mitsubishi Avenue. There was a panic there about things turning blue. I asked her to remain in the car while I went to find out what was happening. When I returned, she had disappeared.'

'And then?' asked Shankarlal.

'I thought that perhaps she had become frightened waiting there in the car alone and had returned home. I got a cab and went back to my place. But she wasn't there.'

'When did she come back?' asked Indra.

'She still hasn't. I don't know where she is! I contacted all the hospitals to find out if she had an accident or something, but it was no use. I read that you were here, so I came to you for help.'

'How did you know where to find us?'

'I bribed a newspaper reporter. Three hundred yen.'

'Where do you think your wife is?'

'I think she's been abducted,' said Mudikondan.

'Was she wearing a lot of gold?' asked Indra.

'She only wears a lot of gold on screen. She left all her costly jewels back in India.'

'Was she carrying money?'

'A little change, perhaps. She wouldn't have been abducted for that. I am sure I'm going to be contacted soon by the kidnappers.'

'So how did you come to the conclusion that she's been kidnapped for ransom?'

'This is my reason. A week ago, she appeared on television here and was interviewed about the Indian film world. That interview was telecast all over Japan. She had many visitors after that, especially Japanese women. She struck up a friendship with one of them – an insurance agent. Neelavalli found her charming.'

'Did she ask Neelavalli to insure herself?'

'Neelavalli has already been insured for a huge amount in India. But this woman told her about a new scheme.'

'What scheme?' asked Shankarlal.

'Everybody knows that Neelavalli is extremely wealthy. Because of that, there's always a risk of her being kidnapped. This woman offered a scheme whereby in such a case, the insurance company would pay the kidnappers to release her.'

'How strange! How could the police allow such a scheme?'

'Without receiving a ransom, a kidnapper would not let the person escape alive. The police allow the scheme in order to save lives. Then, they set traps to catch the perpetrators after the ransom has been paid.'

'What if the person is still murdered, even after the ransom is paid?' asked Indra.

'It could happen, after all,' said Shankarlal. 'They might kill her, fearing that she would be able to identify them.'

Mudikondan was visibly shaken.

'That's why I need you. You have to help me get her back alive,' he begged.

'Who knows that she has taken this insurance policy?'

'No one but me. The Japanese insurance saleswoman assured us that it would be kept confidential.'

'How much has she been insured for?'

'She has been insured for 70,00,00,000 yen. The policy is valid for the duration of her stay in Japan.'

'You are convinced that she's been kidnapped. Well then, there's not much we can do until you are contacted,' said Shankarlal.

Just then the telephone rang. Shankarlal answered it.

'Is this Shankarlal?' asked a Japanese woman at the other end.

'Yes.'

'Listen carefully. Neelavalli is safe. Get the 70 crore yen ready within two days. I'll call again and tell you the drop spot; you'll come there alone and hand over the money. This is the only way you can help Mudikondan. Understand?'

'Yes,' replied Shankarlal.

'The money should be brought in notes of 100.'

'Yes. Can I ask your name?'

'My name?' she laughed. 'My name is Tokyo Rose.' Then the line went dead.

Shankarlal turned to Mudikondan. 'They must have known you were here. They want 70 crore yen as ransom.'

'What are we going to do?' asked Indra.

'I'm going to collect the money from the insurance company and take it myself,' said Shankarlal.

He took Mudikondan by the arm and rushed with him to the car.

They drove to the Government Medical Hospital. There were a pair of police vans waiting outside. The policeman escorted Mudikondan alone into the hospital, while Shankarlal waited in the car. When Mudikondan returned, his face had gone pale.

'What is it?' asked Shankarlal.

'I had a look at the body. It's her – the Japanese woman, the insurance agent. They have riddled her beautiful body with bullets. How sad!' replied Mudikondan.

They drove away. After some time, Mudikondan broke the silence.

'Who could have killed that woman?'

'There's no way of knowing for sure yet,' replied Shankarlal. 'But I have a guess.'

'Can you tell me?'

'She must have been killed by the same kidnappers who took your wife.'

'I don't get it.'

'I don't think it stayed a secret that Neelavalli had taken out this huge insurance policy.'

'But we haven't told anyone!'

'I'm not saying you did. It could have been the Japanese woman herself who spilled the information. Maybe that was why she was killed and your wife kidnapped. She must have called me earlier in an attempt to save herself.'

On hearing this theory, a tremor ran through Mudikondan's body. 'What do you plan to do next?' he asked.

'The kidnappers asked me to get 70 crore yen ready. You get in touch with the insurance company.'

'You'll drop off the money yourself?'

'Any other option?'

'I am very grateful for your help and for your courage. I have faith that you will bring my wife back alive.'

'Man survives because of faith. Come and meet me tomorrow.'

'I certainly will. There is one thing I can't understand though. How could they have known that I had contacted you?'

'You'll understand very soon. Please note down your address for me,' said Shankarlal.

When he returned home, Indra and Madhu were waiting eagerly.

'What happened? What did you find out?'

'Quite a few things! Mudikondan identified the dead Japanese woman as the insurance agent.'

'What was the name of the other woman who spoke to you on the phone?' asked Indra.

'She said her name was Tokyo Rose. That's a well-known code name. During World War II, there was a female radio announcer who went by that name – no one ever knew her real one.'

'How strange! How can there be a connection between her and this case?' asked Indra.

'There is a connection. At the beginning of that war, Japan was victorious in many battles. That was because they had been preparing for war for a long time. They had spies all over the world, so Japan was informed in advance about the movements of the American and British troops. In Tokyo Rose's radio broadcasts, she talked openly about all the secrets the Japanese had discovered. It was Japan's way of thumbing their noses at the enemy; the Japanese thought it was a big joke. But America and Britain did not find it funny. This woman is teasing us with that pseudonym,' explained Shankarlal.

A little while later, the police commissioner arrived.

'I've been expecting you. If you hadn't turned up soon, I would have called you myself,' said Shankarlal.

'I heard that you went to the morgue,' said the commissioner.

'I brought another person along with me: Mudikondan, an Indian, husband of the actress Neelavalli. She disappeared this morning. He suspected that she had been kidnapped. While he was here, the kidnapper contacted me with the ransom demand,' Shankarlal informed him.

'It's amazing how many people in Tokyo seem to know your phone number,' laughed the commissioner. 'We've verified that the dead woman was in fact an insurance agent. Her name was Tohiko Isawa.'

'Was she married?' asked Shankarlal.

'Yes. Her husband seemed to have been very much in love with her. He was devastated at the hospital. They had only been married a few months ago.'

'What is her husband's name?'

'Sutomu Takaya.'

'What does he do?'

'Presently, he's unemployed.'

'Why?' asked Shankarlal.

'The wife was earning good money. So, he felt he didn't need to.'

'Maybe he decided not to work because he wanted to do the cooking at home,' Indra suggested.

'Nothing like that. I think he's just an idle sort of chap,' said the commissioner.

'We should keep an eye on him,' said Shankarlal. 'There is every chance that Isawa told him about Neelavalli's insurance policy.'

'True,' agreed the commissioner.

'Do you suspect that *he* is behind the kidnapping?' Indra asked her husband.

'It could be! Isawa called us for help. He could well have knocked her off,' said Shankarlal.

'Then why don't you arrest him?' Indra asked.

'Not until Neelavalli has been found,' replied Shankarlal.

'Is there any proof that she actually has been kidnapped?' asked Indra.

'I'm still guessing. We have to find out what happened to her car,' said Shankarlal.

'I'll make enquiries about abandoned vehicles and let you know if anything comes up,' said the commissioner.

When the commissioner left, Shankarlal called the number Mudikondan had given.

'Mudikondan, I need some facts.'

'Please ask,' said Mudikondan.

'What kind of car was your wife in?'

'A Datsun – a Japanese car. We bought it here.'

'What's the license number?'

Mudikondan told him.

Half an hour later, the telephone rang and Shankarlal answered it. It was the police commissioner. 'We found the Datsun abandoned at the foothills north of Tokyo, thirty miles from here.'

Shankarlal thanked him.

'We're going to give you control of this case. Tell me the next step.'

'Come over tomorrow evening and I'll tell you my plan,' replied Shankarlal.

'So, what are you going to do?' Indra asked him the next morning.

'I'm going to wait until Tokyo Rose gets in touch. Anyway, the insurance company will need a day to get the cash ready.'

Shankarlal's patience was legendary. He never broke a sweat. As he got up, his cowlick flopped forward into his eyes.

Indra laughed. 'You may be able to handle an army of criminals, but not your own hair.'

'I'm going to check Neelavalli's house and Isawa's house. I'll be back soon,' he said as he left.

Mudikondan was not expecting such an early visit from Shankarlal. Neelavalli's bungalow was huge and luxurious. There were many Japanese servants and maids buzzing around. Shankarlal guessed that the rent must be astronomical. But then, Neelavalli was a film star. It was not really surprising that she would require such luxury.

'I came to see Neelavalli's room,' said Shankarlal.

The room was beautiful, befitting a princess. Such a lavish room for such a short stay! Shankarlal noticed the costly upholstering of the furniture and the jasmine perfume on the dressing table.

When he came out, he saw a Japanese servant sweeping up cigarette butts from the floor. Shankarlal laughed. 'So, you didn't get much sleep, I take it?' he asked Mudikondan.

'How could I? I don't think I will sleep until Neelavalli is back safe. I smoke cigarettes the way you drink tea.'

'Why is it that you have so many servants?'

'My wife had too many visitors; we needed all these servants to take care of all the guests. But I don't need them any more. I'll send them off today,' replied Mudikondan.

'I've made arrangements with the insurance company to collect the cash. Then we'll wait for the next call.'

'I hope you don't run into any danger,' said Mudikondan.

'My car will be wired by the police. They will follow a mile behind me.'

'I'm happy with the plan. But you must make sure that this brings no further danger to Neelavalli,' Mudikondan requested.

'I will take full responsibility for that,' Shankarlal reassured him.

Next, he went to check on Isawa's house. It was a tiny one, surrounded by a neatly kept lawn. There were two constables outside. He took their permission before entering the house.

Inside, Takaya was reading at the table. Rising, he asked, 'Are you Shankarlal?'

'Yes.'

'Please, you must help me. I have lost my wife – but the police are keeping me here under house arrest. Please tell me who killed my wife. I will avenge her death myself!' he sobbed.

'I'll do my best. Can I see Isawa's room please?' asked Shankarlal.

It was a simple room, but modern and comfortable. Shankarlal noticed a lingering scent of jasmine. He saw a handkerchief under the bed. He picked it up and sniffed it. Jasmine! But here, on the dressing table, there was only one bottle of perfume: rose. Neelavalli must have been here, recently. But why?

He returned home without a word to anyone.

The promised telephone call came that night: it was Tokyo Rose on the line. 'I hope the cash is ready. You can start now. Come alone. Take the highway west out of Tokyo for forty miles. You will find a big rock outcropping on your left. There will be a note left for you there which will instruct you how to proceed.'

'I'll start now. What about Neelavalli?' asked Shankarlal.

'We'll return her to you by tomorrow morning. But you must ensure the cash is there in full. And no one should accompany you. Understand?'

'Yes.'

Shankarlal put the bag of money in the back seat of his car. He switched on his wireless set and informed the police of his plan.

Behind him, three unmarked police cars followed at a distance.

Forty miles further on, Shankarlal got out of the car to search around the rock. Eventually he found the note, written in English. 'Drive north. Stop when you have driven twenty miles. But tell the policemen following you that they must go south, or you'll all be in great danger.'

Back in the car he told the police over the wireless, 'I'm supposed to head south. Meet me twenty miles from here.'

But he turned to the north instead. Twenty miles ahead, he slowed down; the car was travelling up a rocky incline. Suddenly, he heard a sound from the back seat of the car, but before he could turn around, he felt a pistol pressed against his neck. He did not look around at the person in the back seat.

'Who are you?' he asked. He got no reply. He brought the car to a halt. Silently, his right hand moved to the door handle; with a sudden move, the door flew open and Shankarlal rolled out of the car to the ground. The pistol went off. Shankarlal jumped to safety behind the rocks. The person who had hidden behind him clambered into the front seat and drove off at a great speed.

The police cars that had been sent in the opposite direction had realized by now that Shankarlal was missing. Coming back up the road, they met the detective walking down the hill.

'What happened? Why are you walking?' asked the commissioner.

'The kidnappers got the money. I rolled out of the car to avoid being shot,' said Shankarlal.

'Are you hurt?'

'No. Let's go.'

'What? Don't you want to chase down the kidnapper?'

'No. I know who it is. Tomorrow Neelavalli will be back, safe.'

'How do you figure?'

'Wait and see. Let's meet tomorrow, early morning. You'll have a few surprises waiting for you.'

The following morning, Neelavalli's house was buzzing with excitement. Neelavalli was home and safe and her husband welcomed the police commissioner and Shankarlal with a smile. 'Thank you so much for bringing my wife back!' Mudikondan exclaimed.

'And I must thank you for saving my life,' said the actress. 'When the kidnappers took me from Mitsubishi Avenue, they forced me to drive the car at gunpoint. I got a look at the man holding the gun, but after that, they kept me blindfolded – I didn't see anyone else. But, Shankarlal, why didn't you bring Indra along?'

Shankarlal replied with a smirk. 'Initially Indra did want to meet you. But this morning, she decided she could wait and meet you later – in prison.'

'What? Prison?' squawked Neelavalli.

'That's right.'

'Why would we go to prison?' Mudikondan demanded.

'You know very well why. But the commissioner still doesn't, so I'll explain. You've been living a very lavish life here in Japan. The Indian government does not allow endless foreign exchange to be taken out by Indian tourists. Even I was only allowed a limited amount. That's why I brought Madhu with me, rather than hire Japanese servants.'

The commissioner interrupted him. 'But you are our guests here! We would have been happy to give any assistance you needed.'

'I know, but it wouldn't be fair for me to accept. Anyway, Neelavalli was in a cash crunch here. It was around this time that Isawa sold her the insurance policy. Takaya came to know about it; his wife was unaware of his criminal connections. He contacted the Indian couple and together they came up with a scheme to make an easy 70 crore yen. He thought his wife Isawa would cooperate with the plot, but she turned out to be an honest woman. When Neelavalli was being kept hidden in her house, Isawa threatened to go to the police. Then she reconsidered; if she went to the police, her husband would go to jail. So, she called me instead. That was when Takaya, her husband, shot her down in cold blood.

'Then he shifted Neelavalli to a new location. They abandoned the Datsun and moved her in with Takaya's gang. Now Mudikondan made his move; he contacted me and gave me this tale about his wife being kidnapped. He prearranged the Tokyo Rose call. I didn't figure it out until I saw a handkerchief, scented with jasmine, in Takaya's bedroom. If he had forcibly kidnapped her, then there's no way he would have taken her to his own house.'

'So, where's the money, then?' asked the commissioner.

'Not to worry. Takaya was under house arrest, so it must have been Mudikondan who snuck into my car while I got out to find the note. Therefore, the cash must be in his possession,' said Shankarlal. 'I'm sure it's right here in this bungalow! Arrest these two, please. They're now your responsibility,' smiled the king of detectives.

He strode away, ignoring Neelavalli's screams: 'Please don't arrest us. We'll return the money!'

DETECTIVE

Rabindranath Tagore, tr. Shampa Roy

'I work as a detective in the police department. My life has centred around just two things: my wife and my profession. Earlier, I was part of a joint family, but the lack of respect shown towards my wife led to a quarrel with my older brother and subsequently to our moving out. All along, it was my brother who had been earning money to take care of me, so forsaking that sheltered set-up with my wife was a particularly bold step on my part.

However, I've never lacked belief in myself. I felt certain that just as I had managed to tame my beautiful wife, in time I would also be able to bring around an indifferent lady luck. Mahimchandra was not going to lag behind anyone in this world. I joined the police department in the usual manner and eventually, it didn't take me long to get promoted to the position of detective.

In the same way that the brightest of flames emits black soot, every now and then, my wife's love would release inky fumes of jealousy and suspicion. Soon it began to interfere with my work, especially since the field of policing does not allow one to be picky about time or place; in fact, where timing and places are concerned, it's bad timing and places that are par for the course. This only led to my wife's jealous nature becoming exacerbated and increasingly hard to control. In an attempt to goad me, she would say, 'You go off willy-nilly, spend time in all sorts of places and get to see me once in a blue moon. Don't you feel suspicious about me?' I would reply, 'Suspicion is the stock-in-trade of my profession. That's why I don't bring it into our household.' To this my wife's retort was, 'Being suspicious is not part of my profession but of my nature and if you give me the slightest reason to feel suspicious, I could do anything.'

I was determined to become better than others in the field of detective work and had vowed to make a name for myself. I read up every bit of descriptive prose and fiction related to the area. But such reading only intensified my dissatisfaction and restlessness. For I felt that the criminals in our country are cowardly and foolish, their crimes dull and unimaginative, neither hard to crack nor capable of posing insurmountable challenges. Try as they might, the murderers here simply fail to conceal their gruesome excitement at shedding someone's blood. Clueless about the wily strategies required to step out of the nefarious mazes of crimes, fraudsters often get entangled, from head to toe, in the very nets that they spread to ensnare others. There is no joy or honour in the work of a detective in such an unexciting place.

After effortlessly nabbing a Marwari crook in Burrabazar, I would muse, 'O you blot on the tribe of criminals, only gifted masterminds are blessed with the ability to ruin someone; ignorant clods like you would be far better off becoming saints and mendicants.' Upon arresting a murderer, I would address him thus in my mind: Have the government's highest gallows been constructed for unworthy creatures like you and your ilk? You have neither the required breadth of imagination nor the steely self-restraint; so how dare you fellows aspire to be murderers?

On the other hand, whenever with my mind's eye I gazed at the cloud-kissing array of lofty mansions on the crowded streets of London and Paris, my entire being would pulsate with excitement. I would think to myself: Just as there are myriad streams of people, professions, festivals and beautiful things flowing through those buildings, streets and lanes, there's also an all-pervasive, darkly sinister and viciously cunning undercurrent of criminality relentlessly making its way; and it's this proximity to darkness that makes European humour and culture so fiercely entertaining and awe-inspiring. In our Calcutta, it's never anything but cooking, spice-grinding, domestic chores, exam preparations, card games and chess, or at best, marital squabbles, fraternal feuds and heated discussions about litigation that carry on endlessly in the houses that line the streets. Not once, while looking at any of the houses, does one get the feeling that at that very moment there might be a devil lurking in one of its corners, intent on hatching its inky black eggs.

Quite often, I would walk about on the streets and closely observe the faces and mannerisms of the passers-by. As soon as someone would strike me as being the least bit suspicious, I would follow them on the sly. I would even dig up information about them, only to discover with a crushing sense of disappointment that so impeccably virtuous were they, their friends and relatives had never even been able to spread false rumours about them. Of all the passers-by, the one who seemed like he might be the worst kind of cold-blooded criminal – indeed whose very appearance left me in no doubt that he had just returned after committing a grisly crime – turned out to be a second-grade teacher in a local school for scholarship students, doing nothing worse than going back home from work. Had these very men been born in some other country, they would undoubtedly have become notorious thieves or bandits; but in this country, the absence of much-needed dynamism and valour compels them to spend their lives as teachers who go on to draw a pension and die of old age. Even the pettiest of thieves had failed to arouse the kind of deep disgust I felt towards that diffident second-grade teacher who rendered all my investigative efforts fruitless.

Finally, one evening, under a lamp post not very far from my own house, I spotted a man pacing anxiously about for no apparent reason. No sooner had I clapped eyes on him than I knew without a shred of doubt that he was there on a sinister mission. I hid in the dark and carefully scoured his face; he was both young and good-looking. I said to myself, 'Now, this is undoubtedly the most appropriate kind of face for someone who wants to commit a crime. Men whose very visages are like hostile witnesses should immediately abandon all their criminal activities. While they may or may not find success in virtuous pursuits, as miscreants they have little hope of ending up as anything but failures.' But that young fellow's face, I noticed, gave him an all-important edge. I stood marvelling at him for quite some time and thought, 'God has gifted you a rare advantage indeed! If you can use it well, I'll definitely say bravo!'

Stepping out of the darkness, I went right up to him, thumped his back and cried, 'There you are! Are you all right?' He jumped out of his skin and turned completely pale. I said, 'Forgive me, I have made a mistake. I thought you were someone else.' Meanwhile, to myself I said, 'I haven't made the slightest mistake. I was absolutely spot-on in my assessment.' But it didn't behove him to get startled in that manner; that was quite annoying. He should have been able to exert greater control over his physical reflexes; but then flawless perfection is rarely to be found even amongst criminals. Mother Nature can be quite parsimonious even when it comes to helping a thief become the best of his kind.

When I returned to my hiding place, I saw him leave that spot under the lamp post in an agitated manner. I followed him and saw him entering Gol Dighi[5] and then lying flat on his back on a grassy knoll beside the lake. I thought that was indeed a good place for pondering over one's strategies, so much better than lurking under lamp posts. Should anyone cast suspicious glances at him, they would conclude that the young fellow was conjuring up his beloved's luminous face on the dark, moonless skies above. The more I saw of this young man, the more drawn I felt towards him.

Then I did a bit of research and found out where he lived. His name was Manmath. He was a college student and after failing his exams, he was spending his summer vacation roaming around.

---

[5] Gol Dighi refers to a lake in the heart of Kolkata.

All his hostel mates had left to go back home. Usually, during any long vacation, students tend to flee from their hostels, so I vowed to find out what evil star was holding him back.

I disguised myself as a student and rented a portion of his hostel. On the first day when he saw me there, he looked at me with an expression that I wasn't quite able to interpret. It was one that suggested he was taken aback, as if he had fathomed my reason for being there. I realized that hunter and prey were evenly matched and that there was no way I was going to catch him in the blink of an eye.

But when I tried to forge a bond of friendship with him, he seemed to walk right into my trap with alacrity. And yet, I had the feeling that he was watching me with keen-eyed intentness and was trying to take my measure. That kind of alert watchfulness and curiosity are the marks of a criminal mastermind. I felt immensely pleased to detect that kind of cleverness in a fellow of his age.

Then I thought, unless I bring a woman into all this, it would be difficult to unlock the doors to the extraordinary young chap's precociously cunning mind. So, one day, I said to Manmath in a voice choked with emotion, 'You know, brother, I love a woman, but she doesn't love me.'

At first, he looked at my face with a shocked expression and then said with a slight smile, 'Well, that's not at all an uncommon predicament! I sometimes feel it's only for the sake of having fun at our expense that god, a veritable prankster, has created differences between men and women.'

I said, 'Well, I need your help and advice.'

He acquiesced.

I regaled him with all kinds of made-up stories, all of which he heard with avid interest but didn't say much. I'd always assumed that the quickest way to get close to someone was to share one's deepest secrets with them, especially the kind related to love. But I couldn't see any signs of that happening in this case. If anything, after engraving in his mind everything that I uttered, the young fellow seemed to become even quieter than before. My admiration for him grew by leaps and bounds.

Meanwhile, I remained utterly clueless about what Manmath was up to behind closed doors every day and also about how far he advanced in his secret mission. For advancing he was, of that I had no doubt. One look at his face was enough to tell me that he was part of an extremely complex plot that was maturing with each passing day. I had even used a secret key to open his desk, but there was nothing to be found in it other than a notebook full of obscure poetry, some college notes and a few inconsequential letters from his family. The only thing I could gather, as evident from those letters, was that his family had been vehemently importuning him to return home. And yet, despite their repeated pleas, he seemed to have some very convincing reason for not going back. Had the reason been a legal one, surely it would have slipped out by now in all that he had told me. But in fact, just the opposite had happened and this fuelled my excessive curiosity about the fellow's movements and his history.

The young fellow, I was sure, was a part of that all-pervasive, enormous and eternal tribe of anti-social beings that hides itself completely in the dark underworld and keeps the entirety of human society out of joint. No mere student, he was playmate and accomplice to the forces of destruction that rampage across the world; at present, he was operating in the guise of a bespectacled and harmless Bengali scholar pursuing his studies in college. The horror he embodied couldn't have been greater had he arrived in the form of one of the dreaded cult followers of the fierce Goddess Kali with a garland of human heads around his neck. I couldn't help but become his devotee.

Eventually as part of the plan, I had to get hold of an actual flesh and blood woman who could make an appearance before him. Harimati, a salaried employee of the police department, came to my aid. I told Manmath that I was a wretched seeker of Harimati's love and that it was with her in mind that I repeatedly recited the poem 'Why has the moon risen again at night?' while walking with him around Gol Dighi. Harimati announced in a manner that was part sincere and part coquettish, that she had lost her heart to Manmath. But our plan didn't succeed since Manmath did little but watch us with a distant, detached and impassive curiosity.

And then one day, around noon, I picked up the torn-up fragments of a letter lying on the floor of his room. When I joined all the bits together, I was able to retrieve the line, *'Today at seven at your place.'* Despite searching long and hard, there was nothing else that I could find.

My very insides churned with joyous excitement at what I had read; my feeling was comparable to the euphoria that ignites a palaeontologist's imagination, when he discovers the bone fragment of a creature belonging to some extinct species.

I knew that at ten that night, Harimati was slated to make an appearance at our hostel. What then was this about seven in the evening? The young fellow was as sharp-witted as he was bold. While planning a secret crime, it's best to wait for the right moment on a day when there's some special occasion at home. For one, everyone's attention is diverted to the main event at that time and second, people assume that nothing secretive can go on in a place where there's a gathering of people.

All of a sudden, it occurred to me that Manmath had decided to use both his recent friendship with me and my feigned love for Harimati to fulfil his own ends. That was the reason why he neither displayed any sign of being attached to us, nor did he detach himself from us completely. We helped keep his secret machinations well-hidden. Everyone thought he was busy with us and it suited him not to dispel that illusion.

Consider this for a moment. It's only natural to assume that a student who's an incomer and who ignores his family's desperate pleas only to languish all by himself in an empty rented house, must have, without doubt, a very special reason for seeking that kind of solitude. And yet, when I started going to his hostel, intruded into his private space, created new and serious disruptions by bringing a woman in our midst, he did not become resentful and leave the hostel, or try to avoid our company. At the same time, it was clearly evident that he had not developed even the tiniest bit of affection towards either me or Harimati. In truth, when I watched him in his unguarded moment, it seemed as though there was an intense loathing growing in his heart towards both of us.

The only possible reason for this had to be that in order to enjoy the advantages of solitude while putting it about that he was not alone, he needed to keep his recent acquaintances close to him. Besides, there can be no better decoy than a woman when one wants to pursue something without being disturbed by people. Manmath's earlier behaviour, so inexplicable and suspicious, changed completely once we entered his life. The fact that a youth born in our very own Bengal was capable of such foresight, quick judgment and calculating cunning, made my heart race with excitement. Had Manmath not taken offence, I would probably have clasped him in a tight embrace.

That day, as soon as I met Manmath, I said to him, 'I have decided I want to take you out for dinner today at seven in the evening.' He gave a start when he heard this, but then quickly recovered his restrained manner and said, 'Please forgive me today, my friend, for my digestive system is in a fairly grievous state.' Never before that moment had I seen Manmath display the slightest bit of distaste at the suggestion of a meal at a hotel. I felt sure that his mind was caught up in some extremely complex matter.

That day I was not meant to be in his hostel in the early part of the evening. But like an annoying, unwanted guest I hung on, prattled about all kinds of things and refused to evince the slightest inclination to leave, even as the evening wore on. Manmath became extremely restless, agreed wholeheartedly to everything that I said and refrained from arguing over any of my statements. Finally, he turned to look at the clock and then stood up and said imploringly, 'Aren't you going to fetch Harimati today?' Feigning surprise, I said, 'Oh yes, yes! I had completely forgotten about that. Please get the food and everything else ready, my friend. I'll get her here at exactly ten at night.' And with these words, I departed.

The blood rushing through my entire body throbbed with intoxicating feelings of joy. I was no less keen about 7 p.m. than Manmath. I stood hidden in a spot not very far from the hostel and looked at my watch constantly, like someone waiting with breathless anxiety for a rendezvous with their paramour. Then, just as the twilight hour began deepening into darkness and it was time to light the gas lamps on the street, a closed palanquin entered the gates of the hostel. I experienced a delightful frisson as I imagined the smooth, unimpeded arrival of a moist-eyed and veiled sinful figure at the students' hostel like an embodiment of tragedy borne aloft on the shoulders of Oriya palanquin bearers with their customary shouts of *hnai-hnui*.

I couldn't hold myself back any longer. After just a short while, I crept up the stairs very slowly to his room on the first floor. I had planned to hide near the stairs and watch everything secretly, but that was not going to be possible. For Manmath was sitting in a room that faced the staircase, while a veiled female figure was seated at the opposite end, talking to him in a low voice. When I realized that Manmath had spotted me, I marched into the room and said, 'I think I left my watch here. I've come back to get it.' Manmath looked so shocked, I thought he might collapse on the floor. Feeling rather tickled, I said, 'Why, are you feeling ill, brother?' He couldn't utter a single word in reply. Then I turned to the veiled woman in the room, who had become as stiff as a wooden doll and asked, 'How are you related to Manmath?' I got no response. And then I saw that she was not related to Manmath. For she was none other than my wife. What followed after that is known to everyone. This was my first experience of nabbing a crook while working as a detective.'

After a while, having listened to all this, I said to detective Mahimchandra, 'It's quite possible that the relationship between your wife and Manmath was not an illicit one.'

Mahimchandra said, 'That's a definite possibility. This letter from Manmath was found in my wife's suitcase.' Saying this, he placed a letter in my hand; it was as follows:

Dear virtuous one,

Perhaps, by now you have all but forgotten about a wretched man called Manmath. As a child, whenever I visited my maternal uncle's house in Kajibari, I would visit your house in the neighbourhood and we would play several games together. However, in due course, our playhouse and our bond as playmates were both shattered. I'm not sure if you know this, but at one point, I threw aside all my inhibitions and unabashedly attempted to fix our marriage. But since we are almost the same age, the elders in our families refused to agree to the match.

After that, once you got married, I got no news of you for the next four or five years. Five months ago, when I learned that your husband had got a job in Calcutta police department and was transferred here, I searched and found out where you lived.

I had no audacious hopes of meeting you, and as god is my witness, I did not have any insidious plans of intruding into or disrupting your conjugal peace. In the evenings, I would simply stand under a lamp post in front of your house like a sun worshipper. At exactly seven thirty, every evening, you would place a lighted kerosene lamp at a window of one of the south-facing rooms on the first floor and for a few moments your face, illuminated by the lamp, would rise in front of my gaze. That's the only crime I have committed, in relation to you.

Meanwhile, in the course of events, I got to know your husband and gradually even got close to him. Based on what I saw of his character, I was left in no doubt that your life could not be a happy one. It's true that I have no socially sanctioned right to ask anything of you, but the same providence that made your sorrows mine, has also entrusted me with the responsibility to try and alleviate them.

As such, if you forgive my temerity and secretly come to my place on Friday in a palanquin, for just twenty minutes, I would like to tell you a few confidential things about your husband; if you disbelieve me, I can even present you with evidence provided you can bear to look at it and follow it up with some advice. I hope with all my heart that you'll take my advice and be truly happy one day.

My aim is not completely selfless. To see you before me for a few moments, to listen to you and to have my room transmuted into a place of eternally happy dreams, with the touch of your feet, I long for these as well, in my heart. But if you don't trust me and if you want to deprive me of even this little bit of joy, then write to me saying so and I'll disclose everything in a letter to you. And if you feel you can't trust me enough to write a letter, then show this missive to your husband and I'll convey to him whatever I have to say.

Your eternal well-wisher,
Manmath Majumdar

A DEATH CONSIDERED

Anil Menon

An attempt (at controlling the narrative).

So I'm stuck. What to do with my love triangle? Satya, Padma and Rafiq. I still don't see how things will play out, even after a week of brooding. I'm really afraid I'll run out of time. I'll try 'writing aloud' and see if that helps. I'll just put down my thoughts and thoughts on thoughts and see where it leads. Life imitates art, etc.

> I wake to sleep and take my waking slow.
> I learn by going where I have to go.
>
> –Theodore Roethke

I want an *existential* detective novel. And what is existential here are the situations, not the characters. The characters are roles, in that sense. Husband, Wife, Third Party.

But what is an 'existential situation'? I'm having real difficulty getting some clarity on that concept.

Idea #1: it is a situation which forces you to realize that the self is a fictional entity.

Idea #2: it is a situation which involves life and death questions, such as: should I put my mother in a nursing home?

Idea #3: it is a situation in which survival means destroying something true and good and beautiful about yourself.

All three definitions seem quite distinct. But I don't know. Maybe they're connected. But each leads to a different novel, I think.

The Current Situation

Satya is a pathologist by education. He cuts up dead people. Why? Because my husband is one, that's why. Write what you know. Solid useful occupation; decent money. Perhaps it's an ideal career for a murderer (that's a joke). It's certainly great for Padma, who bases all her stories on his cases.

Satya is just an ordinary, good-natured doctor with a dangerously beautiful wife, Padma. A much younger wife. Again, this parallels my situation. I am quite sure I'm only a danger to myself, but just last week, at the hospital mixer the new HOD thought I was hubby's daughter! Write what you know.

Rafiq is an assistant superintendent of police, which is the first posting of an IPS officer. He'd taken a forensic class under Satya. He's got a certain animal quality: hairy, large feet, deep-set eyes, flat belly. He's younger than Padma and they met at a writing workshop. Padma loves metafiction. Rafiq, who's not really moved beyond murder mysteries, finds it interesting that his former prof, who cuts up dead bodies, has a missus who cuts up texts (TODO: think of something different from what had happened—as far as meet-cute goes, this one is really lame). Rafiq's sexiest quality is that he *listens*. God, he's a good listener.

What's in it for Rafiq? Beyond the 'dangerously beautiful' pussy (ha ha), I suppose the reader will see that, on first inspection, Padma offers the simultaneous satisfaction of multiple fetishes: the married woman fetish, the older woman fetish, the teacher's wife fetish, the classmate fetish and not to mention, the piquant taboo thrill of engaging in *dharmabrasht* (they roleplay this, the shameless creatures).

Ironically, it was Satya who had persuaded Rafiq to attend the fiction workshop with him. He dropped out of the workshop, leaving Rafiq to 'keep my wife company'.

Now, it might seem this will lead to the kind of story with characters who are basically 'physical description + traits', which is the hallmark of the worst kind of writing. That is true. When I started, I thought I'd set up their characters and then work in situations to show these people aren't who the reader thought they were. But that's the old bait-and-switch game and I don't like that stunt with my warranty policies, nor with stories I read. I'm not interested in character traits any more than I'm interested in Ayurveda's obsolete model of health (hubby takes it seriously though).

I despise it when people bring up personality as an explanation. It explains everything and therefore, nothing. However, I think we do all have a personal philosophy of life, as it were. And this personal philosophy drives how we move about in the world. I don't know whether that's true or not, but that's what I use in my writing.

So: Satya is someone who has great faith in an ordered universe; that is, he assumes things happen for a reason. He's not religious or anything. It's just a matter of training, job experience and preference. It's a useful philosophy to have when things get too stressful in his job. Like the time he was doing an autopsy of an Indian teen who'd been abducted, murdered and then dumped into the ocean. He had begun with a standard Y-shaped incision starting from the shoulders, joining at the sternum and then a midline incision to the pubic bone. He had separated the skin, subcutaneous tissue, fascia, the linea alba and transversalis fascia and the peritoneum, finally exposing the rib cage and abdominal cavity. It was then a mess of Indian long-tailed sand-eels flopped out.

He told me this story in his usual absent-minded drone, over dinner, while we were having spaghetti marinara. For a short, balding, rather ordinary man, he is very vain.

If I were him, I'd find another profession. But I suppose he likes his little mysteries. His boat floats on the ironwood keel of a rational universe. Ships need the storm to feel like ships.

Padma, his wife, is cursed with self-awareness. She thinks too much. It has always kept her on the straight and narrow. Good daughter, good sister, good wife. Good, good, good. Her philosophy is: you'll always be haunted by the road not taken. Or like the Frank Sinatra song:

regrets, I have had a few,
but then again, too few to mention.

I introduced her father in Chapter 2. He's a corrupt *tehsildar;* a loving, vicious, pot-bellied tyrant. Now I'm not sure if he serves any purpose. That story about how her father would return home from work and after dinner would cryptically announce to her mother: 'six'. Sometimes he'd say: 'seven'. Or: 'five'. On these days, he would pet Padma, bring her gifts, indulge her whims (she always kept them reasonable). But if it was a 'three' or anything lower, her mother was in for it. Evidently, the numbers were indices to the magnitude of his ill-gotten gains for the day. Her father had died of old age, respected, surrounded by family. Her mother wailed an ocean. Satya now wears his father-in-law's gold watch. Padma's father had gifted it to Satya along with a quote: 'A clock keeps good time; a good husband makes time...'

All this sounds terribly significant, but I have a sinking feeling it isn't. I think I need to make Padma more likeable. Make her relatable. Give the audience someone to root for. Most readers of detective fiction are men and men (in theory) like women who're a little helpless. God, it makes me want to vomit. Are readers *that* stupid? Listen, Padma's father used to slap her mom, okay? Open palm, on the face, this way, that way. You know how humiliating, how soul-destroying, how suicide-inducing that is! Is she helpless enough now?

I see Rafiq as an idealist. That is, Padma sees Rafiq as an idealist. It's one of his attractions. He believes in all the stuff he was told in police training. He stands ram-rod straight when the national anthem is played in cinema theatres. He knows first-hand that violence can solve many a tricky problem.

Satya knows about the infidelity. That's where Chapter 3 left off. Inciting incident. I think I need to redo it.

The Inciting Scene: The Department's Diwali Party
(check: do these departments have such parties?)

Satya watches (in the window's reflection) Rafiq (seemingly) moving his hand to get a napkin to remove some stains, losing his balance, reaching for support and his hand landing on the inner sanctum of Padma's salwar-covered thigh. Specifically, the inner deltoid, that forbidden Eden formed by the sartorius, gracilis and the inguinal muscles.

Rafiq takes his time removing his paw. He slides his hand away, instead of lifting it away. A definite grope. Her face is flushed with a colour Satya has never seen before. The blood he's used to seeing is usually congealed and dead and rust brown. But she smiles, her gaze locked on Rafiq's, hands him a napkin, then as they continue talking, she leans over and brushes crumbs off Rafiq's t-shirt. Chest, pecs, muscular arms: she's quite thorough.

This is the scene that rocks Satya's ship. It gets Satya looking for reasons. He imagines Rafiq's body, spread out on the autopsy table. But yeah, I don't know. It seems forced. Who's taken the first step on the road here, for example? Rafiq, right. But it's Padma who should make the first step. Perhaps she had, in her act of thorough grooming. If she hadn't, perhaps none of this would have happened and life could've continued being harmonious. If only, if only.

I need to think about it, but the flow of words is good now and this writing-it-out shit is really helping to clarify my situation.

I am at a fork in the road. Someone is going to die. But who? I see six possibilities.

Option A: Satya can murder Padma.

Option B: Satya can murder Rafiq.
Option C: Rafiq can murder Padma.
Option D: Rafiq can murder Satya.
Option D: Padma can murder Rafiq.
Option E: Padma can murder Satya.

That's why I like Dostoevsky. The bugger has no idea where his novels are headed and writes them as if he's taken all options. But forget about writing like him. I have six roads. Which one do I take?

The Problem

If I were Satya, I'd go with Option A (Satya murders Padma). Of course, if I were really Satya, then I don't know if I could go through with it. Satya loves Padma and it's the kind of gentle love where all a husband really wants is to grow old together. He's hurt, not angry. Agreed, hurt is a form of anger, but how does killing Padma take it away? If he does kill her, then I suspect he will kill himself soon after. His world (which is just him and Padma) no longer makes sense and it's this world he'll try to end.

Option B (Satya murders Rafiq) doesn't seem plausible to me. Rafiq would flatten Satya with one punch. But, chalo, assume Rafiq is somehow dispatched. What about the next Rafiq, Doctor-saab? While you're chakki-pissoing in jail, 'your' missus will be grinding on her next mistake. I think it's more likely that Satya will sabotage Rafiq's career. Rafiq has expressed to Padma more than once his worry about that possibility. A forensic pathologist with a vendetta can really screw up your cases. Okay, so Option B is out.

Option C (Rafiq murders Padma) is more than a possibility. Padma is just a fling for Rafiq. He is planning to marry a shy Bohra Muslim girl who'll give him a passel of kids and look the other way at his affairs. He's even given his mom the go-ahead. Padma was fun, but now she's just this whiney, needy, psycho bitch. She even fantasizes about marriage. Seriously? God knows how many affairs she's had. She's damaged goods, *bheedu*.

Return to Amazon. And her *chutiya* stories! Autobiography is not metafiction, okay? Characters should stop trying to escape the story. Something will have to done about Padma.

This is how Rafiq, Padma's Rafiq, her sweet and hairy ape must surely think. In short, this is a live option.

What all this means is that Padma's life is in danger from both Satya (Option A) and Rafiq (Option C). Naturally, Padma has to protect herself.

Option D (Rafiq murders Satya) is a possibility. A pissed-off husband is always a threat and Rafiq is a man of violence. But that may only create more problems, since Satya's removal would only fuel Padma's hopes. Option D is really just a delayed form of Option C (Rafiq murders Padma).

Option E (Padma murders Satya) isn't really an option. He's her ATM. What are the odds of a 30+ year old woman hooking a stable, hygienic, under-40 male with a great credit rating, dead parents and no siblings? No, Padma can't murder Satya. It's too self-destructive.

That leaves Option F (Padma murders Rafiq). Aha. Oh, my pretty morsel of probability. Rafiq's death would perhaps appease Satya. With Rafiq gone, things could return to stability. She would shower Satya with love. Any sin can be forgiven so long as it is wrapped in a white, chiffon sari and sleeveless blouse. He would forgive her, yes he would. Also, Rafiq *deserves* to be murdered. Some people just do. Yes, so it is possible. But is it feasible? If Satya is physically not capable of murdering Rafiq, what makes Padma any more capable? I suppose Padma would have access to poisons, but frankly,

TODO: research accidental death while cleaning firearm.

We thus have a 'hate triangle', so to speak.

My commitment for the next two days is this: I will figure out Padma's choice in Chapter 6. The triangle must be broken; I simply cannot bear this tension anymore. And like I said, I'm running out of time.

That said, I wonder if I should postpone her decision to Chapter 7. One question that readers will have is: why doesn't Padma simply run? Why the hell is she waiting for Rafiq or Satya to make up their minds?

I have alluded to the reasons in earlier chapters, but perhaps a full chapter on how trapped Padma is might be necessary. Padma isn't independently wealthy. She's dependent on Satya. She can't divorce him. She's pretty sure he has PROOF of the infidelity.

Sure, she can give up Rafiq. But the thing is, he won't believe it. He's convinced Padma will settle scores. Hell hath no fury, et cetera. Wait – where have I demonstrated her vindictiveness?

Oh god.

I haven't shown it! I have to show that Padma isn't all sugar and spice and all things nice. Sugar has a dark history. Sugar was once manufactured in slave plantations. Padma's sugar has a dark history.

I think I have an idea for that. Remember what Jane Austen says in *Sense and Sensibility*: the greater hurt is forgiven sooner than the lesser one. That's me! I can understand, even forgive, my husband and lover wanting to murder me, but I can't forgive, say, someone cutting me off or buying the last of something I'd wanted. I persuaded Satya's mom that she should get checked for oral cancer because she didn't like my cooking. And I waited two whole weeks to spring the scare on her! I feel terrible about it; Satya didn't speak to me for a week when he found out. But I am not a bad person. I know I have this seriously vindictive streak. I've tried to control it, but it anyway, point is:

TODO: incorporate the cancer incident.

Somebody will be murdered this week. I'm so tired, I'm finding it hard to care. It's ridiculous and worrying I am this lost! It means the planning isn't as tight as I'd imagined. There's this uneasy feeling I've forgotten something. I just hope Patricia Cornwell and P.D. James had similar problems with their novels.

The Real Problem (with detective stories)

Maybe I should slow down. What am I trying to do? Reinvent the detective story.

Oh, please. What am I, Chekhov? Jane Austen? Agatha Christie?

Okay, what am I really trying to do with detective novels?

I am not famous enough to be invited for a panel discussion and therefore I have panel discussions with myself. I ask myself why I want to write detective mysteries. Why can't I be like the other genteel Indian women authors, content to write stories with recipes and life gyaan from their fucking grandmothers? Life would be so much easier.

Answer #1: in a detective novel, everything and everyone is unreliable. Everybody lies. Every character is an 'unreliable narrator' as we writers say in our lingo. That is also exactly how it is in life.

And death.

Hubby told me something deep once: even the dead can lie. He gave the example of a woman, a schoolteacher living near Worli Sea Face. She hung herself, but made it look as if her husband had murdered her. Screaming fights the night before, broken furniture, etc. After her husband was arrested, tried and executed, her attorney, bound by prior contractual agreement, sent a letter she had deposited with him. In the letter, the wife gloated. She chortled. She made a full confession.

Who can you trust then in a detective story? Can even the Reader be trusted? Think of all the experts who 'read' the dead body of that woman, gently swaying in the afternoon breeze from Worli's seaface? Hadn't that schoolteacher *relied* on Unreliable Readers? I don't think any other artform is so reliant on uncertainty.

Answer #2 (all the other panelists are stunned into silence): the other reason I love writing detective stories is because the actual murder is the least important aspect of the story. Everything lies in the detection (pun intended, ha ha). Detective stories make death significant, but irrelevant. Spinoza said: 'The free person thinks least of all of death and his wisdom is a meditation not on death but on life.' The detective story is truest to that vision of living purely.

I get another question from the audience: *Loved your novel, thank you for writing it and for your fascinating analysis of detective stories, what in your opinion would make the perfect detective story?*

Thank you. Well, it would be a story with the highest possible stakes. The kind of stake that would make the reader truly, truly care about the victim. Perhaps (*I* wouldn't say 'perhaps'; one has to be certain in life) it wouldn't be a whodunit, but a whomtodoin. It's not about framing the least likely suspect. It's about finishing off the maximally safe character. And isn't that person the reader? This asshole, this vulture, this gloating fraud who pretends to feel our pain, this sink of all narratological motives: if only they could be murdered and made to detect for themselves the inevitability of their end, what a terribly wonderful and just story it would be!

Sigh.

How I love to dissect.

The fact is that the situation is intolerable. The triangle must be broken. Three disjointed sticks have been arranged to create the illusion of a triangle. As long as one stick remains, the illusion of closure remains.

I must write a detective story that creates a sense of closure without, while destroying the closure within. Every story, Ricardo Piglia claimed, is actually two stories: the told story and the untold story. I will describe one of these stories in words; what is read will be the story of the other, written on the world.

THE DESIRE OF THE DETECTIVE

Tanuj Solanki

November: the month when Bombay breeze turns cool and longing has narcotic ripples. From the sliding window of my fourth-floor apartment, I see a big, grey cloud hanging in the evening sky. The monsoon is long over, poor chap's just been left behind. I feel for it for a second, then I remember how I hate this city's rains. Not too far below the cloud, little rectangles of light are beginning to glow in a faraway building. How many people get to fuck in that building tonight? I wonder. Then I look away, down. Autos gurgle anxiously on the road right below, like they always do. For me there isn't much to do this evening, nowhere to be. I let the crime begin a conversation with me again. A man with a bullet pit in his head, brains splayed on the desk inside a room of his twelfth-floor apartment. He was in his mid-thirties, like me. Neither young nor old: potential beginning to peter out, hope still squirming. Perhaps he would have put it better himself, for he was a writer, although not a terribly famous or important one. That he was a writer living alone in a high-rise means that he had rich parents. You need a bit of comfort for paperwork.

The writer was writing when he was shot. The murderer, it can be deduced, was known to him. There were no signs of forced entry. No signs of a struggle either. It is possible that the murderer had a spare key to the apartment and entered on his/her own. It usually is the ones you trust. That also makes it interesting for cops like me. The shared-key hypothesis and the dramatic betrayal embedded in it – these things have their gossipy allure. The writer was shot in the temple and not in the forehead, which means that it was no execution. No revenge or retribution or 'Look, I warned you this would happen and now it is happening.' Anyway, the point is that the moment before he was shot, the writer was oblivious to the intentions of the armed man/woman standing next to him.

Earlier in the day I had gone to the supermarket. I had to buy kitchen knives, underwear, a tiffin box, cereals, daal. After I paid, a saleswoman approached me and tried to sell me a credit card. She was wearing a cheap white polo with red collars and her breasts were distorting the red rectangle of the bank's logo. She had large pleading eyes, had her curly hair tied in a hurried bunch and had a forehead that was too high and wise for someone in her profession – a fake smile producing two horizontal lines on it. I didn't say a word to her, just stared into her eyes and lifted the polybag in my hand and twist-tied it with a swift motion. She accurately decoded my single-handed gesture as one of aggression: the pleading in her eyes turned to trepidation. This pleased me no end and I hummed a song as I walked out of the supermarket's deathly light and into the burst of the afternoon. There was an array of eager autorickshaws at the exit and I got *myself* into one.

My *autowaala* turned out to be talkative. He gave a little speech about how kids knew no shame these days. I asked him to elaborate further. He told me of a guy and a girl who entered his auto at Powai and fondled each other all through the JVLR (Jogeshwari Vikhroli Link Road). The guy got off somewhere in Andheri and a hundred or so meters down the road another guy got into the auto. The girl then made out with this new guy before dropping him off at the Oberoi Mall in Goregaon. 'All the spit the first guy had left on her hadn't even dried, sir,' the *autowaala* said. 'That girl's mind wasn't working. But her other things were working fine. I could smell it. I'm not joking, I could smell it. She was wearing such a tiny thing. It was making me dizzy.' After he had dropped the girl off at Kandivali, he had taken a break from his shift and gone to his wife. 'I couldn't control myself, sir, I needed some fucking. You understand, right?' His word for fucking was *chudai*. He went on to talk about how it was difficult for him to drive an auto in Bandra during the night: 'Every girl is half-naked, every girl looks like a model.' By the time we neared my locality, he had peppered me with a couple more stories about girls without morals. I didn't like his crassness, but I sort of agreed with his subject matter. The crime branch makes you see the world clearly, deduce all the hidden logic in it, make rules to live by. One of those rules goes like this: attractive women can be fatal.

Life doesn't edit itself only to moments of significance: a detective lives a whole life, eats, shits, fucks, scratches, reads, runs, buys, sells, etc. The crime-solving obsession we detectives are routinely portrayed with is fake. That consuming angst, those high-nicotine late-nighters, those photos and maps and bank statements and insurance claims pinned to boards, clues prepared to slug it out – all that stuff never happens. Truth be told, I have never felt too strongly pulled by the other side of a mystery. If a case seems unsolvable, or if solving it becomes irrelevant, I am always keen to let it go, or to let an easier solution fit. This is, of course, not what happens in detective novels or movies. Most of these show us detectives in the heat of problem-solving, almost erotically charged by the elusive heart of the mystery, as excited about finding the real murderer as the audience watching us. In life there is no audience and finding the murderer is a predominantly bureaucratic exercise. Every day, there are fresh crimes; every day there are files to update, magistrates to cajole, bribes to accept or deny. I have genuinely solved some cases, though; I have seen my fair share of murderers. They fit a fuck-all type after they are found: their face becomes expressionless, their nervous tics vanish, they sniffle once or cough a couple of times and then they start to breathe as deeply as possible. All actual murderers I have seen, till date, acquired a dumb sort of opaqueness after being discovered, an aura of unapproachability, like they all belonged to a world where life did indeed edit itself to moments of significance and I, their revealer, the one who was going to condemn them to the vagaries of our justice system, at once became a nobody for them, someone who would always be removed from the final reels of their personal narratives. That isn't a great feeling, I must say. Imagine: you solve a case and you find the murderer and right there, right before your eyes, and the fucking thing starts forgetting you. Even in solved murders you will be no protagonist. Someday you will kill someone for that.

An erudite senior once gave me a theory explaining this. The successful solving of a case, he claimed, is nothing more than the detective's artful imposition of a narrative on what really happened. For a detective, this fiction is the solution; the identity of the murderer is merely the remainder of the fictionalizing process. For a murderer, however, there is no fictionalizing. What happened is hard reality and the detective is nothing but an irritant that will never quite get all of it.

Also, if I allow myself some honesty, between committing a murder and finding a murderer, the first is more operatic, more visceral, ever more efficient at removing boredom from life. The latter might be a minor thrill that persists for a few days, if at all, until a new case is at hand and the monotony of investigation begins anew.

This is the last text the victim wrote, hand-written on a sheet of paper on which some parts of his brain had come to rest:

The nuances in an ending are many.

There is the problem of agency. Just who shall bring about the end to a story? And how should this agency contrast with the agency that propelled the middle of the story? Or the agency that began the story?

There is also the problem of inclination. Mathematically speaking, if the mood of the story was a function, then in which direction is this function differentiated at the end. Does the ending spike the mood in one direction, or does it do so in the reverse? How big is the spike?

And sticking to mathematics, we might as well pose the question: When does an ending begin? Is it the last sentence? The last para? The last third? When does a part that is not the story's end end and when does the end end begin? The ending of the pre-end is also an end and so on and so on, till one reaches the beginning of the story.

A subordinate of mine found this text utterly ridiculous and suggested that the murderer had read it and had no option left but to shoot the guy in the head, saying something like, 'This is the end.' I had to feign laughter, but I knew that the murderer had read this text before pressing the trigger. Because the text is complete. Wouldn't chance instead demand that the last sentence, or even the last word, not be complete, that the violent severing of thought, a bullet unloaded into a brain while its owner was still putting a sentence on paper, cause incompleteness?

But that didn't happen. The murderer acted only after this coherent stream of questions had been written. It is even possible that the text was completed in the murderer's presence, that the murderer, for the sake of form, had allowed the victim to finish the text. And yes, it is possible that the murderer even discussed the text with the victim.

So, what if the murderer hadn't liked the text? Did the murderer's views on endings differ? Was the murderer also a writer? Or what if the murderer hadn't liked the fact there was such an interesting text at all, that the victim was a writer?

After I was done looking out from the window, I prepared a chillum and took long drags while lying on my bed. I thought of Ankita, of how she fucked. Ever ready, that's what she was. Which I came to know much later as a bad thing, for she was ever ready for it with others as well.

Her latest novel lay dog-eared on the bedside table. The Amazon rankings were pathetic. I was not surprised. Two reviewers had trashed the novel, one of them nearly imploring Ankita to stop writing.

The novel is about a young woman who, now tired of disappointments with Indian men, has decided to spend some of her savings on a long trip to Europe. The European incidents are banal, the men all too sweet and chivalrous and the final redemption – enduring love with a pectoral-endowed Italian villager, what else – phony. When I first read it, the novel angered me. I found it to be filled with feminist hubris that was strategic when it came to Indian men and tactical when it came to European men. It ultimately proposed fucking men as a solution to having to fuck men.

But it is these silly convictions that I have always liked in Ankita.

One of the follies during an investigation is to go too deep into the details. The detective, working under the injunction of imposing a narrative, cannot quite know which parts are relevant and which are not. Because as long as the centre of the mystery is hidden, every point is a contender for dilation, everything seems deserving of attention. But this is where instinct comes into play. One cannot chase every notion, one cannot have too many hypotheses; one needs to choose the right one early.

The text was complete; was allowed to be completed. Which feeds the possibility that the murderer may have known the victim as a writer. Which feeds the possibility that the murderer had a sense of irony. Which feeds the possibility that the murderer may have been a writer himself/herself.

Video footage from CCTV cameras on the ground-floor lobby shows one hundred fifty-seven people entering the building in the twelve-hour time window before and after the murder and one hundred forty-nine people exiting the building in the same window. Out of the one hundred fifty-seven who entered, ninety-four have been classified as residents in the building (forty-four of them are visibly children). Out of the remaining sixty-three, forty-three are regular or irregular visitors deemed outside the first circle of suspicion. These are maids, food-delivery boys, electricians, plumbers, massage boys, a well-known prostitute trying to wiggle out of dance bar duties, etc.

The victim's parents, who are from Delhi, cannot come up with any possible suspect. They don't know any of the twenty faces who are possible suspects.

Now to the writing business. I contacted some friends of the victim, identified either through his parents or through his social media. Most confirmed that the victim had big writing ambitions and that he had even managed to publish some short stories in reputed online journals. Fourteen of the victim's friends were writers themselves. Of these fourteen, one had entered and exited the building in the appropriate time window.

The sky above is bloodshot, the roads below the veins of my desire and all the roads lead to her.

Ankita is the prime suspect, but the evidence is only circumstantial. I have actually never understood what the word circumstantial means and what it adds to the classification of evidence. Is circumstantial evidence the evidence implicit in the circumstances? But then, isn't all evidence, whether true or false, produced by circumstances, by *someone's* circumstances?

I know I could have her questioned by one of my subordinates right now, but I am lazy and the effect of the chillum has yet not receded. This case, from where I look at it, could be open and shut. I like it when cases are open and shut and when the shutting is done slowly. The end should be flawless.

The victim and Ankita were in a sexual relationship. She would visit him every other day, presumably to fuck, presumably to write, presumably to listen to him read his texts to her and fuck, presumably to have him fuck her while she wrote... there are many combinations possible. Not many of the victim's friends knew about this relationship. The secrecy had obvious reasons: Ankita was cheating on her husband. Her infidelity had been going on for many years, with multiple partners. She never kept one lover for long and so maybe she was beginning to distance herself from the victim as well. Things must have gotten ugly; there must have remained no other option.

Classically speaking, Ankita's husband should be the prime suspect. Creating the right set of circumstances around him would almost ensure conviction: rage and jealousy are the judges' favourites. Of the people who entered the building that day, there are at least half a dozen unidentified men, three of them wearing caps or hats of some kind. It wouldn't be impossible to argue that Ankita's husband had been one of those six. One could then make a claim that he had followed Ankita into the building and found her and her lover in a compromising position. But then the judge would say that the victim was found fully clothed, that Ankita's husband wouldn't have been allowed to enter the building in the first place, et cetera. And here we come to an irritating truth: that the creation of circumstances can itself require a testimony. In her husband's case, that testimony can only come from Ankita.

If the testimony became available, the rest would be relatively easy. Because Raman Verma, a respectable mid-to-senior-management employee in a major insurance company and by all accounts a decent, even if sexually tentative, man has an ingredient that can thicken the circumstantial soup like nothing else: a gun.

The story behind it is simple. Raman's father, a *tehsildar* with a career in several districts in Uttar Pradesh, had two gun licenses: one for a twin-bore rifle and one for a Colt pistol. Months before the father died of cancer, Raman surrendered the twin-bore's license but got the Colt license and the weapon transferred to himself. And he even carried the gun to Bombay. For vague sentimental reasons (apparently having to do with shooting two bullets in the air every Diwali) – Ankita had told me this about a year ago when some of her afternoons were spent fondling my gun.

The Colt's calibre is of course the same that bore through the victim's head from contact distance. Since the time of the shooting cannot be known precisely, the differences in time between Ankita's entry and exit, and Raman's entry and exit (which is to say, the entries and exits of the six unidentified men) and the moment of the crime itself are not relevant beyond a point. That there was entry, that there was exit, that there was a weapon, that there was a situation, that Raman is a cuckold and Ankita is a deviant wife – all of it points to Raman as the murderer. The only hiccup to this theory could come if someone cited the ground floor security's SOP of calling the intercom for an apartment whenever an unknown visitor came. This is where Ankita's testimony assumes importance. She could declare that it was she who had asked her lover to let her husband in, to amicably discuss getting into an adult's agreement, or even to discuss a divorce and a subsequent remarriage.

Alibis are not a problem. The day of the murder was a Saturday, a holiday at Raman's insurance company. Raman was in Bombay. After these macros, all that is needed to squash any irritating alibis is to adjust the phone's location data. Kadam at Cyber does that kind of thing for a rum quarter.

I was content and dizzy before going to sleep last night. I slept for nine hours, the longest I have slept since Ankita and I split eight months ago. In my sleep I dreamt of the victim's text, his text about the beginning of ends, and the text swirled around till it evaporated and I saw an image of a murderer on a motorbike. I somehow identified the man on the motorbike as a murderer. Dreams can convey such information; they are both cinematic and novelistic. The murderer was riding his motorbike on a mountain road. The frame of the dream was set behind the murderer's back and he was moving away from it. Far in the background, set against the blue-grey sky, there was a giant cement structure that had no shape for a while. But after a bit of visual trickery, that jumbling and reconstruction peculiar to dreams, the structure came to resemble a half-built bridge. It seemed the road would eventually lead the murderer there, to the edge of the half-built bridge and after that, there would be nowhere to go but below, down to the depths of the ravine.

Today I will have a subordinate get in touch with Ankita, to tell her simply that she is the prime suspect. This, I am certain, will terrify her. My subordinate will warn Ankita not to leave Bombay at any rate, for that would be damning. Then, just before letting her go, he will convey, nonchalantly, that I am the head of the investigation for this case. Ankita will contact me and then I will tell her that my subordinate probably made a mistake. That it is not she but her husband who is the prime suspect, that the evidence against him is strong and that all it will really need is a testimony from her, doing nothing more than tying the story's loose ends. As to her failure to immediately contact the police about the crime, it will be attributed to her shock and her love for her husband. The judge will take a benign view: she will probably go to jail for a few months, if at all, after which she will find me waiting for her.

Needless to say, Ankita might even find it plausible that her husband committed the murder. A confused witness is the most easily convinced.

Imagine the dourness of the procedures involved even in this open and shut case. Twelve hours of CCTV footage had to be carefully seen and documented; scores of people had to be interviewed; the gun-licensing records of all these people had to be checked; the neighbours had to be asked if they really did miss the report of the gunshot; the published stories of the victim had to be read; Google and Facebook had to be requested to allow some access to the victim's accounts; and much more…

After two hours of convincing, Ankita agreed to testify against her husband. I told her that to make the story even more plausible, she had to find access to the weapon and hand it over to me. I told her I needed to check if the shot had been fired from the same gun.

Even for detectives, it is better not to leave trails behind, which is why I prefer public transport to the official vehicle. As of now, I am in a taxi going towards Bandra, where I live, from over the Sea Link. An hour back, I was with Ankita at a restaurant in South Bombay, where she handed me a packet with the pistol and all the bullets. To assure her I held her hand in mine, and she smiled nervously. I made her sign my copy of her book with her lips. Her top showed ample cleavage when she bent to kiss the page. She knew I remembered this top. She knew I loved this top.

On the Sea Link, I ask the taxi driver to take the car to the left-most lane, close to the side of the bridge. I throw the packet over the bridge as hard as I can: I see only the first part of its parabolic descent. The taxi driver, curious, asks me what it was. I tell him that it was a thing that belonged to, and reminded me of, a dead friend of mine. The driver nods. Rid of the packet, I suddenly realize that I am in the mood to talk and so I tell the taxi driver that I had only come to know my friend a few days before his death and that we had become very close very soon.

I tell him that my friend was trying to be a writer. At this, the taxi driver interjects me and launches into a monologue about a Hindi detective novel that he read recently and enjoyed a lot. He is intent on telling me the plot of this novel. I want to tell him just how I befriended my now-deceased friend, how I loved the stories he wrote, how we came to spend time together, how he was kind enough to invite me to his house sometimes, how he would read his stories aloud to me. But the driver does not let me say any of that. He goes on with his plot, with his twists and turns. His is a murder mystery and I don't really care. Soon I stop listening to him, allowing my mind to go to the last text of the victim. Could it be that the murderer had loved it?

I let the thought pass and look outside the window. I feel the speed of the taxi.

SHE HAS MY NAME

Timeri N. Murari

She waited exactly where she had told him she would. Round the corner from the metro station, down the quiet, residential street with free parking. She was prepared to wait all day. She had her phone, a book, a thermos of coffee and samosas. He would come. Would she recognize him? He would have to change his appearance as his bearded features were recognizable in the newspapers and on television. But he would not be able to disguise those heavy-lidded, piercing eyes. It had been many years since she had seen him in the flesh.

He came into the country for the body of his daughter. He knew it was a trap, but he believed she should lie in the land of his birth and not in the enemy's. She had been killed, so young and beautiful, to pay for his sins against the State. The State had alienated him on the murder of his father, a man of wisdom and steadfastness of purpose against the injustices of the State, when he was around the same age as his daughter. It had murdered his daughter to draw him out, knowing that he would not rest until he had recovered her body to lie beside the graves of his father, mother and grandparents. His brothers too lay in the same graveyard.

The men who helped him enter the country on his new passport, with a false name and in the photograph clean-shaven and so youthful, did not ask for money. They wanted only a favour, to kill a man for them and then they would take him and his daughter's body safely back to his homeland. They were from his country, exiles who claimed to support the cause and were overly deferential to him. You are our hero, they said in unison and bowed in unison, expecting him to be swayed by such flattery. They gave him the photograph of the man he would kill, a gun and left him outside the building, telling him they would wait for him in the car. When he returned to the street, the car had gone. This betrayal didn't surprise him. He expected that, always.

He didn't drop the weapon but tucked into his waistband and walked unhurriedly up the street towards the metro station. It was winter and he wore a light leather jacket, pressed jeans and an open neck shirt. He didn't look out of place but a good citizen. It was mid-afternoon and the street deserted. The town and the streets were familiar. The homes were behind high walls, the gates protected by sleepy guards in crumpled uniforms.

He passed a parked car in which a man and a woman were arguing fiercely with the windows closed. He didn't pause when the man slapped her hard and only hesitated when he heard the shot, a muffled crack. He glanced back as the woman climbed out of the car. Inside, the man slumped against the window.

She asked him if he would help her. He said nothing but returned to the car and helped her heave the body onto the back seat. He guessed it was a shot to the heart, no sign of blood, quick and clean. He took the gun, a .38 automatic, levered a round into the chamber and returned it to her. She dropped it in her handbag.

Ride with me, she said and he climbed in. The imprint of the man's palm on her cheek was fading as she drove.

You don't say much, she said as she steered quickly through traffic, but then you never did.

He nodded and, knowing he was safe, fell asleep. When he woke up, it was dusk and they were deep in the country.

I'm taking you home. Is that okay? He merely closed his eyes in agreement. How have you been, she asked.

She turned into the drive, a long one, to a house set well back. It showed no lights and she was not bothered that he hadn't answered.

We'll bury him in the rose garden, she said. He loved roses and he'd like that. She pointed to the side of the house. There are gardening tools there.

Obediently, he went and found them. They took turns digging up the rose bed, the soil was soft and loamy. She took the dead man's feet, he took the shoulders. They dropped him in the grave and shovelled the earth back. When they finished, he meticulously patted the earth flat and then helped her re-plant the roses. He couldn't tell the colour in the darkness, but their smell reminded him of his homeland where roses blossomed to the size of a fist and caressed the air with their perfume.

Why did you marry him, he asked when they were sitting in her catalogue kitchen, gleaming with gadgetry, all wasteful in his eyes. His taste in food was austere and simple – leavened bread, spiced vegetable, pungent onions – enough to sustain him in the mountains. He noted but said nothing, that she had used a key to open the front door while the kitchen one was unlocked. She poured herself chilled Chablis but didn't offer him any as she knew he didn't touch alcohol.

I fell in love, I suppose, why else does one marry?

She had a worn beauty, like a well-rubbed coin, still revealing the profile of a queen or a princess.

He was gentle in the beginning, she continued, then he became a beast, as all men do with the passing of time. He knew you were coming and he knew I'd be waiting for you. I never stopped waiting for you and he knew that too. He knew my password, it's her name. When I typed it in, I thought of her and now when I do, I am reminded of her. You took your time.

I have time, he said.

So do they.

How did they kill our daughter? He waited until she refilled her glass, the wine sending a faint blush through her cheeks.

They had found her hanging from the clothes hook on the back of the door in her room, she said in a whisper. They said it was suicide, young people do that in their depression and then they said it was a drug trip. My heart broke into small pieces when I saw my dead daughter, and it will remain in lost pieces until the day I die. I didn't know until then how frail the heart is, it broke like dropped china.

He waited, letting her weep, without consoling her. Always patient. He knew what she would say before she said it.

You're to blame because of who you are! she screamed at him. They killed her knowing it was the only way to hurt you but they don't know you as well as I do. That you can't be hurt by your daughter's death. You feel nothing, nothing, you never did.

He waited until she stopped crying, poured himself a glass of water from the tap, savouring its cool sweetness, envying her only for that convenience. He had forgotten the ease of such a life, a tap, clean water, the very simplicity unavailable in his land. He drank slowly, remembering the times he had thirsted for water.

Remembering too, despite his reluctance to recall the past, that she was wrong in her screamed accusation. He had felt, he had experienced love. She had forgotten that in her anguished rage. There was that long winter of tenderness in their lives, the winter in which she conceived the daughter who was now dead. He had felt love for her, though he had not articulated his emotions. And that was his fault, love needed to be spoken out aloud and not confined to the heart. He had not spoken it so long ago, when they were young, because he knew he would not remain in her country long. She would not survive in his; the harshness would have killed her.

When they assassinated his father, he had left her, without saying goodbye, never expecting to return. Knowing he had left a part of him in her body. He had underestimated her determination to make him remember and had sent him photographs of the daughter, wrote about her too and sent those messages to an email address that was not in his name or even remotely connected to him, except through layers of intermediaries.

From that distance, he had watched his child grow into a beautiful young woman who also wrote to him. She wanted to know her father, meet and embrace him, though she knew too, from reading the newspapers, that he was considered a dangerous man, incapable of human warmth. His replies to her long, longing letters were curt, dismissive of her suggestions, not knowing that rejection to a woman's heart only increased her loving. The daughter knew, despite his curtness, that she had touched him and he had read her letters, otherwise he would never have even replied. By doing so, he realized now, even his curt replies had endangered his daughter's life. He had revealed, to those who watched for such signs, his vulnerability. If only he had stayed silent.

He rose and washed the glass, letting the water run, listening to its music and then wiped the glass clean before placing it in the rack. She remembered that he had always been meticulous in his movements, keeping them minimalistic, never wasting energy. He had the slight stoop of a man who crouched close to the earth in his movements, which brought him down to her height, almost. He'd lost some weight but wasn't skinny, just lean and muscled and tried to imagine what kind of a haunted life he led. When he washed his hands under the running tap, she thought he was trying to wash the blood off his hands as he used the soap to scrub them, like a surgeon before an operation. Of course, his hands could never be cleansed. When she had known him long ago, he had not killed anyone and was just an innocent boy she fell in love with. A solemn young man, yet with a wry sense of humour and honeyed skin she loved to caress. That skin looked coarser, tiny scars criss-crossing the backs of those cleansed hands and his eyes no longer held any humour. She could not see any laugh lines.

Breaking the silence to distract him from hearing them approach, she said, my daughter insisted on using your name, you know, insisted, even though she had never set eyes on you and knew you only through my bitterness. I wanted her to use my husband's name. He had adopted her, but when she reached eighteen, she dropped his name and changed it to yours. You had no right to her life and she lived only another 18 months with your name.

He nodded. Yes, she told me and I advised her strongly not to. It would mark her out for life. She was reckless.

She heard beyond the question he asked, for the first time showing some curiosity for his daughter. She was brave, she replied and she was beautiful and clever; she danced and sang and laughed with abandon. She was so alive, unlike other girls her age who walk and talk as if they're dead and she had a halo of friends who surrounded her wherever she went. She couldn't, wouldn't, commit suicide, especially by hanging herself from a hook on the back of her bedroom door. The coroner said she had, no matter how much I insisted that the authorities murdered her because of her father. The coroner was one of those kindly looking men with metal hearts. He said I was mad with grief, as she was my only child and I was fantasizing such conspiracies. The authorities are kindly people too, he had said, they lived by the law and would not, could not, murder an innocent child for the sake of punishing her father. The State would not do that, as it upheld high moral codes, respected human rights and practised democracy. It was men like her father who murdered the innocent, that's what he told me in front of everyone.

I begged him to order an autopsy, but he said it was unnecessary. She had committed suicide. The Investigator and here she used two fingers of both hands to place that word in quotation marks, sat in the front row and he too looked at me with kindness and sympathy, as if understanding my unremitting pain. The Investigator was the one who broke the news of my daughter's death to me. He came to the house early Sunday morning with his mourning face to tell me that there had been an accident, that my daughter had hung herself from the hook on the back of her bedroom door. I didn't believe him, she had called me the evening before, she called every evening and told me she was going to a party with her friends as she had finished her assignments. She had that discipline too; she wouldn't party until her work was completed.

He listened without any movement, wishing he had met his daughter. She had wanted to meet him when she changed her name, but he had coldly discouraged her. A curt no.

You married when you went home, didn't you? Did you fall in love? And when he shook his head, just once, she continued, how many children?

Three, two boys and a girl. He paused, not wanting to continue, but he did in spite of his reticence. A missile hit our home when I was away. It was the rumour I was there that killed them.

In the silence, she wondered whether he had mourned that loss and poured herself the third glass of wine, giving herself the false courage to continue with the evening.

You've come to avenge my daughter's death, haven't you?

No, he said, revenge against the State is futile. As she has my name, she must lie in the graveyard in my home. Where is she now?

She had to laugh aloud at his audacity, though she knew the dangers of her contempt. I buried her in the land of her birth, in the town's graveyard. She was my altar when she was alive, now her grave's my daily pilgrimage. She will remain here. Who would she know in the graveyard of your ancestors? She didn't even know your language and I will not allow her to lie among such strangers. Please, I beg you, allow me that, she said, though he heard no pleading note in her voice. It was more mocking.

He felt no remorse when he knew that, because of her defiance, he would have to kill this woman he had loved. His daughter had to lie in the family graveyard, even as one day he will lie beside her there.

Despite their years apart, she still knew how he thought and waited for them to come for him. They were near, just beyond the door. They both waited as he had been listening to the silence and knew it had been disturbed and, seeing her look, knew they were here.

You told them, he said.

Yes, I told the Investigator you would come for her. You knew that?

Yes.

Yet, you came.

For you and for her. She has my name. What did they promise you for me?

I wanted you to take your revenge but you won't, will you?

No, I told you that.

He still had the gun in his waistband; it felt so heavy, dragging him down. She saw, for the first time, that he was tired, not so much physically but spiritually.

The Investigator came through the back door, not quickly but cautiously and two armed men, who remained in the shadows, followed him. Their guns aimed at him. The Investigator stood facing them both with all the authority of his State. A square man, with a square face, receding dark hair and unforgiving eyes.

Give me your weapon, he said quietly to the man and accepted the gun slid across the polished table. He picked it up, hefted it, a 9 mm automatic, then freed the clip. It was full and there was one round in the chamber. He sniffed the barrel. It hadn't been fired recently. He placed it far out of reach from the man and sat down. He had a gentle voice, it calmed the spirit of the listener.

I've waited many years for us to meet. Patience pays off.

You killed my daughter?

The State ordered me to. You are too famous and protected in your land. Unreachable. It was unfortunate, but how else could I get you, so well-hidden away in your land. Like a serpent in its hole, I had to tempt you out, somehow. I know your culture and your traditions; you couldn't allow her to remain here. It was my persistence. I did not know you had a daughter here until she changed her name and it came up on our computers. I traced you back to the days when you were here and read your communication with her. Even though your responses were brief, I knew she had touched you. Otherwise, you would never have exposed yourself.

He sat very still facing the Investigator and she knew the men would kill him as soon as they could. He knew that too. They would call it an 'encounter'. He glanced at her and she caught the tiny glint of admiration in his eyes.

The Investigator turned to the woman and said, thank you for helping me and keeping me informed on his movements. Otherwise, I could never have brought justice to this terrorist. Of course, he will be tried in a court of law. We believe in our democracy and just rule of our laws.

And found guilty?

That is up to the judge.

And justice for my daughter?

There is a reward of course, he smiled.

There are only three of you, she asked. He's a dangerous man, as you yourself said.

Three are more than enough.

When he turned to one of his men, she opened her purse that lay on the table. She took out the gun with which she had killed her husband and killed the Investigator first and then his two companions.

I believe in revenge, she said in the silence that followed the explosions. I wanted him here alone; I wanted to hear him boast about my daughter's murder. I knew he would come himself so he could boast about catching you.

You had to do it, not me, to free you of the hate for the man who killed our daughter. I can never be free of that. You will look after our daughter?

Yes, I will.

He reached over and took the gun. Carefully, he wiped it clean of her fingerprints and then gripped the weapon in his hand, pressing down firmly on both the butt and the barrel, then placed it back on the table between them. He smiled, reminding her of that youth and she felt it gentle as a goodbye kiss.

He rose, picked up his own weapon, tucked it into his waistband and walked through the door. She thought of offering him a lift but knew he would find the way back to his own land.

DEATHGPT

Navin Weeraratne

'That's why, Detective, I killed her,' he said.

The radiator rattled to show it still mattered. It filled the room with that awful smell that I've always thought was burnt dust. White paint peeled from the walls of the interrogation room. Underneath, they'd been pastel blue. Someone thought this place would've been cheery? Some fresh officer trying to make a difference… Dumb bastard. The mould patches were the record of their achievement. It was mid-morning and I was questioning the star of last night's crimes – Rahul Das.

Rahul was a thin, small-built fellow with the compulsory moustache that men like him always had. His hair was neat. His shirt and trousers clean; he could have been going to work, just another person on the subway you'd never remember. His ID, a few small bills and a picture of his young wife and their infant son were in his wallet. Just the type who'd shoot a woman in the head.

'How did you know Ms Nitya Anand?'

He frowned at the name like it was politically incorrect to say.

'She goes by Sandy.' *She goes by Sandy*. In his mind, she hadn't moved to past tense yet. 'It was the only name she went by on the sites. That's how we knew her.'

'We?'

'Her fans. Everyone knew her; there aren't that many South Asian adult stars. Didn't you know her?'

'No,' I lied. 'Did you arrange to meet her at Victoria Road junction?'

'Yes.'

'How?'

'I used a disappearing message service.'

'How did you make contact with her in the first place?'

'I went to her fan page. She's good with emails, answering within a few hours. We became friends.'

Within hours? Idiot was friends with a chatbot.

'Why did you destroy your phone's SIM and memory cards?'

'I didn't want anything traced. That's why I destroyed her phone, too. I didn't notice the CCTV.'

The cadence of a rehearsed line.

'You mentioned sites. What websites did you see her on?'

'Femjoy, Hegre Art, Holly Randall.'

'And you have subscriptions to these adult sites?'

'Yes. For years.'

Finance had uncovered that, too. He'd wrecked his credit and had bills out to collections. Yet, he also had years of unbroken, recurring payments to international porn sites... He'd joined each one on a different month. Yet, always on the first of the month.

'What was your phone plan?'

'I didn't have one. I only bought prepaid cards.'

'HighTel has a postpaid plan for just 400. LotusNet, as well. Why didn't you just get one of those?'

'I can't afford postpaid.' There was outrage in his voice. It was the outrage of someone who'd been led to believe life would have a bag of sweets for him behind every door.

It was the first honest answer he'd given.

'Then, how could you afford $150 monthly in porn subscriptions?'

There it was: the first look of worry on his face.

'What were the porn sites you subscribed to?'

'Femjoy, Hegre Art, Holly Randall.'

'You said Femjoy, *Rylsky* Art, Holly Randall,' I lied.

'Sorry, yes, I meant Rylsky Art.'

'What was the exact fee for each site?'

'I didn't pay close attention.'

'You didn't pay close attention?' I held up the printout of his financial records. 'Not even the City's greatest accountant could manage these payments while collapsing into financial ruin. Where's the income?'

'I used credit cards!'

'Which you never applied for?'

'I didn't want my wife to know!'

'Your *wife*?' Inane reasons are last-ditch straw-clutching. 'You can keep anything from your wife, Rahul. She's pretty stupid to have married you. But you can't hide anything from *me*. What were those four porn sites? *What were the sites?*'

'Femjoy! Hegre Art! Holly Randall! Playboy!'

The day's lunchroom story would be how he got it wrong each time. *Open and shut, sir*, I'd been told when I was handed the case file. *Camera footage and all, sir.*

To my right was a pot of tea. I poured him a cup and set it in front of him. He stared in amazement as I uncuffed his hands.

'Let's talk about Sandy,' I lit a cigarette.

'All right,' he sipped the tea. He was regaining his composure.

'You've been a fan of hers for how long?'

'Years.'

'Can you say how many?'

'Three? Maybe four.'

'So, you've looked at pictures of her for three or four years?'

'Yes.'

'What colour are her eyes?'

He froze.

'Brown.'

'Just brown?'

'What do you want from me?' he glared.

'Tell me about her eyes! Her face! You like looking at naked pictures of her, yes? What did she look like?'

Das folded his arms and said nothing. He started trembling, suppressed rage. People will tell you everything, whether they like to or not. You just have to ask.

'Her eyes were green, Rahul. I've looked at them many times.'

Late last night, the victim, identified as Nitya Anand, aka Sandy, walked to a deserted intersection in an industrial park. Footage shows her looking about, nervous as any woman walking a deserted street. She pulled out her phone when she reached the intersection and began texting.

She was well-dressed, too well-dressed. A wide-brimmed hat obscured her face. Beneath it, sunglasses (at night). Facial recognition couldn't confirm her identity, but that wasn't because of the headwear. It was because Sandy seemed to know exactly which way to turn to hide her face from every CCTV along her route.

Then the killer, Rahul Das, arrives. He does nothing to hide his face. Both seem to expect each other but still react as if seeing one another for the first time.

Then, Sandy turns her back to take a call.

Without hesitation, Rahul pulls a gun and shoots Sandy in the back of her head.

He then loads her into the trunk of a stolen car and drives to an undeveloped lot outside the City, where he went on to pour petrol over the car and set it alight.

Evidence shows he bashed her face in with a rock and special attention had been given to her teeth. Too many American crime shows? Dental records weren't a thing in this part of the world.

His arrest was routine. Security AIs scanned and flagged the CCTV footage within an hour. The police were informed; Traffic tracked down the car. We reached him just as he had finished. He had no getaway vehicle. He didn't seem frantic or angry that an associate hadn't come to collect him – or surprised it was the police instead who did.

The arresting officer noted that Rahul seemed relieved. That he'd then slept so soundly in lockup that they thought he'd died.

Someone had died. I just didn't think it was Sandy.

Sandy had no known family members. Any identity documents the victim might have had were destroyed in the fire. There was no phone number on Sandy's website. The site's domain registry was also hidden, so there was no way of knowing who owned it. We were getting that information released, but I wasn't optimistic. There were ways to stay hidden if someone tried hard enough.

Someone had tried *very* hard. Sandy had no social media presence except for promotional posts. It was a typical AI-managed account, connecting only to other adult industry professionals or fans. Calls to those people drew a blank; no one had ever *met* her. The only person identifying the victim as Sandy was her killer.

A man who'd never seen Sandy before in his life.

All the same, someone had taken a great deal of trouble to fake her death. Bank records had been altered. CCTV locations mapped. Das had been coached on what to say – and how to shoot.

Cracking Das was easy. He was just another who'd looked up at the City's glitz and not noticed the shit he was standing in. He'd spent beyond his means and become a bank serf. I'd requested a warrant to check his wife's finances for any sudden, life-changing sums of money. I doubted it would come to anything. You can't have corruption without cash and the City loves its cash.

As for the victim's identity, I doubted I'd ever find out. There's no shortage of poor, young women in the slums. Being asked to wear something nice and go for a walk might have been the least she'd been asked to do.

I kept questioning Das, but we'd seen it all before. Anonymous fixer. Untraceable payment. Hidden client. Criminals even have apps for that now. Clients, vendors and intermediaries had no idea who they were doing business with. It was an age of add-to-cart crime.

The real planner would've known none of this would withstand serious scrutiny. However, they'd been careful not to leave clues.

Or had they?

I watched looping footage of the victim in the street. She was walking in heels awkwardly. She kept adjusting her scarf like she didn't know she could wear it any way she liked. Were the clothes the clue?

I took screenshots from 20 different angles and ran a search.

What are these clothes? I asked.

A 'Chateau de la Croix' wool scarf in a deep navy blue, finished with a bold, geometric design and a faux-fur pom-pom trim.

A 'Gemstone Couture' necklace featuring a solitaire pendant suspended from a delicate white gold chain. This necklace is the epitome of classic elegance and would be perfect for any formal occasion.

A 'Vivienne Atelier' handbag made of the finest Italian leather. The bag is a structured, envelope-shaped clutch with a removable chain strap and a magnetic snap closure.

'Manolo Blahnik' heels. Known for luxury, elegance and quality, this pair of heels are made of velvet, with a pointed toe and a stiletto heel. The deep green colour is perfect for a formal event.

How many stores sell these in the City?

Eight.

List them. Also, their contact numbers and the numbers for the security firms that handle their CCTV footage.

It did so.

The larger stores cooperated. The smaller ones grumbled: they didn't want us seeing their clients buying fetish wear for their mistresses... I said it would be best if social media didn't think they weren't cooperating in the #JusticeForSandy investigation. That did it.

I wasn't comfortable crunching the footage on the department's cluster. Whoever had faked Sandy's death was powerful. Powerful people have friends in the police. Instead, I uploaded the footage to my cloud storage and paid a cluster in Estonia to do the work.

At 4 a.m., the Estonian AI found something.

'Who is this?' asked Chawla, my friend on the Financial Crimes floor.

'Adlan Narain, freelance programmer. Lives in a large house in Sandhurst.'

'*Sandhurst?* Must be *some* freelance gigs he's landing! Why is he buying women's clothes? Dude, vice crimes aren't a thing any more.'

'I think he's involved in the Sandy disappearance.'

He frowned.

'Chief is calling it a murder.'

'There was a murder. Just not Sandy's. I think Adlan Narain is holding her captive.'

'Ha! Jilted fan kidnaps sex goddess, imprisons her in a sound-proofed dungeon, right in the middle of posh Sandhurst? You should write detective stories!'

'I'm serious. Look at where he lives.' I showed him on City Maps. 'Look at how *big* the house is. Whatever he's doing, it's not programming.'

'You want me to look into his accounts?'

'Quietly.'

He raised eyebrows.

'If you have to ask, that means you shouldn't be asking.'

'Narain killed someone!'

'So? Why should I get in trouble? If you don't want people to make phone calls about the police looking into their financial crimes, don't ask Financial Crimes to look. You're smart, Vikram. Find a way. We all do.'

The hardest thing to understand is your own culture. That's because you're raised in its unspoken assumptions and inane taboos. To understand them, though, in the first place, you have to notice them. You won't till you are dumped somewhere else. Among the alien, you notice what you didn't in the familiar. From seeing follows assessing. Only then can you measure how much your world has been shaped by the ideas it questions so rarely that it doesn't know they're there.

In the city, that unquestioned idea is corruption. We're aware of it as its beneficiaries and its victims. What we don't understand is how corrosive it's been. So used to seeing the scars in the mirror, we've forgotten the acid attack.

It spreads to and infects every layer of society. The politician learns he can help himself, both hands outstretched, to a foreign loan. The bureaucrat beneath him sends what's left to a contractor – himself. His staff insists on bribes for paperwork to go forward. The businesspersons paying the bribes become proactive; why compete when you can grease? Research and development budgets shrink and *entertainment* budgets rise.

The honest then complain that the crooked are getting ahead. They console themselves that they, however, have remained honest.

Their children regard their poverty and make their own opinions about honesty.

You can imagine the difficulty of being a policeman here. Everyone you count on is underpaid. People don't trust you because they know you'll shake them down like the bandit you are (how else can you pay your bills)? If you can be counted on to accept gifts, you will rise. You'll find yourself in an ecology of friends, favours and even more gifts: you have become a beneficiary.

If you try to do your job, though, those friends become nervous. They call in favours from other people.

Your career ends.

I'm Detective Vikram Reddy. As Detective Reddy, I go by the book. This often gets me nowhere. That's when I stop being Detective Reddy. Instead, I become Myuran, the Fixer. Myuran couldn't care less about the book.

Myuran is a beneficiary.

'Why do we have to meet here?' said Sajin, the bank clerk. 'Why do we have to meet *at all*?'

The noon sun beat down on the open-air food court. The lunch crowd had emerged from their unlicensed construction sites and gloomy basement shops.

A group of construction workers was clustered around a rice stall. They pressed, one against the other, each with an outstretched arm holding a phone, a cash card, or a printed QR code from the day's employer. Not making eye contact as he served them, a sweating chef tossed rice in a blackened wok and turned up the heat. Flames blue as neon flared, then turned dirty yellow.

Three teenagers in the prim and proper cardigans and jackets of a private school too greedy to expel them sat on monobloc plastic stools around a crate. A man set down a tray of steaming filter coffees in front of them. One student pulled out an imported cigarette and lit it. Another pulled a bottle of Old Monk and spiked his drink.

Tenements rose on either side of the illegal food court. Brown grime collected in recesses. Green algae stains followed leaks from unmaintained ACs. A woman in a nightgown began hanging laundry outside her window.

'There are cameras,' said Sajin. He motioned to one right above us while trying to hide his face. 'Myuran, if that's even your real name, we could have done this online.'

'It's my real name,' I replied with a truth he wouldn't understand. 'Don't worry about the camera. It hasn't been working for the past 10 minutes. It will only start again after we leave. Same as all the other cameras on this table.'

'This very table?'

'Only this table. That's why Auntie Mehta reserved it for me,' I motioned to a large, older woman standing at a stall of bubbling clay pots. She harangued a man working alongside her, caught my eye, smiled and then returned to haranguing him.

'She's really quite sweet. So, do you have what I asked for?'

Sajin pulled out a folder and passed it across the table to me. I opened it and began flipping through; it was row after row of bank transactions.

I saw the end-of-month balance.

'Adlan Narain is filthy fucking rich,' said Sajin. 'Not Rolex and BMW rich. Not fly-first-class-but-complain-about-the-price-of-onions rich. He is buy-a-foreign-passport-and-a-private-jet rich.'

'He hardly buys anything expensive!'

'He's that kind of person. His biggest expenses are computer equipment – and property. Yet, he pays rent for a small flat in Chandi.'

Chandi was a good, upper-middle-class neighborhood. The kind of place you'd think someone like a freelance programmer might live if he was fairly successful. Why was he renting it?

'His friends and family don't know about his house in Sandhurst,' I said.

Sajin smiled and nodded. He would have made a good policeman if only he didn't like money so much.

'Then, there's how he's moving money around,' he leaned forward, his voice becoming quiet. 'Large payments coming from Ninja & Pirate Private Limited, in Singapore. It accounts for ninety-nine per cent of his money.'

'Did you dig them up?'

'Yes. The address is a Singapore corporate law firm. N&P's only assets are a couple of accounts in a Chinese bank.'

A shell company. There was no knowing how many others he was bouncing money through or in how many countries. That he still brought so much into his City bank account was eye-watering. He would have had so much more offshore.

'There is something else,' I flipped through the pages again. 'The spending on computer hardware.'

'You said he's a programmer,' Sajin shrugged.

'Surely, he can't need to spend this much on it?'

'Surely, he does. Given that he only buys apartments and junk food, he must need the hardware to make his money. He really is a programmer.'

What was Adlan Narain doing? Fake news bots? Selling likes? Plain old spam? It didn't matter. What did matter was that his spending was pathologically sensible. If he spent money faking Sandy's murder, it was a business decision.

How was faking a porn star's death a business decision?

'Here's your money,' I handed Sajin a brick of banknotes in a paper bag.

The man who dealt with money for a living reacted like I had handed him a rabid rat.

'Are you mad?' He glared at me. 'I can't take cash! How am I supposed to carry around all this?'

'It's all right; I do it all the time. Don't broadcast you're carrying cash and no one will mug you.'

'You could've deposited this into my account.'

"But then someone could just look into your finances.'

'No! No one *ever* looks into accounts until they become a person of interest to the police.' The words had a practised rhythm. 'It's not possible, even with all the power of modern computing, for governments to screen every financial transaction to see what you're doing. The *Americans* can't do it! Millions upon millions of transactions each month. And that's if the laws allowed it. We can move money between bank accounts, Myuran. No one will ever know unless you are a real idiot.'

'And what if someone like me comes to someone like you and just asks? All it takes is a paper bag filled with cash.'

As Myuran, I had established that Narain was crooked. That he had the money to fund the murder. That he also might have had the IT skills to cook Das's banking records. If I'd gone through the channels as Detective Reddy, someone would have tipped off Narain – and I'd still not have the information.

Nothing good could come from Narain owning a house his friends and family didn't know about. A large house in a quiet, exclusive neighborhood. A house for which the building plans at the land registry showed a large basement.

Was he holding the real Sandy captive in his basement?

It was just the sordid sort of thing that happened in the City. I had to enter his house to find out. I couldn't conduct a raid; my financial findings were inadmissible. There was also every chance someone would call Narain and tell him the day and time we'd be turning up (it happens). I had to go on my own.

Myuran had to go on his own.

I parked a street away from Narain's house and waited till 3 a.m. No one is up at that time but death squads. Then, I walked over.

Narain's house was a neoclassical mansion from the colonial period. The original high wall and wrought-iron gate might have kept me out, but the rich and powerful of Sandhurst didn't need walls. They'd passed a building code getting rid of them. In doing so, they'd shown the rest of the City how much safer they were – than us and from us.

I walked right up to the large wooden front door.

'Good morning, sir,' it said. Above my head, one of several cameras swiveled to look at me. 'It's late. Why don't you make an appointment and come back later? Mr Narain would not like to be disturbed at this hour. Thank you for being understanding.'

I held up my badge, ensuring the QR code could be read.

'I'm Detective Reddy of the City's police department. Authenticate my voice pattern: "One, two, three, four, five. The quick brown fox jumps over the lazy dog."'

'Thank you for the voice sample, Detective Reddy. I'm sorry, but this is quite irregular. I'm sure this can wait till morning. Why don't you come back tomorrow? Mr Narain can see you as early as eight.'

'This is not a conversation. This is the *police*. Open the door now, or there will be legal consequences for both Mr Narain and the security contractor.'

Behind the door came the dull, dragging sound of metal, anti-riot bolts sliding into place. Black shutters came down over the Victorian-era windows.

'Uniformed police have been notified of this unwelcome visit,' said the door.

An alert beeped on my phone.

I checked it; it was a request from Emergency Dispatch for an officer to investigate a possible disturbance – at Narain's house.

I marked the alert as 'claimed'. A QR code with the event data came up; for better or worse, I was now on record as the man on the spot.

I regarded the house. There was no getting inside; the riots after the financial crash had taught the rich how to keep the thieving, dirty hordes away from the silverware. I wasn't getting inside through a concealed basement entrance, a loose window, or even with a tac team using explosives.

I had to convince the gatekeeper.

'You have notified the police and asked them to respond, yes?'

'That is correct, Detective Reddy. I'm uncomfortable letting you in until a first responder turns up.'

'If the first responder says they would like to come in and talk to Mr Narain, will you allow it?'

'It is very late. Why doesn't the first responder come back at eight in the morning? Mr Narain will be happy to see them then.'

'The first responder will want to come in to check that Mr Narain is alright. He may be in danger.'

'If Mr Narain is in danger, I will do everything I can to help.'

'I am the first responder,' I held up my phone and showed the QR code from Emergency Dispatch. 'Detective Reddy of the City's police department. Authenticate my voice pattern: "One, two, three, four, five. The quick brown fox jumps over the lazy dog".'

The metal bars slid again and the door opened.

'Thank you for coming,' it said. 'Mr Narain is on the second floor, third room to the right of the stairs. Please hurry!'

'How dare you! This is against my rights!'

Adlan Narain was a small man with a well-groomed beard and moustache. Both of those were pressed against his bedroom's marble floor. He tried lifting his head, but I shoved it back down. He groaned as I shifted my knee, pressing into his back. We knew just how to make that hurt and leave no bruise.

'Police? Ha! I know the mayor! When this is done, you'll be begging to clean toilets!'

'Where is Sandy?'

He froze.

'*Where is she*?' I dug my knee in.

'I don't know what you're talking about.'

'I know all about you, Narain. The money you get through Singapore. How you paid Das to murder a woman. The shops you bought her clothes from. It's over, Narain. Where are you keeping the porn star?'

'You can have my money! As much as you like! Let me go; I'll transfer it right now!'

I looked at the stairwell. It went down to the basement.

'*Whatever* I find down there, she'd better be *alive*.'

With a key from the safe in Narain's room (some people have a *very* low pain threshold).

In the basement, vintage wooden stairs ended at a modern metal door. Narain had been reticent with the key code, but I had been forthcoming with pain. We'd reached the inevitable middle ground. I entered the digits. The door clicked, unlocking.

I pushed it open.

Cold, dry, air-conditioned air hit me. I saw no sound-cancelling tiles. No blood on the floor. No hanging chains with manacles. Instead, there were four tall, metal wracks that ran along most of the basement's length. Crammed on each shelf were computers, case after identical case. All had green status lights. The sound of a hundred whirring computer fans filled my ears.

At the end of the room was a workstation with three monitors. One showed a female ragdoll rendered in, shall we say, an artistic video sequence. The second screen, in windowed boxes, showed nine human adult industry performers. I recognized several. One of them was Sandy.

Each performer mirrored the ragdoll's sounds and movements. The mirroring was perfect.

'What's all this? Where is Sandy?'

'There is no Sandy,' said Narain. 'I created her.'

This took more than a moment to settle in.

'She's… artificially generated? She's *content*?'

'She's *art*!'

'How did you pull this off? There are so many videos of her. Pictures. She *talks to fans*.'

He smiled as he saw me realizing.

'Why did you fake her… death?'

'One of the sites I sell to became suspicious. They wanted her to fly down for a live event. I was protecting myself – and them! And all the other websites I sell content to. If this got out, they would have to take it all down. Think of the losses! The money, the reputation! Hundreds of millions of dollars…'

I tuned out his justifications. Humans always tell themselves reassuring lies. The last one we may tell ourselves is that machines can't do what we do. Yet, at every turn, they've shown us that we're hardly special... They took on mindless tasks. Then, dangerous ones. We let them; who cares about the working class? Their jobs deserve to be automated! Beneath human dignity. Besides, we'll always have art, culture, genius.

Then AI showed that genius was nothing special, either. AI started coding and wrote better programmes than us. It tried drawing and won our art awards. Silicon-written dreams uplifted us, while writers walking in our shoes could not.

Some people saw AI as a useful tool. Transforming in the way a solid gold mountain would allow us to upgrade every electrical wire on earth.

Others reacted like Swiss bankers. They protested the advance of cheap, easy-to-use, easy-to-learn AI technology levelling every playing field down to sea level.

Those afraid of learning won.

Later that morning, Adlan Narain confessed to the murder of Aisha Khan. I cannot tell you how delighted I was to learn her name. She would be remembered now and her family could find peace. Corruption only protected so far; Narain would have got away with murder, but not with the media circus around it – and the collapse of his pornography empire.

My fellow officers cheered me on. My superiors smiled quietly, disturbed. This was how it was; I wondered how much longer I would be allowed to be a detective. Detective Reddy had been a bit too successful for the City's liking.

However, attacking AI didn't make the technology go away. It just went underground, finding its full appreciation in the hands of criminals. It wasn't the City's corruption that had made Narain a murderer; there were Narains everywhere. He was just another programmer – quiet, hard-working and minding his own business. It was because his work was made illegal that he became a criminal.

Once you become a criminal, you realize just how easy it is.

I checked the air conditioner. At last, a rat trap in the corner had nothing to show. The ceiling panels had been removed to give the electricians better access. Looking up, all I could see was a tangle of shiny, black power cables and ancient piping.

The whirring of a hundred computer fans was the only sound. On the table was a workstation and three monitors. It was amazing what you could get out of evidence these days.

I stepped over to the window and parted the blinds. Down below, Auntie Mehta was stirring one of her pots of curry. She dipped a finger into one and licked it, frowning. She looked up and her eyes met mine. She smiled and nodded.

Myuran smiled back.

I sat at the table. The centre monitor showed images of attractive men and women. All I had to do was select a headshot and begin.

I cracked my knuckles and got to work.

ANDHERI NAGRI

Kehkashan Khalid

Red is scattered throughout my chronology: the silk-red of your embroidered sari, the wine-red spilling out of your victims, the lush scarlet of your lips, the berry-red of your nails, the mahogany of your entreating eyes that always fool me. I see imprints of you in years you never visited. As if you were a star and I gazed at you for too long.

The first time I see you, you are dismembering an unfortunate. The *pallu* of your sari cascades over your midriff as you bend over the body in its own living room. The grin on your face when you catch my eye is feral.

'Are you going to kill me, detective?'

'I'm not a detective… any more.' I add that last word in barely a whisper.

'I know,' you whisper, 'You tell me that in 1996.'

And then my gun is slipping out of my hands and you are breaking into fragments of light.

It's not easy being the only police detective in a small hamlet on the outskirts of Karachi. All the forensic technology resides in the big city – though even that isn't enough to solve most crimes – and they don't deign to share. So, when the boys, up on the moors, amidst a heated game of *Chor* Police, discover a woman burning what look like human remains, my first instinct is to groan. But the boys, running into the police station screaming with equal parts delight and outrage, force me to investigate.

The hill is shrouded in watchful trees and darkness, except for that small, faraway ember that burns like an innocent bonfire. I hike up my khakis and, grumbling to myself, begin the steep climb.

I didn't know at the time that it was you. You must have seen me coming because you flee into the forest. Your guilty retreat awakens something of the policeman in me, because I give chase to the shadow that is you. You are lithe and speedy and I am… a graceless potato sack. You leave me behind, of course. And by the time I climb to the ruins of a fortress that loom at the top of the hill, grave and otherworldly, you're gone.

I am seven years old when I first dream of you. Dark, almond eyes framed with lashes that follow their shape. Sultry smile, painted red. You look much older than that first time I had seen you, slicing through a man's guts. It is a comforting dream, like I have been visited by someone familiar. In fact, for some time after, I believe I had been visited. I stay awake many nights after, straining my eyes in the darkness to see if there are any feet under the curtains. And then, you simply become a part of me. There is no love then, but eventually, years later, Amma asks me what she should look for in my bride and I describe you.

But it turns out, your looks have nothing to do with it. My wife has big eyes and ample curves and for all that her appearance means to me, she could have been a cow. Still, we take care of each other. We provide the village with the kids it asks us for year after year. That's how families are built here – if the pieces don't fit together, you hack and hew until they do. There was a power in your physique, an intellect sparkling behind your eyes, that no one could match. But years go by and you never appear. I have to concede that you were a fantasy. All men have them, don't they?

Desire can be doused with affairs or asceticism. But how does one appease cravings of the soul?

I give you up. I settle down in an ill-fitting marriage and a disappointing job. I allow the *tarka* that floats above my wife's cooking to fatten my belly. And then, I run into you.

It happens completely by chance. I am walking the perimeter of the fortress, after you elude me. A couple of kids standing on some tumbled stones from the fortress wall sing loudly: '*Andheri nagri, chaupat raja, taka ser bhaji taka ser khaja.*'

They scamper when they see me, squealing and bleating like sheep who've spotted a wolf. I grunt as I take their place upon the corroded stones. Nothing here except a hollow building, abandoned by time. I glance around. I have to shield my eyes from a single beam of the setting sun as it tears perpendicular to the sky and lights up the rubble in the fortress behind me. Then the brief illumination is gone. And yet, I do not leave. What do I have to return to anyway? My cheap cell phone buzzes in my pocket. I ignore it. I don't need to pick it up to hear my wife's high-pitched, nasal voice ask me to get yogurt and bread on the way home. Yogurt and bread, to dip in meat and oil, to add to the layers of adipose already hampering my movement. I bite my flashlight between my teeth and step into the empty fort.

You can only see the door once you stand in the middle of that forlorn space. I would study it, years ago, or years later – however you want to look at it. It was called Badal Gate. Badal – the Urdu word for clouds, I think. It doesn't occur to me that, depending on inflection, it could also mean change. It is such an unassuming archway on the eastern side of the fort. Useless too, for it leads nowhere. There is the tiniest ledge where the doorway begins and after that, nothing but an endless drop.

That night, the moon lights up that gate of change and I see the intricate motifs carved into the stone on all sides. I don't know what possesses me, but I step out onto the ledge. Tempting providence is not the same as suicide. The sheer drop makes my vision blur unpleasantly and within the second, I have stepped back through the gate. I feel sick and lean my hands against the carvings to let my nausea subside. I shake my head and walk away from the fortress and it is only when I reach the foot of the moors that I realize my village looks different.

That is my first time through the gate. I walk through the vaguely familiar town ignoring the people who cast strange looks at my uniform. But as I approach the police station and catch sight of myself, twenty years old, grinning in the face of my lieutenant's censure, I panic. I duck out of the way before anyone sees me and snatch up a newspaper from the nearest vendor. 1997. The date blurs before my eyes, and then I black out.

There is a small crowd gathered above me when my eyes refocus. I sit up.

'Why is he dressed like a policeman?'

'Might be visiting from another town. Are you okay, Sahib?'

I nod and then regret it when pain shoots across my temples. Someone hands me a metal cup full of cold water that tastes wrong. Then slowly, the crowd disperses and I am left to find my way in a place where I should not exist.

I spend weeks stumbling about in the moors, scrounging for food and sleeping in the warm crevices where tree trunks meet. Somewhere out there are people who know me, but they don't know this version of me and so I cannot turn to them for help. I catch small animals and roast them over measly fires fuelled by old leaves and dry branches. And, on every moonlit night, I make a pilgrimage to the ruins at the top of the hill. But the fortress remains dark and impervious.

It is on such a night, frustrated by the silence of the ruins, that I spy movement in the foliage. Starving and desperate, I lunge towards it. But what emerges from the bushes, struggling in my grasp, is not an animal. It is a child with a sharp, little, mud-caked face and wild-cat eyes, angry and bright. They are so familiar, but I gave you up too long ago to think of you now. Besides, she isn't you yet.

She is my salvation. She gives me a place to rest my head, food to warm my stomach and occupation to idle away the hours. I chop firewood, mend the plumbing of her run-down cottage and, at night, I nestle between the cows in the barn, grateful for their pungent warmth. Most days she follows me around as I do the chores, perching on a wall or a fence, sharing the strange and desultory thoughts that flit through a child's mind. Between those stories I learn that her father is a bricklayer, who spends the better part of his day in the town tavern and ever since her mother's untimely demise, she spends her days alone. And prefers it that way.

Together we carry lilies to her mother's grave, where she squats and cries, pressing the heel of her hand into her eyes. I feel woefully inadequate, standing there as she hugs herself pitifully.

'How did she die?' I ask, once we are home, seated on the wooden table dipping hunks of dry bread in broth.

'Everything is all wrong,' she mutters, wiping her nose and her eyes with her sleeve and glaring at me through the dirty fringe of hair that falls across her forehead. I have no idea what she means.

'Do you want to hear a story?' I ask, hoping to distract her. She doesn't reply, so I continue, '*Andheri nagri, chaupat raja, taka ser bhaji taka ser khaja*. Do you know what it means?'

'Dark is the fortress, insane is the king. A paisa for wheat and a paisa for cake?' She repeats and then shakes her head.

'One day a great guru and his disciple arrive in a strange land. On the surface it is a glorious place, with a vivid bazar where rich desserts were as cheap as grains. But, on closer inspection, the people there look starved and thin and they tremble under the thumb of their autocratic and whimsical ruler. The guru advises the disciple that they should not stay long, but the disciple, spurred by greed, wants to stay and enjoy the spoils of the beautiful city. A few weeks later, the teacher hears news that his disciple will be sent to the gallows. He rushes to the city and finds a group of people bickering in the King's court about who is to blame for a minor crime. None of them want ownership of the mistake and yet the King has ordered the noose to be readied, for someone must take the fall. It is a fat noose and can only fit the neck of a fat man. But all the residents of Andheri Nagri are emaciated with fear, except the disciple who has been splurging at the market. And so there he was, for someone had to be punished for this crime. So, the guru, who was well thought of throughout the lands, announces that the hanged man would be taken straight to the halls of heaven. At this, of course, the King insists that he should be the one to be awarded such an honour. So, he steps up to the gallows himself and, in this way, the guru saves the anarchic city from its foolish ruler.'

I could see by the way her eyes light up that my story has intrigued her, 'He killed the king and changed the world.'

'I don't know if that's the moral of the story.'

She looks unconvinced. She stares incredulously at her hands, and whispers, 'Someone had to be punished.'

The idea of it seems to engross her completely and we often end up debating the end of the story. It is my opinion that the King would only be replaced by another idiot from the crowd of bickering people, for their cowardice and complacency as an innocent man was brought for his execution are the true fault. But her view is different.

'The people don't know any better. They're silly and violent and scared. The King should have done right by them. And they needed the guru to hold him accountable. The system was broken and they needed the guru to come and fix it.'

And so, our days pass by, until I nearly forget the old ruins on top of the hill. In my absence, the moonlight pricks the motifs embroidered on its walls and ignites the gate. But I am not there to use it.

One day her father lurches home before I have a chance to retreat to the barn. He is incensed to learn that she has been harbouring a strange man in their home. He grabs her arm and slams the door. I hear their yells ascending to the first floor. I kick the door and when it does not give way, I grab the axe. I rush into the house and there they are, his huge frame hovering above hers at the top of the staircase. His shoulders heave like pistons in a frantic machine.

'She would still be alive if it weren't for you,' he sobs through his drunken madness.

'No, no, that was your fault!' she yells. A desperation descends into her eyes, followed by frightening resolve. And then she is barrelling into him. They tumble down the stairs in a heap of arms and legs.

'No one is going to believe me. I'm already an outcast from the whole town. The daughter of the drunkard and the abused woman,' she whispers in the aftermath, her teeth gritted, her head in her hands. I stare at the impossibly angled body on the floor. My head spins. I have to act as a caretaker, not a policeman.

'Let me take the blame,' I suggest, even though the idea of being arrested and executed in front of myself makes me giddy.

'Just go,' she says, her voice muffled. The moon splits through the clouds and illuminates us with one long beam. I glance over my shoulder at the hills.

'I have a better idea.' I pick her up and throw her over my shoulder and we walk away from the sad little cottage.

I am alone when I step back through the gate. And this time, the fortress is plunged in darkness. It takes me a few gasping moments to realize that someone has built a frame around the ruins. I spin around. The girl is nowhere to be seen, but a sheer cloth flutters across the archway of Badal Gate, a veil punctured with scattered dots of lights. I lift my hand to touch it and feel a cold metal slice across my wrist. Someone yanks my hand rudely downwards – a motion I am familiar with. I have been handcuffed.

They blindfold me so I only see their square, clenched jaws once we are already at the police station. They look nothing like the overgrown lads in rumpled *salwar kameez* I am used to working with. They are all crisp suits and gleaming watches. Is this even my station? It certainly looks upgraded. A tall woman standing to the side, gives me a look of intense displeasure. Everything about her – from the gleaming cufflinks on her suit to the sharp upward strokes of her eyebrows and her hair – spell authority. She is a lynx and I am the rabbit caught between her jaws.

'So, he's finally here.'

'Looks like it.'

She sits down before me.

'I know you must be disoriented, but we need to ask you a few questions. How did you find the gate?'

'The gate's always been there, that old fort is nothing but a pile of ruins where I'm from.'

'And where are you from?'

Something tells me they'll understand the way the 1985 people never could, '2012.' I shrug.

'We need your help with something.'

I glance from one impassive face to another.

'Show him.'

They have a morgue full of bodies you've mutilated. Or so they say. I am sceptical. A skinny little thing like you, murdering grown men? They ask me all sorts of questions about you. Who you are, why you would do something like this. I don't know, I don't know, is all I can say. I didn't know. I didn't know you. It will be many trips through Badal Gate later that we discuss anything and everything with each other.

'The girl I met… I don't really think… She couldn't do this.'

'Oh, but she does.'

'Who are you people?'

They exchange glances. Years of reading the faces of petty liars tells me they are apprehensive.

'You're all responsible. Aren't you? You messed about with that old ruin and made this happen. What did you do?'

'It doesn't matter what we did. What you need to know is, the gate is an access point to different locations in time and she has been using it, murdering at whim. For all we know, she's the serial killer every century is looking for – what better place to escape than an alternate dimension. And none of those people have the resources to find her except for us.'

'An alternate dimension?'

'Oh yes, she's manipulating her existence, weaving herself through time like a vicious needle. And we're the only ones who can bring her to justice. You're the one who will bring her to justice,' she says this with finality, as if it were something that has already happened, 'You're going to be our bounty hunter.'

'Why can't one of you go?'

'You don't think we've tried?' The lieutenant's eyes soften, 'She trusts you. You can do what none of us could. You can lure her in. You might even be able to make her see reason.'

'And if I do?'

'The moment you've dealt with her, we'll send you right back to 2012.'

'Well, what if I don't want to go back?'

'I only have jurisdiction this far, if you decide to linger here, I'll have to inform the rest of my station and they might not be so lenient with the man responsible for unleashing the world's worst serial killer.'

And just like that I am enslaved to a hopeless cause by this new lieutenant.

By the time my physical training is complete, I have become an alter ego of myself. Firm abs and a belt full of weapons I can skilfully use. I swing my gun at the lieutenant once and the only reaction I get is a raised eyebrow. It is programmed to react to your DNA and your DNA alone. It cannot aid my escape – not that I know how the veil of fireflies on Badal Gate even work. They purposely withhold that knowledge from me. They send me where they think I'll find you and I see you for the first time: red *chanderi* sari and all. I am so mesmerized and horrified to see you – the woman from my dreams, the girl from my past, astride a desiccated body – that I do nothing. You escape and I return to my owners.

The next time they send me out, it is 1947.

Their sorcery always dislocates me in time to make sure I follow you. I am your own personal stalker. A little dog on a leash, pulled along after you. I find myself in the middle of a train station full of frantic crowds. There is no way to find you amongst that press of bodies. I am swept perforce towards the metal mouth of a train ready for departure. As the horns blare and overlapping mechanical voices announce incomprehensible destinations, I feel the gentle scrape of cold nails on my arm. I glance down. Neatly filed, crimson nails. The crowd surges and your body pushes up against mine. I feel the brush of your breasts against my back and a tingle reverberates through me. You whisper in my ear, 'Don't get on that train. Follow me.'

The train explodes. We are nowhere near when it happens. I will find out about it later, in the recordings made by survivors of the migration during the fracturing of the subcontinent. Lives torn apart by British fingers like tea cake. I am already in your *haveli* when it happens, sitting like a dumb sheep on an ornate chair, across from the criminal I am supposed to be chasing. My eyes follow the hypnotic way you play with your bangles, the gold clinking thoughtfully against itself.

'You don't know who I am,' you whisper.

'I know who you are. You're the girl I rescued. And you're a killer.'

'You don't know who I am,' you repeat with a breath of laughter.

'Why'd you kill all those people? You should turn yourself in. Save me the hassle.'

'You really think I could do something like that?'

'I saw you.'

'You really think I could kill a bunch of *innocent* people?'

'So, you've made yourself judge, jury and executioner?'

Your eyes flash at that, 'Fuck you. Get out of my house.'

'If I'm going, you're coming with me.'

You are quicker than I anticipated. Your kick knocks my gun from my hand, sending it spinning under a piece of furniture. I reach for my blade and you throw yourself at me. And there we are, grappling on the floor in an aggressive mockery of how we will make love years from now. Even when you have me pinned against the tiles, you never reach for the knife I can see strapped to your thigh.

'Come with me. Follow me. I'll show you,' you beg.

I was a fool. And you were clever. I should have known.

The first time we make love is on a grassy hillside in 1996. We sit with our backs to Margalla Hills and speak impossible dreams between kisses. We'll have a family, we'll have a house. No, we'll travel the world together. We'll be free. I believe you by then. How could that version of me have known you would show me only what I wanted to see?

'You took it literally,' I say, as you lie on the grass, biting into an apple as red as your clothes, one arm stretched overhead, tugging the lace of your blouse upwards to reveal silky skin.

'What?'

'The story. You took it literally.'

'I just saw the world for what it is. Despotic leaders and the cowards who support them. And mobs full of idiots who can't tell right from wrong.'

Your words reverberate with passion and descend into my soul. I am proud of you. You are no vapid policeman wasting away in a mindless town and blaming everyone else for the stupor of his life. You have grasped opportunity with both hands and propelled yourself into your future.

'How did you do it?' I lean closer to you, imbibing your unchanging scent. As if you have freshly stepped from a pool steeped in jasmines. You turn towards me, your eyes laughing, strands of dark hair escaping your braid.

'Come with me and I'll show you.'

We land in a cobbled street under a brooding sky. Bleak lamplight outlines the facades of massive, colourless houses.

'What is this place?'

'We're in London.'

You put a finger to your lips and we move through the shadows towards one of the houses.

'You've been here before?'

'I've been to lots of places.' There is a thrilling gleam in your eyes. I am awed by the possibilities. You hand me a rolled-up newspaper. The air is damp and the ink bleeds into my fingertips. I scan the page and see the black-and-white photograph of a man floating face down in a wide river.

'He tricked and killed women who had no one else looking out for them. The police couldn't catch him.'

'But you did…'

You nod.

'Why are we here?'

'We've come to stop a man who is going to be responsible for thousands of deaths. Remember that train explosion? That wouldn't have happened if it weren't for him. He sailed in from far away and arbitrarily broke a country into two, with no thought of the consequences.'

'And he lives here?'

You nod again and then squeeze my arm, 'Just be ready when I return. Our escape will have to be quick.'

I nod and it is only when you slip away into the darkness that I call out after you. I saw that train explosion happen in front of my eyes, would that never happen if we go through with this?

'Are we here to stop him or punish him?'

But my words are swallowed by the night. You never hear my question or you choose not to answer it.

I ignore my misgivings and focus on the good you've done. I am deliriously happy. The woman from my fantasies, the woman my mind conjured up all those years ago, in my arms. Suddenly, even returning to make false reports to the lieutenant seems worth it. I follow you through time and space and we leave pieces of ourselves in every place we visit – a lock on a fence, a carving on a tree, initials scribbled on walls – until the lieutenant outsmarts you.

'Never send a man to do a woman's job,' the lieutenant is waiting for me and her expression warns me that my excuses will not work this time. 'This is your last chance, detective. If you're too enamoured with our target, I'll simply have to incapacitate her myself.'

'We don't have to do this. I've seen what she does, she's changing the world, she's fixing it.'

'Wow, she's really done a number on you, hasn't she? She can't change a thing.'

'I've seen her catch criminals that have eluded the police,' I argue.

'And what gives her the right to judge them? Have you forgotten so much of your duty as a law enforcement officer that you applaud vigilantism?'

Her words are a slap in my face, a reminder that I have never been much of a policeman. 'But she hasn't told you everything she's done. Your beloved is quite the narcissist. Maybe we should have given you a little bit more information about how all this works.' She pursed her lips and watched me keenly, as if she's trying to assess what it would take to convince me. 'Let me show you something.'

I admit I am a fool. I just don't realize how much my foolishness will cost me until I see the wife I never loved weeping with unbridled grief over the burned body of a son I didn't know well enough. 'Yes, this is the body she was burning that day,' the lieutenant says grimly, 'But don't worry, it's not that she's singling out your children. She extrapolates the life trajectories of many of her victims and determines that they don't deserve to live. But who's drawing the line? Are we killing only potential killers and rapists? Or mob-men? If you're killing thieves, what about a one-time shoplifter? Who draws the line, detective?' Her words pierce me. Her voice recedes into the background, replaced by the heavy sound of my own breathing. I cannot reconcile you with this crime.

You are older the next time I see you. Closer to forty, with strands of grey hair amongst the mahogany. And you know that I am onto you.

'I'm not going to justify myself to you.'

Anger at your betrayal, irritation at your calm rejection of me – something I still cannot manage to do with you – war inside me.

'You're crazy,' I utter through gritted teeth. I know I've triggered you. You charge at me, but I am ready for it. Our bodies have been intertwined too often. I know every movement of yours like the back of my hand. I lock your wrists behind your back.

'The system was broken, so I broke the system,' you spit the words out. 'Someone has to take the fall for a broken system. People are violent and unjust and you can't control the horde. But you can tame it. You can push the trajectory of the world in certain directions. Like the guru.'

'You killed people who have done nothing wrong.'

'And now they never will.'

'Have you killed my son yet?' Would killing you now save him?

'I always kill him.'

Tears spark in my eyes and I let your wrists fall.

'How?'

'That's how it works! Remember you asked me on the hillside how I did it? It's because I was meant to. I was meant to be there! You can't change the past or create a future. Time is infinite and immutable.'

The lieutenant's words ring harshly in my head. We're the only ones who can bring her to justice.

'It was never about stopping you…' The realization staggers me, 'I've ruined it. I've ruined it all.'

How can I feel such grief for a family I never valued? How can I ruin a life I never desired? I don't even hate you. How can my heart be divided so between two things that are meant to destroy each other?

'You were never changing the future, were you?'

You hold your palms out desperately as if to shield yourself from my pain.

'I was meant to change the future. If they weren't supposed to die, there was no way I'd be able to kill them.'

'That's no justification.'

'Then you should never have saved me that day,' you whisper, your eyes begging me to disagree.

'But it's like you said… I will always save you.'

There is a knock on the door of the *haveli* and when the servant opens, I hear a familiar voice. The lieutenant. She's given up on me and followed me here.

'Listen,' you plead, 'Don't let her take me, kill me, please. I've tried to travel farther than this and I never can. This is where our story ends. Whether you kill me or she does, you won't be seeing me again.'

I stare at this portrait of you, the warm tones crumbling away, leaving behind only jagged, sadistic strokes. I raise my gun.

'Then, I guess I don't have a choice.'

And that is how it ends. I become responsible for taking the lives of the woman I love and the child I ought to have loved.

Back in 2012, my wife wraps her arms around me and sobs with relief. Her husband returned to her just in time for her son's funeral. I shed tears, but I don't know who they are for. Maybe it is just the oppressive heat of unnecessary relatives crammed into our tiny house with arms full of over-spiced food. I take the sledgehammer from the shed and retreat to the moors. I want to knock down that fortress, like breaking the lieutenant's teeth. But when I stand in front of the door, watching the sunset beyond the ruined walls, all I see is the dirt-streaked face of a skinny girl laughing and laughing. And I cannot bring myself to.

1984.

A boy stirs in his sleep. The curtain billows with the night wind and a lithe shadow steps out from behind. It is a tall woman in an elegant sari, her mahogany hair streaked with grey, knotted at her neck. Her dark eyes glimmer in the feeble light of the mosquito lamp. She pauses beside his bed and the clinking of her bangles as she strokes the hair away from his forehead, wakes him. He opens sleepy eyes, barely registering the scene before him. He won't remember anything except the sensation she leaves behind. And the words she whispers to him, that don't make any sense.

'I forgive you.'

DEATH OF AN ACTRESS

Sumit Bardhan

A dirty ceiling. Below it a grimy ceiling fan moving languorously with jerks. This is what I watched for a few seconds with a hazy sight after forcing my eyes to open.

My head felt heavy, the temples pulsing with some deep-seated ache. It took me another few seconds to realize that I was lying on my own bed. It also took some effort for me to push myself up into a sitting position.

The bed sheet felt damp. My body was sticky with sweat. When did I sleep last night? The stupor massed inside my head did not allow me to remember.

On the bedstand, my phone pinged. Stretching out my hand, I picked it up. A message from Sohini. Rajib da wanted me to meet him.

An empty glass rolled away with a tinkle as I got down. Bending to pick it up I saw two empty whiskey bottles. The reason for the stupor nestling inside my head was evident.

I opened the only window in the room. A whiff of pollution-tainted air brought in the busy sounds of the lane below. Was I drinking too much? Was booze becoming my sole companion? To avoid the uncomfortable questions bubbling up inside me, I quickly left.

A small sign outside a flat in a dingy house in a narrow Bowbazar lane declared it as the office of the *News Wave* news portal. Inside sat Rajib da and Sohini at their respective tables. These two, along with me, consisted of the portal's entire staff.

Having seen me, Sohini peeked out from behind her laptop. 'Wow! Right on time! Set an alarm before going to sleep, did you?'

'No,' I shook my head with an expressionless face. 'Someone I was sleeping with woke me up.'

Sohini laughed derisively. 'You must have been dreaming. Given your state, someone will sleep with you only in a dream.'

Dreams bring no one near me, they just bring a sense of foreboding, I thought. Not answering her, I sat down at Rajib da's table.

He threw a file on the table. 'Take a look. Sohini put together some information from the internet and old newspapers.'

I picked it up. 'What is this?'

'Paromita. TV actress. Was acting in a number of TV serials. Died last week.'

'What happened?'

'Hung herself.'

'What's your angle?'

'Section 306.'

'Abetment of suicide?'

'Yes! Successful actress, lead role in the high-TRP serial *Lonely Roses*, why should she want to kill herself?'

'Connections?'

'Maybe some of the Tolly actors…,' Sohini started to say.

'Forget it!' I interrupted her. 'It will be impossible to approach them. Give me something doable.'

'You can try Abhishek Guha. Paromita's doctor.' Rajib da said.

'Doctor? Why?'

'He told the police that Paromita was suffering from depression. Maybe there is some story there?'

'Story or dirt?'

'Call it whatever you will. To eat, we produce what sells.' There was a touch of bitterness in Rajib da's voice.

There were some printouts on Abhishek Guha in the file. Among them was a list of the places where he saw patients. I took a photo on my phone. 'I will start digging.'

I made a trip to Milon Nursing Home first. It was the closest one from the list.

A board outside the nursing home listed the days and timings of the galaxy of doctors who visited the place. A glance at it made it clear that I would not be finding Abhishek Guha here.

But I still had a job to do. Putting on a dumb expression, I walked up to the security guard standing at the large glass doors. 'Dr Abhishek Guha is in already, no?'

He shook his head, 'No, he doesn't come today.'

'Oh!' I pretended to be surprised, 'But I just saw his car in the parking lot. Silver Honda City.'

'That is Dr Sen's car. Dr Guha's is a black Toyota Camry.'

'Oh! My mistake then.'

A quick look at the photo on my phone of the list of clinics Abhishek Guha visited told me where he would be available now. Leaving Milon Nursing Home, I took a bus to Shyambazar and walked through a winding lane to reach Nirog Polyclinic.

Nirog's parking was in the basement. Among the cars, there was just a single black Toyota. I stood in a corner, keeping an eye on it.

After nearly half an hour, a man came out of the lift on the other end and pressed a car remote. The Toyota beeped in response.

'Doctor! Doctor Guha!' I moved towards him. His face flashed with irritation as I intercepted him between the lift and his car. 'Who are you?'

I dropped any pretensions as I blocked his way. 'I am from *News Wave*. Wanted to talk to you about Paromita's death.'

'I don't talk to third-rate portals. Get lost.'

I decided to push him off balance. 'We are planning to do a story that Paromita's suicide was a result of a broken love affair with you.'

His expression became ugly. 'Do it and I will drag your forefathers to court.'

I ignored the threat. 'Why else would a successful actress take her own life?'

'Not because of me!' He said angrily. 'Go and check her family background. You...' He added a string of expletives as he pushed past me.

I came out of the basement and messaged Sohini, asking her for Paromita's home address and instructing her to look up her family background.

Paromita's flat was in one of the upscale high-rises on the outskirts of the city. Using the combination of my press card, a five hundred rupee note and the lure of printing a story with his name in it, it did not take me too long to convince a pliant security guard to take me to it.

Inside the flat, the look of the otherwise richly decorated drawing room was marred by a stack of crates piled right in its centre.

I took a closer look. They had the stenciled logo of some logistics company on them.

'What are these?' I asked the guard.

'Goods for madam's boutique. The shop is closed now, so the transporter has left it here.'

'Shop? She had a shop? Where?'

The guard gave me a location.

The bedroom door should have been sealed by the police, but it wasn't. There was not much to see though. On the bedside table stood a vase with some wilted sunflowers and a garish table lamp with a shade that had star-shaped holes. Through the room's large glass window, the green eastern fringes of the city could be seen. I took a few photos and left.

I got a call from Sohini as I came out. 'Paromita owned a boutique.'

'Yes, I just learned.'

'Her business partner was Sudip Ghosh.'

'Who is he?'

'Real estate guy. Owner of Emerald Properties. Controversial man.'

'Controversial how?'

'The usual. Money, muscle, political connections.'

The hope of a juicy story glimmered in my mind. The narrative of a real estate shark and a glamorous actress spiced with the right amount of innuendo would make a heady mix.

'Where can I find him?'

'Hold on.' I could hear the clicking of keys as Sohini searched the net. 'Emerald Properties' website lists multiple offices. But they are developing a property near you. You could inquire there. Sending you the location and his photo.'

I was lucky. In the words of the very worker at the property site, to whom I was trying to sell the rather watery story of wanting to buy a flat, the boss had in fact arrived at the site sometime back. He pointed towards a shipping container that functioned as the site office.

Knowing where the owner of Emerald Properties was one thing and approaching him was quite another. Any wrong move would result in a thrashing and probably being picked up by some policeman in his pay. A couple of rough looking characters with dyed hair and thick gold wrist chains standing in front of the office was as loud a warning as any.

I decided to keep a discreet watch. There was a partially complete building just opposite the office. The day's shift was changing and workers were coming and going in groups. Taking advantage of the jostling, I picked up a yellow hat and donning it, climbed up to the wall-less first floor of the building. This floor was empty, the work being concentrated on the upper storeys. I went to a corner where the floor met empty air and stood behind a pillar, watching.

I did not have a solid plan. My hope was to accost Sudip Ghosh as he came out of his office on the pretext of doing a story on his company and then slowly diverting the discussion to his partnership with Paromita.

But even after a long wait, Sudip Ghosh did not emerge. Instead, something else happened for which I was not prepared. A familiar black Toyota Camry drove up to the office and from it emerged Abhishek Guha. As he walked towards the office, with a small bag in hand, one of the bouncers held the door open for him. From the man's body language, it was evident that Abhishek Guha was a regular here.

Abhishek Guha came out after a good twenty minutes and drove off. Curiously, he no longer carried the bag he had brought.

I waited for some more time, but there was no sight of Sudip Ghosh. Afraid that standing there any longer was risky, I was about to leave, when a small pickup van drove in. A look at the decal painted on the side of the van stopped me in my tracks, for it bore the logo of the same logistics company whose boxes I had seen in Paromita's flat.

Whoever had come must have been quite important, because one of the bouncers opened the door a bit and spoke to someone inside and a man came out hurriedly. I recognized him as Sudip Ghosh from the photo sent by Sohini. A little later another well-dressed man jumped out of the van and handed over a large bag to one of the bouncers. The newcomer and Sudip shook hands and went inside, the bouncer following behind with the bag. I just had time to take a couple quick snaps before they vanished inside.

I waited for some more time, but neither Sudip Ghosh, nor the newcomer emerged. With the day now ending, I left the now darkening building and after I had sent Sohini the photos, I headed home.

Next morning, I entered the office in a rush. I could sniff a major scoop beyond the dirt that generally keeps us afloat.

Rajib da lifted his eyebrows as I narrated my findings. 'So, where do all these lead to?'

'Something major, I hope. When three people connected to the late actress meet at a construction site, something definitely must be going on. Sohini, did you get something about Paromita's family background?'

'Not much. Parents died early. There is a brother, but the chap seems to be a complete wastrel. I found some passing remarks on social media on his being sent to some rehab about three months back. Sending you the photo.'

I forwarded the image to the security guard at Paromita's apartment and called him. 'Yes, yes, your interview will get published soon. In the meantime, could you take a look at the photo I just sent and tell me anything that you know.'

The guard confirmed what Sohini had found. This *saab* used to come once a week earlier, but in the last few months he has not seen him.

'This looks very fishy. Abhishek Guha tried to divert me in the wrong direction, while he himself had something going on with Sudip Ghosh. Any information on who that other man with Sudip Ghosh was?'

Sohini handed me a printout. 'That's Barun Shaw. The owner of Sunrise Logistics. And check this.'

The printout was of a six months old news article. It spoke of an income tax raid on the premises of Emerald Properties, Sunrise Logistics and another company named Olive Enterprises.

'So, there *is* some relationship between Barun Shaw and Sudip Ghosh. I think there could be some hidden financial motive behind Paromita's suicide.'

'Let's not jump to conclusions,' Rajib da interjected. 'Barun and Sudip may be involved in some shady financial deal, but that does not connect them to Paromita's death.'

'There *has* to be a connection. I am certain that it will come out. Do we know anything about Olive Enterprises?'

'They are distributors for fast-moving consumer goods and have ties with many well-known brands.' Sohini answered.

'Who is the owner?'

'Tapas Dastidar. His office and residence are both in central Kolkata. I just messaged you the address and his photo.'

'Aren't we going somewhat off track? Shouldn't you concentrate on trying to find out why Paromita committed suicide?'

'It will become clear as we unravel the financial connections.' I was adamant. 'Sohini, in that list of nursing homes that you gave me yesterday, is there one that Abhishek Guha owns himself?'

Sohini got busy with her laptop. 'I think this is the one. Skyview Nursing Home. It's owned by Abhishek Guha and two other doctors.'

'What has that got to do...' Rajib da started, but I did not allow him to finish. 'I have a hunch.'

Skyview Nursing Home was on the fringes of the city. A place where armed gangs of real estate sharks fought daily for supremacy and a share of the land and money pie. The glass-panelled building looked out of place among the half-built structures and plots of land overrun by weeds. Mustering as much a goonish swagger as I possibly could, I sauntered into the almost empty reception. The receptionist, engrossed with his mobile, just raised his eyes in a questioning glance, not bothering even to greet me.

I leaned into him over the counter. 'I need to get surgery done. How much?'

'You yourself?' he asked.

'No. A friend of mine.'

'What kind of surgery?'

I lowered my voice in a conspiratorial whisper. 'Injury. Bullet.'

The man didn't even bat an eyelid. 'Two lakhs. Cash. Advance.'

'What about fifty–fifty, before and after?'

'Nothing doing. Either pay in advance or get lost.' He sounded irritated.

'Fine. When?'

'I will have to ask the doctor. Come back in the evening.' He went back to his mobile.

I came out and called Rajib da. 'My hunch was correct. Abhishek Guha takes cash payment. I think he is involved in some type of cash dealings with Sudip Ghosh. It's possible that Barun Shaw also has the same relationship, maybe on a bigger scale.'

'Could be. But what does it have to do with Paromita's death?'

'I don't know yet. But I am sure to find it out. Can you check the financial status of her boutique business? Maybe we will find something there.'

'Fine. And what about you?'

'I will check out Tapas Dastidar.'

Tapas Dastidar's office and residence was in a three-storey building at the corner of a narrow lane and the main road. The building was easily at least a century old, but had been reinforced with iron grilles on windows and iron gates. Cameras poked out from its every nook and cranny.

Sitting on the bench of a footpath tea stall, I casually chatted up a few locals. Yes, that was the house and office of Tapas babu. Oh yes, he is very helpful indeed. Look at Babun, just a small-time private taxi owner and Tapas babu got him so many rich clients. And then when Soumen, the physiotherapist got picked up by police after Master moshai's suicide, Tapas babu used all his influence to pull him out.

Another suicide! I got such a jolt that it took me a few minutes to get my balance back and ask the right questions.

Mastermoshai, as a teacher is often respectfully addressed, was Bijan Datta, a classical vocalist who ran a music school. A descendant of one of those old musical families of Kolkata who practised art for the sake of art, he had devoted himself to teaching music after retiring from his government job. For some reason that is unknown and perplexing to everyone, he had taken his own life about a fortnight ago by hanging himself in his room.

No, no, he had no financial troubles, lived quite well on his savings and his government pension. No, no family issues either; he had never married and lived all by himself. No, of course not, he got along quite well with everyone. In fact, he was quite respected and revered here. No, no, no health problems either, apart from a few age-related pains and aches for which he was taking physiotherapy from Soumen.

Today there is a memorial meeting at his house – organized by Tapas babu who else! You should cover it. People like Master moshai, who have dedicated their lives to music, deserve recognition.

So, I went. Perhaps this would give me more insight.

Bijan Datta's home was at the end of a winding lane. A hand-painted sign outside it read 'Young Stars Music School'. A small crowd had gathered outside. Inside, after a flight of steps was a small room. Here, Bijan Datta's garlanded photo rested on a small stool, flanked by sticks of incense and tall vases of *rajonigandha*. The sun had crossed the zenith and very little light entered from the window that opened east, though its yellow curtain had been rolled up. On the white sheets spread on the floor, a few people sat in respectful posture, while in a corner a young man sang a melancholy tune with a *tanpura*. After bowing my head respectfully with folded hands and taking a few pictures, I left.

Coming out, I introduced myself to the crowd outside with a half-truth. I was a reporter and having learnt of Master moshai's death had come to do a story. It lent me the credibility I needed to interview Soumen, the physiotherapist. His story did not differ much from what I had learned earlier. He had visited in the evening to take Bijan through his exercise regime. Next day, when Bijan did not open the door despite his maidservant knocking on it for the better part of an hour, the police were informed. They broke open the door and found him hanging from the ceiling fan. Since Soumen had been the last person to have seen him alive, the police picked him up and detained him, probably to threaten him with a case unless he coughed up some cash. Fortunately, Tapas babu had stepped in and got him released.

'Tapas babu seems to be very helpful,' I remarked.

'Yes indeed. He had helped me earlier also. I was struggling to get enough patients when he put in touch with many of his high-flying friends. Now I am a pretty well-known physiotherapist.' Soumen proudly handed me a fancy blue visiting card.

'What kind of friends?'

'Sudip Ghosh of Emerald Properties for one. And then…'

Soumen reeled out a few more names, but I felt somewhat dazed to hear it all. Was it a coincidence that the name of a man linked to a death I was investigating had cropped up in another?

'He helped me in the same way.' Soumen was interrupted by another man.

'And you are?'

'I am Babun. I own a few taxis.' He pointed towards a couple of white cars parked on one side of the lane. They had 'Ma Tara Taxi' written across them in bright red decals. 'My business was running at a loss and I had a huge bank loan. Then Tapas babu got me connected to his friends and I started getting steady business.'

'Must have been all big shots.'

'Oh yes!' And Babun gave me a veritable list of the who's who of the city. This time I was careful to note them down.

There was some commotion behind me as the crowd parted to give way to a man. I recognized him from Sohini's picture. This was Tapas Dastidar, the owner of Olive Enterprises. He folded his hands as he approached me and I repeated the half truth about having come to do a story on Bijan Datta.

'Of course! Of course!' He said and continued to give me a monologue on Bijan Datta and his family's musical legacy. I nodded dutifully and made a show of noting everything down.

His lecture completed, he again folded his hands and nodding to everyone in the crowd, proceeded towards Bijan Datta's house. I waited, giving him the few necessary minutes to reach the door. Then, as soon as he had crossed the threshold, I ran up to him and said, 'Sir, I had a request.'

'Yes, yes, please tell me.' He was the epitome of politeness.

'Soumen told me that you know Sudip Ghosh of Emerald Properties.'

'Why do you ask?' He raised an eyebrow, his veneer of politeness suddenly dropping a notch.

'Just that I was planning to buy a flat, sir. So, I was wondering if you could put in a word and maybe I could get a special price.'

'Of course, of course!' Tapas Dastidar was back to being his polite self. 'I will definitely introduce you to him and put in a word. In fact, why only him? I have many friends in high places. I will introduce you to them all. Come and meet me someday.' He smiled at me and went in.

As I walked back towards the main road, I caught up with Babun. Putting on an excited air as I approached him, I said. 'Tapas babu has agreed to connect me to his friends.'

Babun nodded in agreement. 'See, I said so, no? He is indeed very helpful.'

Lowering my voice to a whisper, I asked in a concerned voice, 'I was wondering though, do we have to do something in return?'

'No, no, nothing.' Babun waved me off. 'Nothing serious. Maybe once in a while he asks us to pick up or drop off something when we are visiting his friends.' He added with a breath, 'Just simple stuff. Maybe a book. Or some documents. Perhaps a bag once in a while.' He made it sound trivial.

I bade him goodbye, messaged Sohini the list of names I had received from him and went in search of a drink.

Sohini's call woke me up in the morning. 'Do drop in today. We found some stuff.'

When I reached the *News Wave* office, Rajib da's table was strewn with papers and printouts.

'Why the urgent summons?' I asked.

'I will tell you.' Rajib da answered. 'But your story first.'

His brows knitted as I recounted all I had learned. 'Another unexplained suicide!'

'Probably just a coincidence.' I said weakly, not even too convinced myself. 'I think we need to keep our focus on the financial aspect.'

Rajib da did not look too comfortable but did not argue. 'Fine, we will come back to this later. Take a look at this.' He pushed a printout towards me. 'Sohini went through the list you sent and from a financial angle, this name jumped out like a red light.'

I glanced at the paper. It was the profile of someone named Sandeep Tibrewal. The bio was accompanied by a photo.

'He is one of the top investors of Kolkata. Owns Greenfield Capital.' Rajib da pointed out.

I nodded. 'So, the connection runs deep. From real estate shark Sudip Ghosh to Tapas Dastidar to Sandeep Tibrewal.'

'It runs the other way also. I pulled out the details of Tibrewal's investments. He holds a stake in a new start-up. Coincidentally, Sudip Ghosh also holds a chunk of shares in this same company.'

'So, you think that the cash that Sudip Ghosh collects is routed to Tibrewal and converted into shares?'

'Most likely.'

'And what about Abhishek Guha and Barun Shaw?'

'Some of those shares may actually be theirs. Sudip is holding them in his name. A *benami* holding.'

'Shall I approach Tibrewal and see what comes out?'

Rajib da shook his head vigorously. 'Don't even think about it. He is too powerful. One word from him and the police will close us down on flimsy charges. And anyway, there's little chance you could go even a mile near him.'

Sohini had been doing something on her laptop as we talked. She now glanced at me. 'Tibrewal is scheduled to address an investment seminar today at Hotel Novo Regency.'

'When?'

'A couple of hours from now.'

I jumped up. 'This could be a good opportunity to get some information.'

'Seminar or not, you still won't be able to approach him.'

'Let's see.'

I ran out of the room, ignoring Rajib da's 'Don't get us into trouble' shout.

The seminar room was deep inside the bowels of the hotel. Outside it, people jostled to get in. I waited, knowing how these seminars worked. I would have my chance when they broke for tea.

The crowd finally entered the room and the doors closed. Soon after, flanked by a couple of bouncers, Tibrewal sauntered in and went inside. A couple of waiters came and started laying down the tea service. I hung around in a corner, pretending to be engrossed in my mobile.

The doors reopened exactly after forty-five minutes and the crowd spilled out, followed by Tibrewal and his bouncers. After picking up their tea, people stood in groups talking to each other. The largest of these was, of course, around Tibrewal, but there were smaller clusters too. I quickly snapped a few pictures as discreetly as I could and approached a couple of young looking men standing a little apart.

'Isn't that Sandeep Tibrewal?' I feigned surprise, 'The big investor?'

One of the guys nodded. 'Yes, he is.'

I decided to try a direct approach. 'My friend runs a start-up. Could he hope to get an investment from him?'

The man shook his head. 'Not unless you come through a reference.'

'Reference? Whose reference?'

With a knowing smile, his companion glanced at the two men standing at a distance. 'Them for one.'

'Who are they?'

'Manoj Gupta and Vishnu Chawla. Tibrewal's golf buddies.'

I was trying to build a credible story in mind with which to approach them, when I suddenly observed one of Tibrewal's bouncers coming towards me in long strides.

I quickly turned and walked away. One did not mess with these people.

I went back to the office. 'Got two names. Manoj Gupta and Vishnu Chawla. Check them out.'

It didn't take Sohini too long. 'Both are big businessmen. Manoj Gupta is the owner of Carmine Motors. They sell top-end luxury cars. Vishnu Chawla owns Azure Ayurville.'

'What's that?'

'Upscale health resort. Specializes in Ayurvedic therapy.'

'Good. But what's the connection?' There was no mistaking the irritation in Rajib da's voice.

'Let me check.' Sohini got busy with her laptop.

Rajib da glared at me. 'I am not sure where you are going with this. You were supposed to find out a reason behind Paromita's suicide.'

'The motive is financial.'

'But how?'

'I pulled some details from the corporate affairs department's website,' Sohini interrupted, saving me from the embarrassment of being unable to answer Rajib da's question. 'Manoj Gupta also holds some shares in the company Sudip Ghosh has invested in.'

'So?' Rajib da said angrily. 'This could be just a coincidence. It proves nothing.'

I thought for a moment. 'Check the customer page on Carmine Motors' website.'

'Olive Enterprises is listed as a customer in the Carmine Motors website.' Sohini informed us, after checking.

'See!' I remarked with a broad smile.

'I see nothing!' Rajib da retorted. 'What are you driving at?'

'Let me explain.' I said smugly. 'Sudip Ghosh collects cash from people he knows, such as Abhishek Guha and Barun Shaw and passes it on to Tapas. I think Tapas runs a money-laundering scheme. He uses ordinary people like Soumen and Babun as his cash couriers.'

'How do you know this?' Sohini asked.

'He tried to recruit me.' I answered. 'Anyway, Tapas then sends the money to Tibrewal, who invests it in start-ups and gets them to sell their shares at a highly discounted price to the people who gave the cash. And he himself also gets to buy a stake at that reduced price for his services.'

'What about Manoj Gupta and Vishnu Chawla?'

'I think they act as brokers. In the course of their businesses, they would be coming across businesspeople either having money or wanting money. They push them to Tibrewal who plays the matchmaker.'

Rajib da had sat in a huff while I had been answering Sohini. Now he burst out in exasperation. 'Fine, you have unearthed a money-laundering scheme. So? How is this connected to Paromita's suicide? And what about Bijan's death?'

I fell silent. I had no answer to either question.

Rajib da let out a long sigh. 'You have gone off the rails. Even if this financial fraud that you have sniffed out is true, I can still do nothing.'

'But why?'

'We have no proof, just pieces of information. Tibrewal is not someone you mess with without solid evidence.'

I tried to say something, but Rajib da stopped me with a raised hand. 'Let's not forget that we are dealing with two cases of unexplained suicide. Let's not just ignore them.'

Sohini, who was still at her laptop, now looked up. 'Actually, there may be three suicides. Not two.'

'What?' I almost shouted.

'Yes. I suddenly remembered an old news story about Ayurville. This is what I was checking. A few months back, a guest had hung himself in his room. A painter named Janak Roy.' Rajib da nodded. 'Yes, I remember this story. Janak Roy was a very successful painter. Sold his paintings to the rich and famous. It was a complete mystery why he killed himself.'

I felt shaken. 'No reason for suicide found?'

Sohini shook her head. 'None whatsoever. In fact, he should have been celebrating. The day before a gallery had sold his painting *Morning Bouquet* for a huge sum. Here, take a look at this article.' She turned the laptop screen towards me.

The article wondered why Janak Roy had taken his life and shared the details about his death. Before the break of dawn a waiter had found the door of his room slightly ajar. He had knocked and then peeped inside to see Janak Roy hanging from the ceiling fan. Police had come in the morning and cut him down. There was neither any sign of struggle nor a suicide note. Post-mortem had ruled it a case of suicide.

There was a photo of the crime scene. The sky outside the large window was tinged red. A body covered in white sheets lay on the bed. A basket of bananas on a table and a large replica of Van Gogh's *The Starry Night* on the wall gave the scene a somewhat surreal appearance.

Rajib da fixed me with a hard stare. 'We now have three unexplained suicides. We can't just ignore them. And unless we can understand why they killed themselves, we cannot tie them to this financial corruption. Get back to basics, start with Paromita's brother.'

I knew his words were final. In my excitement I had indeed ignored the basics.

It took some effort to locate Paromita's brother. After her death, he had fled rehab to avoid talking to the police and was now living in a tenement house at the largesse of friends whom he had convinced that he would soon have his hands on the wealth of his late superstar sister. From whatever I could glean from his drug-fuelled raves and rants, he squarely blamed Sudip for Paromita's death. Apparently, Sudip used to frequently force her to accompany him to a live music bar in Hotel Ascott and must have done something to her there that forced her to take that extreme step.

The possibility of finding the connection between a real estate shark and a dead actress gleamed in my mind once.

I made a trip to Ascott. Ascott's bar, in a spirit of double entendre, was named the Ace of Clubs and had the picture of a playing card of the same denomination painted on its glass doors. Live music shows were held there during the weekends. With the lie that I was writing a biography of Paromita for a major channel and a large tip for the waiter, I was able to learn that after

Paromita's death, Sudip had gathered a rising starlet as his new escort and the couple was regular visitors to the live music shows.

The weekend was a few days away, so I decided to check out the other two deaths. However, in both cases I made absolutely no progress. Janak Roy's family had moved abroad, so there was no one I could speak to. Attempts to talk to some of the galleries that had sold his paintings just brought me cold stares and pursed lips.

Enquiries about Bijan Datta also brought me to a dead end. He had worked in the government's horticultural produce department and his mundane job of tabulating data and creating routine reports did not expose him to any kind of pressures or enticements that would cause him to take his own life.

On the weekend, I walked into the Ace of Clubs bar. A music band was playing some garish tune under pulsing psychedelic lights when I arrived. Casually taking a stroll through the crowd, I noticed the upcoming TV starlet I had learnt to be Sudip's current companion sitting alone at a table. Her face was heavily made up, but that did not hide her look of boredom and distaste. I sat down at a table near her and ordered a drink.

As the waiter lowered my drink on the table, I glanced at the young woman and asked with a tone of familiarity, 'Divyani sitting alone! Didn't Sudip Ghosh come with her today?'

The waiter silently pointed at the bar counter with his head and quickly turned away, but not before I could notice the smirk on his face.

I looked towards the bar counter. Sudip was sitting on a high stool next to a young man wearing mascara and ear piercings. They were almost leaning into each other. As I watched, the man whispered something in Sudip's ear. As if in response Sudip lowered his hand and slowly caressed the man's thigh.

I called for the bill, gulped down my drink, paid, and left. The meaning of the waiter's smirk was clear. There would be no story involving a relationship between Sudip Ghosh and the late

Paromita. Sudip was gay. He brought along a glamour woman just as a cover.

I called Rajib da after leaving Ascott. 'Did you get anything on the financial status of Paromita's boutique?' I knew I was clutching at straws.

'Thank you for suddenly remembering me after a whole week.' He sounded caustic, but still answered my question. 'I got a tax consultant to dig up the tax returns of the boutique. It was running at a minor profit.'

There went my straw. 'Should I check up on Barun Shaw now?'

'No motive.' Rajib da sighed. 'Paromita's serial was topping the charts, but after her death it has gone south. I heard from some studio sources that Barun Shaw had invested a large sum in it. She was more useful to him alive.'

Another straw went even before I could make a grab at it. I bought myself a bottle of whiskey before going home. I would need to drink myself to sleep.

The alcohol did not help. I tossed and turned, dreaming of psychedelic flashes of colour, strange symbols and impossible geometries.

Finally, when I woke up sweating, unable to sleep any more, it was still dark. As I switched on the light to check the time, I saw the bill from the Ace of Clubs lying on the bedstand, where I had casually thrown it earlier. I noticed that it had a picture of an ace of clubs playing card printed on it. Next to the bill lay Soumen's visiting card. I kept staring at them. Some strange thoughts dredged from the now barely remembered dream started floating up in my mind.

I don't know how long I had sat looking at the three leafed clover printed on the bill and Soumen's visiting card, but when I came to myself, the sun had already climbed the sky. Stuffing the bill in my pocket, I left.

I ran and stumbled into the office where Rajib da was going through some documents with Sohini.

'What is the rush?' He asked, surprised. 'Found something useful at last?'

'Yes.' I nodded slowly. 'A connection, a pattern, I don't know what to call it. I still don't know why these people took their own lives, but I think I have found some things that connect them.'

'What things?'

'Colour for example. Specifically yellow. In the room where they died.'

'I don't get it.'

'In Paromita's bedroom, there were a few yellow sunflowers. Bijan Datta's room had a yellow curtain. And in Janak Roy's case, it was a bunch of bananas.'

Rajib da looked dumbfounded. 'Are you joking? These are common items that can be found anywhere. This is rubbish!'

'Is it?' I shook my head. 'Then there are stars. Star-shaped holes in the lampshade in Paromita's room, the word "stars" on a sign outside Bijan's house, Van Gogh's *The Starry Nights* in Janak Roy's room.'

Sohini snickered, Rajib da let out a heavy sigh. 'You are displaying a classic case of apophenia.'

'Apophenia? What's that?'

'It is the tendency to see patterns among random things. The stress of the case has got to you, I think. Or the drinking.'

I went on nonetheless. 'Stars and then flowers. Paromita was acting in a serial called *Lonely Roses*, Bijan worked for the horticulture department and Janak Roy had just sold a painting named *Morning Bouquet*. Then windows, yes windows. All three rooms where these people died had a window to the east.'

'When something keeps on repeating, can it any longer be called random?' I kept the Ace of Clubs bill on the table. 'Look at this three-leaf clover that stands for clubs. Our case also has three sets. Three victims and three sets of people connected to them.'

'Are you not barking up the wrong tree again? The question still remains, what made these people take their own lives?'

'I still don't know. But I feel if I can understand the deeper pattern underlying all this, maybe I will understand their deaths too. Three dead people. All connected to some form of art. One an actress, another a singer, the third a painter. Each associated with a set of three people, one kingpin and two lackeys. The kingpins are associated with the colour green. Sudip Ghosh owns Emerald Properties. Emerald is a green gem. Tapas Dastidar's business is called Olive Enterprises. Olive is a shade of green. And Tibrewal runs Greenfield Capital. One set of lackeys are from the health profession. A doctor, a physiotherapist and a health spa owner. Their colour is blue. The blue of the sky in Abhishek's nursing home, Skyview, the blue of Soumen's visiting card and a word for blue, Azure, in the name of Vishnu Chawla's business, Azure Ayurville. The other set of lackeys are in the transport business. Logistics, taxi service, car showroom. They have red as their colour. The red sun in Barun Shaw's company name, Sunrise Logistics, the red decal in Babun's cars and carmine, a shade of red, in the name of Manoj Gupta's company Carmine Auto. Red, blue, green, yellow. It is as if all the different types of characters across the sets have been colour coded.'

I had expected a retort from Rajib da, but he nodded. There was no response from Sohini. She suddenly seemed to have frozen still. Like a mannequin, her open eyes stared blankly at nothing.

'You have finally got most of it, I see.' Rajib da said with a sigh. He seemed relieved.

'Got what?' I asked. 'I still do not know why they died. Maybe this repeating pattern has got something to do with it?'

Rajib da shook his head. 'The deaths are inconsequential. Their only purpose was to provoke you to detect the patterns. It took you some effort, but you finally did it. We have to improve quite a lot before you can be deployed of course, but it's definitely a progress over the previous attempts.'

I stared at him, not understanding.

'You see, this is all a simulation. We actually are from a time where crime has become so sophisticated that subtle hidden patterns in data must be found in order to detect them. A job that is done by detection algorithms. Like you.'

I suddenly felt very sleepy; Rajib da's voice seemed to be coming from a great distance.

'But a detection algorithm has to be trained first. And what better framework to train it in than constructing it as an investigative journalist and embedding it in a simulation of the society of the previous century? A time when technology was still primitive and no sophisticated monitoring instruments were available. It would force the algorithm to rely on its investigative skills alone to detect patterns.'

A rich, deep darkness seemed to be descending upon me, enveloping me. I quickly lost all sense of space and time in its thick folds.

I opened my eyes with an effort. A dirty ceiling. Below it a grimy ceiling fan moving lazily. This is what I saw in a haze.

My head was heavy. The bed sheet felt damp, my sweaty body sticky. When did I sleep last night? The stupor inside my head did not allow me to remember.

WITCH HUNTING

Kiran Manral

My head was splitting. It felt like it had been cut into two. I gingerly put up a hand to check if it was indeed intact. It was, but my hand came away sticky with blood. I was bleeding from a wound I could not check. There was blood on my bodysuit. It was my own, I knew. I was in a strange place, it seemed like an alleyway, completely unfamiliar. How had I landed here, who had assaulted me, why had I been left here? I patted down the pockets of my bodysuit. One of my weapons was missing, the ancient bullet gun useful for these times, but the concealed communication channel, embedded into my skull was still active, connected to my palmtronic, the communication device embedded into the skin of my palm. I pressed down on my palm, activating the channel.

PSYCHE, what happened?

You got attacked as soon as you materialized.

By whom.

Earth people of the time.

Where's my weapon of the times?

They took it. You still have your ray tube. Check.

Where's my transponder?

You won't need it. You will get another.

Sometimes PSYCHE didn't make sense. PSYCHE wasn't a person, not an artificial interface. She was me communicating with an elevated sense of consciousness of my own through telepathy.

It was something we had honed from the time we were picked as infants to be in The Force. It kept functional even across distances as vast as to be immeasurable and when traditional channels of communication were inaccessible. I communicated with the me I had left back at the base, floating in a liquid suspension pod, suspended in a vacuum field. I was there. I was here.

I felt in the chest cavity of my bodysuit. There it was – my ray tube. No bigger than what humans back then would call a 'lipstick'. It looked like one too, a sleek steel tube. Perhaps those who had attacked me would have thought that it was a lipstick and not taken it, perhaps they had not bothered to check.

I held on to a rusting pipe and hauled myself up to my feet inch by inch, every single bone in my body was weighed down like I had crash landed into a world with thousand gravities. But I was here and it looked like the old earth I had studied, the earth before the arks, the huge intergenerational interstellar space ships, had left the toxic skies, a seedy section of it no doubt. I looked up, the sky above was already sooty like the grains on a television channel of the times switched to nothing. Dead channel. The toxicity of the skies would increase over the years, until humans had no option but to step out wearing filtration masks and then portable breathing apparatuses. And then, of course, humans stepped off the planet. I had studied enough of the past surface to understand that where I was now is a city called Bombay, along the western coast of a country called India and this was after 1995 when the name of the city was changed to Mumbai from what it was previously, Bombay, or the good bay. I moved slowly to the road ahead, reading the signboards of the shuttered store fronts and figured I was in the area then called Pydhonie. Now, of course, it did not exist. The city had long been submerged in the shift when the seas claimed the land.

I racked up the data on it. It had the famed Mumbadevi Temple translocated here in the 1700s, from where the city got its present name, Mumbai. It derived its name etymologically from 'py' and 'dhone', which meant to wash one's feet, in Marathi, which was the language spoken in this part of the world and it was conjectured that the name originated back when the area was still the small creek at high tide at the Great Breach when the city was still many islands. This area, like most of the city, was reclaimed from the sea to make a continuous city that eventually joined with the mainland beyond the Mahim Creek. Settled primarily by immigrants from Gujarat and Rajasthan, the buildings reflected the architecture of the lands they had left behind, with *jharoka*s and murals, ornate lintels and balconies, all decrepit and faded, the newness long gone from them, the years weighing heavily on the flaking plaster and faded paint.

There was absolutely no one around the narrow alley I had landed in, and the roads ahead that it led out to were completely deserted. The alarm bells went off in my head. I had been dropped into a time when the mother planet was teeming with humankind, landing bang in the midst of the most populous city in the world, of which this was amongst the most densely populated areas. But where were all the people? Why was the city bereft of all living things, not even a bird was fluttering past, the leaves were still and not even a light breeze moved the still air, there was a hush, one that was almost ominous. Every living creature was behind locked and barricaded doors and shutters. I was the only thing that was moving.

I had landed in 1984, to be precise, April 1984, 22 April 1984, Bombay, Pydhonie. that was what the tracker had shown us. Map coordinates – Longitude: 72° 50.0959' and Latitude: 18.954235°. I had been flung here to find an escapee, a law enforcer gone rogue from the Federation Force, the consolidated law enforcement of the settlements in the clusters beyond what was the immediate sol system where man had moved out to from centuries ago from the here and now I had landed back on. The escapee was someone I knew. Someone they hoped I could convince to return to our times, an ex-lover. We were not allowed to go back without purpose, we ended up altering too much of the streams of the past, making the present untenable.

If you think finding a needle in a haystack is easy, try finding a time escapee who has travelled back in time hundreds of years and found one of the densest places on the mother planet to hide in. The population teeming so much here that people were scattered like microbes on the surface of the city. Or supposed to be. I had landed in an empty city, where I couldn't see a single creature alive, not even a gutter rat. The shutters of all the shops were down, the lane was wet with the remnants of an earlier drizzle. What year was I in, what date was I in, where had the one I'd been chasing gone, was he here contrary to the tracker, had they changed my coordinates at the last moment, and who had attacked me and taken away all I needed to survive in this alien time and land? There was no two-way communication once one had entered the time turner. I was here, I had to find the one who had escaped the high-security containment zone at the Althimea 1 settlement on Vulcan, a terraformed asteroid used as a security headquarters for the highest level of Federation prisoners and I had to figure out how to get him back. I rested a bit leaning against a wall. My bodysuit, with all its sensors hooked up to the system back home in my time and my space were useless here. I had only a ray tube but that was to be used only in dire circumstances, it would vaporize whatever it was aimed at. For now, I had only my bare hands and my wits. And my detective instinct. I had all the other things that detectives of this era had never benefitted from – enhanced sensory inputs, muscular power implants that gave me the strength of ten humans and of course, my training. I was, what they called, an elite squad detective on the force. I was an elite squad detective of the Force.

PSYCHE, where do I go?

Turn right. Go into the clinic. He went that way too. Take what he left behind.

Two days had passed, there was no telling where Darren had disappeared to in the hive that was Bombay. He would have most probably covered up the bodysuit with clothes of this time, if he had been able to find clothes that would be commensurate with his height. We were taller as a species now, much taller than what folks on the original mother planet used to be, almost twice the average height of the current generation in that time span. Humans had gotten incrementally taller as a species over the centuries. It was difficult for us to blend in when we went back. Where had he gone? How did I track him down? I did not know.

I stepped out of the alley way onto the main road. Here, too, everything was deserted. The streetlights were on, a pale white that filtered down through the drizzle shimmering with the refraction. I pressed my palm against the wound at the back of my head, trying to staunch the bleeding. To my right, I saw a sign board: Dr Chunawalla Clinic, it said simply. There was a faint light visible inside, although the door was shut. All the doors and windows of all the tenements, crowded around and on top of each other had no lights and were shuttered resolutely against the world. Some windowpanes gleamed dimly, as though they had been blacked out by paper. Metal strips were welded across the frames. Fear hung in the air, a stench that overpowered the rotting garbage and the sludge in the blocked drains along the roads. There was an uncanny silence in the air.

I went up to it and knocked, feeling the dizziness threaten to swamp my consciousness again. I was still retching, both from the shifting through time and space and reassembling and then from the knock to my head. There was no response. I heard a sound within. I knocked again. Again, no response. I pulled out my ray tube and trained it down the front of the metal strip that had been locked from within. It vapourized with surprising ease. A horrified gasp and a terrified scream came from within. A thin man with a pinched face accentuated by a thin goatee was huddled in a corner, with an equally terrified looking young man who had crawled under a table and was covering his head with his arms.

'Who are you?' the thin man asked, puzzled, getting up from the corner and walking up to me.

The other man turned around and looked at me, surprised and then his eyes goggled with what was an expression which had remained constant across millennia when men looked at women.

'Is this the *chudail*?'

'Don't be silly,' the older man told the younger man. 'If you looked at the *chudail*, you would be frozen, you wouldn't be able to ask that question.'

The older man came forward and shut the smashed door firmly behind me and put a chair against it. It would be no defence should anyone choose to push it and enter.

'Dr Chunawalla?' I asked. The man with the goatee nodded.

'Can you treat this?' I asked, pointing to the wound on my scalp which had stopped bleeding now but was still throbbing with a dull ache. My body had already begun pumping painkillers through my bloodstream, along with a blood clotting agent.

I wasn't sure if he could understand what I said, my language was not of this time, but I could understand what they spoke because of the translator chip embedded in the Wernicke's area, just behind my ears, in the temporal lobe of my brain. It was an essential part of my equipment as a federal law enforcer, given the numerous dialects and languages which had evolved all of a sudden over all the settlements.

'Let me take a look,' he replied, moving hesitantly towards me, like one might move towards a dangerous wild animal, albeit a wounded one. I caught a glimpse of myself in the reflection within the glass-fronted cabinets. There was blood dripping down my face, down the shoulders of my bodysuit. I was terrifying to look at.

The doctor examined the wound on my scalp and nodded; then the younger man brought out a tray with all the first aid equipment on it.

I sat on a stool and faced the wall while he worked.

'You are not from these parts, where are you from?'

'From very, very far away.' I didn't bother to elaborate.

'Why is everything shuttered down? Didn't the city always stay open 24 hours every day of the week? What is this *chudail* your assistant was scared of?'

'Don't say that word… even saying it might bring it here,' he shuddered. So did the assistant. They looked through the open door, locked it and then drew up a heavy desk to block the way in.

'It will give us some more time to escape in case she comes.'

There were inner rooms I saw, every room had a door that had metal strips welded across, making them impenetrable.

The fear came off the two men in waves. The silence weighed heavy in the room. He worked deftly with a needle and thread on my scalp. Thankfully I couldn't see him working and the local anaesthesia was working well enough.

'Another like you had come in just a couple of days ago.'

That would have been the approximate time lag between us deciphering his coordinates and flinging me here across the void of time space. Strangely enough, the time had differed from the time we were now in, although in our time we had moved barely a few hours later.

'He was dressed in a similar manner to you, with this body-fitting suit and he was like you – perfectly fit, as tall, perhaps taller. You don't see many people so tall and fit. Like Dara Singh was. And his one eye had a screen like yours where it felt like some screens of information were constantly rolling down. He came from very far away too, he told us.'

'Why did he come here?'

The younger man laughed. 'That we don't know. He asked about the *chudail* and her habits. He told us you would be coming and to give you something. And that he would wound you and we were to treat you when you came in. We were not to use any disinfectant on the wound that would mask the smell of the blood. He was very clear about that.'

The doctor opened a drawer and pulled out what looked like a completely solid block of metal, as thick and wide as perhaps what they understood as a metallic cigarette case back in their time. A cigarette case that did not open. Engraved metal. I knew what it was. The etched lines and notches on it lit up when my gloves touched it, sending pulses into my brain, waiting for my command. When I did, it would whisk me and whoever else touched it with these gloves back to where we came from, pulling us apart into individual fragments of our atoms, reassembling us back into what we were, a process fraught with immense risk if it went wrong.

He handed over the box, the teleporting device. He wanted to be tracked, Darren did. That was the only reason he had left this behind, he had left me a way to find him. I took it and pressed it where it needed to be pressed. It lit up with a million lights, like I knew it would. They gasped and stepped back, hiding behind me. This was a cutting-edge teleporter: regular federation citizens would never be able to get their hands on one of these. Regular teleporting stations were singular pod platforms within immense teleportation terminals, given the amount of energy required for the process, sometimes using more energy than was used in interplanetary Federation ships. Whoever had handed him this device was someone extremely powerful in the scheme of things: to gain access to this and the port that it was operated from. For protocol, that had first been put into place back in the distant 1990s and theorized even earlier by the ancient scientist Albert Einstein. We had managed to build on the technology quite a bit in the recent centuries to split selves and transfer each across vast distances of time and space. It was protocol that was earlier reserved for important people who needed to be physically present at multiple places at the same time in the course of their official duties but was now being used to maximize manpower.

'He told us it was precious and it seems like it.'

I nodded.

'I don't know what it is for, so I guess I should give it to you.'

I did not know where this was connected back to, which terminal had offered it to him to enable him to port himself out of the Containment Zone at Althea 1, but the coordinates would be set right back to it, should he choose to return. I would figure that out later, right now my job was to find him, to convince him to return and get us both back using this teleporter. The Federation could not afford to lose him.

PSYCHE, I have his teleporter.

Use it to find him and come back. All of you.

All of us? Sometimes PSYCHE spoke in riddles.

Where is my teleporter?

She lost it.

Who is she?

There was no response. PSYCHE did speak in riddles and at times she chose not to respond. I would have to figure this out for myself.

I pressed down on the teleporter and transmitted the individual coordinates to the control. I put it into my pocket. It would take me back when I pressed on it again. I rose and thanked them and went to the door that I had wrecked and which the assistant had carefully shut behind me.

'Where will you go now, after dark?' the doctor asked. 'Nobody steps out after sunset in the city now. The *chudail* roams and feasts on whoever comes in her path.'

Chudail. That was a new one. I scanned my databank.

Chudail: English translation of 'चुड़ैल'

चुड़ैल

/cuḍaila/

nf

witch countable noun

A witch is a woman who is believed to have magic powers, especially evil ones.

/cudaila, cudail, chudaila, chudail, cuDaila, cuDail, chuDaila, chuDail, cuḍaila, cuḍail, chuḍaila, chuḍail

I snorted in amusement. This lot was terrified of a witch roaming around the city after dark, a *chudail* who feasted on whichever hapless soul she came across when the sun had sunk into the sea. The ancients continued to be superstitious long after we'd assumed they had moved into the scientific era.

'What is this *chudail* you speak of? Have you seen it?'

'No, we haven't but we've heard she's taller than the tallest man and has the strength of ten men. Her face is so beautiful that you are frozen when you look at her and you cannot escape her if she sets her eyes on you. She tears humans into bits and eats them raw. No bullets can kill her and no nets can trap her. The police force is baffled and everyone stays within their homes after dark, because she steps out only once the sun sets. I recommend you stay here and step out only when it is daylight. We live here, my son and I, and we keep a light on in case there is an emergency and someone needs urgent medical help.'

'Thanks for the warning, but I have a task to do, a person to find.'

I stepped out of the clinic into the hushed stillness of the night, glistening and damp with rain. The clouds played a juvenile game of hide-and-seek with the satellite of the planet which was in its full phase at the moment, reflecting all the light it received from the sol of this system. The system to coordinate locations was inaccessible to me, whatever had taken my weapons and identification had jammed my systems as well. I was all alone in a strange time with only my wits to get me out and back. And the one I had come hunting for.

Darren Kommandant. We bore our titles in lieu of what ancients had as surnames. Why had he chosen Bombay, I wondered, as the destination he'd chosen to return and this time and year? Had his ancestors stepped onto the ark from here back when we began moving out to settlements? Did he have ancestral family here? He was a rare criminal, one from the Elite squad who had been on a special mission and then gone missing. Members of the Elite squad were not allowed to travel back without permission. He was also my ex-lover, which is why I had been deputed to catch him. A trial of sorts, I knew, to see if I was worthy of being in the

Force, if I put duty over everything. Which I did, that is why I was here, wasn't I? And saying no was never an option. Had I said no, I would have been organic manure feeding the plant fields on Vulcan right now. Where would Darren have gone?

Pydhonie was a tangled warren of streets, densely packed with buildings, each containing a multitude of people, crammed into quarters which weren't meant to contain so many in so little a space. The odours were overwhelming, the stench of rotting, uncleared garbage, the sludge of drains, the smell of people, so many people. Sometimes, we could sniff out a runaway, given we had the enhanced olfactory abilities that humans had never had in the past, almost on par with that of the ancient African elephant which had over 2,000 genes dedicated to the task of detecting and differentiating through odours in the environment. This was also why unpleasant odours affected me so. They would have Darren as well, he had been similarly modified genetically, as had all of us. Why then, would he have chosen this place.

PSYCHE, where is he? Where do I go?

Go straight down this lane. Stay in the shadows. Switch on visual deflect mode.

The bodysuit had the benefit of what the ancients would have called an invisibility cloak. A switch activated the particles built into the bodysuit which deflected the light around the wearer. I pulled the hood over my head and became well on invisible, only thermal imaging could spot me if they chose to use it. These were ancient times though, no one would have access to thermal imaging technology here on the street, or would they, one could never be sure.

PSYCHE, where is he, locate him.

He is still in these coordinates. He hasn't moved from here since we last tracked him, he has been here for three solar days.

72 hours, 4,320 minutes, 2,59,200 seconds. Darren had spent more time in the past than any of us had ever done so far, how was he able to even survive on this gravity, breathing this air.

It was long enough a duration. Yet it was too short for it to have affected him. I would find him. How on earth would I find him? The night was dark and damp. I had no shelter. There was something curious called a '*chudail*' running amok in the city devouring the humans. I had to find a fugitive I once had loved, although love as a bond was considered rather outdated by the current standards of human interaction where children were no longer raised in a family unit and therefore were encouraged not to form an emotional bond with any other human. It weighed humans down, this attachment to others. Darren. I sighed, moving swiftly down the deserted street scanning it manually for any bleep of response from the tracker implanted deep within Darren's brain. I had his teleporter and it would take me to him. There was no way he could have got the tracker removed here, the time did not have the technology to either implant it, or remove it. He was still traceable, only if one got within the immediate periphery of a few hundred metres.

It was ominous, the still unrippled night in this part of the city. Noises were hushed, lights were out or dimmed behind closed doors and windows. Most doors were barricaded with additional metal grills. The *chudail* could not get through metal, I assumed. Nothing beeped as I moved through. I hadn't accounted for hunger when I had packed for my journey through space and time. The reassembled body was hungry. What could I find for food here that would suit me. I had some food capsules somewhere in the bodysuit. I patted myself down, found the little pocket with an assortment of pills for a variety of hunger and cravings – meat, dessert, snack – and pulled out a random pill and swallowed it. It ballooned in my stomach into a full meal of meat and potatoes with gravy. Damn. I would be sleepy now and there was no space I could lay down and sleep. Perhaps I should have waited at the clinic until daybreak. The gravity on earth was different too, heavier and more annoying. It weighed my steps down. I dragged myself forward. The night was still dark and ponderous, stray clouds floated across the sky casting strange shadows on the ground as they crossed the satellite of the earth called moon, with its feeble pale purple light, reflected off their sol. I could sense rather than see something following me. I picked up a scent, a familiar scent, something so strangely familiar that it felt oddly comforting in the chaos of the ambient smells around which were unpleasant for the most. I turned around, I could see nothing. I walked towards the scent, keeping in the shadows, wondering what it was that I was seeking. Something moved in the darkness swiftly, movements that were not the litheness of any human of the times and moved up a wall, jumping over it, disappearing into the crannies that made up the jumble of walls and buildings. The scent I had picked up was my own. The fragrance of my body and the metallic stench of my blood.

There was nothing to be seen, even when I switched on my enhanced night vision. Whatever it was had disappeared from sight, even the faint trail of the particular body odour I had picked up had now disappeared or was swamped over by the other smells that made up the olfactory bouquet of this area. How had humans survived this onslaught of smells before we decided to sanitize living spaces of ambient sounds and smells, I wondered.

PSYCHE, what or who was that following me?

We could not track it.

Why was the body odour so familiar?

We could not identify odour from this distance. We get only visual inputs.

Sometimes I wondered why PSYCHE spoke in the third person when she communicated with me. After all, she was a single person. Me. Or an alternate version of me, the disembodied psyche of me, encased in a synth bodysuit, further immersed in a liquid tank. Back into the womb at a time when none of us were born out of the womb anymore, we were grown in petri dishes and planted into gestational pods. We were created to specifications, we were no longer the casual results of the roll of the dice.

How would I find Darren in this maze of buildings and people? I had nothing to go with; I was working blind in an alien time and space that did not support the technology I had been trained in. Perhaps the only thing to do was to be so visible and obvious that he found me. He would come to me if he found me. I walked down the street knocking on doors that would not be answered. The shutters of all the stores were down. There were no people sleeping outside. There was also the teleporter in my pocket, I remembered: that small square metallic case that someone could have mistaken for a metallic engraved cigar case. I switched the teleporter on again, it would tell me when he was near. The teleporter would also tell him when I was near. That was how it worked. And just then, as I thought of it telling him about me being around, it beeped. A soft beep, but one that made me jump. We were within ten metres of each other. I looked around, cautiously. He would be armed. I had only my ray tube and I didn't want to use it on him; it would vaporize him immediately.

A hand came out of nowhere and clamped down on my mouth and another grabbed my arm. I slammed the elbow of my free hand into what I assumed was the torso of whoever it was who had grabbed me from behind, it was like slamming it into granite. Nothing gave, it wasn't the soft flesh of the unprotected humans of yore. This was the Kevlar strong bodysuit of the kind I had on; the hand grabbing me too, I realized, was at level with me; the humans of the time and of this place were much shorter; any human grabbing me here would have been at waist level. I recognized his scent, a scent that had not been layered over with fragrances produced in laboratories.

'Darren.'

'Hush,' he replied and drew me close to him, withdrawing step by step into the canopy of a stairway we were standing in front of. We had to bend to fit within, it was not made for those of our height. The morning star was not yet out. A mosque, lit up with lights shone like a beacon in the distance, above the low tenements. Soon, the muezzin would call the faithful for prayer.

Would they step out, I wondered, if night hadn't withdrawn into itself by then?

'Shhh...,' he whispered into my ear.

He had been tracking me even before I realized he was. Slowly he lowered me, so we were both squatting behind a decrepit staircase that led up into the maws of a building which looked like it was about to collapse any minute. It smelled disgustingly of human sweat, urine and excreta, thanks to the common toilets which were located at every landing. I could feel the vomit rise to my throat. I had eaten nothing to bring up and so I brought up bile. Darren wiped my face where the blood spilled with what felt like cloth. He was holding a handkerchief in his hand. It was the first time I felt the fibre of pure cotton, as grown from the earth and spun from the loom, touch my skin. It felt like the kiss of the earth, soft and gentle. He was wearing the same bodysuit I was wearing, Federation issued, but he was carrying a handkerchief of these times. I turned to look at him in the dark, he was much the same as I remembered him after all these years.

'Sorry about hitting you on the head. I needed to spill blood.' He balled up the blood-stained handkerchief and threw it out onto the street.

'I have to take you back,' I told him, realizing he held me in a grip that was stronger than a vice.

He shook his head. 'You've got it wrong. I needed you here so I could take you back.'

'I don't understand. What are you talking about?'

There were footsteps coming down the street, they echoed ominously in the silence. Even the night insects went still, as did the soft breeze. Everything paused, held its breath. The steps were heavy. A shadow approached, its presence accompanied by heavy breathing and a miasmal stench I gagged again.

He tapped my palm and thought into it, no words.

'Work with me on this. Stay calm.'

The shadow approached.

PSYCHE, I found Darren. Rather, he found me.

She's approaching you, she has smelt you. Capture her.

Her? You mean capture him, right.

No. She is coming towards you.

Who is she?

You will see.

The shadow lengthened as it approached. It sniffed us and turned towards us. I froze, a sense of dread running amok in her veins, freezing her blood into icicles. Darren did not relax his grip on my mouth, I could sense my heartbeat racing unpredictably and my bodysuit releasing relaxants into my skin to calm me down.

What was casting the shadow had almost reached up to us. My heartbeat was now regular, my breathing no longer ragged and uneven, my body had just about become accustomed to the weight of the true gravity that I had never experienced all my life on the settlements and in transit, except for brief training periods in simulations. What approached us came to the front of the building and stood there, sniffing. It was tall, it was a woman, it planted both feet on the ground and stood, swaying confusedly. It looked around, the darkness obscured its face. It bent down to its knees and seemed like it would topple over, staying there for a long moment and then raised its head again, looking around discombobulated. Heroin nod, that's what they called it back in the day when humans ingested substances that took them onto chemical highs, substances which then took over their systems and led them to their deaths. Its hair streamed down the sides of its head, obscuring its face. It let out a heart-rending scream that echoed through all the heavens and the seven hells. Then it stood up straight and looked up straight at me, a face more beautiful than I could ever remember, even though I saw it every time I looked at a reflection of myself. She smiled, revealing teeth stained with blood, blood that trickled down the side of her lips, blood from a fresh kill, a hapless human who had probably had the mischance of crossing her path. The moon was behind the creature, full and gibbous at the same time, casting two shadows of the same creature. I knew, somehow that the moon had stayed unchanged, hanging twice in this sky, ever since this creature had come here. Time had gone out of warp, she had been stuck here for months, perhaps years. And now, I was here and the creature was here. We were both in the same time. It was my voice screaming. The creature screaming was me.

Darren pushed me out of the stairway, out into the light of the moons, out from where we were hidden in the shadows. The creature turned to face us sniffing the air for the molecules of our individual odour. She sniffed the scent of blood riding on the air, the blood from my wound. I had been wounded to have her find me. She screamed again, a scream that tore open the silence of the night and rent the clouds above into ribboned shards, that dissipated into rain all around us. She swayed in place. Then bent down as if her backbone had turned into jelly, her head almost touching her knees, staying that way for a long, unending moment, nodding in and out of consciousness with the high that the scent of blood gave her. Then she stood up and looked straight at me putting her hand out, fighting with something primeval within her, something that had driven her to become what she had. Her eyes were drenched in a raw pain that I felt viscerally, I had been suffering and I hadn't known.

Darren injected additional calming doses directly into my body suit, pressing through his own. I pulled out my ray tube. He plucked it out of my hand.

'You will die too, if you do that.'

I felt the calm go through me, I saw her calm down too, standing, waiting, unsure.

PSYCHE, why was I not informed of who it really was that I was to get back.

Would you have believed us, until you had seen it?

Seen her, you mean?

Now incorporate and collect.

I reached out and took her hand, gathering her into me, assimilating myself back into one body. I felt myself scattering and assimilating simultaneously. This couldn't be. I was a detective of the Elite squad, but I had been used as bait to hunt a forgotten fragment of myself down. A forgotten fragment of me that had evolved into a monster and needed to be extricated back into her proper time and place, to let this city live as it had, to let the people emerge any time of the day and night, without fear of the *chudail*. And exterminated in her own time and space.

Now I knew. I had to bring the discombobulated half of myself back to my times. I had gotten stuck here after an error in transmission, the blackest part of my psyche deposited amongst humans. What and how that had happened I did not know; there was a blank in my memory where it should have been.

Darren held on to me, taking the transponder out from where I'd kept it in the side pocket of my bodysuit. The plasma field enclosed us in a flash, all three of us, sweeping us across oceans of time and space, buffeted on waves of energy we could not see, only feel for the long, long never-ending drop into the now we had all come from.

When we stopped, I opened my eyes, all of me in me now. PSYCHE. She. Me. Me in the now and here. The three of us, entangled across distances of space and time. The original, the copy and the conduit. The me, the dark rage of the monstrous me, the transparent acuity of telepathic me. When we stopped, I knew they would end us, all three of us.

A MESSIAH OF TEARS AND BROKEN THINGS

Shweta Taneja

Stars hang heavy overhead, the moon deflated and dead. Freezing wind blows from the snow-capped peaks of the Himalayas, searing the Chandrabhaga river valley and tearing bits off my skin. Above me, ravens circle and caw. Across the holy pyre of the Aghori tantriks, someone screams in agony. The wind howls. The man clutches his throat as though a snake were writhing inside. He gurgles.

Suddenly, the wind stops. The man drops.

'He isn't breathing!' bawls his companion, Ghimari, an aghori who likes to take newcomers under his wing. Ravens circle above, croaking and drowning out his voice. I get up, sway and walk around the pyre, crouching near the body.

'Just half an hour ago, he had haggled with Hingi. I offered him some herbal tea. Did he overdose?' Ghimari frowns. I turn the body around. I know this one. When alive, the body was a failed musician in his 30s, always desperate for opium. A week ago, Hingi had even made him eat his own finger to get some. I check the body. No needle marks, no blue throat or popping eyes. No other signs of overdose or poison. His four-fingered hand is fisted, but he has a darned smile and a horrible smell I can't shake off. I go closer, sniff. Sweet like bubble gum and bubbly memories. Ugh.

'It's not overdose.' I've seen too many deaths by opiates. Aghoris love them all. Those popular with the regular crowd: opium or heroin. Those popular with tantriks: charak made of *chandaali's* blood and *dhrash,* fine powdered bones of *yalis* – both powerful magical supernaturals. 'This is a murder.'

'Princess is dramatic as usual,' snorts Hingi, the arrogant ass of an apprentice who hangs out with the alpha aghoris on the other side of the outcrop by the riverbank.

'Weren't you the one who chatted with him just half hour ago?'

'I've the best opiates, of course he will come to me,' he says dismissively. 'Ghimari, stop being a pussy and drag the body down to the river.'

If I were who I used to be, I would've drunk him dry before breakfast. But no, that's not who I am any more. I don't know who I am any more.

'Fifth dead in three days,' I say. The first was a family man, laid off from a job in Bengaluru, with empty eyes and a crooked tie that he wore without any other clothes. He died the same night a teenager did. The teen had escaped his murderous classmates in a madrassa after they discovered he was gay. Yesterday were two white-skinned Canadians, depressed, high on opiates, waiting for the apocalypse. Now the musician.

Five hopeless misfits with nothing in common. Except they were all lost causes. Something dark I'm trying to ignore rises in my sternum. Not bile; anger, a furious energy. I don't like it when people abuse nobodies and get away with it.

'She's a natural, Chitti!' cackles a hunchbacked ancient woman, looking at me but talking to an animated skeleton that chitters around her. I know her name. Dhuma. I've seen her sometimes at aghori all-nighters. Always loud, always cackling, dancing without a beat with a *damru* and that clunky skeleton of hers, getting on my nerves. She squats by my side, grabs my left hand, pulls out a boneblade, cuts my fingertip to let a few drops fall on the dead body's forehead. 'Oi!' I cry.

Red mist rises from the body's forehead just as a raven perches on her ash-covered shoulder. *Caw-caw!* Dhuma hoots. 'My bloody tears. What an artistic kill. The human was killed by an Ashru!'

'You can do mantras?' I frown, eyeing her boneblade. Sharp, shiny, beautiful. Only men have tantrik weapons in my world.

'No, *you* did that,' she says.

'That's impossible,' says Haala, the head tantric of the aghori clan. He glowers at me, his ape-like body glistening with sweat. The black hair on his chest move like micro-sized snakes as he makes his point, agitated. 'None of our Aghoris would use an Ashru. They're not that *weak*.' He spits out the last word in disgust.

My hand itches towards the blade. Dhuma sees my attempt and cackles, her pendulous breasts flapping on her protruding stomach. Ugh.

'Find the killer, Anantya,' she grins, toothless, 'and Dhuma will teach you how to use all that shakti you brim in.' I frown. How does this crinkled hunchback know what I'm called? I haven't heard anyone use my name since I came to this clan. It's been what? A year? Maybe more? Can she teach me how to become a tantrik? Use my own shakti?

'What's an Ashru?' I ask instead. For the first time in months, I feel like doing something. 'I'll find it.'

'A low-level *bhuta* that feeds on broken souls till they drop dead,' says Haala. He whacks his beard, hollers. 'Used by weak *desperate* tantriks. Not possible, not possible.'

'The one who calls for Ashru,' Dhuma gets up, brings out her damru and starts to turn it. *Tak-tik-tak-tik*. 'Desires *raktashru*. Blood tears. The collective shakti of the ones without hope!'

'But it demeans and destroys you…' cries Haala. 'No one in my clan is desperate enough!'

'Bhila talks about *raktashru*,' says Ghimari.

'Aha. Bhila. All that desire for power,' cackles Dhuma.

'But he won't, no, no,' Ghimari shakes his head, eyeing Hingi who walks towards us. Hingi swings a *rudraksh mala*, broken, like a noose.

'I heard my name.' Bhila emerges from the shadows behind us. Alpha aghori of the clan, Haala's favourite pupil, Bhila is ripped with a ripped body made to fuck. Yum.

'I wasn't saying you will kill for it, Bhh... Bhila. You know, *raktashru*...' mutters Ghimari. 'You were saying how it would be a useful shakti to tap...' He lets the last word hang, looking at Hingi and then Bhila, shaking. 'I'll deal with the body.' He quickly grabs the feet of the dead and drags it away, breathing hard from the effort.

'You think one of us dares seek blood tears?' says Bhila. 'None is as desperate for power.'

'Like you?' cackles Dhuma. 'You reek of ambition! You drink her...' she points at me with a *jhaadu*. The raven on her shoulder ruffles for dramatic effect. 'You source *yalis* illegally, you've even killed for power. Maybe your greed makes you desperate, aghori? Or are you too cowardly even for *that*?'

Bhila's beautiful eyes darken with anger. He pulls up his bone staff, his pouch of ash. Dhuma grins lopsided, unmoving, the boneblade swinging temptingly on a string around her waist. He doesn't attack though, instead he turns to me, vengeance shining in his eyes. Oh shit.

'What's my name?' I mumble, daring the aghori who likes to mind-fuck me as he fucks me.

'You're my little princess,' he grins. His arm snakes around my shoulder and he offers me something. 'Here, take a drop of charak.' I try to wriggle him away, his grip tightens. He brings his bone staff between us and thumps it in the sand.

'Take the charak and come with me, princess.' The words leave his lips and become a whip that wraps my mind and body with a cold dead hand. *Think nothing but me.* Bhila's command wraps my mind. A psycho serial killer in the Aghori clan? Not my problem. A bunch of despairing freaks, edged out of society, hoping for respite. Death is the best thing that can happen to them. I turn away from the crime scene, from the hunchbacked woman who knows my name and start to walk with Bhila and Hingi down towards the bank of river Chandrabhaga, on the other side of an outcrop, where the alphas sit.

'A mind controlling Vashita?' laughs the old hag from behind. 'Tonight, the stars will tear away your puny power, aghori!' The hag raises her hands and ululates like a hurricane. She starts to sing, flicking her damru and her *jhaadu*, back and forth in her two hands. 'Come, Chitti! Tonight, we dance to find the one who seeks bloodied tears.'

Tak-tik-tak-tik.

Come here, you lout.

Tak-tik-tak-tik.

Bhila's fawning apprentices sit in a circle, snorting *dhrash,* a powerful magical opiate for aghoris to find shakti. Two white women, their skin bare and snow, writhe inside the circle. Bhila joins the women, curling up his legs around their bodies. Fresh meat from the streets of Rishikesh, he had whispered to me earlier, his dimples deep. I sit down in the circle, cross-legged, my head dropping into the hollow bone I'm given. I sniff the last few drops of charak. Red, glistening, bubbling, it's a *chandaali*'s pure blood. Shakti courses through me, curdles my blood.

'What's my name,' I ask aloud, the question shining through the cobwebs that crawl into my mind. Bhila pulls his head up from snogging, grins.

'Princess. That's who you are,' he says, as the women kiss his neck and shoulders. 'Come, rub yourself on my feet.' His modulated murmur creates a denser web in my brain, pulling me. My fingertips curl into fists as I crawl to his orgy and rub my breasts at his feet. He kicks me. Laughs. 'She left her royal court in Banaras to be my royal whore,' he tells the white women, pronouncing the last word as 'whorey'. His apprentices laugh. The women smile vapidly. They're high on heroin, their mind filled with cobwebs like mine. Vashita, the controlling spell Bhila likes to use and is good at. I wipe off the sticky, salty wetness from my cheeks.

Tak-tik-tak-tik.

Grab my boobies and scream aloud!

Ailailalalalalalala! Anantyaaaaaa!

Jazz plays wild in my mind; the ravens spiral above cawing incessantly. Before I know it, I've picked up his bone staff and am pointing it at him. Bhila smirks. The two women stop their writhing.

'Did you murder them for power, Aghori Bhila?' I ask. He rises up, his face feral, a razor smile sharpening his jawbones. He pulls away the staff from my shaky fingers and dramatically points it to his chest. It glistens like tears.

'Why? Are you turning from an assassin to an avenger?' It's like he has read my mind – which he has with his mind-fuck mantra. 'Go on, make me confess.' More people have gathered. His followers laugh. 'Or do what papa taught you,' he cups his erect penis. 'Suck it.'

'Here's more to suck, princess!' says Hingi. He leers at my nipples, offers his dick. Cackles, back slaps, laughter. I gulp, trying to find my way through a maze of shiny webs.

Grab my boobies and scream aloud!

Tak-tik-tak-tik.

Ailailalalalalalala! Anantyaaaaaa!

Dhuma's ululating voice pierces through my skin, crawling up my spine. Ravens circle high above, in sync with the hunchback, round and round, spiralling down through the bawdy song, faster and faster, eating the stars.

'Forgive her.' Someone comes in the middle of the two of us. Ghimari. 'She's just a consort! Girls can't control shakti.'

'She's useless like you, you mean?' Bhila pushes Ghimari away. He falls. 'Come to alphas after you've learnt how to handle your bone staff.' A weak tantrik is a treat for them. A few sniggers, a few snorts. Dhuma's bad singing. The ravens.

Tik-tak-tik-tak.

Grab my boobies and scream aloud!

Ailailalalalalalala! Anantyaaaaaa!

'Did you know Hingi spoke to the musician?' I say. 'He desires shakti, like you.'

'I'm going to kill her!' exclaims Hingi.

'Wait, I'll break this mare,' answers Bhila. He closes the distance between us, getting his pouch of ashes ready. I don't need to be broken into. I'm broken. I've been broken ever since I escaped my murderous father and found his pale carbon copy – Bhila. My broken soul starts a murmuration like the spiralling ravens above. It makes me think of tears and broken things that the Ashru *bhuta* drinks. The ones with no hope. Casually culled by an aghori who is desperate for power. Sounds like I've heard this story before.

This time, I desire a different ending.

'No,' I say. Electricity barks through my blood, uncoiling at the base of my spine at that one word. The bone staff strums with power, sparks feed into Bhila and his body flies upwards, back arches as he lands with a resounding thump into the sand. He's sprawled, shocked, hurt, his breathing shallow.

Silence curdles the air. Hingi runs to his bestie, crouches. The bone staff slips from my sweaty fingers. Someone pulls me away from the fire, into the shadows.

'Come,' whispers Ghimari. He drags me, unresisting, away from the bank, into the outcrops. We run up. I falter, fall, I'm shaking. I'm weak and scared. Was that me who just rammed shakti into Bhila's face? Can I channel my shakti like the old hag says? Arms around my shoulders. Ghimari takes me along an inlet among the rocks. 'Stay here, till he has calmed down.' He hands me a waterskin. I sniff. 'It's tea,' he says. I chug, shake, wonder if I will unravel now that I've let my shakti loose. 'I'll be back with some food,' he says.

What have I done? Stupid, stupid. You're a girl, papa comes alive, you cannot lose control, your shakti will consume you. Only my sexual partner can use my shakti. I can't. That's what the ancient tantrik texts say. That's what my dad's clan, the Kaula tantriks say. I've been learning the art of controlling my shakti, storing it, allowing a Kaula tantrik to absorb it since I was ten. What happens now? How will I be punished to have let go of my control?

The waterskin tumbles, tea leaking into the sand. I pick it up, my blood mixes with it. I see the colour, sniff. Memories rush into my head. Shit. I get up and run into the dark, blindingly.

Behind the outcrop, I can hear calls. Cajoling, threatening, soft cooing ones.

'Oh… princess… where are you?' Hingi. 'Don't be a tease.'

I flatten against a rock, pressing myself invisible, put both my hands on my mouth, trembling, wondering when I became so weak. I've fought for men, became their weapon. But I know I can't escape. If they catch me, I'll be mind-fucked and fucked. Again. My shakti extracted by power-hungry tantriks. No! I'll find the murderer and learn how to use that freaking boneblade. If it's supposed to kill me, well, I'll take that chance. I follow the ravens to the other end of the riverbank.

Dhuma sits on her hunches, singing by the dead body, a *jhaadu* in her hand. She's talking to a raven, while her skeletal consort chitters next to her. Was I mad to believe this unhinged crone? I tap on Dhuma's ash-covered shoulders.

'I…' I gulp, chew my lower lip, 'I hate abusers. Let's find the fucker.'

'Go find.' Dhuma grins, nods, hands me a beedi. 'Come Chitti, let's dance to Chandrabhaga.'

The skeletal consort heads after their mistress, chittering. She starts to sing and shudder. 'Grab my boobies… *Ailailalalalalalala!*'

'What in Shakti's tits?' I spit, irritatingly I light up the beedi and take a long drag. I'm alone with the murdered musician. The victim. His face seems at peace, as if death was the best thing that happened to him in a long while. I crawl closer to the body.

I sniff. The smell again. I've smelt it before. Ghimari's tea. I smile. He's kind.

Further away, Dhuma's hollers as a raven comes and sits on her shoulder. Caws. Dhuma runs towards me and hits me with a *jhaadu*. 'Ashru gets two tonight. One plus one free.'

She grins, waiting for me to acknowledge her joke. It's such a bad pun. Just my luck to find someone who won't know a joke even if it hits them on the face with the speed of light.

'Chitti will give you mantras. You ask,' she waves her *jhaadu* like she's Harry Fucking Potter. She hands me her boneblade, saunters away. The skeleton creature towers above me, his skull set into a perennial grin, waiting. I look at the boneblade, turn it around, whip it, look down at the dead. The dead musician looks up in the sky, his eyes like beads, face calm, fingers closed into a fist, waiting. I don't know how to give orders. I've only taken them.

'Know any mantras to find a murderer in a line-up?' Chitti shakes their head, their vertebra hitting a broken rib. Ting-ting. 'To find where the *bhuta*'s hidden?' Ting-ting. Who thought solving a murder would be a twisted guessing game? 'To find the living who touched a body last?' Tang-tang-tang. Lumbar to sacrum. That seems to be a yes.

'Tell me how to do it.' Chitti hits my head with their ulna.

'Shakti's tits!' I exclaim. 'Woah,' I say, realizing the mantra's been airdropped in my head. And here I thought there will be a book somewhere. 'What now? I just speak it?' Tang-tang-tang.

'Khol kha bhool bha sab dikha!'

Nothing happens. I look back at the grinning skeleton. Are they laughing at me? Clack-clack-clack. Another whack to my head. 'With blood and belief? How am I to bring *belief* into a mantra?' Bloody Dhuma. I've landed with the worst teachers in the history of tantrism. Just my luck. I frown at the dead, swipe the boneblade on my fingertip, cringe and let a drop fall on the dead musician's face. Against everything anyone has told me all my life, I try to believe that I can use my shakti.

'Khol kha bhool bha sab dikha!'

The musician's hands remain fisted. The fists! I turn back, pry open the frozen fingers. A rudraksh seed. Shit of a *shatoot.* In both hands. I know where these come from. Was it the mantra? Or did I just notice the fists? Tang-tang-tang.

'Fine, maybe the revealing mantra did it.' I get up, flick my boneblade, turn around and walk to the other side of the bank, the alpha side, forgetting to feel fear.

'Oi, Hingi,' I cry out, 'I found beads of your mala.' I show him the beads, allow everyone else to see them too.

'He…' I say, pointing at Hingi. 'He is the aghori who controls Ashru. He seeks *raktashru*.'

'Arrgh! You pest, I'll kill you!' sneers Hingi. He rushes at me like a bull. I swing the boneblade, twist and duck and swipe it on his chest. Blood erupts. He rages, attacks again, blindly. Angry, but not every intelligent. I sidestep, extend my leg; he trips and falls on his face. I pull the boneblade high up in the sky, my back arched and with all my body's weight, aim the blade into his carotid.

'Stop it! You'll kill him!' Bhila hauls me away. 'Control yourself!' he cries. He's scared. Fuck, I'm scared. What was I doing? Hingi looks at me as if he's seeing a monster. I've made a bully piss with fear. Bhila carefully takes the boneblade from my unresisting hand. He pulls me up, cups my face.

'Hingi placed the beads in the dead's hands to find the murderer. We know someone's killing the new joiners, but we don't know who. We've investigating, princess.'

'You are?'

'Yes. But you shouldn't. You're vulnerable. Your heart is evil. You cannot use shakti. You were about to kill him! You can't trust yourself.' His voice is soft, cajoling. He's right. Your shakti, my father's voice says, is dangerous for you, my princess. It needs to be extracted. Bhila and my father merge with other men who have done the duty of taking my power, to protect me. Maybe father's right. Maybe Bhila's right. Even by using the power, I can only murder and kill and become the murderer I want to catch. I can only become a reflection of the men who I have grown up with. There's no hope.

'But, Dhuma…' I begin.

'Honey, that mad crone is dangerous. She's a red tantrik. She sacrifices animals for shakti. She's not even human. We tolerate her because Aghori Haala is friends with her. My little princess, come here.' He hugs me, smiles, his eyes filled with love. 'Go, clean yourself, puppy, wipe off the blood.'

The soft whisper becomes a burning blade, branding me. I look down at my breasts covered with muck and sand and blood. I'm filthy, I need a bath.

I walk down to the bank, into the roaring, icy waters of Chandrabhaga. The river dances an eternal dance – constant, steady, powerful. I want to join it. There's no hope for the likes of me. My soul's evil. Who am I to fish out a murderer? At nineteen, I'm a fucking murderer. I've killed for my dear father. I've killed for Bhila. That's who I am. A weapon. Dangerous without someone in control wielding it. Tears roll down my cheeks as I plunge into the choppy icy river. I walk out, drenched, shivering, sobbing. Full moon dances silver on the beach. Ghimari sits on his haunches, shows me a waterskin. His calming herbal tea. I sit, take the tea. It's warm and fragrant, sweet like memories of my time with Neel, the only joy in my life.

Ghimari stares into the river, forlorn, tired, worried. The alphas tease Ghimari, call him mother hen, always protecting the weak, taking in the hopeless cases. I sip the tea, wondering why I end up with all the shitbags of life.

'Do you want to give it all up, princess?' he says, his voice so soft. I look at him, all concern, all love. So, that's his approach.

'Yes,' I nod. 'Yes.'

'Ok,' says the kind aghori. 'I'll help you.' Ghimari takes out his pouch of ashes, pours some in his hand, turns to me and puckers his lips to blow it towards me. Bhila's right, my mind's a twisted thing. *Clamp your ears, girl. Don't listen to mantras,* father had whispered. I had pretended not to listen, but I had heard and I had remembered them all. I am bad. I am evil. There is no hope for me. But my sense of smell. Oh, that's fantastic. Couldn't doubt it. I've learnt to smell lies since I was five. Pretty lies smell saccharin sweet, laden with hope and happiness, like the herbal tea Ghimari offers.

I pull out the boneblade Bhila had tried to pry from my hand and duck, just as the ashes from Ghimari's palm become the Ashru *bhuta* which roars towards me. Slash on my fingertip. A drop of blood. Add belief, like Chitti had said. This time I do. Believe in my power, that is.

'Bhuta pishachi darke bhag!' I cry. The Ashru *bhuta* freezes midway. I can't see it but smell it all right. That sweet smell of nostalgia. It vanishes into hell. Good riddance.

'No!' cries Ghimari, anguished, like he has just lost his best friend. 'You useless girl!' There might be no hope for me, but useless, that I'm not. I pounce on him, we roll in the sand, limbs askew. He's powerful, drunk on the power of five helpless souls. He gets on top of me, grabs me by my neck and hollers in anger. Oh yes, let it all out Ghimari. Show me who you really are. The truth. That's what I'm always after. I've been waiting for that ever since you whispered sympathy with that sweet-laden tea.

'You're such a pest,' he shouts. I can understand why he's pissed. He was expecting a distressed little hopeless girl he could feed on. He found a gritty idiot instead.

'*Die*! Why don't you want to leave your miserable life?'

'For I want to deal,' I gag as he chokes me, 'with real shits like you!' Both his hands are around my neck, focused on squeezing, so I'm quite surprised when someone hits me on my head with a *jhaadu*.

'What,' I cry out as I struggle with the aghori on top of me, 'in Ghor's fuck!'

'Use angry blood!' hollers Dhuma. She sits a few feet away, behind. Chitti clacks somewhere. 'No, we can't force her. She needs her own tears and blood.'

She has to be the queen of incoherence. Why in Bali's burnt balls are they not helping me out? I don't have time. For some reason, Ghimari's anger has made him forget that I'm a killing machine. I don't need weapons, though they're nice to have. I'm angry enough. I grab a handful of sand and fling it into his eyes. He hollers, leaves my neck. I launch at him, flailing, biting, clawing. I grab a rock, hit it on his forehead using all my rage. A bleeding Ghimari realizes he's weaker than this girl, stumbles back, grabs his bone staff, points it at me.

'Naadi naadhi vishphotha!'

Chitti moves and comes between me and the deadly black mantra, which would've blasted my veins open, bleeding me to instant death. As it hits them, their bones fill up, their body fleshed, many layered – of a man, a girl, a yaksha, a daitya, a wraith. They fall, becoming a heap of bones.

'No!' I cry, anger making my blood bark.

'Yes! *Kroudha, kroudha!* The angry blood!' hollers Dhuma. *'Ailaiaiiallala!'* I pounce, grab the boneblade, twist and point it to Ghimari.

'Aim hreem ashru kheem!'

That one I know, thanks to Bhila. Every time he extracted my shakti, that's the spell he used. Much to my surprise, I feel the tingle again as power rushes from the aghori towards me. Oh, that power. It feels good.

Ghimari falls onto his knees, bursts into tears. Blood pours out of his eyes and nostrils and other orifices. Fuck. That feels good. All the power. I'm brimming with the tears and blood he has stolen from five souls – that I now take from him. I fall on my knees, my head rushes like it's a rocket thrusting to Mars. So that's how all those men felt when they stole my shakti. I feel like ants are crawling up my ass, like I've had a whole river full of charak. Fuck. This would be addictive.

'There she is!' We hear cries as aghoris tumble around the corner.

'It was Ghimari!' cries Haala. His hairy chest bristles. 'He never could do mantras right. Jima, take him to the kitchen. We will think of a punishment.'

A few of them leave with the exhausted, bleeding aghori. The others circle around me, the woman who has just drunk the evil aghori.

'Look at what he's done to you!' That's Bhila. Ever my saviour. Others fall away as he pulls me up. 'Your face!' he exclaims. I have a few rashes and gashes. I don't see Dhuma, but I hear her cackle from the other side of the rocky terrain. They're moving away.

'You should've come to me, princess. It was dangerous to face that aghori on your own. Only I can protect you. Come with me.' The last sentence is a leash, a brand sent to my fuddled mind. He wants my shakti. The shakti I stole from the evil aghori. Oh, I know your game, my dear ambitious Bhila.

But tonight, his cobwebs won't work. I've avenged five hopeless who died and that's given me hope. The ravens activate again, circling above us. Their cawing drips in my ears. *Ailailalalalalalala.*

I point the boneblade to his face.

'No,' I say.

'Where did you find that? It's dangerous! Don't you know? You're evil. You can't control your power.' He reaches out, tries to grab it. I twist, fall, shakti coursing through me, up my spine.

'What's my name?' I ask as he falls on top of me, his hands on both my arms. 'Give it to me!' he commands, pouting, using a Vashita-laden command. Not tonight, my boy. I move, flit the boneblade, hit his groin with my knee, surprised it's so easy to twist his body, to make it dance to my tune. I come on top, saddle him, pushing him down into the sand. He stares at me, surprised, shocked, but he won't call his apprentices for help. He can't. He's the alpha. He forces himself to smile, as if we're playing a sex game. I grin back. The ravens spiral with the stars. 'What's my name?'

'Princess, you need help!' he says, his voice oily, curling up like a snake through my ears into my mind. I twist my boneblade towards him, its tip touching his neck, almost, tantalizingly. I stop. 'Speak my name,' I say.

'I...' Bhila starts. I make a soft gash on his Adam's apple, ever so gently, scoop the blood with my fingertips and suck on it. Its metallic and smells of dhrash.

'You're being evil!' he says.

'My name,' I say, 'is Anantya. Speak it!'

'Fine, fine! Anantya,' Bhila cries. His apprentices hover. They can see it's gone wrong, but should they intervene, or not? They also know I'm powerful right now.

'And I am a tantrik,' I say.

'Girls can't...'

'Say it!'

'You are a tantrik.' *Ailailalalalalalala!* I get up, pull Bhila up. It's time. Dhuma's calling me. But I've to do one last thing. I walk through the circle of aghoris. They part to make way. They smell of fear and awe. I walk to the alpha fire and pick up the two women. I turn, look at Bhila.

'Free them,' I say. I don't use a mantra to say it, but he nods. He mutters a spell, their eyes widen. The women look around like they've just woken, fear filling their eyes. 'Leave,' I say to them. They turn and start to run in the other direction. I head towards the opposite direction, to the other side of the riverbank, where Dhuma's ululating. Bhila and his apprentices are back by the fire. 'If you try to use Vashita on women again, I'll scoop out your eyeballs and feed them to the ravens.'

'You're mad,' spits Bhila, 'like that fucking crone! Go, destroy your life for all I care!'

'Yes,' I grin, feeling light as I begin climbing the rocks. The skies spiral around me. On the other side of the riverbank, Dhuma dances. Chitti has been put back together. They clank and clatter too, chattering away, probably discussing a mathematical probability or what gruel to have for breakfast. As I walk towards Dhuma, for the first time in years, since those terrible months that are a daze to me, I laugh. I'm free. I walk down, sit by the fire, feeling the hum in my blood. The hum of shakti.

'Here,' says Dhuma, offering me a skull-cup filled with gooey crap. 'Tears of blood. The best remedy for a broken heart.' I gulp down the liquid, chomp on the tiny feathery bones that curl in the sludge. It tastes and smells horrid. Like truth.

As we snake through the other aghori pyres by the banks, moving northward, I turn back to the river. 'Remember my name!' I cry, to them, to the skies, pointing my boneblade to the grumpy moon. 'I'm Anantya Tantrist and I will be back.'

THE DETECTIVE OF BLACK KORAIL

Saad Z. Hossain

Texas Mok was having tea on the lawn. Greenery stretched on all sides, shaded by mango trees, irregular patterns that faded into aperiodic tessellations. Mok looked well, relaxed. He was reading a book on the occult called *Golems: The Seven-year Itch*. He had not expected witch–golem erotica to be a thing, but there it was, in his benefactor's library. In fact, she had all manner of esoteric books, as if the entire repository of magical tomes in the world was somehow dumped in this one house. That most of them were frivolous and fanciful was a source of great comfort to him.

The tea was accompanied with biscuits. He did not eat them, because he knew his tormentor would come soon to claim tax.

Kira was ten, endlessly ten. Here in the witch's mansion, this orphanage of the nearly extinguished, they thrived in the moment between life and death, a sanctuary made timeless by the power of the witch Bibima, herself the first victim. She had warped a mirror version of the Korail Mansion[6] into this pocket universe, first to save her own life and then the lives of all the children hovering on death's door, all the victims of brutality.

When Mok, former sheriff, had come to kill her, she had turned him; in that crucial moment, he had chosen to fight his own men. He had taken a bullet in the neck that exited through his cheek, blowing a hole in his face, a neat circle that should have

6 The Korail Mansion is a massive structure in the middle of the slum zone – a brothel, gaming and opium den – a pleasure garden for all tastes.

killed him. Bibima poured silver in his wound, a living molten mercury that shone in the light and granted him a terrifying beauty. Her magic wrapped him in loving gossamer. His watch stopped and he lived again. He had not been a believer in the occult before. It seemed only polite to show interest now.

The mansion sat slantwise within the great slum of Korail, twisted in space and time, inaccessible to most. Mok was the guard dog, snarling at the gate, yearning to visit more slaughter upon his former brothers, being one of those violent men who required a patina of justice over their handiwork, some valid reason to use their natural gifts, his gaze now turned towards the real perpetrators of violence: his own police force.

Kira's face was almost entirely silver, because a policeman had carved her up for fun. She had a precocious spirit however, which permitted her to almost entirely forget the senseless savagery committed on her person. The other children were not so resilient and avoided Mok; to them all adult men were dangerous. No one except for Kira ventured out of the walls of the Black Mansion[7], not even Bibima. She was the centre of the magic and it moved with her, she claimed, like gravity. Mok suspected she was not yet reconciled with her half-ruined face and preferred the dark.

Ergo, by process of highly evolved detection, the patter of running feet could only be Kira. She grew stealthy when she came close, barely making noise and then made an almighty leap at the end, like a ferocious housecat, upending the table and absconding with the biscuits, trailing maniacal laughter. Mok, who was very fast, managed to salvage his cup and the porcelain tea pot, but was forced to forgo the milk and sugar, which went tumbling down.

Kira stopped at a distance from him and ate her snacks. She pushed the biscuits wholly into the space where her mouth ought to be and the molten silver caved inwards to accept it.

---

[7] The Black Mansion is a mirror copy of the Korail Mansion created by the witch Bibima in a hidden pocket realm, where she housed the near-dead orphans of Korail. It exists in a slightly different dimension, inaccessible except by invitation or magic, where time does not affect the denizens.

What method of nourishment or pleasure this gave her was beyond his knowledge. He himself had been here a month and wanted neither food nor rest. They were alive, but had none of the concerns of the living, save what the mind craved.

'We have a visitor,' Kira said, once the biscuits were demolished.

Supplicants often came to Bibima with their hopes and needs. In the Korail slum of reality, injustices were rife and there was a growing cult of the witch, to cure, to save, to avenge when all else failed.

Mok motioned for her to continue with his teacup. He didn't like speaking. It felt funny to move his mouth around the silver that coursed inside.

'Mother is asking for you,' Kira continued. 'I don't know why. You're pretty useless. You just lie around here, eating all of our biscuits.'

'You have an endless supply,' Texas Mok objected.

'Still.' Kira grabbed his hand and pulled him up. 'Hurry up, mother is waiting. And don't try to flirt with her.'

'What do you know of that, little witch?'

'I grew up outside the big brothel, idiot,' Kira said with justifiable scorn.

They went into the house through the great hall, a vast expanse with black and white checkered marble. Bibima waited in an antechamber, which was reserved for supplicants. She sat on a simple divan, half reclining and gurgling on a hookah, pointy slippers on her feet, draped in black shawls, inescapably beautiful from where Mok stood, hair obscuring most of her face. Darkness swirled around her like barely perceptible smoke. It was a role she played, he thought; the visitors expected it, a show of eldritch power.

The lady sat in front of the witch was middle aged, exuding an aura of fashion and drama. Her black and white sari was covered in bold patterns and adhered only loosely to the precepts of mourning.

'Sheriff!' she uttered when she saw him. She had a theatrical voice which presaged a highly charged inner life. 'They said you died in a gunfight! I am relieved you are safe!'

'Nearly,' Mok said. He often forgot how well known he had been in Korail. 'Bibima saved me.'

'I asked for you, Mok,' Bibima said in her deep voice. 'Because Mrs Ademan has a peculiar problem which might interest you. She wants us to solve a murder.'

Mok sat down at the foot of the divan, prompting Bibima to sit upright. Kira squirmed into the space between them, ostensibly to serve as chaperone. They regarded Mrs Ademan like a trio of demons.

'It's my husband,' Mrs Ademan said, without blinking. 'He has died.'

'Congratulations,' Kira said, earning a cuff from mother.

'With his head cut off,' Mrs Ademan looked sternly at the girl, making it clear that the presence of impressionable children in a murder investigation was highly irregular. 'And this object lodged in his neck.'

'Object?' Bibima asked.

Mrs Ademan produced a printed picture, it being well known that electronic devices did not function correctly around djinns and Nephilim. This was not, strictly speaking, true, because Mok's reaper drones[8] seemed to be working just fine, considering the way they had atomized the last team of homicide detectives who had come this way, to investigate his 'demise'.

'A black *tabeez*,' Mok said, flicking through the plastic snaps. 'Parchment inside? Arabic spells? Black magic.'

'Exactly,' Mrs Ademan said. 'Which is why I am here.'

'Where was the body found?' Mok asked.

---

[8] Reaper drones: small marble-sized kinetic drones with anti-gravity techonology which can be controlled by a military grade ECHO implant in the brain. These are cutting edge weapons used by police or paramilitary forces for urban suppression. Almost all humans carried the neural implant called the ECHO, part communications device, part AI, part visual augment.

'In the car. He is the driver, sir, to the Commissar himself.'

'Commissar. Our Commissar?'

'Your former boss,' Kira piped up unnecessarily.

'The Commissar himself!' Mrs Ademan gushed. 'Such a handsome man. And so brave! He would go everywhere with just my Ademan for protection, not a single bodyguard in sight. None of those hulking blue monsters[9] for him. Why, plenty of nights, Ademan would go to drive him on secret missions, just the two of them.'

Mok's face tightened. The Commissar had carved up Bibima himself, before his promotion and it was clear his obsession with witch-hunt was centred on her. Mok badly wanted to kill this man.

'Why, then, are the police not investigating this?' Bibima asked. 'Surely it would be a priority.'

'They have investigated,' Mrs Ademan said with awful dignity. 'And concluded it was a robbery gone wrong. They are "searching for the miscreants".'

'That sounds like a cover up. Where was the car?' Mok asked.

'Parked at the Korail gate. The Commissar had come here for a police drive. Against witches,' Mrs Ademan beamed at Bibima. 'Of course, no one in Korail would *dream* of giving you up, dear.'

That meant they had almost certainly told him all about the hidden orphanage of Black Korail.

'Thanks,' Bibima said.

'So, it's the official car? The black Toyota?' Mok asked.

'Yes, sir.'

'That car is full of sensors inside and out. There is no way they didn't get a glimpse of what happened.'

'All video-audio surveillance showed nothing,' Mrs Ademan said. 'According to the detective.'

'What's his name?' Mok asked.

'Barek.'

---

[9] Blue Monsters: Bio-engineered enhanced police recruits, often called Blues, due to the blue tinge on their skin.

'Political guy,' Mok said. 'He's not going to investigate shit. This is definitely a cover up.'

'Well?' Mrs Ademan said. 'Are you going to take the case?'

'Well?' Bibima looked at Mok. 'Are we?'

'Yes! Yes! Yes!' Kira clapped her hands. She forgot her role as nemesis and gave Mok a big hug. 'Our first case!'

Having settled with Mrs Ademan regarding payment – an arcane fee best known to Bibima – they ushered her off and settled down in the study.

'We need the case files from Barek,' Mok said.

'Is he a friend?'

'Hardly. He's the commissar's man. He won't be doing me any favours. Besides, I'm dead as far as they know.'

'At least you got a hero's burial,' Bibima said.

'One thing, he's a terrible coward. Known for it. If I can get near him, I can frighten it out of him,' Mok said. 'Can I leave the boundary without dying, that's the question?'

Bibima hesitated. 'Not far. I don't know how far the magic can stretch. I have never been outside.'

Kira raised her hand. 'I have.'

'Outside the gates?'

'Yes. Way outside. At night.'

'Kira! I told you not to do that.'

'Yes, mother, but I was bored.'

'Well, how did it feel?' Mok asked.

'Like I was losing weight. Becoming like air. Also, the clock in my head started ticking again.'

'Dying, Kira, that's what you were doing,' Bibima said.

'How long did you stay out?' Mok asked.

'The longest I've stayed out was an hour,' Kira said. 'I went all the way to the Korail Gate, but I felt really funny then, like I was going to float away. I ran back in and I was fine,' she shrugged. 'It's easier at night.'

'Okay, looks like I could do this, if we can get Barek inside Korail,' Mok said.

'That is simple,' Bibima said. 'Mrs Ademan will call him with new information. He will come at night.'

'How do you know?'

'This is Korail. Cops only come here at night.'

'Don't worry, Mok,' Kira patted his hand. 'I won't let anything bad happen to you.'

That night, Barek duly came to continue his investigation. He was a desk man, cautious when he left his fortified office and an augmented recruit followed him everywhere, half a head taller than the average Bengali, carrying a riot issue shotgun and sporting full body armour. There wasn't much in Korail to combat, at least not in plain sight.

Mok armed himself lightly, the matching guns on each hip and his reaper set forming a necklace around his throat. Bibima said a prayer over him and kissed his forehead, as if he was still a child.

'Think I'll manage the job?' Mok asked. He fretted about his appearance. In his previous life, he had carried a surfeit of weapons and a gunslinger's scowl, which he wore as a uniform.

'Don't worry,' she said. 'You look terrifying.'

Kira led him out of the mansion, 3 left turns and 3 right turns, into ethereal streets of mist, a warp of space and time that spat them out in front of the Black Mansion's mirror image, the infamous Korail Mansion – part brothel, part gaming arena – the beating heart of the slum where all things were possible. If the Korail Mansion was the Taj Mahal, then Bibima's Black Mansion was the ethereal matching mausoleum that Shah Jahan had yearned to build and never started.

Mok felt sharp, alert, but instantly lighter, as if his mass had halved. He clutched Kira's hand unconsciously, fearing she would float away. She skipped down the road and he followed.

'They won't notice us unless they look directly at us,' she said, as they passed a couple of off-duty police officers, come to throw their wages into the thresher that was the Mansion.

'Are we ghosts?' Mok asked.

'No, but we are almost dead,' Kira said. 'Mother stops time in that moment right before you die. Isn't she clever?'

'Very,' Mok said.

'She's lonely,' Kira said, glancing at him. 'I've noticed.'

'You notice too much.'

'She smiles more now that you're here,' Kira continued. 'Secretly, so you can't tell.'

Mok felt himself smiling in turn, despite himself.

Mrs Ademan lived in the respectable part of Korail, three lanes from the gate. Mok saw the blue-skinned recruit lounging on the street, bored. His eyes passed over them with disinterest. Mok had been prepared to kill him and felt a little twinge of disappointment when this proved unnecessary. It was a four-storey building made of prefab material, printed on site and therefore well-fitted to the weird configurations of the street. Mrs Ademan, childless, had a two-room apartment in the back.

This part of Korail had the full services, running water, electricity, even full air scrubbers and meters which read out the maltech count in the atmosphere. It hovered around a light orange most of the time, indicating a bearable threat. Almost all the nanotech produced in the warm bodies of Korail were pushed into the rich neighbourhoods next door, of course, but they kept enough here to maintain a microclimate. Microclimates were the defence against the maltech in the air, good nanotech fighting bad nanotech and climate change in a continuous invisible battle.

Even as Mok and Kira walked in, Barek barely noticed them, his eyes glazing over in boredom as Mrs Ademan waffled on about diaries she had found in her husband's secret shelf, chronicling romantic conquests from his youth and whether this was possibly a cause for his decapitation. The detective was a portly, balding man, in an expensive suit that still failed to fit properly. He was sitting on a couch against one wall, while Mrs Ademan sat upright on a narrow bed opposite him. All of the furniture was of good quality print and the room was spotless and smelled faintly of antiseptic.

Mok, prepared for violence, stood beside the door and coughed gently, shielding Kira from sight.

'What the hell?' Barek started. 'Who are you?'

'You know me. Look closely.'

'Texxxxas M-m-m-ok. You died.'

'Not quite.'

'I saw the casket. I was at the funeral.'

'You didn't see the body though, did you? Never mind. I want to know about the headless corpse. Your pardon, Mrs Ademan.'

'It's a mugging gone wrong,' Barek said, arms crossed in fear. Mok could almost feel him reach out with his ECHO desperately trying to call the newbie.

'I'd not call for help, if I were you,' Mok said. The reaper drones took to air, forming a halo around his head. It was a sight all of the police force knew intimately. No weapon was faster or deadlier in their arsenal and Mok had the best one. 'I just want some answers and then I'll go away. If not, you'll both die.'

Barek pointed a shaking finger at him. 'Y-you're not real! You're a ghost!'

Mok moved forward smoothly and slapped the detective across the face. The back of his hand made a satisfying crunch. There was blood and swelling. He felt a bit of relief. He wasn't sure he had retained his former strength. Barek recoiled in horror. Not from the blow, but rather from the improvements to Mok's face, now visible in the wan lamp light.

'Why are you silver? You've become a monster.'

'I always was,' Mok said. 'I just changed sides. The case files. Give them to me.'

There was a ring on his ECHO and Barek shunted over a pile of data.

'Everything?'

Barek nodded. 'Why are you doing this, Mok? He's just a driver.'

'That.' Mok felt an enormous rage. 'Because of that.' He had his gun in his hand, unbidden. 'Because drivers and peons die first and no one gives a shit.'

'Don't.' Barek closed his eyes, held his hands up. They were trembling. 'Please. Mok please. I don't know what happened to him. I swear.'

'You won't even try. Why?'

'The Commissar wants it put to rest. He's up for bonuses. By the corporates. Doesn't want his rating to go down,' Barek said.

'The official report says he died from a fright-induced heart attack,' Mok said, rifling through his ECHO. 'Why lie?'

'The Commissar's got heat for the witch shit. Lot of the Corporates think he's gone nuts. They don't want to hear about anything magic. *So, I left out the beheading and the tabeez*. Does it matter? Dead is dead, right?' He turned to Mrs Ademan with a pleading glance. 'I got you full severance, plus double his pension. Why are you doing this?'

She looked at him scornfully.

'I'm going to let you live, Barek,' Mok said. 'And I'm even going to do your work for you. If Mrs Ademan gets any heat, or anyone comes looking for me, I will visit your house in the middle of the night and slaughter your entire family. Do you understand me?'

'Yes.'

'I have done it before. You know that, right? Killed innocent people?'

'Yes.'

'Your Blue didn't even see me coming. You're not safe *from me.*'

'I know. Er, I don't have a family or a wife, but I am terrified just the same.'

'Okay, go.'

Later, as they walked back home, Mok, lost in the case files, felt a small hand stealing into his own and an insistent tugging from his nemesis.

'Did you kill lots of families?'

'Yes,' Mok said.

'That means children too.'

'Yes,' Mok said, hiding a smile. 'Specially kids. Always get them first. They're the hardest.'

'Because they're cute?'

'No, because they run around a lot.'

'You're lying,' Kira said blithely. 'Because you didn't kill me at all when you had the chance and instead you shot your own men.'

'I should have,' Mok said. 'That was an error.'

'*I* think you like killing cops more than you like killing children,' Kira said. 'We are home. You can tell Mother about the case. I am tired.'

Bibima was waiting up for them in the library, a high-ceilinged, cheerful room at odds with the general spookiness of the mansion. Here, like everywhere else, there were toys strewn and other evidence of vanished children. Mok sat across from her leather sofa and accepted a cup of tea.

'The car was parked near the entrance gate of Korail. It was nighttime, so the gate is typically closed. There were no other vehicles near it. It is covered by 13 different camera feeds, both satellite and ground. Nothing and no one came near the car. The Commissar finished his visit at 8 p.m. and was heading back. That's when they discovered the body inside,' Mok said.

'There are things which can avoid electric eyes,' Bibima said.

'Like us?' Mok asked. 'We walked through the front door at Mrs Adelmans, the Blue outside didn't bat an eyelid.'

'Yes,' Bibima said. 'Because you are imbued with my spell now. All manner of magical creatures might avoid surveillance; djinns, golems, ghosts: to name the obvious examples. There are plenty of books here relating to their qualities.'

'Or the surveillance might be tampered with,' Mok said. He still thought like a policeman and jumping to supernatural murder was anathema to everything he had been taught.

'Thirteen of them?'

'Unlikely,' Mok admitted. 'Well, let's look at method of death then. Head cut off clean with a sharp instrument. Must be a sword or an axe, a knife wouldn't manage that cleanly. I'm leaning towards sword, as the wound indicates a flat, sharp blade rather than a wedge.'

'Inside a car though?'

'Hmm, so it has to be a short sword of some kind. There are no nicks on the seats or sides and you can't swing a big blade in there. In fact, you can't even swing a short sword in there without hitting some part of the vehicle. Then there is the issue of blood.'

'What issue?'

'There isn't enough of it. The roof of the car should be drenched. It is not. There isn't enough arterial spray.' Mok rubbed his head and wished he had a glass of whiskey. Bibima did not keep booze in the house. Probably because Kira would drink it all if given the chance. 'Finally, the object found in his neck. Multiple policemen saw it, but when the forensics team tried to fish it out, it disintegrated to dust. Not even dust, something finer. There was literally no remnant left. All agree that it seemed like a tightly folded piece of parchment with writing on it.'

'So, who killed him and how he was killed are both impossible.' Bibima laughed. 'You're not doing very well here, Texas Mok. Are you sure you were a policeman?'

'Then we ask why. Why kill the driver?'

'Was he always a driver?'

'For the last twenty years,' Mok said. 'Got the Commissar's car seven years ago. Before that he used to drive a transport vehicle for Dhaka north.[10] He's literally held no other job. No record of any kind. Model citizen. So is his wife. They have no children. I want to question her again tomorrow.'

[10] The City is bisected into two municipalities, North and South.

'No sleeping, no eating, just work!' Mrs Ademan said. 'The bloody man just worked. He was the most loyal man in the world. And now they've killed him like a dog.'

'When you married him, he was already driving for the Commissar?' Mok asked. He was conducting the interview alone, Kira and Bibima apparently had pressing business elsewhere. He suspected they were already tired of the case. A policemen's greatest characteristic was persistence in the face of awful boredom.

'Yes, he was stuck to him. Followed him everywhere. The Commissar took him at night even though that is against normal regulations,' Mrs Ademan said. 'We barely had any time to ourselves, he was on duty so much.'

'He has no records, not even any parking fines,' Mok said. 'Well, I suppose the Commissar would have taken care of those. Can you tell me if he was in touch with anyone odd, if he had any run-ins with criminals, any fights, anything at all?'

'No, he never left the car,' Mrs Ademan said. 'That's what he always repeated to me. Commissar said never leave the car. He would say it like a mantra.' She sniffed. 'He was a bit odd I guess, but he was a good man and every month he would give me his entire salary.'

'Did he get paid over-time?' Mok asked. 'For the night duties? It would have come as a separate cheque as per regulations.'

'No, there was just the salary,' Mrs Ademan said with a sniff. 'I knew he was getting ripped off! Always the same, the good people get stiffed while the wicked prosper! He would never keep a penny for himself, my dear love!'

Mok frowned. 'Nothing for vapes, or booze, or anything? No simulations? Not even money for a favourite snack?'

'I told you he was a good man. He was kind-hearted too. Never said a cross word to me.'

'Seems so,' Mok said. This was already getting suspicious. Mrs Ademan, with her shrill voice and diva attitude, should definitely have driven someone to curse words regardless of how kind his heart was. 'Did he have any friends? Relatives?'

'My poor Ademan was an orphan,' she said. 'And what friends he had faded away as he focused on his career. You know how people in Korail are. They can't stand it if someone gets ahead. By the time I married him, he was quite alone. He was a very restful man. He'd be quite happy to read a book or watch a show when he was home.'

'What about the djinn? Did he ever speak of the supernatural?'

Mrs Ademan pursed her lips. 'I'll have you know we are a good Muslim family. None of this djinn fornication!'

Why is it always fornication that springs to mind? She didn't answer the question really.

'Was it arranged, this marriage?'

'He was our neighbour. He asked my father's advice about getting married and my father introduced us that very day.'

'I see. And would you say you were happy, Mrs Ademan?'

'Certainly,' she said. 'I had my own household and a loving husband with a great career. We were going to move soon, out of Korail altogether. Do you know they haven't even returned the body? How am I supposed to have a funeral and show respect to my beloved?' She started sobbing loudly.

The poor always spent the most on funerals.

'May I ask something personal?' Mok asked. *Not that I'll give you a chance to say no.* 'Have you and your husband ever consummated your marriage?'

Mrs Ademan went pale and then hissed with rage, her fingers clenching into fists. If there was something within her reach that she could have smashed, she would have undoubtedly done so. She got up and stomped out, muttering incoherently, which in itself was an answer.

Later, Bibima received a call from their employer and summoned Mok to her study. He found her laughing uncontrollably.

'What on earth possessed you to ask her that?' Bibima finally said between gasps. The miasma of darkness around her was gone entirely, replaced by a silvery light.

'Her place. It's two rooms and there's a bed in the front room. Meaning, they must have each kept a room instead of sleeping together,' Mok said. 'Also, in all her reactions, she's lamenting losing a man with a steady job. Not talking of love or affection.'

'You really are a detective,' Bibima said. 'Texas Mok, investigator of the bed chamber! Policeman of love! Detective of…'

'All right, all right,' Mok said. 'Very funny.'

'Well, you seem to have touched a nerve, so it probably is true. But what does it have to do with the case?'

'It's just a weird case. The guy is weird. He died weird. But he also lived weird. I'm just pulling at threads. I'm going to the crime scene tonight. I want Kira to sniff around.'

'Kira?'

'Yeah, don't you know? She can sniff magic.'

'Really? I didn't have the faintest idea.'

Mok grinned. 'Looks like I'm a better detective than you at least.'

At night, Kira and Mok made their way to the Korail Gate, with her skipping as usual to match his stride. He didn't expect trouble this time and there was none. The night was patrolled by drones and they were invisible. The car was gone, but there was still crime tape marking the spot, the fussiness of the procedural lab guys over-riding the desire of the Commissar to clean up the whole mess and forget about it.

Kira literally sniffed the air and shook her head. 'What were you expecting?' she asked.

'Like a vampire who can turn invisible and chop a man's head, clean in half and also drain the blood without missing a drop.'

'That would be like big magic,' Kira said. 'It would smell fresh.'

'So, what *can* you smell?'

'Just something old and sad and dead.'

'The victim then, maybe,' Mok said. 'Bibima said djinns, golems and ghosts. Feel anything?'

Kira shrugged. 'Golem smell just like dead people. Djinns smell like fire. Ghosts smell like regret.'

Mok nodded. He blinked out a call on his Echo.

'Who're you calling?' Kira asked.

'I want Barek to come here. I have some questions for him.'

'We don't have much time,' Kira objected.

'Don't worry, he's close.'

'How do you know?'

'He's at the Mansion most nights.'

Sure enough, within ten minutes they saw Barek waddling over at a brisk pace, his face torn between irritation and fear. He stopped a good distance from Mok and stood there panting, hands on his hips.

'The Commissar hired this guy seven years ago. Did he come from the academy?'

Barek frowned. 'No, funnily. It was a personal hire.'

'Is that normal?'

Barek shrugged. 'No. Normally the drivers would come from academy noobs, or the driving pool. And to get the top job he'd have to rise up the driver pool ranks. The cushy jobs are given by seniority. But it's the Commissar. If he wanted his own man, who's gonna say otherwise?'

'Did they know each other from before?'

'How the fuck should I know?'

'I'm asking because his file is like paper thin before this job,' Mok said. 'Just bare bones shit you'd find on a basic search.'

'He must have known him, right? To handpick him as number one driver?' Long dormant detective muscles began to fire up in Barek.

'He used to drive a transport van for Dhaka North city corp. Not even a car. A bloody chips delivery van,' Mok said. 'How on earth did their paths cross? What possessed the Commissar to hire him?'

'I know what you're doing,' Barek said with a pained look. 'Stop sucking me into your weird vortex.'

'I can't leave Korail,' Mok said. 'You have to find out the answers. Investigate this shit for real, for god's sake. I'll bet my life that they never met before. Something drove the Commissar to hire Ademan on the spot seven years ago.'

'What happened to your face?' Barek asked.

'My number two shot me.'

'Why?'

'I suppose I was shooting him back.'

'Personal or business?'

'You remembered that story where someone carved up a Korail kid and left him for dead? Remember the pictures?'

Barek shuddered. 'Yeah, who could forget?'

'Her brother,' Mok motioned at Kira. 'Did the same to her, except she lived. Turns out it was my team who did it, off duty. Bragged about it too.'

'I see.'

'So, I put them down like they deserved.'

'I see.'

'Sometimes you have to take a stand. Right?'

'Okay. I'll look into it.'

'Oh, and Barek, can you bring me a copy of the old police handbook? The huge one with the terms of employment.'

'It's all online now,' Barek frowned.

'There's one from two hundred years ago or something. The original. It's still given out as copies to officers when they're sworn in. Everything else is amendment.'

'Yeah, I remember, the doorstop,' Barek said. 'Fine I'll get one. Damn thing is heavy. You're a damned peculiar cop, Mok.'

'Thanks, partner.' Mok began to walk away.

Barek frowned. 'Hey!' he shouted. 'You shot your last partner!'

Three days later, Bibima called Mok to her study, this time gurgling with laughter. 'Where on earth did you find this man? The poor dear is about to faint.'

Barek was sitting bolt upright in a chair, clutching his knees, petrified with fear. Having eschewed all offers of refreshment, he then found himself unable to speak and had to clear his throat three times before any sound came out. He was carrying the old police handbook, an encyclopaedic tome which he thrust at Mok.

'I found him loitering around outside,' Kira said proudly. 'So, I brought him in.'

'He looks like he's about to be eaten by crocodiles,' Bibima laughed.

'He's a big coward,' Kira said. 'I could hear him blubbering.'

Barek hesitantly raised his hand. 'M-m-ma'am. May I speak?'

'Oh, go on, we're not going to hurt you,' Bibima said. 'And ignore Kira's manners, please, she grows wilder by the day.'

'Easy, partner,' Mok said, sitting down next to Barek. 'This here is the lady Bibima, our host and the director of this orphanage. There are other kids here, but they avoid adults. You can breathe, Barek, you're safe here.'

'I… I'm sorry, madam, I did not expect you to be courteous,' Barek said after a moment. 'Nor this house to be so cheerful.'

'She grows on you,' Mok said.

Bibima smiled at him.

'I looked into it,' Barek said. 'The Commissar was transferred to the Gulshan station as chief detective seven years ago. Kurail was his main beat. He was touring the slums the day he hired Ademan. The paperwork was filed at night. They have been inseparable since then.'

'Inseparable,' Mok said. 'They used to go out alone. No bodyguards. Do you remember the Commissar as a particularly teched-up man, Barek?'

'Like drones? Military-grade Echo?' Barek frowned. 'No. That was you. You were the department tank. He's basically top-of-the-line civilian. Makes sense. Wants to be a politician. Can't move in Corporate circles with a head full of killer hardware.'

'Yet he'd come to Kurail with just his driver for protection. Was this Ademan trained in combat?'

'Nothing on file,' Barek said. 'And he can't have been on the sly; you know how closely they track military implants.'

'Right. Where is the body, Barek?'

'Body?'

'Ademan. They haven't given it back.'

'Well, morgue or lab I guess.'

'Find out please.'

Barek called back that very night, in a tone of rising panic. 'It's gone!'

'Body?'

'Taken from the morgue that very night. The Commissar signed off on it being sent to the pathology lab in Dhaka Medical, but somehow the body has disappeared en route. The van broke down, the driver went for repairs, came back to find it looted, tyres and all.'

'How strange,' Mok said with a smile.

'Why the hell would he send it to Dhaka Medical? Gulshan station has the best lab in town.'

'He sent it there because it's clear across town,' Mok said. 'To stage this little charade.'

'Why?'

'Because he wants the body back. And the head. We must not forget the head. I trust he sent that in a jar. Full of nanotech broth?'

'Yes, he did and yes it was taken too,' Barek said, calming down. 'How do you know? Why put a dead head in a nanotech broth? That's for organ transplants.'

'Because he doesn't want too much damage to it. I think I know what happened.'

'What? I'm going crazy with this case.'

'If you come tomorrow, I will tell you.'

They gathered again in the formal living room. Bibima wanted to add gravitas to Mok's reveal. Everyone attended with a sense of solemn purpose. The witch wore her customary black silk, embellished with a fabulous, embroidered shawl of what appeared to be black brows against a black sky. Kira wore her favourite blue dress which brought out the sparkle in her silver face. Mrs Ademan attended in due pomp with a bright red-and-blue sari, having dispensed with mourning altogether. Even Barek wore his best suit, having correctly determined that the Black Mansion of Korail was a much fancier place than he had hitherto had the privilege of visiting.

The formal living room, with a black and white marble checkered floor, was furnished in the Turkish fashion with a plethora of divans, upon which the guests reclined. Low tables held fruits and other delicacies and beside their feet were long necked hukkas, a smoking apparatus delicately wrought in silver and gold leaf. The inviting smell of apple tobacco wafted gently around the room, creating a cloud of smoke around Bibima, who was happily gurgling away.

Mok entered last, feeling nonplussed without his weapons. Kira had picked out his wardrobe, scavenged from long abandoned closets. He wore a dark silk suit, mercifully with no embroidery.

'As you all know, I've been living here for the past three months. Bibima saved my life, as she did for all the children gathered here,' Mok said. Bibima glanced at him under her cascade of hair and smiled. 'At her insistence, I've begun to read a lot. Her words: "I'd go mad pacing around the house and drive everyone else mad with me." So I have taken her advice. The first book I have finished is *Golems: The Seven-year Itch*. Very interesting. A romance between a golem and a witch.'

Bibima blushed.

'Another interesting book I've read is the old police handbook, particularly the sections on wages and overtime regulations,' Mok said. He pulled out the book. 'It's actually from the British colonial era. It says here that all non-human members deputized shall still receive a living wage, each to his kind. Dogs employed full-time, for example, shall receive food and shelter in official cantonment kennels and one large thigh bone per week. Non-human officers such as djinns, golems or demonic-natured creatures shall receive full pay and benefits but no overtime, as they do not require sleep. No overtime. Interesting.'

'It's true, the British police force in Darjeeling employed two djinn officers in 1866,' Barek said. 'And there are still drawing pay to this day! It's right there in the payroll. I was astounded.'

'A second interesting thing I learnt was that Kira, who can smell magic, found no trace of violent death at the site of the crime,' Mok said.

Kira, ever happy to be at the centre of attention, took a bow.

'A third interesting fact, pardon me Mrs Ademan, was the lack of personal relations during the marriage,' Mok said.

Mrs Ademan opened her mouth, but Mok wisely railroaded on.

'My conclusion is, unfortunately, in this case, there *was no murder*.'

Mok waited for the general furor to die down.

'No murder at least recently. Mr Ademan was not a human, he was a golem. He has been one for the past seven years, ever since he entered the Commissar's employment. The seven years is significant because golems live in bands of seven. Seven years for a level one, made by novice, 14 years for a level two, 28 years for a level three and so on. This I learnt from the golem–witch erotica book, but I believe it is still true,' Mok said. 'You see, his head wasn't cut off… it just fell off, at the line. It explains the parchment in his neck. Seven years ago, the Commissar killed his new driver in a ritual by precisely bisecting his neck and created a golem – the perfect bodyguard to take with him at all times, in his crusade against witches. Well, I don't know about the *killed* part, Ademan might have died of natural causes or in an accident and the commissar merely livened him up again. Regardless, I strongly suspect that the commissar has the body and the head and he will shortly be reconnecting the body and the head with another geas and Ademan will walk once again, perhaps under a different name.'

'How dare you!' Mrs Ademan sprung to her feet.

'Ma'am, are you not an attractive woman?' Mok asked.

'Of course!'

'How can you explain his lack of interest then?'

'Actually, golems are thought to have higher-than-normal libidos,' Bibima whispered. 'It's why us witches prefer them…'

'*Will* you shut up?' Mok hissed at her.

'Ma'am, I can assure you, that the behaviour shown by your husband indicates irrevocably that he was in fact a golem during the entirety of your marriage,' Mok continued. 'However, as he was gainfully and formally employed, the pension and accrued benefits Barek offered you are safe.'

'Oh,' she said.

'Furthermore, if you were to want him back, you could probably approach the Commissar and work something out. For the next seven years, at least.'

'Back? He'd be living with me again?'

'Certainly.'

'Thank you, Mr Mok, you have done a splendid job!' Mrs Ademan said, with a flutter of her long, painted nails. 'The case is closed! I believe I shall take the pension!'

LIST OF CONTRIBUTORS

Ambai has been an independent researcher in Women's Studies for the last forty years. She has a PhD from Jawaharlal Nehru University, New Delhi, and has several books and articles to her credit. She is also a creative writer who writes about love, relationships, quests and journeys in the Tamil region and elsewhere under the pseudonym Ambai.

She has been writing from the age of sixteen and is a well-known writer in Tamil. Her stories have been translated in five volumes entitled *A Purple Sea*, *In a Forest, a Deer*, *Fish in a Dwindling Lake*, *A Night with a Black Spider* and *A Meeting on the Andheri Overbridge*. The second book *In a Forest, a Deer* shared the Hutch Crossword award 2006 for translated fiction. She received the Puthumaipithan Memorial Lifetime Achievement Award for her contribution to literature from the US Tamil cultural organization Vilakku in 2005. She was awarded the Lifetime Literary Achievement Award of Tamil Literary Garden, University of Toronto, Canada, for the year 2008. She was awarded the Kalaignar Mu. Karunanidhi Porkizi award for fiction awarded by the Booksellers and Publishers' Association of South India in the Chennai book fair, in January 2011. The University of Madras awarded her for excellence in literature in the centenary celebrations of the International Women's Day in March 2011. She was awarded the Sahitya Akademi Award in 2021 for her book *Sivappuk Kazhuthudan Oru Pachai Paravai*. She is also the recipient of the 2023 Shakti Bhatt Body of Work Prize and the 2023 Tata Literature Live! Lifetime Achievement Award.

She is currently the Director of SPARROW (Sound & Picture Archives of Research on Women). She lives in Mumbai with her filmmaker friend Vishnu Mathur, who also happens to be her husband, in a small third-floor flat with a view of the sea, along with her twenty-seven-year-old foster daughter Khintu and her two brothers Krishna and Akendra who brighten up her life.

Anil Menon's *The Inconceivable Idea of the Sun: Stories* (Hachette India, 2022) is a collection of his speculative short fiction. His novel *Half of What I Say* (Bloomsbury, 2015) was shortlisted for the 2016 Hindu Literary Award. His debut novel *The Beast with Nine Billion Feet* was shortlisted for the 2009 Crossword Prize and the Carl Baxter Society's Parallax Award. Along with Vandana Singh, he co-edited *Breaking the Bow* (Zubaan Books, 2012), an international anthology of short fiction inspired by the Ramayana. His stories have been translated into more than a dozen languages, including Arabic, Hebrew, Igbo, and Romanian. He is the chief editor of *The Bombay Literary Magazine* and a co-founder of the annual Kolam Writers' Workshop. His novel *The Coincidence Plot* (Simon & Schuster) was published in 2023.

Anirudh Kala is a psychiatrist by profession and lives in Ludhiana, Punjab. He was a member of the expert group tasked by the Government of India with writing Mental Health Policy for the country, released in 2014. His book on addiction titled *Most of What You Know About Addiction is Wrong* was published in March 2023. He also writes fiction. *Unsafe Asylum: Stories of Partition and Madness* and *Two and a Half Rivers*, a novel based on terrorism in Punjab were published earlier. Anirudh Kala has been instrumental in forging cross border links between two sides of Punjab and is founder of 'Indo-Pak Punjab Psychiatric Society.' He is fond of Urdu poetry, travelling and photography.

Ankush Saikia was born in Tezpur, Assam in 1975. He worked in journalism and publishing in Delhi for over a decade and is currently based in Shillong. He is the author of eight novels, including *The Forest Beneath the Mountains*, *The Girl from Nongrim Hills* and *Tears of the Dragon*, the latest in the Detective Arjun Arora series. His articles and longform stories (mostly on North-East India) have appeared in *FountainInk* magazine, *Scroll.in*, *Indian Express*, *The Hindu*, and *Hindustan Times*, among others.

Arunava Sinha translates classic, modern and contemporary Bengali fiction and non-fiction from Bangladesh and India into English. He also translates fiction from English into Bengali. Over 70 of his translations have been published so far in India, the UK and the USA. He has won India's top translation prize, the Crossword Award for translated books, twice. He teaches at Ashoka University, where he is also the co-director of the Ashoka Centre for Translation and the Books Editor at *Scroll.in*.

Chandana Dutta is an author, editor, and translator. She holds a PhD from Jawaharlal Nehru University, New Delhi. She has been Assistant Director for Katha Vilasam, the publishing wing of Katha, an organisation that pioneered translations in India. She set up the publishing outfit Indialog.

She was Editor, *Indian Horizons*, a quarterly journal on art and culture published by the Indian Council for Cultural Relations, New Delhi. She has been Adjunct Faculty for the master's programme in publishing at the Ambedkar University Delhi. She translates from Hindi and Bangla into English. She is the author of *My Other Half: Krishna Paul in Conversation with Chandana Dutta* (Red River, 2019) and co-author of a monograph on *Joginder Paul* (Sahitya Akademi, 2021) and editor of *Joginder Paul: A Reader* (Sahitya Akademi, 2023). She is series co-editor of the Writer in Context series being published by Routledge UK and has edited the volume *Joginder Paul: The Writerly Writer* (2022) under this series.

Gita Subramanian taught English, English Literature, and History at the senior-most levels in international schools in Hong Kong for several years. She was Head of History when she opted for early retirement and came back to India in 2001 to look after her aged parents. On her return she took up a fresh career as translator and has since published a number of English translations of novels and short stories written by renowned Tamil writers. Her translations include works by Nanjil Nadan (*Against all Odds*, 2008), Yuma Vasuki (*Blood Ties*, 2008), Imayam (*Begetter*, 2013), Vaasanthi (*Prison,* 2010), Ambai (the first of Sudha Gupta Investigates series, *A Meeting on the Andheri Overbridge*, 2016) and Tamil Sri Lankan writer Sharmila Seyyid (*Ummath*, 2018). In 2010, she won the Nalli Thisai Ettum award for the best Tamil-to-English translation. Nanjil Nadan's short stories, translated by Gita, have been brought out as a web series by Juggernaut Publishers. In 2018 the Sahitya Akademi published *A New Beginning,* Gita's translation of a collection of Nanjil Nadan's Award-winning short stories.

A passionate theatre buff, Gita has participated in many amateur productions both in Hong Kong and India as actor, director as well playwright, apart from doing a leading role in a successful commercially produced English play in Hong Kong. She now lives in a retirement community in Trivandrum with her husband.

Gopa Majumdar is a well-established translator from Bengali into English. She has translated Ashapurna Devi's *Subarnalata*, Taslima Nasreen's *My Girlhood,* and Bibhutibhushan Bandyopadhyay's *Aparijito*, Sahitya Akademi award winner in 2001. She has translated all of Satyajit Ray's Feluda stories for Penguin.

Kehkashan Khalid is a writer and illustrator from Karachi. Her stories have been published by *Fantasy Magazine*, Neon Hemlock Press and *Translunar Travelers Lounge*, among others. She is also a slush-reader at *Clarkesworld* Magazine and co-editor/Art Director at *Tasavvur* Magazine. Her work has been featured on Tor.com and *Locus*. She works full-time as a revisions editor at New Degree Press, and part-time at FRAG Games to design the narrative for Pakistan's first historical fantasy video game. She can currently be found in Jeddah, working on her first novel, spending time with her three young children, and searching for calm amid chaos. You can see her in action at www.instagram.com/artworkbykehkashan

Kiran Manral is a writer, author and novelist based in Mumbai. In previous avatars, she has been a journalist, researcher, festival curator and entrepreneur. She has received multiple awards, such as the Women Achievers Award by Young Environmentalists Association and the International Women's Day Award 2018 from ICUNR supported by the Ministry of Women and Child Welfare, Government of India, for excellence in the field of writing and Womennovator 1000 Women of Asia Award 2021. In 2022, she was named amongst the 75 Iconic Indian women in STEAM by Red Dot Foundation and Beyond Black, in collaboration with the Office of the Principal Scientific Advisor, Government of India, and British High Commission, New Delhi.

Meeti Shroff-Shah is the author of the Temple Hill Mystery series, the first of which – *The Death of Kirti Kadakia* (published as *A Mumbai Murder Mystery*, internationally) – was longlisted for the CWA New Blood Dagger in 2022 and shortlisted for the *Times of India* Women AutHer Awards in 2023.

Prior to this, Meeti has written the critically acclaimed memoir – *Do You Know Any Good Boys?* – a funny guide to the Indian arranged marriage, which has also been optioned for screen.

When she isn't plotting murder, Meeti works as a creative consultant and copywriter, and has had an award-winning career in advertising spanning over 16 years, including with global agencies such as DDB Mudra and Rediffusion Y&R.

Meeti lives with her husband and daughter in Mumbai. Her new book, *A Matrimonial Murder*, will be out in 2024.

Navin Weeraratne is a professional miniature painter. That is to say, he's not miniature, but he paints miniatures – toy soldiers to be precise. People do indeed pay him to do this. He also writes Hard Science Fiction, and is the author of *Zeelam*, *The Hundred Gram Mission* and *Planet 9*. He plans to escape climate change by growing his own vegetables in the mountains, where his neighbour, fellow Sri Lankan science fiction writer, Yudhanjaya Wijeratne, is doing just the same thing across the street. They're really doing this. Sri Lankans are mad.

Chennai-based **Pritham K. Chakravarthy** is a translator, theatre practitioner, storyteller and activist. As a freelance scholar she has taken up research assignments at UC Berkeley, the London School of Economics and the University of Toronto. She has translated *Zero Degree* by Charu Nivedita, among others.

Rabindranath Tagore (1861–1941) was a Bengali poet, short-story writer, song writer and composer, playwright, essayist, and painter who was highly influential in introducing Indian culture to the West, and he is generally regarded as the most outstanding creative artist of early 20th-century India. In 1913, he became the first non-European to receive the Nobel Prize for Literature. Knighted by the ruling British Government in 1915, he subsequently resigned the honour as a protest against British policies in India. Tagore had early success as a writer in his native Bengal. For the world he became the voice of India's spiritual heritage; and for India, especially Bengal, he became a great living institution.

Tagore wrote successfully in several literary genres. Among his fifty volumes of poetry are *Manasi* (1890), *Sonar Tari* (1894), *Gitanjali* (1910) and *Balaka* (1916). His major plays are *Raja* (1910), *Dakghar* (1912) and *Raktakaravi* (1926). He was also the author of several volumes of short stories and a number of novels like *Gora* (1910), *Ghare Baire* (1916) and *Yogayog* (1929). Besides these, he wrote musical dramas, dance dramas, essays of all types, travel diaries, and two autobiographies. Tagore also left numerous paintings and songs for which he wrote the music himself.

Radha Chakravarty is a writer, critic and translator based in Delhi, India. Her books include *The Essential Tagore*, nominated Book of the Year 2011 by Martha Nussbaum, *Mahasweta Devi: Writer, Activist, Visionary*, *Feminism and Contemporary Women Writers* and *Novelist Tagore*. She has translated Tagore's *Gora, Chokher Bali, Boyhood Days, Farewell Song*, *Four Chapters* and *The Land of Cards*, Bankimchandra Chatterjee's *Kapalkundala*, Kazi Nazrul Islam's Selected Essays, and Mahasweta Devi's *Our Santiniketan* and *In the Name of the Mother* (nominated for the Crossword Translation Award, 2004). She has edited *Vermillion Clouds: Stories by Bengali Women* and *Crossings: Stories from Bangladesh and India* and several anthologies of South Asian writing. *Subliminal*, a collection of her poetry, was published in 2023. She has contributed to *Pandemic: A Worldwide Community Poem* (Muse Pie Press, USA), nominated for the Pushcart Prize 2020. She was Professor of Comparative Literature & Translation Studies at Dr B.R. Ambedkar University Delhi.

Saad Z. Hossain is a Bangladeshi author writing in English. He lives in Dhaka. His war satire, *Escape from Baghdad!*, was published in 2015, and included in the *Financial Times* best books of 2015. It was translated into French, as *Bagdad la Grande Evasion*. This book was a finalist for the Grand Prix de L'imaginaire 2018. His second book, *Djinn City*, released in 2017, was also translated into French. His third *The Gurkha and the Lord of Tuesday*, was published in 2019 by Tor.com. It was a finalist for the Locus Awards as well as the Ignyte Awards 2020 by Fiyahcon. It is translated into Spanish by Duermevela Ediciones. His fourth book, *Cyber Mage* was published by Unnamed Press in America and ULAB Press in Bangladesh. His fifth book, *Kundo Wakes Up*, is also out now, published by Tor.com, and is longlisted for the British Science Fiction Awards 2022.

Saradindu Bandyopadhyay was a lawyer by profession, who gave up his practice to write. He wrote novels, short stories – including crime and detective stories – plays, and screenplays. He was actively involved with the Bengali as well as Hindi film industries. Bandyopadhyay created the fictional Bengali detective Byomkesh Bakshi, whose stories have been adapted for television and movies in multiple languages.

Satyajit Ray (1921–92) was one of the greatest auteurs of the twentieth century. He was awarded the Bharat Ratna in 1992, the year he received the Oscar for Lifetime Achievement Award. He worked as an advertising professional to begin with and was a talented music composer and illustrator. Besides many critically acclaimed films, his creative writing in varied genres such as detective fiction, featuring Feluda and science fiction, featuring Professor Shonku for younger as well as adult readers continue to have a wide-ranging appeal in the original Bengali and in translation across the world.

Shampa Roy is an Associate Professor in the Dept. of English, Miranda House, University of Delhi, India. Her articles on topics ranging from Victorian memsahibs' writings to postcolonial pedagogy have appeared in international journals like *Feminist Review*, *Interventions*, *Studies in Travel Writing* and *Clues*. She has co-edited and contributed to *Towards Freedom: Critical Essays on Rabindranath Tagore's Home and the World* (Orient Longman, 2007) and *'Bad' Women of Bombay Films* (Palgrave Macmillan, US, 2019). She is also the author of *Gender and Criminality in Bangla Crime Narratives: Late Nineteenth and Early Twentieth Centuries* (Palgrave Macmillan, UK, 2017) and *True Crime Writings in Colonial India* (Routledge, UK, 2020). In 2019 Roy was awarded the Charles Wallace India Trust Translation Fellowship, a well-established residency programme offered by British Council to one Indian scholar every year for working on a literary translation project of their choice at the University of East Anglia, UK.

Shweta Taneja is an award-winning author who writes science and fiction for kids and adults. Her latest novel, *Kungfu Aunty Versus Garbage Monsters*, is a wacky climate fiction for young readers. Her bestselling books include an entertaining non-fiction on Indian scientists, *They Made What? They Found What?*, graphic novel *Krishna: Defender of Dharma* and the critically acclaimed fantasy fiction series Anantya Tantrist Mysteries. Her sci-fi short story 'The Daughter That Bleeds', was shortlisted in the prestigious French award Grand Prix de l'Imaginaire and was awarded Editor's Choice Award in Singapore.

She is a Charles Wallace Writing Fellow and has given talks at international sci-fi conferences including Worldcon in China and Ireland,

Eurocon in France and the Cartoon Museum in London. Her work has been translated to Kannada, French, Romanian, Italian and Dutch.

When not writing, Shweta wanders in forests, hikes on trails and eyes birds through binoculars. Find her online at www.shwetawrites.com or with her handle @shwetawrites on most social media.

Suchitra Bhattacharya (1950–2015), a major Bengali writer, was born in Bhagalpur, Bihar, and graduated from Jogamaya Devi College, affiliated to Calcutta University. After some odd jobs, she opted for public service, but gave it up in 2004 to become a full-time writer. From the late 1970s, she regularly published short stories. In the 1980s, she took up novel writing and shot to fame with *Kancher Deyal*. Some of her well-known novels include *Dahan*, *Hemanter Pakhi*, *Neel Ghurni*, *Chhenra Taar*, *Palabar Poth Nei* and *Rangeen Prithibi*. She wrote on urban themes, and often focused on contemporary social issues and women-oriented subjects. For her detective fiction, she created the figure of Mitin Mashi, one of the few women detectives in Bengali literature. She also wrote for children. Her novels have been translated into several Indian languages and adapted for cinema. She received numerous awards, including the Katha Award, the Tarashankar Award, the Sharat Puraskar, the Bharat Nirman Award and the Dinesh Chandra Smriti Puraskar.

Sujan DasGupta was born in Kolkata, India. He graduated from Jadavpur University in Mechanical Engineering and completed his PhD in the US where he resided for more than 50 years. After retiring early from Bell Labs/ Lucent Technologies, Sujan worked on establishing a Bengali language keyboard, Haraf, and founded Abasar.net, an online Bengali informational website, in 2002. He began his writing career with puzzle-based stories for young readers. In 1992, he launched his bumbling detective 'Ekenbabu' for readers of all ages. The series achieved widespread success after it was picked up by Hoi Choi television in 2018. The Ekenbabu stories have been converted to six streaming seasons and two full-length feature films. Sujan has nearly 25 books to his credit. On 18 January 2023, Sujan unexpectedly passed away.

Sumit Bardhan is a Bengali science fiction author, reviewer and translator. He has written and regularly writes SF stories and novellas in Bengali for print and web magazines. He has also penned reviews for *Scroll.in* and contributed to translated anthologies of works of H.P. Lovecraft and African Speculative Fiction. His published books include *Arthatrishna,* a steampunk novella, *Nakshatrapathik*, a collection of two SF novellas, *Asishapta*, a science fantasy novel in the Japanese *jidaigeki* style, *Chitribichitra Manush*, the first official Bengali translation of Bradbury's *The Illustrated Man,* and *Ak Dojon Kalpabigyan*, an anthology of twelve science fiction stories.

Tamilvanan (1921–76) founded and edited the Tamil magazine *Kalkandu*. He was associated with the Dravidian movement and wrote detective stories in pure Tamil featuring Shankarlal, a stylish and well-travelled amateur sleuth who became an iconic presence in Tamil pulp fiction of the 1960s and 70s.

Tanuj Solanki is the author of four books of fiction. In 2019, he was awarded the Sahitya Akademi Yuva Puraskar for his short-story collection titled *Diwali in Muzaffarnagar*. His last two novels, *The Machine is Learning* and *Manjhi's Mayhem*, have been longlisted for the JCB Prize for Literature.

Timeri N. Murari began his career as a reporter on a Canadian newspaper before moving to London to write for the *Guardian* for 20 years. He also wrote for the *Sunday Times, New York Times* and other newspapers, and magazines. His first novel, *The Marriage,* was on the tensions within the Indian community in England. He wrote a memoir about his relationship with an orphaned child, *My Temporary Son*, an orphan's journey, and a travel book *Limping to the Centre of the World*, his 200 kms trekking pilgrimage to sacred Mount Kailas and Lake Mansarovar. He has written 15 novels, five non-fiction books, the *Axxiss,* young adult trilogy, a children's novel, *Children of the Enchanted Jungle*, stage plays and screenplays. *Time* included his film, *The Square Circle (Daayra)*, in its top 10 films of the year and he later directed it in Leicester, UK as a stage play, starring Parminder Nagra. His novel *Taj: A story of Mughal India* is translated into 25 languages and *The Taliban Cricket Club* into eight. Niyogi books will publish his new novel, *Chicanery,* early 2024.

COPYRIGHT ACKNOWLEDGEMENTS

Satyajit Ray, 'The Locked Chest' in *The Complete Adventures of Feluda*, vol. 1, trans. Gopa Majumdar, 2000, rev. ed. New Delhi: Penguin, 2004. Reprinted with permission from the publisher.

Saradindu Bandyopadhyay, 'The Rhythm of the Riddles' in *The Rhythm of the Riddles: Three Byomkesh Bakshi Mysteries*, trans. Arunava Sinha, New Delhi: Puffin, 2012. Reprinted with permission from the publisher.

Rabindranath Tagore, 'Detective', trans. Shampa Roy. The story is reprinted from *Metamorphoses*, Volume 29/Issue 2, Fall/Winter 2021 issue, 123–31 with permission from the editor.

Tanuj Solanki, 'The Desire of the Detective', a version of this story was published in June 2016 in the Painted Bride Quarterly.

Ambai, 'The Death of a Sarus Crane' in Sudha Gupta's Adventures in Detection, translated by Gita Subramanian, New Delhi: Speaking Tiger, 2023. Reprinted with permission from the publisher. Original title in Tamil 'Poovadi Chethil' in *Saras Paravai Ondrin Maranam: Sudha Guptavin Thuppariyum Anubavangal,* Kalachuvadu, 2019.

Tamilvanan, 'Tokyo Rose' (1967) in *The Blaft Anthology of Tamil Pulp Fiction*, trans. Pritham K. Chakravarthy, in Rakesh Khanna, ed. 2008, rpt. Chennai: Blaft Publications, 2018.

ACKNOWLEDGEMENTS

Bringing together some of the best classic stories as well as contemporary writing from India and the diaspora in such a double volume of mysteries has been quite a challenge. At the outset, I would like to thank Thomas Abraham, managing director and detective fiction aficionado, who has been an invaluable interlocutor and source of suggestions and insights. Anupama Manral as inhouse editor at Hachette India has enabled each individual contribution to become the best version possible. Sini at Hachette India has worked tirelessly to ensure that all the permissions are in place. Many thanks to the designer, Mia Jose, as well for the striking cover design.

Along the way, conversations with Alok Bhalla, Arjun Raj Gaind, Manjula Padmanabhan and Vaibhav Parel were especially illuminating. As ever, Manjula has exceeded expectations with her endpaper design. Vaibhav's generous sharing of books of criticism of the genre was really helpful as I began thinking about Indian detective fiction. Arjun was unstinting in sharing the addresses of fellow writers in the detective fiction community in India and abroad. I appreciate the careful and critical reading of drafts of the introduction by Professor Bhalla, Professor Supriya Chaudhuri and Professor Suvir Kaul, besides good friend Suman Gupta.

Thanks to all the contributors, who responded to the concept note in distinctive ways, ensuring a high standard of writing.

Finally, I would like to dedicate this double volume to my late father Chand Kishore Saint, always supportive of such creative initiatives, and my mother Sudesh Kumari Saint.